CULTURAL POWER, RESISTANCE and PLURALISM

CULTURAL POWER
RESISTANCE
AND
PLURALISM

COLONIAL GUYANA
1838-1900

BRIAN L. MOORE

The Press University of the West Indies
Barbados • Jamaica • Trinidad and Tobago

McGill-Queen's University Press
Montreal & Kingston • London • Buffalo

The Press University of the West Indies
1A Aqueduct Flats Mona Kingston 7 Jamaica W I
ISBN 976-640-006-7

Published simultaneously in Canada by
McGill Queen's University Press
3430 McTavish Street Montreal PQ H3A 1X9
ISBN 0-7735-1354-X

Printed in the United States of America

99 98 97 96 95   6 5 4 3 2 1

CATALOGUING IN PUBLICATION DATA (JAMAICA)

Moore, Brian L.
    Cultural power, resistance and pluralism :
    Colonial Guyana, 1838-1900 / by Brian L.
    Moore

    p. cm.
    Includes bibliographical references and index.
    ISBN 976-640-006-7
    1. Guyana—History. 2. Guyana—Civilization
    —History. 3. Pluralism (Social sciences)—
    Guyana. 4. Guyana—Social conditions.
    5. Guyana—Civilization—European influences.
    6. Guyana—Civilization—African influences.
    7. Guyana—Civilization—Hindu influences.
    8. Guyana—Civilization—Chinese influences.
    I. Title.
    F2384.M66 1995   988.1 dc—20

Cover and book design by Robert Harris
Set in 10.5/13 Garamond x 25

For my parents,
Irene Iris and the late Edwin Wilfred,
without whose love, dedication and care
none of this would have been possible

CONTENTS

Illustrations / *viii*

Glossary / *x*

Preface / *xii*

Chapter 1   Introduction / *1*

Chapter 2   Guyanese Society after Emancipation / *7*

Chapter 3   Elite Victorian Culture: Material Culture, Social Attitudes and Values / *17*

Chapter 4   Elite Victorian Culture: Leisure / *51*

Chapter 5   Afro-Creole Folk Culture: Material and Temporal / *85*

Chapter 6   Afro-Creole Folk Culture: Spiritual / *137*

Chapter 7   Indian *Bhojpuri* Culture: Material and Temporal / *155*

Chapter 8   Indian *Bhojpuri* Culture: Spiritual / *207*

Chapter 9   Portuguese Latin Culture / *241*

Chapter 10   Chinese *Hua-Qiao* Culture / *265*

Chapter 11   Conclusion: Cultural Power, Resistance and Pluralism / *295*

Appendix / *309*

Notes / *311*

Bibliography / *355*

Index / *369*

ILLUSTRATIONS

Maps

Map of Guyana[p] / xiv
Map of the plantation (coastal) belt of Guyana[a] / xv

Plates

Cover	Stabroek market, Georgetown[n]
I	A typical sugar estate (Plantation Château Margot)[c] /10
II	The Public Buildings, Georgetown, c 1860: seat of colonial legislature[f] / 14
III	Elite residential area in Georgetown (High Street) c 1860[f] / 20
IV	Typical elite mansion[d] / 20
V	The planter's chair: known in Guyana as the Berbice chair[m] / 22
VI	Typical dress of white elite males[g] / 25
VII	Government House (governor's residence) c 1860[f] / 33
VIII	St. George's Anglican Cathedral (state church) c 1860[f] / 37
IX	St. Andrew's Scots Kirk (state church) c 1860[f] / 37
X	Elite gentleman and wife with retinue of servants[c] / 43
XI	Aerial view of Georgetown, c 1860 (Water Street)[f] / 49
XII	The Tower hotel, Georgetown, c 1890[c] / 50
XIII	The Sea Wall, Georgetown (promenade for urban elites)[c] / 52
XIV	The Queen's College (elite boys' grammar school), c 1890[c] / 58
XV	The Assembly Rooms, c 1890 (principal venue of elite cultural events)[e] / 64
XVI	The Parade Ground: site of ritualistic military parades[f] / 77
XVII	The Parade Ground: venue for elite cricket matches[b] / 77
XVIII	Typical flooding in rural villages after heavy rains[q] / 87
XIX	Urban ghetto woman (Tiger Bay, Georgetown)[h] /90
XX	Creole woman plaiting hair in the yard[g] /96
XXI	Everyday dress of Creole working-class women[d] / 97
XXII	Sunday dress of Creoles[e] / 98
XXIII	The coalpot: stove on which food was cooked[a] / 99
XXIV	Typical Creole method of preparing food[q] / 100
XXV	Creole village string band[q] / 119
XXVI	Artist's impression of masquerade revellers[l] / 124
XXVII	Creole children playing the imperial game: cricket[j] / 131
XXVIII	The Wesleyan Methodist church, Georgetown, c 1860[f] / 135
XXIX	*Cumfo* drummers[q] / 141

XXX   Type of immigrant dwellings on the estates: double-storied
           ranges[c] / 157
XXXI   Type of immigrant dwellings on the estates: single-storied
           ranges[r] / 159
XXXII   Wattle and daub (*kacca*) house[d] / 159
XXXIII   An Indian immigrant family[d] / 165
XXXIV   Typical dress of an Indian woman[d] / 166
XXXV   Indian musicians[i] / 200
XXXVI   A typical East Indian village[j] / 206
XXXVII   A Hindu temple (Albouystown)[o] / 210
XXXVIII   An Islamic mosque (Queenstown)[o] / 210
XXXIX   A Portuguese immigrant family[k] / 242
XL   The Brickdam Roman Catholic Cathedral, Georgetown,
           c 1860[f] / 247
XLI   The Sacred Heart Roman Catholic church[k] / 250
XLII   Chinese immigrants[h] / 269

Sources

[a] From the author's collection
[b] George W. Bennett, *An Illustrated History of British Guiana* (Dem., 1866)
[c] The Henry Bullock papers
[d] L. Crookall, *British Guiana* (Lond., 1898)
[e] Charles W. Eves, *The West Indies* (Lond., 1956)
[f] A. Hartman and M.J. Casabon, *Album of Demerara* (Paris, c1860)
[g] James Johnson, *Jamaica: The New Riviera* (Lond., 1903)
[h] H. Kirke, *Twenty-five years in British Guiana* (Lond., 1897)
[i] W. Look Lai, *Indentured Labour, Caribbean Sugar: Chinese and Indian
     Immigration to the British West Indies, 1838-1918* (Balt., 1993)
[j] Allister Macmillan (ed.), *The Red Book of the West Indies* (Lond., 1922)
[k] M.N. Menezes, *Scenes from the History of the Portuguese in British Guiana* (Lond.,
     1986)
[l] National Advertising Co., *Guyana: A Nation on the Move* (Bridgetown, 1969)
[m] From Velma Pollard's (UWI, Mona) collection
[n] James Rodway, *Guiana: British, Dutch and French* (Lond., 1912)
[o] P. Ruhoman, *Centenary History of the East Indians in British Guiana 1838-1938
     (Georgetown, 1947)*
[p] R.T. Smith, *British Guiana* (Lond., 1962)
[q] R.T. Smith, *The Negro Family in British Guiana* (Lond., 1956)
[r] The Sugar Industry Welfare Fund, *Forward with Sugar Workers* (Georgetown,
     1950)

GLOSSARY

Accourie	a kind of guinea-pig
Anansi(e)	the crafty spider hero of Afro-Creole folk tales
Batteau/bateau	round bottomed boat
Bitt	four penny piece worth eight cents
Bottom-house	space under a house elevated on stilts
Buck	Amerindian (*pejorative*)
Buck-shot	seeds of a caladium
Buckra/buchra	white man
Calabash	gourd made from the fruit of the calabash tree
Cassareep	boiled juice of bitter cassava used for making pepperpot
Chefa	Chinese lottery
Chinese hell	Chinese gambling and opium den
Coal-pot	iron charcoal stove, shaped like a large egg-cup, with its base open to allow a free draught of air. A grill separates the base, where the coal fuel is burned, from the pot containing the food to be cooked.
Coolie	Indian immigrant (pejorative)
Crapaud/crapeau	frog or toad
Creole (s)	(adj., n.) In its generic sense, this term is used in the lower case to mean local, local-born, or indigenous. When used in the upper case, it pertains to the black and coloured native population (called 'Creoles' or 'Afro-Creoles'). The terms 'Anglo-Creole' and 'Euro-Creole' pertain to the local white population.
Creolese	Creole language or patois
Cutty-cutty	vegetable soup with plantains, saltfish, and hot peppers
Coo-coo	a Barbadian Creole dish made by boiling Indian cornmeal with okras/ochroes
Festereiros	lay promoters of Portuguese Roman Catholic feasts
Foo-foo	boiled plantains, pounded
Ganja/ganga	marijuana/cannabis
Greenheart	local hardwood
John Chinaman	Chinese immigrant (pejorative)
Jumbi	spirit (Afro-Creole)
Kenna	Creole belief that some foods are unwholesome
Koker	sluice
Labba	hollow-cheeked paca
Logie	shed
Manatee	sea-cow, dugong
Manny	Portuguese immigrant (pejorative)
Marooning party	a hunt

Mauby	drink made from the bark of the Carob tree
Maugre	thin
Megass	sugar cane refuse
Michahan	Chinese gambling game
Mora	local hardwood
Mortar pestle	thick wooden club used for pounding foo-foo
Obeah	Afro-Creole magic, medicine and witchcraft
Ole Haig	witch
Palm-loaf/-board	the spine of the branch of the coconut or palm tree used for channeling water from a house roof to a water tank or vat, and as boards for walls of huts
Patwah	local river fish
Pepperpot	stewed meat flavoured with cassareep and peppers
Pourri	Indian roti (bread) made with ghee and split-peas
Quashie/Quashy	black person (pejorative)
Querriman	a large scale-fish
Sammy	Indian immigrant (pejorative)
Senghor	Portuguese immigrant (pejorative)
Stelling	wharf
Swizzle	Cocktail
Tadja	Indian religious festival
Tannia	kind of yam
Tie-head	cloth tied around the head (headkerchief)
Toddy	alcoholic drink made from the sap of the coconut flower bud
Vat	large cistern used for storing drinking water
Wallaba	wood used mainly for shingles
Yager	dog handler in a hunt

PREFACE

When I wrote *Race, Power and Social Segmentation in Colonial Society* (New York 1987) I was conscious that the one area which, due to constraints of space, could only receive scant attention was culture. Consequently I decided to do further research with a view to writing a companion volume that would focus exclusively on the cultural history of Guyana after emancipation. This book is the result.

It has taken several years to complete mainly because of the extensive and diverse range of documents and other materials which I have had to consult in order to produce a reasonably coherent study. What was at times tedious and frustrating, however, has in the end proven rewarding especially since this under-explored subject area has provided invaluable insights for both social and political history. My hope is that this work will stimulate further research into the cultural history of the Caribbean.

As usual the course of research leaves a long trail of indebtedness. A number of archives and libraries deserve mention for the source materials which they provided me. These are the Guyana National Archives, the University of the West Indies (hereafter U.W.I.) Main Library, Mona, the National Library of Jamaica; and in England, the Public Record Office, the Essex Record Office, the British Library, the Royal Commonwealth Society, the Congregational Council for World Mission, the United Society for the Propagation of the Gospel, the Society of Jesus (English Province), and the Methodist Missionary Society.

I would especially like to thank Bridget Brereton and Barry Higman who once again did a thorough job of critically commenting on the first draft and offering sound advice on improving it. Special thanks are due to the following persons for assisting me in obtaining some splendid photographs from Britain, Guyana and Trinidad: Allister Hinds, Raymond Eytle, Doreen Holder and the staff of the Caribbean Research Library of the University of Guyana, and Maureen Henry of the U.W.I. Library, St. Augustine. I must also express my gratitude to Velma Pollard, who tolerated several disruptions of her living room in an effort to photograph her "Berbice chair"; and to Hazel Forsythe and Pamela Moore for so kindly trying to trace the provenance of that chair. Thanks too to the Campus Research and Publications Fund Committee (U.W.I., Mona) for generously making available a small grant towards this project.

Finally, a special word of thanks must be reserved for the staff of The Press U.W.I. who made the task of transforming the manuscript into a book relatively 'painless' and pleasant by their professionalism and friendly cooperation. With quiet efficiency, Linda Cameron (Director) was instrumental in, among other things, arranging for the joint publication with McGill-Queen's University Press; while with seemingly boundless enthusiasm, Pansy Benn (Production Manager) practically left no stone unturned in her tireless efforts to ensure that the final product was of a very high quality. To all those other persons who had anything to do with the progress of my work, however small, thanks very much.

BRIAN L. MOORE

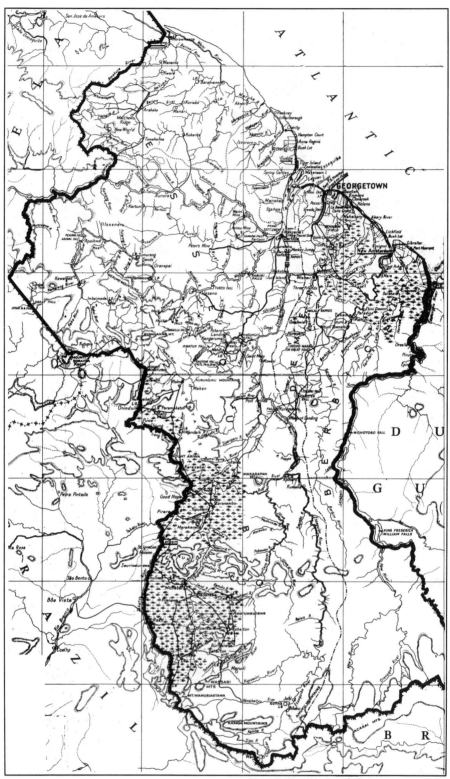

Map of Guyana

Source: R.T. Smith, *British Guiana* (London 1962)

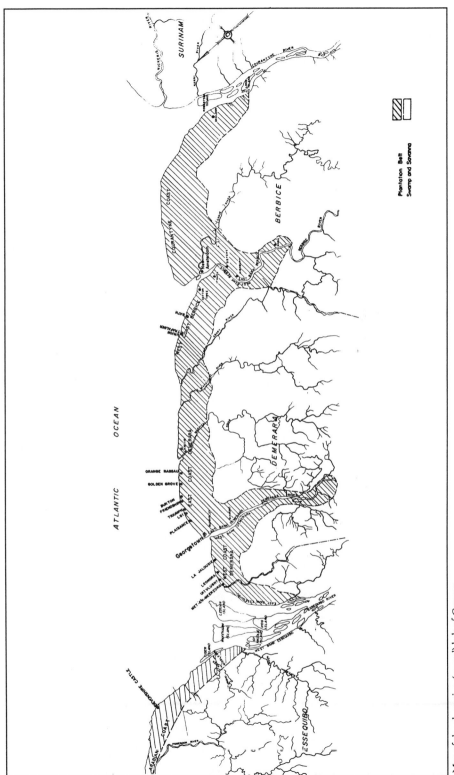

Map of the plantation (coastal) belt of Guyana

INTRODUCTION

Cultural history was for a long time the Cinderella of historical writing. It was treated lightly as merely the history of manners, leisure, and a whole range of 'exotic' cultural activities, "conducted outside political, economic, military and other institutions which were the concerns of specific kinds of 'real' history". In other words, as simply the record of past everyday life in the home, the work-place and the community, it was regarded more as antiquarianism than serious history, and was accordingly criticized as "an inchoate amalgam of fashionable fads" and trivialities such as "clothes, hunting, sex, weddings, houses, eating and sleeping". Seen thus, cultural history "provided mere light relief, the tail-piece for proper history".[1]

Over the past two decades, however, this attitude has changed remarkably, particularly in Europe and North America, but there still remains a bias against this genre of history in the Caribbean. Consequently Caribbean historians have not to date bothered much with cultural history. This is not to say that it has not received any attention at all but, in so far as that has happened, it has been treated essentially as an adjunct of social history rather than as a separate, viable branch of Caribbean historical writing. So while there are some social histories which have dealt with different aspects of culture,[2] no full scale or comprehensive cultural history of any Caribbean territory has hitherto emerged. In many respects it would be true to say that the study of past culture in the Caribbean has been very much the preserve of ethnography/cultural anthropology. This book, therefore, is intended to fill a major lacuna in the historiography of the Caribbean.

Primarily a historical study of the religious and secular culture(s) of the *plantation society*[3] of postemancipation Guyana (1838-1900), it aims to address three major concerns: first, the way in which the colonial elite classes manipulated their culture to create a consensus of values throughout the society designed to support the ideology and practice of imperial rule and the existing social order that it spawned. Second, it will examine the responses of the subordinate ethnic categories to this attempt at cultural imposition and its impact on their traditional cultures. Third, it will analyse the cultural fabric that emerged from this dynamic interplay of counteracting forces----the extent to which it was integrated or pluralistic----and assess the role that culture played in determining the organization of the society.

Most Caribbean societies have been largely influenced by the dominance of the plantation system. It was the production regimen of the sugar plantation, both during and after slavery, which determined the composition and structure of these societies. Already biracial by the end of slavery (1838 in the British colonies, 1848 in the French West Indies, 1863 in the Dutch West Indies, 1886 in Cuba), the societies of the larger, less densely populated territories (most notably Guyana, Trinidad and Surinam) became increasingly multiracial thereafter as immigrant workers from India, China, Madeira and West Africa, among other places were imported to supplement the local labour force which had decreased after emancipation, as many ex-slaves vacated the plantations in search of a more lucrative and self-sufficient way of life. The immigration of new ethnic categories of workers radically altered the composition of those societies. This immigration brought in its wake new social problems, conflicts and instability associated with the divergent economic, social and political interests of the several ethnic components; and these were further exacerbated by racial jealousies and animosities among those groups.

In an earlier work I showed that in such an environment the dominant white minority in Guyana placed primary emphasis on political controls and military coercion to maintain social stability, budgeting between 14 and 25 percent of annual revenues for expenditure on the police and judiciary alone, as opposed to just about 7½ percent on education. Those statistics did not include expenditure on the militia and on maintaining imperial troops in the colony. It was strongly felt that the reality of everyday life in the colony demanded forthright, at times even brutal, action for dealing with a mass of 'barbarous', potentially hostile, natives and immigrants. Yet although it was given relatively low priority in nineteenth century Guyana, the idea of building value consensus was never ignored by the colonial elites; but they clearly were not prepared to rely too heavily on its efficacy especially in a society open to regular introductions of fresh immigrants. Cultural consensus was conceived as a long term goal, achievable only after a prolonged and sedulously administered process of propaganda, religious proselytization, education, and practical example.[4]

Following Antonio Gramsci, Pierre Bourdieu, and the Centre for Contemporary Cultural Studies at Birmingham, England, who have all shown that in Europe elite cultural institutions, beliefs and tradi-

tions are valued by the masses even if they do not actively participate
in them, Brian Stoddart has espoused the concept of *cultural power* in a colonial situation. This he defines as "the set of ideas, beliefs, rules, and conventions concerning social behaviour that was carried throughout the empire by such British servants as administrators, military officers, industrialists, agriculturalists, traders, financiers, settlers, educators, and advisors of various kinds". He argues that these characteristics were fostered in an informal manner within carefully selected sections of the colonial populations, and that success of this cultural power depended on how well the bulk of the client population inculcated the transmitted social tenets as appropriate forms of behaviour and social ordering.[5]

Stoddart's conceptualization, however, suffers from two significant weaknesses. First, his exclusion of formal authority systems such as the bureaucracy and the military, which stems largely from his restricted concern with the transmission of imperial culture through sport, seriously limits the use of the concept of cultural power as an analytical tool in the colonial context. Second, by focusing on the *characteristics* of the transmitted culture rather than the *instruments* of transmission, his definition does not come to terms with the essence of *power* which is the ability to act in order to exercise control or command over others. In this study, rather than seeing cultural power merely as certain characteristics of imperial culture and ideology transmitted in an informal manner, the emphasis will be placed on the ability and willingness of the cultural elites to exercise the power derived from their position of political, economic and social hegemony to repress expressions of non-British culture and to promote their own imperial culture. Accordingly, it will include both formal and informal authority systems representing the state, private institutions and individuals. Hence cultural power encompasses the use of legislative and executive instruments, the forces of legitimate violence, propaganda, elite public opinion, religious proselytization, the cultural content of colonial education, the invention of imperial traditions and symbols, the control of the leisure time of the colonial population, as well as the transmission of sport ethics.

On the other hand, the colonial populations, whether native or immigrant, were generally powerless—politically, economically and militarily—and by nature of the social order of imperialism were relegated to the bottom of colonial society. They were therefore vulnerable to elite cultural power to which their resistance was dependent on a range of variables relating to their material and spiritual condition. Some, therefore, succumbed and became fully assimilated into the elite culture; others inculcated selected aspects of that culture to produce a syncretic or hybrid culture; still others resisted resolutely and held on faithfully to their parent traditions. As we shall see in nineteenth century Guyana, cultural resistance was not uniform among the different subordinate ethnic groups,[6] and each of the above conditions was present. This meant, therefore, that the cultural power of the elites was only partially effective, and this in turn had important consequences for the cultural integration of the colonial society.

After emancipation, Guyanese society not only became highly segmented racially, but this condition coincided with cultural compartmentalization as each ethnic group sought to insulate and isolate itself behind exclusive socio-cultural boundaries. One of the major objectives of this study, therefore, is to examine and analyse the nature of this compartmentalization and to determine the extent to which elite pressure and social contact across ethnic boundaries promoted cultural change, and perhaps contributed to cultural integration in the sixty years under review.

This work will thus describe, explain and analyse the cultural institutions, behaviour, customs, habits, religious beliefs and practices, superstitions, music and dance, marriage and family relations, rites of passage, dress, festivities and pastimes, food and language, and so on, of each ethnic group in the society. It will show how and why these differed from their respective parent traditions, and what role these modified cultures played both in moulding ethnic group consciousness, cohesion and identity, and in defining the socio-cultural position of the group in question within the colonial society. The study will also examine the issue of cultural integration from two angles: first, the impact of elite cultural power in promoting a consensus of values around the idea of the superiority of British culture; and, second, the extent and impact of interculturation among the different ethnic groups.

The question of cultural integration will be examined against the background of the old debate which contraposes it against the notion of cultural pluralism as enunciated mainly by M.G. Smith, Leo Despres, Pierre van den Berghe and R.A.J. van Lier. They argued that composite societies such as Guyana are composed of exclusive cultural groups or sections which merely coexist with one another, lack value consensus, and are consequently characterized by conflict. These societies, therefore, are considered to be inherently unstable, and to be only held together by force under the political hegemony of one group or section, usually a cultural minority. Smith further asserted that cultural or institutional differences are critical to the divisions in these societies. Hence they take precedence over racial differences in determining social status.[7] This priority assigned to culture as the key social determinant is problematic and thus forms an important issue under examination in this book.

Crucial to the consideration of the plural society thesis is the distinction which Smith makes between basic, alternative and exclusive instutitions, and their implications for the societal form. Basic or compulsory institutions are common to all members of an ethnic group; alternative institutions are optionally participated in; and exclusive institutions are shared only by members of a given ethnic group. If all members of a society share a common institutional system, a condition of cultural homogeneity ensues. If the members of a society share the same basic institutions, but practise different alternative or exclusive institutions, then there is cultural heterogeneity. If there are no shared basic institutions in a society, a state of cultural pluralism prevails.[8]

The other side of the debate is influenced by the Parsonian sociological tradition and includes such advocates as Lloyd Braithwaite, Raymond T. Smith, Malcolm Cross, et al. In a nutshell, these argue (with some differences) that although seemingly divided racially and culturally, composite societies, especially those in the Caribbean, are in fact held together by a set of shared values derived from a common 'creolized' experience in the contact situation of the plantation.[9] In other words, great emphasis is placed here on cultural integration rather than on cultural divergence.

I have shown elsewhere that though radically different in their conceptualizations, in reality these two broad theoretical positions are by no means incompatible with one another, and actually describe hypothetical models at different poles of the same societal continuum. In general terms, a composite society develops from a condition of 'pure' pluralism into a class stratified social system integrated by certain basic elements of a shared culture. But at any given point in time, it may exhibit combinations of the features and characteristics of both polar societal models.[10] Apart, therefore, from the numerical composition of the ethnic components, and their power and status relationships with one another, which are not unusually based on racial criteria, the other important factor in determining whether these societies are pluralistic or class stratified is the extent to which there is *cultural* divergence or integration. And to a large extent that is dependent on how successful the exercise of elite cultural power has been in moulding a consensus of values or, vice versa, how effective the cultural resistance of the subordinate ethnic groups has been. These are the primary areas of focus of this book.

As an historical work, most of the data are drawn from a wide range of primary archival and secondary contemporary sources. Perhaps more so than other branches of history, the sources for culture history tend to be very dispersed, sketchy, patchy, highly selective in what they treat and consequently not comprehensive. Throughout this work there is a certain degree of unevenness in the coverage not only of different ethnic groups, but also of aspects of the culture of specific groups. There is, for instance, a sad dearth of cultural data on the Chinese in particular and to a lesser extent on the Portuguese. What concerned contemporary commentators in relation to the Creoles was hardly the same with respect to themselves. This thus makes comparison of some cultural features between different ethnic groups very difficult. By far the greatest attention was paid to the two numerically largest groups in the society, the Creoles and the Indian immigrants. But even where they are concerned, the data are patchy on certain aspects of their cultures.

The cultural historian is also faced with enormous inaccuracies in the data largely on account of the cultural biases and ignorance of contemporary recorders. Very often these scribes did not know, care about, or understand the phenomena which they were recording. Ethnographical findings have thus been used to provide explanatory insights into some of the raw historical data. Despite these shortcomings of the historical sources, the results have been rewarding, and what was indeed a very rich cultural environment has been reconstructed for the reader. I am myself convinced that the social history of any given area cannot be properly appreciated without a clear and full understanding of the culture of the people: how they lived, worked, played, and worshipped. That is the focus of this book.

GUYANESE SOCIETY AFTER EMANCIPATION[1]

The sixty postemancipation years of the nineteenth century witnessed a radical demographic transformation of Guyanese society. In 1838, the year of final emancipation, the population of the plantation areas of Guyana was approximately 95,000 of whom about 97 percent were black and coloured (the mixed progeny of miscegenation between whites and blacks), and the remaining 3 percent white, roughly 2.5 percent British and a few hundred newly migrated Portuguese. (These statistics exclude the indigenous Amerindians who lived in the hinterland outside the plantation culture sphere, and who consequently are not treated in this book.) By the end of the century, this essentially biracial composition had been significantly altered. The total population had increased by 183 percent between 1841 and 1891 when the last census of the century was taken, but this was mainly due to the large scale importation of immigrant workers to meet the labour demands of the plantations. The black and coloured population increased by 58 percent to 144,619 in 1891, but much of this increase was on account of 55,077 immigrants from the West Indies and Africa.[2] If one excludes those, the native black and coloured population (hereafter called **Creoles** or **Afro-Creoles**) would actually have *decreased* by 1.7 percent. So the black and coloured population owed its increase to immigration rather than to natural increase.

The white population also owed its increase mainly to immigration. Less than half (ranging between 42 and 45 percent) of the whites were born in the colony. Hence although the Anglo-Saxon white population increased by 64 percent between 1841 and 1891, the local born whites increased by only 31 percent. During the postemancipation period, the total white population was also augmented by the arrival of 32,216 Portuguese immigrants. Although several of these died shortly after arrival, they significantly boosted the total white population at a very critical period of the social development of the colony. In 1891 the Portuguese numbered 12,164. What is clear, therefore, is that the original biracial creole (i.e., local born) population was barely able to sustain its numbers naturally during the second half of the nineteenth century, and that without fresh immigrants its numbers would have suffered a decline in absolute terms. Guyana's total population at the end of the century, therefore, would have been smaller than in 1838.

This means that the phenomenal increase in population after 1838 was entirely due to immigration. At the end of the century, new immigrants and their descendants exceeded the native population. The significance of this phenomenon cannot be overstated as it was bound to have very profound consequences for the society. This situation is a serious indictment of the population and economic policies of the planter-dominated colonial regime which promoted the stagnation, nay, decline, of the native black and coloured population while spending large sums of public money to import new immigrant labourers. Nothing was evidently put in place by the colonial government to ensure the material prosperity and physical well-being of the native population which could encourage its natural increase. This reflected the persistence of antediluvian slavocratic ideas that labour was expendable and easily replaceable by large numbers of fresh importations.

So by means of a policy of neglect, the emphasis during the postemancipation years was not on keeping alive the native population, but rather on importing labour from wherever in the world it was most readily obtainable. Even costs did not seem to matter too much, since the natives were required to bear most of the brunt through indirect taxes on essential items of consumption. By 1900 a total of 270,448 immigrants, nearly three times the native population of 1838, were brought into the colony at public expense: from Madeira 32,216, although not many of those were required to work on the plantations— another indication of how public money was misspent; from India 210,639, from Africa 14,060, and from China 13,533. This cynical and very narrow-minded population policy transformed Guyanese society beyond recognition not only numerically, but also in terms of the new racial and cultural diversity which it produced. So narrowly focused was it as a means of providing dependent manual labour for the plantations (except of course for the Portuguese who were valued mainly for their numerical contribution to the total white population), that even these immigrations, as we shall see later on, were sharply skewed against women, resulting particularly in the case of the Indians and Chinese, in severe shortages of females, with all the adverse social and cultural consequences of that.

Immigration played a very major part not merely in keeping the plantation system alive, but in expanding it tremendously during the later nineteenth century. It enabled the planters to overcome the initial challenges of emancipation posed by the ex-slaves' demands for higher wages and their attempts to lessen their dependence on the plantations by setting up independent peasant village settlements. Coupled with the move towards free trade by Britain which threatened to deprive the West Indian planters of their guaranteed market, the British Caribbean plantation system looked extremely vulnerable. Guyana and Trinidad, however, were able to do rather better than their neighbours, since they were much less debt-ridden and still had a considerable amount of land space for expansion, provided an assured and controllable supply of labour could be obtained. This was provided through large scale immigration and a system of contract labour (indentureship) which, with investment in new technology, enabled the planters to increase sugar production far beyond pre-emancipation levels. In Guyana sugar exports peaked at 116,550 tons in 1891, 80 percent higher than during the 1830s. Prosperity had returned to the plantation sector.

These developments, however, had long-term and profound consequences. Economically, the plantation sector continued to be favoured by both the local and metropolitan governments at the expense of all other sectors. In particular, small farming into which many of the neglected ex-slave population drifted suffered for want of credit, basic infrastructure especially drainage and sea-defence, equipment, and technical know-how to improve methods of cultivation, crop types and yields of production. This was a deliberate policy aimed at forcing the farmers back into full-time plantation employment, and resulted in the strangulation of peasant small-farming until late in the century when ex-indentured immigrants were able to put the ill-drained lands into productive wet-rice production. This policy left a large pool of native Creole farmers impoverished with the result that many drifted into urban slums in a vain search for better opportunities.

The only economic sector outside the mainstream plantations that was not deliberately depressed as a matter of policy was the retail commercial sector. But because of its great potential for lucrativeness, it was skilfully manipulated both through taxation (licences) and credit restrictions to ensure that the ex-slave population would not control it and thus earn their way out of plantation labour and poverty. Consequently, largely on racial grounds, the Portuguese immigrants were facilitated to establish a virtual stranglehold on this area of economic activity. This, coupled with genuine hard work, enabled some Portuguese to achieve considerable and enviable prosperity; but it also led to all forms of skulduggery by several retailers who cheated native and immigrant workers out of their meagre earnings, and consequently aroused considerable animosity towards the Portuguese as an ethnic group. The result was that they were the victims of serious communal

A typical
sugar estate
(Plantation
Château
Margot): symbol of
planter
economic
power

attacks on at least three occasions during the nineteenth century in various parts of the colony: 1848 in Berbice, 1856 in Demerara and Essequibo, and in 1889 in Georgetown.

One of the most striking consequences of these shortsighted and narrowly focused economic and population policies, therefore, was precisely the growth of suspicion and hostility among the several ethnic groups which made the formation of a stable integrated society very difficult. All immigrants came with the objective of becoming rich before returning home, and this conflicted directly with the interests of the native Creoles who felt cheated out of what they thought was naturally theirs after generations of unremitting toil in the colony. Their wages fell, jobs became scarcer, taxation to support immigration rose, they were squeezed out of the lucrative retail trade in favour of immigrants who very often charged them exorbitant prices, their lands depreciated because of the government's refusal to provide essential drainage infrastructure, and in some instances land they had occupied for years was actually taken from them and granted to immigrants. All this left a bitter taste in their mouths which rankled as white newcomers (the Portuguese) increasingly flaunted their growing opulence.

For their part, most immigrants found the host society distinctly hostile. Those who came to work as indentured labourers on plantations had their expectations of high earnings immediately dashed, and found the work onerous, living conditions harsh, and their treatment both by estate personnel and by the wider society decidedly abusive. They were hardly made welcome, and were essentially looked down on as illiterate trash. The laws were stacked against those who were indentured, and there was very little hope of redressing in the courts the numerous injustices which they suffered on a daily basis. For some of them, migration became a nightmare soon after arrival as the climate reduced them to sickness and even death. If the Portuguese fared better in the long run because of the advantages from which they benefited, they too had to overcome the rigours of the climate (many did not), and had to put in many long hours of arduous work before they could build their fortunes (many were not successful). In the process they too had to endure the same abusive treatment dished out to other immigrants, and were the victims of direct attacks on their property.

Nineteenth century Guyana, therefore, was by no means a melting-pot. On the contrary, there was a consistently high level of suspicion, tension and violence which characterized inter-group relations. In addition to the aforementioned anti-Portuguese disturbances, there was also friction between blacks and Indians, Indians and Chinese, Chinese and whites, whites and blacks, Indians and whites, and even among different categories of Indians, and between Barbadian and Creole blacks. The seemingly most trivial dispute between individuals of different ethnicity could degenerate into wider ethnic conflict. There was hardly any consensus among the several ethnic groups as each competed with the others for scarce economic resources—made even scarcer by the gross mal-distribution of wealth in the society. Since the dominant whites controlled the commanding heights of the economy—plantations, large import-export merchant houses, the banks, etc.—they garnered the bulk of the wealth produced in the colony. The dependent workers of the other ethnic groups jostled for the crumbs that trickled down. Only the Portuguese, through their control of the retail trade, stood a fairly good chance of amassing significant wealth.

So ethnic friction and hostility were encouraged by competition over scarce resources. There was literally a 'rat race' at all levels of society as the various ethnic groups, and individuals within them, jostled to carve out a niche for their own material well-being. Within the economy there was a high degree of occupational specialization as certain jobs came to be identified with specific ethnic groups. Thus the dominant British were plantation owners and attorneys, managers and overseers, senior civil servants, senior clergy in the established churches, merchants and store clerks, bankers, lawyers and doctors, police and army officers. The Portuguese controlled the retail trade as shopkeepers and pedlars, though some were small farmers. The Creoles engaged principally as small farmers, plantation workers specializing in certain tasks, unskilled urban workers (e.g., porters, stevedores, cartmen, domestics, and coal women), independent artisans, seamstresses, teachers, low ranking policemen, and junior clerks in government offices. Indians and Chinese were indentured plantation workers, and later on, peasant farmers and shopkeepers. The society too was similarly segmented as each group tended to segregate itself residentially in urban clusters or rural village settlements and mingled very little outside the work and market places or at public cultural events (e.g., horse-racing meetings, cricket matches, street festivals, etc.). Intermarriage was, in this context, an aberration; and as a result the mixed population never exceeded 11 percent during the entire nineteenth century. Such segmentation may have minimized the level of conflict, but it did little to promote social and cultural integration.

In such a segmented social environment, racial and cultural differences were elevated to prominence in determining positions in society. 'Race' and culture became the primary tags of social identification. Individuals were perceived principally as the bearers of the collective personality of their ethnic groups. Not surprisingly, therefore, racial stereotypes, ofttimes pejorative, abounded. Williams argues that, emanating from the hegemonic political and economic position enjoyed by the white elites, such stereotyping was the product of their perceptions of the different ethnic groups (including themselves) based on the allocated economic roles and the levels of success of those groups. The stereotypes were thus largely elite ideological rationalizations (or preferably distortions) of the prototypical experiences of the various groups in the society, but were subsequently reinterpreted and reshaped by the subordinate groups to suit their own perceptions of their position in the colonial social hierarchy.[3]

In the nineteenth century, therefore, *Buckra*, the British white, was a fortune-seeker, coarse but craving high social status, hospitable, pompous, arrogant and extravagant. *Quashie*, the black Creole, was a noble savage, very excitable, lazy and improvident, who especially loved music and dance ('to party'). *Senghor* or *Manny* was the Portuguese immigrant, hardworking but penurious, 'sleazy' and dishonest. *Sammy*, the Indian, was immoral and superstitious, docile but excitable and vengeful, industrious and thrifty. *John Chinaman* was hard working, neat and very intelligent, but an opium addict, inveterate gambler, and prone to violence.

Such stereotyped images and the high level of social and economic segmentation reflected the absence of societal consensus among the various ethnic groups. Unity and stability had to be imposed from above. The overpowering dominance of the plantation system imposed unity over the colonial economy. Even if not employed directly on a plantation, the fortunes of that sector affected the performance of the whole economy, and the well-being of every inhabitant in the plantation sphere of the colony. Over and beyond this, the state played a critical role in stabilizing the segmented society through its laws, sanctions, and very importantly by the show and use of force. Both the plantations and the state, however, were the exclusive preserve of the dominant British minority, and were operated for that minority's benefit. The state was responsible for protecting the economic interests of the plantations, as well as the social and political interests of the white minority. To this end, the legislature, the judiciary, and the armed forces (police, militia, and imperial troops) were employed specifically to coerce the non-white population into subordination to the will of the dominant white minority.

Early postemancipation Guyana thus bore all the hallmarks of a classic plural society: racially determined social segmentation, economic specialization along ethnic lines, political dominance by a small racial or cultural minority, differential incorporation of the ethnically differentiated subordinate majority, emphasis on coercion for societal stability. Those who choose to ignore the appropriateness of the plural society hypotheses for analysing composite colonial societies at the early stages of their development do so at their own peril. Admittedly the theories may be flawed (see chapter one), but that does not negate

The Public
Buildings,
Georgetown
c. 1860: seat of
colonial
legislature

their general analytical usefulness for such societies. Social and cultural pluralism, however, is not an immutable condition. From its very inception, forces are at work in the plural society which, however imperceptible, gradually undermine its structural features and lead to the growth of a more integrated social order. Nineteenth century Guyana was no exception.

By the 1870s such forces were already forging changes that were discernible. The degree of occupational specialization by ethnicity was lessening. Creoles were acquiring education and technical skills which enabled them to obtain white collar jobs in both the public and private sectors, and to enter the liberal professions (law, medicine and the priesthood) in small but growing numbers. Portuguese immigrants had diversified their economic activity by moving into forestry and gold mining. Indian and Chinese immigrants were beginning to free themselves from indentureship, to acquire land and become small farmers and, particularly in the case of the Chinese, to engage in retail shopkeeping, forestry and later on gold mining in competition with the Portuguese. By the 1880s, the subordinate non-white elites and middle strata whites, recognizing that they had much in common as a socioeconomic class, began to challenge the dominant white minority's (mainly planter) monopoly claim on political power. This agitation eventually produced major political change in the 1890s when that monopoly was finally broken. A broad based societal consensus began to emerge among the educated middle classes which obviated the need to maintain stability and unity mainly by coercion. Thus by the end of the century, many of the structural indicators of pluralism were being eroded and the beginnings of an integrated class stratified society were becoming more evident.

Even so, however, many of the scars of ethnic segmentation still persisted, reinforced largely by cultural differences. While 'race' was seen by contemporaries mainly as the physical characteristics----skin colour, shape of nose, shape and colour of eyes, type of hair, etc.—which visually differentiated one person or group from another; culture was critical for providing both individuals and groups with a body of beliefs, values and customs which identified them as different from, if not in their estimation 'better' than, other individuals or groups. Culture therefore provided groups and individuals with a consciousness and identity which helped to define both their perceptions of themselves and their place in the society.

But culture is not immutable and can be interchanged among individuals of different ethnic groups. The process of cultural transmission is thus key to social change. In a colonial context, great consideration needs to be given to the transmission of the dominant elite culture in particular, since that is one of the principal methods of moulding value consensus among different sections of the subordinate population in support of the status quo. The cultural power vested in the colonial elites by virtue of their social, political and economic dominance enables them to promote cultural integration around the notion of the superiority of the imperial culture. How successful they are in this endeavour depends on whether the subordinate ethnic groups equate cultural assimilation with social respectability and advancement within the colonial society. Those ethnic groups which regard the acquisition of elite culture as conferring social respectability on themselves are more inclined to assimilate. Those which do not share that perception tend to be more consciously resistant to elite cultural impositions. Cultural integration in a multiracial society, however, not only takes place vertically, but horizontally as well, across the social boundaries of subordinate ethnic groups of similar social status. This generally depends on the extent of social intermingling among individuals within those groups.

The ensuing chapters will examine in detail *aspects* of the cultures of the several ethnic groups in nineteenth century Guyana, and will evaluate the degree to which the colonial elites were successful in using their cultural power to integrate those groups through the dominant British-derived culture. The chapters will also assess the extent of cross-culturation among the subordinate groups and its impact on the degree of social segmentation during the period under review.

ELITE VICTORIAN CULTURE:
Material Culture,
Social Attitudes and Values

The principal standard bearers of elite Victorian culture in nineteenth century Guyana were the British whites, who were composed mainly of Scottish, English and Irish immigrants serving in different capacities from lowly overseers and bookkeepers on the estates to wealthy planters and merchants, and lofty colonial officials. In between there were professionals such as lawyers, doctors and priests, army and police officers, bank and store clerks, etc. With few exceptions, most of these had middle and lower class origins in the British Isles and were intent on making their fortune in the colony before returning home to enjoy an upper middle class life of luxury and leisure. There were in addition a few Dutch and North American residents representing, one might surmise, the past and future cultural orientations of Guyana. Finally, there was a body of local-born whites who formed between 42 and 45 percent of the total white population. Altogether this dominant white section formed a very small minority in postemancipation Guyana, never reaching 3 percent of the total population, although their absolute numbers increased from 2,776 (2.8 percent) in 1841 to 4,551 (1.6 percent) in 1891. Very importantly, most of them were single males. The number of white women rose from a mere 53 per hundred men in 1851 to just 67 per hundred as late as 1891. Throughout the postemancipation nineteenth century an average of about 60 percent of the white population were urban, concentrated mainly in the capital, Georgetown, and to a lesser extent in New Amsterdam in Berbice.[1]

Elite Victorian culture was not, however, the monopoly of the white population. Even before emancipation, the mixed progeny of miscegenation between white males and black (and later, coloured) slave women recognized that one of the key criteria for social advancement in colonial society was the acquisition of white culture. Some of them (both during and after slavery) were actually sent by their white fathers to Britain to be educated, which accelerated the acculturative process. After emancipation the perception that Victorian cultural attributes were necessary for social respectability and mobility was accentuated and widened by the propaganda dispensed in the daily press, by missionary proselytization, and by the content of education made available locally, all of which stressed the superiority of British culture. Hence not only coloureds, but the freed blacks and their children were prepared to pay the price for progress. They thus sought to educate themselves out of manual labour and grinding poverty in order to become professionals and white-collar workers, e.g., lawyers, doctors, priests, teachers, clerks both in the public and private sectors. A few even became estate managers.[2]

But in the process many sought to purge themselves of their Afro-Creole cultural heritage and value system. This attitude was very clearly articulated by the two leading coloured newspapers of the period, the *Creole* (1856-1882) and the *Echo* (1887-1899) which were no less vituperative than the white press in their condemnation of 'immoral' lower class Afro-Creole cultural forms (as well as 'pagan' Asiatic immigrant cultures). Thus in their desperate quest for social respectability for their middle class black/coloured readership, these newspapers went to great pains to stress loyalty to the British monarchy and to uphold the superiority of British culture. As I pointed out elsewhere, this black/coloured educated elite class:

> felt the need or desirability to inculcate white cultural values, beliefs and mores . . . in order to prove that, despite differences in pigmentation, they were the social equals of the whites. It was a quest for social equality at the price of cultural self-denial. Some of these educated coloureds imbibed so much of the 'superior' airs and graces of their white peers as to attract the label of 'conceited and affected'. Acculturation for these in some cases went so far as to regard Britain as 'home' and to talk about their family traditions, sports crests, coats-of-arms, etc.[3]

The social values which these educated Creole elites (*évolués*) inculcated from the dominant Victorian culture were considered critical to their social advancement and further differentiated them from their lower class brethren. Among the principal values as identified by the black Anglican priest, Rev. J.R. Moore (1874), were energy and persevering industry, moral courage, self-denial, frugality, prudence, carefulness, and the avoidance of false pride. He attributed the absence of these qualities for the non-success and degradation of the Negro race in Guyana after emancipation.[4]

Referring to Trinidad, Brereton argues that this class of *évolués* attached very great significance to the acquisition of white culture because they had no other valuable and valued possession to hold on to:

> They were not wealthy. They owned few businesses and no large ones. With some exceptions, they were not landowners or planters . . . They had no vote, no voice in the government, no political influence. They were not, for the most part, employers of labour. They did not control the economy. But they possessed one attribute which the mass of the population did not have, and which the society, as a whole, valued: and that was cultural and intellectual skills. They elevated

'culture' into a supreme value because, in the circumstances of nineteenth-century Trinidad, this was the only field in which they appeared at an advantage in the society.[5]

This held good for Guyana, and indeed for the entire British Caribbean, as well. Thus as Bryan notes for Jamaica, at the upper level they were culturally indistinguishable from the whites.[6] Elite Victorian culture was, therefore, as much the culture of the educated middle class black and coloured *évolués* as it was that of the colonial whites. In other words, it transcended racial boundaries.

As one will find for all the cultures represented in nineteenth century Guyana, the recording of elite Victorian culture was very random, selective and uneven. While some aspects were reported in considerable detail, other aspects were ignored altogether or treated in a very scanty and superficial manner. This makes the historian's task of reconstruction quite difficult. However, given the nature of the historical evidence at hand, the elite culture will be analysed in two chapters: this one focusing on the material culture, social attitudes and values; the second on leisure activities.

Accommodation

The *raison d'être* of a colony like Guyana was the production of tropical staples, in this case sugar, for the metropolitan market. The plantation was the centre of civilization in the colony. Each plantation had its mansion or 'great house' where the resident proprietor or his agent lived, and quarters for the overseers. The mansion was the symbol of planter dominance on the estate and surrounding countryside. It was usually located in a garden some distance away from the other estate buildings. "Except for the garden, everything on the estate is rough and ready."[7] Barton Premium's mansion, for instance, was:

> large and commodious, with a gallery surrounding, and all those variations of structure resorted to in the tropics to promote circulation of air. A considerable space around it has been planted with those flowering shrubs, and beautiful, though gaudy flowers . . . And amidst them . . . the palm trees which grow also near the house, mixed with the sculpture-like cabbage palm; a little farther off, fruit trees of every variety form an extensive orchard . . . The approach is lined on each side by a regular row of cabbage trees, equal in age and size, which, throwing their branch-like leaves over the road, afford a partial shelter to the passing equestrian or gig traveller from the glare of a noon-tide sun.[8]

Upper class residential areas in the towns were similarly set in a splendid environment. In Georgetown the main sections were the wards of Kingston, Cummingsburg, and Stabroek, with Main and Camp Streets, and the Brickdam the favoured locations. Crookall described Main Street thus:

> In this street are to be found some of the finest tropical residences. Indeed you can hardly call it a street in the sense in which that word is used at home. It is

Elite residential
area in
Georgetown
(High Street)
c. 1860

NLJ photo. Courtesy of the National Library of Jamaica

Typical
elite
mansion

Ken Morgan photo. Reproduced from the collections of the UWI Library (Mona)

more like the entrance to a park. Grand villa residences of various styles of architecture, some with a tower and others with a cupola three or four stories high, and all of them surrounded with a garden, line the street on both sides. A great, broad, fresh-water trench runs up the centre; its banks lined with trees, give a shade and an appearance of coolness that is refreshing. The water is covered with the magnificent Victoria regia, the leaf of which is shaped like a 'frying-pan', and is sometimes two and three feet in diameter. The flower is as large as a man's head.[9]

Camp Street was very similarly laid out with a canal in the middle, trees alongside, and equally fine houses with gardens. The Brickdam and its environs, though structurally different, were no less picturesque:

Carriages run along it, hardly making any noise, for you have no stone pavement here, but a hardened kind of gravel . . . The road is wide enough for three or four carriages to run abreast, and on each side is a little grass plot and beautiful tropical trees. These afford a cool and pleasant shade to the heated pedestrian . . . Passing beyond these we come to the 'Avenue of Palms'. These palm trees, tall and straight, with their feathery plumes, stand like sentinels on each side of the road, making a picture that is only to be seen to be admired.[10]

With some variations in architectural style, both the elite mansions on the plantations and in the towns were similarly constructed. Most were built on stilts to avoid flooding during the rainy seasons. Access was gained by means of a stairway which led to a spacious verandah or gallery "so constructed that when the sun is up its hot rays may be excluded". The gallery was sometimes open, but more often closed in with three or four windows and jalousies. These jalousies were wooden and resembled venetian blinds which could at one's pleasure be opened to let in breeze and light while excluding the sun's rays, or shut to exclude rain and light. Usually the coolest part of the house, the gallery was the major arena for relaxation and entertainment. On the first floor of these houses, there was a tastefully furnished drawing room complete with draperies, engravings and paintings lining the walls, and a few English periodicals and books. Typical drawing room furniture included a suite or couch, whatnot, flower stand, piano, and several types of table—loo, gipsy, papier mâché, centre, sofa, and card tables. European visitors noted the rarity of carpeting which, it was felt, not only attracted insects but also made the room too warm; on the other hand they were struck by the proliferation of rocking and 'Berbice' chairs (called planter's chairs in India) used for relaxation. One noticeable feature of these houses was the multiplicity of windows which could be as many as fifty or sixty depending on the size of the house. Both windows and doors were generally kept open for ample ventilation.[11]

In the middle of the house there was usually a spacious dining room with two side rooms adjoining. The dining room was generally furnished with "a splendidly roomy dining table and chairs. Plenty

Courtesy of Dr. Velma Pollard. Photo by V. Pollard

The planter's
chair, known in
Guyana as the
Berbice chair

abounds everywhere, and the snowiness of the cloth and napkins, the beauty of the flowers and ferns that adorn it, all tend to enhance the pleasures of the table . . ." Other dining room furnishings included a waggonette or dinner waggon, sideboard, chiffonnier (sometimes with marble top and mirror), and by the 1880s a refrigerator or water cooler. Behind the dining room ran a gallery with steps leading to the next floor as well as a pantry, a small room for keeping table linen and service as well as food removed from the table. There were no vaults and underground cellars or basements.[12]

The upper floors were similarly arranged with rooms on both sides of the building. The bedrooms were "airy, lofty and exquisitely clean, with charmingly appropriate appointments", including hammocks. The most glorious mosaic, or sometimes carpet, covered the walls and floor. The four-poster bed generally consisted of a mattress with light feather pillows, and was surrounded with thin gauze nets to keep off mosquitoes. These were securely fastened to a frame at the top and tucked in under the mattress at the bottom. Every adult member of the family had a bedroom. Bedroom furniture included a dressing table (with or without mirror and/or drawers), chest of drawers, wardrobe, bedroom chairs, commode, and clothes and towel horses. Household furnishings were both imported (either from England or the United States) and local, and were generally made of walnut, oak, pine, mahogany, or the local crabwood.[13]

Given the ready availability of a wide variety of local timber from the dense equatorial forests, buildings, both for residences and businesses, were almost invariably wooden with little or no use made of stone. Shingle roofs were generally preferred to tiles because it was felt that they facilitated the supply of better and healthier rainwater to large vats (cisterns). In the absence of running tap water, rainwater was conducted from house roofs by means of pipes to the vats for storage. Wooden structures, however, were more at risk to fire, and consequently kitchens were almost never attached to the main building, but were instead located in specially constructed outhouses. While previously cooking was done on a coal-pot using wood or charcoal as fuel, by the end of the century most elite households had an English or American stove.[14] As a finishing touch, these fine residences were embedded in gorgeous flower gardens with a wide variety of colourful tropical flowers. Boddham-Whetham noted that:

> Many of the gardens are brilliant masses of colour, resembling a rich oil-painting, rather than a delicate water-colour of those of European lands. The tints are so gorgeous and heavy; there are bushes of crimson hybiscus, scarlet cordias, flaming poinsettias, trailing corallitas, the bright flowers of the bois immortelle, the drooping clusters of the red quiscualis, the vermilion blossoms of the flamboyant, all vying in splendour with saffron petroeas, deep blue convolvuluses, abutilons, and the white trumpets of the datura.[15]

Middle class aspirants to elite status, whether white or black/coloured could not afford such luxury. Most of these had to settle for less grand houses which in many instances they did not own. In Georgetown, house rents were reputedly so high that many bachelors, and occasionally even families, lived in hotels or guest houses with few comforts.[16] It was even worse for overseers and bookkeepers on the plantations. Both Wood and Bryan note how harsh the conditions of life were for this class of whites in Trinidad and Jamaica respectively.[17] They were no better off in Guyana. In sharp contrast to the managers and attorneys, living conditions for overseers were decidedly basic and often quite wretched. The overseer's house was generally a long single-storied building on brick pillars about twelve by eight feet. There was normally a gallery in front, about eight feet wide, running along the whole length of the building. Very often the walls of the rooms were bare, though in some cases they were painted or whitewashed. Since the shingled roofs were generally not watertight, in very many instances they leaked badly during the rainy seasons. As a consequence, the rooms were often in wretched condition and in extreme cases the walls were green and black with damp while the wooden floors were rotten. Furnishings were at best rudimentary. Generally the estate furnished a deal table and a bench, but the overseer was responsible for providing everything else. Given the expense and difficulty of transporting furniture, most overseers did very little in this regard.[18]

Generally speaking, the cultural elites made every effort to construct houses that were suitably adapted to the local environment, and made maximum use of local building materials. The layout of their residential areas and the architecture of the buildings were adapted to overcome the problems of drainage along the inhabited coastline which lay below sea level, and of tropical heat and torrential rainfall.

Despite their perception of their residence in Guyana as temporary, they were evidently keen to make their stay in this tropical frontier environment as physically comfortable as possible. This resulted in architectural styles which were unquestionably Guyanese. Indeed the field of architecture was undoubtedly one of the spheres of cultural life in Guyana to which the elites made their most outstanding, creative and long-lasting contributions. More importantly, the white mansion as a symbol of power and status became a desired cultural object for all social aspirants regardless of 'race' and led to its style (though not necessarily its size) being replicated by them.

Dress

In sharp contrast to their efforts to create architectural styles suited to a tropical environment, the dress of the cultural elites seemed wholly incongruous. The newspapers of the period were replete with advertisements which give a clear idea of the items and materials used for clothing. These included for the men, tweed suits, morning coats, trousers, white and regatta shirts, merino and cotton vests, broadcloths, doeskins, linen and cotton drills, serge and flannel. Writing in 1897, newcomer Arthur Sawtell was struck by "the extremely English appearance of the business and professional classes". "Except for the head-gear . . . there is little to distinguish nine out of ten of the whites of the colony from their brethren oversea. Here and there you occasionally see a man in a drill suit . . . But on the whole cloth, frequently dark and heavy-looking, prevails." The only difference was the shedding toward the end of the century of the top hat and frock-coat.[19] Outside of the business and professional circles, however, male dress was less formal, consisting of a complete suit of white duck crowned by a pith helmet. At night, for casual visits to friends where formal wear was not required, a simple change in the cut of the white jacket and the addition of a red scarf round the waist sufficed.[20]

For the ladies, black lace and llama shawls were popular, as were coloured cashmere, coloured and black cloaks, white quilted petticoats, white and coloured muslin robes, hairnets, gloves, hats, chiné mohair, checked satin cloth, checked Mozambique, checked leno cloth, sky, scarlet, green and French delaine, coloured French barège, black Norwich barège, plain Circassian, silk and cotton check dresses. Like their male counterparts, the women dressed informally for casual visits to friends; normally a simple white dress would do.[21]

Several of the above items, e.g., tweed suits, merino vests, serge and flannel, cashmere, etc. were wholly inappropriate to a tropical environment. But for the cultural elites good taste in dress was equated only with what was fashionable in the metropolis; and since one's

Typical dress of the white elite males

appearance was considered important if one hoped to be considered a part of the upper echelons of creole society, considerable attention had to be paid to wearing the latest European fashions. Hence no expense was spared in order to appear elegantly clad in public however incongruous that may have been in relation to the climate. "When light and flowing garments might be worn with comfort, both sexes try to imitate the London fashions, with this difference that their clothes seldom fit them, and they are generally twelve months behind the *mode.*"[22]

If European fashions seemed incongruous in the tropics, they were also capable of shocking the sense of morality of some of the more prudish of these Victorian colonial provincials. During the late seventies, for instance, new dress styles which apparently revealed rather than concealed the lines and curves of the female body aroused embarrassment and consternation in some persons.[23] Towards the end of the century, dress reform was engendering lively interest among some metropolitan women seeking to liberate themselves from the constraints, physically and otherwise, of traditional Victorian fashions, and rational modes of dress tended to reveal more of the female body. This, however, occasioned controversy in Britain,[24] let alone in the more conservative white colonial communities where it was considered critical that women should preserve a high moral image and decorum to avert the lustful desires of black/brown natives.

Be that as it may, however, it is very striking that no local fashions were created or promoted by the cultural elites. The emphasis was on importing forms and styles of dress from the metropolis even if these were wholly inappropriate to the local environment. Superficially, the difference in attitude here as opposed to architecture is striking. The accent in the latter was, of course, on luxury and comfort. But it was probably only because it was neither easy nor practical to import building materials from Britain that the elites did not do so. Where furnishings and dress were concerned, however, the cultural elites spared no effort to import what was fashionable in the metropolis. Yet because of their cultural dominance, they were able by force of example and by propaganda in the press, and even in church, to promote European clothing as the only socially acceptable form of dress in the colony. In fact European dress was equated with Christian morality and civilization. The message was clear: for individuals of any of the subordinate ethnic groups, social mobility within the colonial order entailed conformity with the European dress code. This was a blatant use of elite cultural power to create a standardized form of dress, however inappropriate, within creole society.

Social Attitudes and Values

Wherever Britons migrated, whether to settler colonies like Australia, New Zealand, Canada or the Cape Colony, or to tropical colonies like India and the Caribbean, as far as possible they made every effort to create home away from home and tried to shape their lives to conform to metropolitan middle class standards to which they aspired. As Bradlow notes for the Cape Colony, "the model for the . . . elitist culture was of course mid-Victorian, industrial England, a society whose *zeitgeist* increasingly reflected the ethos of the middle class . . ."[25] Unlike the settler colonies, however, life in Guyana for the British migrants was regarded as a temporary sojourn until they had made their fortune, then they would return home and hopefully gain access to those upper middle class circles which they so desperately sought to emulate. Britain, therefore, remained home for those who either came or claimed ancestry therefrom, *no matter how long they resided in the colony*: "The young Scotchman or Englishman longs for the day when his three or four years will have entitled him to a furlough there, whilst the older planter or merchant looks forward to spending at least the twilight of his life amid the refinements and luxuries always to be purchased in the Headquarters of the British empire".[26]

They made a point of keeping themselves up-to-date with contemporary English affairs, and indeed "England is far dearer to exiled affections than to the cold contents of home".[27] The colonial press played a major role in this regard printing news and features about life in the metropolis. In addition, metropolitan newspapers were also readily available at the elite social clubs. As in other colonies, 'exile' abroad in a far-off colony fostered a strong sense of the imperial idea and identification with the British monarchy[28] even though that was generally lacking among their peers at home until the late nineteenth century. Cannadine has shown how disinterested, indeed even hostile, the mid-Victorian Britons were towards their monarchy until the 1870s. Hence there were few public ceremonies centering on royalty, and very little public pageantry. It was only during the last quarter of the century, particularly following the entitling of Victoria as 'Empress of India' and the acquisition of new colonies, that the monarchy was transformed into a grand national and imperial institution, and every royal occasion became an imperial one—a development which reached its climax in Victoria's jubilees (1887 and 1897) and the coronation of Edward VII.[29]

In the colonies, however, the monarchy assumed tremendous significance from much earlier. In places like the Caribbean, the Cape, and India, it symbolized the might and glory of the imperial power which it was important to extol particularly in situations where white residents were vastly outnumbered by people whom they considered uncivilized and potentially hostile. But it did not merely symbolize imperial military and political domination. It was also a symbol around which a consensus of ideological values could be cultivated to unite both rulers and ruled based, however, on the latter's 'voluntary' subordination to the crown/constituted authority (and to whites in general). Traditions associated with the monarchy were thus invented[30] even where they did not exist in the metropolis, and the skilful manipulation of these placed in the hands of the colonial elite group tremendous cultural power to help promote social consensus and stability. Thus whereas in England for a long time the birthday of Victoria passed almost unnoticed, in Guyana it was celebrated annually in May-June as a public holiday with colourful military parades and gunfire salutes, levees at Government House (the governor's residence), and grand balls. Ships in the port also hoisted buntings in celebration.[31]

Although less attention was paid to the birthday of Prince Albert, the queen's husband, it was still privately celebrated.[32] However celebrations for the wedding of the Prince of Wales (the queen's son) and the Princess of Denmark in March 1863, were marked by a public holiday, although they were somewhat lacklustre, perhaps because the colony was experiencing an economic recession. Hence very few places were illuminated and just a few ships in the Demerara river were decorated with flags. Most people spent the day amusing themselves, though a cricket match on the Parade ground and a fireworks display later in the evening added sparkle to an otherwise quiet day.[33] The birth of a son and heir to the Prince the following year was celebrated with a royal gun salute fired at Fort William Frederick, while the flagstaffs at the Agricultural Rooms and at Government House were gaily decorated.[34] Likewise the first wedding anniversary of the royal couple in 1864 was marked by a fireworks display in the Garrison grounds.[35]

By the late nineteenth century when the monarchy had become a national symbol in Britain itself, the two jubilees of Victoria's reign were celebrated there and throughout the British empire with great festivity. On both occasions in Guyana—golden (September 1887) and diamond (June 1897)—public holidays were declared and the colonial elites organized events not only for their own entertainment, but also to impress upon the subordinate social groups the might, splendour and benefits of the British empire and its empress queen. After many years of witnessing repeated rituals in association with the invented traditions of the monarchy, these were fully internalized by the Creole population. Thus in the words of the coloured newspaper, the *Echo*, "It has been providentially given her to see the growth of her Empire into these imperially magnificent proportions that now astonish the world and honour all who bear the name of Englishman".[36] So with the adulation of the black/coloured colonial 'Englishmen', public buildings and streets were gaudily decorated and illuminated; churches held special thanksgiving services; there were parades of military and civilian organizations, including school children; fireworks displays, dinners for the poor at several churches, entertainment for the Indian immigrants at the Immigration Depot, balls and concerts; and special horse-racing meetings were organized, as were athletic sports meetings. As further tributes to the queen, in 1887 the legislature (the Court of Policy) approved the erection of her statue as a memorial of the jubilee; and in 1897 they approved the construction of a bandstand in her honour at the Sea Wall.[37]

Given their strong royalist sentiments, it is not surprising that the colonial elites should have been utterly ecstatic at the news that the Court of Policy had invited Prince Alfred to visit the colony as part of his Caribbean tour in 1861. Significantly it was the *Creole*, voice of the black and coloured middle class, which asserted that "The inhabitants of all classes look forward with lively interest to the happy day when they may be permitted to receive with loyal welcome on their shores a son of their beloved sovereign". This again demonstrates the extent to which the traditions invented by the white colonists succeeded in cultivating a shared monarchical ideology and vested them with enormous cultural power with which to promote a sense of cultural 'oneness' between rulers and ruled while maintaining social distinctions based largely on 'race', colour and class.

Thus in preparation for the royal visit no objection was made to the extravagant way in which public money, raised by high taxation on items of common consumption by the poor, was spent. Triumphal arches were erected in different locations along the route from the landing place to Government House. The main city streets were cleared and levelled in a style never before known. Expensive additions were made to the Assembly Rooms (the principal venue for elite cultural events) for a grand ball in honour of the prince, and there were militia rehearsals for a grand parade. Imagine the widespread disappointment when it became known that the prince had declined the invitation and would not be travelling further south than Barbados.[38]

In Britain public celebrations of national heroes enjoyed far more popularity that those of royalty among mid-Victorians. Some of these were celebrated by the colonial elites in Guyana too, most notably Trafalgar day to commemorate the famous victory of Admiral Nelson in 1805. Nearly all the leading business houses and most public buildings were decorated with flags and multicoloured streamers. Among the events usually planned to mark this occasion were a thanksgiving service at St. George's cathedral, a parade of the Militia and Police at Eve Leary, and an open air moonlight concert at the Botanic Gardens.[39]

The substantial Scottish (relative to the English) community tried to preserve their own sense of ethnic tribalism by celebrating the Feast of St. Andrew, patron saint of Scotland, annually on November 30. The occasion was usually marked with church services at Scottish kirks, concerts, large dinner parties, and dancing parties or balls where mainly Scottish music was played.[40] Yet for most of the century this was the only occasion on which the Scots seemed to get together as a community. It was not until 1888 that serious attempts were made to form a Scottish National Association in Georgetown. Like its sister societies in Jamaica, London and elsewhere, the object was to foster

social intercourse and mutual assistance, and to organize 'social evenings' in typically Scottish style.[41]

Notwithstanding the conscious efforts of the colonial elites to foster
and preserve an umbilical connection with the 'mother country', the
reality of life in a tropical plantation environment resulted in significant modifications in their attitudes and behaviour which not only
affected their lifestyles, but also their personality and demeanour. Such
creolization was naturally most pronounced among local-born (creole)
whites. Raised in a harsh tropical environment, their tanned bodies
contrasted starkly with the pale countenances of new arrivals, though
that paleness was evidently more valued by those who argued that the
creole whites had "nothing of the freshness of an English face". Power,
wealth and status in a plantation society made the men supremely
self-confident, even arrogant, and relatively informal and easy-going.
On the other hand, perhaps because they were less exposed, white
creole women were somewhat introverted, self-effacing and lacking in
confidence. (As we shall see, white colonial women were largely confined to the home and were strictly subordinate to their men.) Visitors
from the metropolis found it difficult to appreciate the demeanour and
character of the creole whites, and generally considered them crude
and uncultured.

> They are generally considered a self-satisfied, ignorant and indolent class, for the
> most part sprung from low classed parents who have made money. They are
> overbearing towards those who depend on them. They have very little conversa-
> tion. With the men one can talk about sugar and almost solely about sugar; but
> with those creole ladies it is perfectly useless to attempt to make them talk. They
> can answer yes or no and perhaps will venture to ask you if you like the country.
> They are also very shy or awkward.[42]

As in the Cape Colony, the Guyanese colonial elites were driven by
the Victorian middle class desire "to be rich and successful coupled
with a passion for achievement and respectability".[43] But unlike the
Cape, they simply regarded Guyana as a place to make their fortune
and acquire high social status rather than as a place of permanent
residence; hence they made very little attempt to create lasting structures beyond what were necessary to promote their own well-being:
unrepresentative political institutions, a plantation system, and places
of worship. The lifestyles and behaviour of the colonial elites were
also largely conditioned by the open frontier environment of a plantation society far from home, devoid of the 'civilizing' influences and
sanctions of the home society, characterized by a shortage of young
unmarried white women and its attendant consequences on family life
and morality, and where life expectancy was short because of their
susceptibility to tropical diseases. These factors combined to produce a
community marked by such contradictions as fortune-seeking but extravagant spending on material things (e.g., food, drink, clothing),
status-seeking but coarse behaviour and loose morality.

The quest for high social status dominated the social behaviour of these elites. To be accepted in the highest echelons of society was the primary aspiration of those who perceived themselves as the cultural elite. To achieve this, they had to live and dress in a socially approved style and manner, to belong to the right clubs, and associate with the right people. This was often a very unpleasant and humiliating preoccupation which could take years before the desired result was attained. Yet to the casual observer, there appeared to be an absence of exclusiveness in the social life of the elite classes. It could seem as if any white person could rapidly achieve high social status in the colony and become really polished gentlemen and ladies in the process.[44] But in reality the upper echelons of colonial society were very exclusive indeed, and that exclusivity was very zealously guarded by those who belonged. To gain entry, the aspirant had to endure considerable snubs and insults unless he had a natural claim by birth or wealth. Yet that did not deter those who avidly sought such exalted social ranking.[45]

It was mainly young newcomers who felt the greatest need to gain acceptance. Most were of rather humble origin in Britain and whose manners were considered coarse by those in the aristocratic Creole circles. Some also came from neighbouring Caribbean colonies, particularly Barbados. Those almost invariably claimed connections with one of the first families of their native island in the hope of establishing their pedigree. That, however, did not go down well in the local elite circles.[46]

As we noted before, appearance was an important aspect of upper class life. The aspirant to elite status thus found it necessary to dress elegantly in the latest English fashion and acquire a watch and other trappings of bourgeois dress. He would then hire a carriage in order to visit the governor as was customary of newcomers, and also call on other prominent persons with whom he had no previous acquaintance. But in such a class conscious society, he had to be prepared for cool receptions and even insults and not be discouraged, because to be seen associating with the right people was critical to the quest for social elevation.[47] "To cringe and fawn in order to give people, who neither know nor care two pence about you, an opportunity of openly insulting you is a thing none would adopt, but strange to say, there are scores who will undergo this and more, merely for the sake of being thought fashionable."[48]

Officers of the military forces stationed in the colony and of the police force were useful rungs on the social ladder for aspiring aristocrats,

> . . . to be seen walking along the Sea Wall with a beardless sub-lieutenant perhaps just a few months from school, is a social triumph which will furnish one of the[se] youths . . . conversation for a month . . . Newly fledged inspectors of Police are also the objects of great attention; they are paraded about, taken to hotels, treated to swizzles [local alcoholic drink] and other toothsome beverages, and all this for no reason they can discover.[49]

Attendance at high society balls and dinners was regarded as essential if one's quest for social elevation was ever to materialize. The social aspirant would thus go to extremes to ensure that he or she was present whether or not they could afford it. One classic instance was a fancy dress ball organized by Governor Longden's wife in January 1875. Many of those who felt compelled to attend were well known debtors, but nevertheless plunged themselves further into debt to purchase costume and ticket just to be present.[50]

> In a community so small as this, the circumstances of every individual in it are more or less known, and it is a fact that many who were there were decked out in gaudy but expensive tinsel, which if paid for, will in all probability, prevent them from paying their just debts. Nay, it is a fact that there were many there who are overwhelmed with debt, whose daily duns must have rendered them insensible to all feelings of decency and propriety, or else they never would have appeared there to face defrauded creditors.[51]

Even persons who had recently been formally declared bankrupt turned up at the ball expensively outfitted

> . . . with unblushing and bold and brazen countenance, strutting about in all the pomp and pride of a gaudy dress which ill became their position and circumstances. You may see them pushing themselves forward on all occasions, officious everywhere, in the Ball room, on the Cricket ground, wherever they can obtrude themselves; without shame, without remorse . . .[52]

It was this obsession with social status which caused many aspirants to overreach themselves in order to indulge in such extravagance. In creoledom, no matter how distressed one was financially, one could not risk the loss of face and status that would result if one appeared unable to afford to be present at a high society affair. In fact one had to try to outdo one's peers: ". . . I must not only go to it, but I must eclipse that fellow Brown who gave a swell dinner—to which he forgot to invite me last week". Such was the argument which swayed many people.[53]

Attendance at public balls was not sufficient for the young social aspirant. In order to be seen associating with the right people, he generally ignored the young single good-looking, but not particularly well-off, girls for older married women of position. The latter were generally flattered by the fact that they could still attract the attention of eligible young bachelors. But there were certain limits imposed on the aspirant's ambition: he could dance quadrilles or lancers with these women, and might even manage "by dint of taking no refusal . . . a square dance with one of the recognized leaders of local fashion; [but] he never is accorded a round dance, they are reserved for his betters".[54]

Perseverance and imperviousness to snobbery and insult, even the risk of bankruptcy, might after some years pay dividends. The pretender might be elected a member of one of the elite clubs, and then in order to preserve the very exclusivity which for so long kept him at

Government
House
(governor's
residence)
c. 1860: symbol
of British
imperial power

bay, he would do his utmost to blackball anyone whom he perceived to be below his status. Eventually he would go to England to find a wife, and on his return would have to undertake a fresh struggle to get her received in the elite circles. Again, if successful, he would exert all his energies to keep down any youngster who was not willing to grovel before him as he had done.[55] Such were the values of the cultural elites in colonial society.

As a rule, social climbers were avid invitation hunters for high society events. One had merely to whisper an intention of planning a ball or reunion of some sort to be inundated for weeks before the event with requests for invitations "by callers of both sexes, many of them strangers . . ."; and no amount of rebuke would discourage those persons who would persist until granted their wish.[56] This was patently demonstrated, for instance, when rumours began to circulate about Mrs. Longden's proposed fancy dress ball in January 1875. Not finding it indelicate to admit her desire publicly, an excited rural female resident even wrote to the press unashamedly soliciting a formal invitation so that she would not be forced to attend by way of "an outside ticket". Obviously bored and starved of entertainment, she was as early as October 1874 salivating in anticipation and thinking of what she would wear even though she had no invitation.[57] By far the most coveted invitation was that for the annual ball hosted by the governor in honour of the queen's birthday. For weeks before this gala 'extravaganza', the normal Saturday afternoon receptions at Government House would be thronged with unaccustomed visitors anxious to receive an invitation which was issued as a matter of course to every such caller.[58]

In keeping with their efforts to preserve the exclusivity of aristocratic circles in creoledom, it is not surprising that the arts of cutting and snobbery should play a very prominent role in the social etiquette of the cultural elites. This was not unique to the colonies, but could be found in England as well. However, as Bradlow points out, whereas social mobility in the metropolis was determined more by hereditary status than by wealth, both were operative in the colonies.[59] Hence snobbery was accentuated in colonial elite circles to guard against dilution. One did not have to misbehave or do something immoral to be at the receiving end of this practice. One merely had to be seen in the company of somebody of different social rank, particularly if that person were clinging desperately to the fringes of high society. And as Brereton noted in Trinidad, "Real or imagined slights were all-important. Everyone who mattered was known to, and probably related to, everyone else; there was no escape into obscurity".[60]

This might help to explain why duelling which, as a form of settling specific affronts to the male sense of honour and dignity, had by 1850 more or less effectively died out in Britain, remained in vogue until relatively late in Guyana. In 1876, for instance, a duel was called (but later averted) for the simple reason that one man had called another a fool in the presence of a woman. This was considered such a grave insult to the honour of the injured party that it could only be avenged with blood.[61] Very often though, disputes were not allowed to be settled by gentlemanly duels. Instead open brawls among elite males were not uncommon, including even government officials.[62]

Generally speaking, the colonial elites tended to be very informal, even coarse, with those whom they considered their equals. Whereas Victorian middle class English etiquette would require a man to bow politely on being introduced to a woman, and only offer his hand when a certain degree of intimacy had developed, in creoledom it was customary to reach for the woman's arm and shake it vigorously on first introduction. If that struck the visitor as impolite, the behaviour of elites in the ballroom seemed decidedly vulgar; for there was often a mad scramble for the women (of position of course) with no regard to Victorian bourgeois rules of politeness or precedence.[63]

If the urban elites seemed impolite to the cultured English visitor, their rural plantocratic counterparts were of a distinctly boorish vintage. Although considerable improvement was said to have been made in their manners, morality and religiosity after slavery,[64] in many instances their behaviour, conversations and habits could not be "emulated with propriety", and gambling, excess drinking and 'womanizing' (sexual promiscuity) remained endemic.[65] Immorality and coarse behaviour on the plantations were encouraged by the absence of the restraining influence of elite women who were far fewer than even in the towns.[66] The description of a dinner party at the home of a leading planter illustrates how raucous they could become after a few drinks:

But in the status-conscious environment of Guyana and the Caribbean, the colonial elites would incur any expense for both public and
private entertainment. This prompted the following reflection by
Pepps after dinner at friends one evening:

> On my way home did talk to my wife about the extravagance of the dinner we
> had been at, regretting that the fashion now was such that one could seldom bid
> one's friends to dine, so much expense being caused by a single feast; on which
> she did answer sharply that one must do as one's neighbours, and that, for her
> part, her entertainments should be as grand as her neighbours, or not at all.[74]

Sex, Morality and Domestic Life

The reality of virtually absolute social and political power in a frontier
environment, combined with a shortage of white women, and a strong
desire for the pleasures of the flesh, found full expression in the sexual
proclivities of the cultural elites which deviated significantly from the
moral ideals of their Victorian middle class Christian background.
During slavery marriage of white estate personnel was discouraged on
the ground that they would require more domestic servants.[75] Therefore, instead of monogamous Christian marital relationships, it was
customary for estate managers and overseers, merchants and even government officials to have a domestic 'establishment' presided over by a
black or coloured woman who looked after the servants and provided
all 'comforts' for her master. The offspring of such unions though
sometimes sent to England for education were usually debarred from
local white social circles.[76] This created tensions in the society as the
educated coloureds continuously pounded on the doors for admission
as social and political equals.[77]

Such 'loose' mating relationships remained prevalent in the postemancipation period,[78] but there is no indication that marriage of estate
personnel was still either discouraged as in Jamaica or prohibited as it
was in the plantation areas of the Dutch East Indies, even though
similar practical considerations of low salaries and poor living conditions would have ruled it out for most overseers.[79] Certainly, as in
Trinidad, several managers and overseers on estates continued to cohabit with or sexually harass and abuse female workers, with Indian
immigrant women replacing Creoles.[80] Even missionaries from time
to time yielded to temptation and succumbed to the pleasures of native female flesh.[81] But in general marriages among the upper classes
gradually became more regular,[82] particularly when steamships cheap-
ened and shortened travel between colony and metropolis and made
the voyage less difficult. Thus white men returned to England to
marry women of their own kind. As more white women began to
accompany their husbands to the colony and a less unstable white
community was formed, the old 'establishments' were increasingly

St. George's
Anglican
Cathedral
(state church) c. 1860

St. Andrew's
Scots Kirk
(state church) c. 1860

regarded with disfavour and gradually decreased among upper class urban whites,[83] though they remained rampant on the estates.

The increased presence of white women, especially in the towns, reduced the level of intimacy, and consequently led to greater social distance between white and non-white. This was not unique to Guyana. Stoler notes that the same phenomenon occurred in India, colonial Africa, the Dutch East Indies, and in the Pacific islands as well. She observes that the arrival of women usually occurred in conjunction with some immediately prior or planned stabilization of colonial rule. In Guyana (and the British Caribbean) it was related to the efforts to bring about social stability after the upheavals occasioned by emancipation and the economic depression of the late 1840s. New mechanisms were required to restore the social order whereby all the constituent elements would keep their ascribed positions. By reducing the incidence of interracial cohabitation or concubinage, the increased influx of white women not only stabilized the white family structure, but also kept the number of mixed progeny (a major source of social instability) to a minimum. Hence,

> . . . the presence of European women did not inadvertently produce stronger racial divisions: rather, it was in some cases intended precisely to enforce the separation between [non-whites] and whites. Colonial elite concern for the entry of white women was related . . . to 'the real or imagined threat to superiority and status that miscegenation implied'. The arrival (and protection) of women was part of a wider response to problems of colonial control which often antedated the objections raised by European women to miscegenation. It was not sexual relations between European men and [non-white] women per se that were condemned, but this form of domestic arrangement and the social tensions to which it gave rise. The concubines and their [mixed-blood] progeny came to be seen as a danger to the European community at large.[84]

White women were also the 'custodians of morality' in colonial society, and wherever they were introduced in significant numbers they seemed to exert "a civilizing, cultured, and restraining check on the rowdy, crude, and hard-drinking life style" of the rural plantocracy.[85] Thus in Guyana, wherever wives were present there was a fairly high degree of order and decorum. Undoubtedly with some exaggeration, one visitor claimed that the planter's wife

> invariably is a lady of education, and refinement, whose taste, influence, and the results of her tact, are to be seen everywhere . . . Truly is woman's influence best felt in her own sphere, where she reigns the acknowledged Queen, and from whence she sends forth her husband, sons and guests, to fight life's battles with a firmer faith, which is begot of her companionship.[86]

The increased female presence also put religion into a more central position in the lives of the cultural elites. There was certainly more attendance at churches on Sundays, and the women themselves became very involved in the social activities of the churches largely for want of anything else to do with their time. As a British colony, it was natural that the Church of England should be the established church (meaning that it was supported out of public revenues); but there was such a substantial Scottish community in the colony----Heatley regarded Guyana as "essentially a Scotch colony"[87]----that the Church of Scotland was also on the colonial payroll. So there were two state churches in nineteenth century Guyana, each with a major centre in Georgetown (Demerara) and New Amsterdam (Berbice), and the parishes were equally divided between them. The Roman Catholic church had a smaller presence until the arrival of the Portuguese immigrants, while the Dutch Reformed church rapidly faded out of existence because of the disappearance of Dutch residents after emancipation. Among the white population there were a few Jewish families, but no synagogue. Generally speaking, however, the expansion of the established churches and the increased number of priests helped to improve the moral and religious tone of the white community.[88]

If the increased presence of white women and priests caused an upliftment in the morality of the colonial elites by discouraging concubinage particularly in the urban centres, it did not materially curb their sexual promiscuity because there was always a substantial number of young men who did not consider themselves sufficiently well off financially to get married and enjoy a lifestyle befitting that status in creole society: ". . . salaries are small and, until they are in a position, the boys are shy; to occupy a small house and to work honestly together to endeavour to make provision for the future never seems to suggest itself to the *jeunesse dorée* of the colony . . ."[89]

The craving for high status reinforced a tendency among middle class British men against early marriage. According to Hyam, in the mid-nineteenth century the average age of marriage for British men was twenty-nine, while about 10 percent never married at all. Whether in Britain this was attributable to the same reason as in Guyana—the desire to become economically and socially established before getting married----is not clear. What is certain, however, is that in both places it created a social environment in which young men simply played the field, with both single and married women, including prostitutes,[90] until their middle years when they would decide to marry much younger women of suitable status. Young elite women on the other hand, while being courted by men young and old, were generally only likely to receive an offer of marriage from a much older man. In Guyana age did not matter----men as old as seventy fancied themselves with girls fifteen or sixteen.[91]

'Womanizing', therefore, was rampant among the male elites of Guyanese society. Contrary to Stipendiary Magistrate Hancock's impression in 1845 that the phenomenon of the roving single white male with a series of female connections had decreased,[92] the white stud or lady-killer was very much alive until and beyond the end of the century. As the *Royal Gazette* put it, instead of early marriage, "the young men here indulge in dissipation . . . Libertinism seems to be accepted here as a thing of course; in fact a young man without a touch of Don Juan in composition is said to be a 'duffer' or an 'impostor'. To lead a regular and virtuous life exposes a man to the ridicule of society in general".[93]

Kirke recalled the case of one man, resident at Beckwith hotel (the leading hotel in Georgetown c.1872), who was caught by the owner making love to the ladies' maid. Although ejected, bag and baggage, within the hour, he could not curb his libido. "His amorous propensities got the same gentleman into further trouble, for going to St. Thomas, and being caught by the Governor of that island making love to one of his daughters, he was ordered to leave the island within twenty-four hours and never return".[94] In 1878, the gossip columnist 'Argus' reported that a reputedly decent Christian man awoke one morning to find himself in the bedroom of another man's wife. While this sort of occurrence was evidently by no means unusual, it appears that it may have in this instance resulted in the husband's suicide.[95]

No less interesting is the strong hint that sexual promiscuity was not limited to heterosexual activity: the *Royal Gazette* actually labelled Georgetown the Sodom of the nineteenth century![96] Homosexuality would not have been abnormal for, as Hyam notes, many colonial officials and male colonists were sexually initiated in British public schools where they frequently shared beds; and even though middle class Victorian Britain developed a pathological abhorrence of homosexuality, literally driving homosexual groups underground, the colonies offered ample opportunities for, and fewer sanctions against, such 'deviant' sexual behaviour.[97] In Guyana, this would have been made easier by the power which managers and overseers had over young boys working on the estates.

Not all young men were equally placed to enjoy a profligate life. There was a sort of pecking order associated again with one's socio-occupational status. The plantation overseer ranked lowest, with the Water Street store clerk a cut above. The civil servant enjoyed relatively high social status and appeal although his salary was low; bank clerks, who were privy to the financial state of many of the leading citizens, were avowed lady-killers of creoledom. But undoubtedly the most eligible bachelors among the colonial elites were the uniformed officers of the military regiments stationed at the garrison in Eve Leary, Georgetown, and those of the police force.[98]

The high incidence of sexual promiscuity and the unwillingness or inability of men to get married at an early age naturally affected elite women who, like their middle class peers in Britain and in other colonies, were socialized to consider marriage as their natural destiny. This problem was courageously aired in the press by a young woman, pen-named 'Clarinda' who, while desirous of getting married, had no intention of doing so to an old man. Clarinda's letters to the press provide us with a unique picture of what some young elite women thought and how they attempted to fight against a social order which reduced women to being sexual objects. She disliked those married men, old bachelors and widowers whose flirtations discouraged or inhibited young men, whom she considered preferable, from courting. She was, however, most distasteful of those males whom she called the

> set of young and old rakes whose estimate of themselves is unbounded. They fancy they are quite killing and make love alike to married and unmarried, but the truth is they prefer married ladies if young and good-looking because then no questions are asked and the stupid henpecked husband looks on complacently, or keeps his feelings to himself for a quiet life.[99]

It has already been observed that this preference for older married women by young men was clearly exhibited at high society balls. It was obviously more related to their uninhibited quest for high social status by association than to sexual attraction since the young attractive single women were ignored. One consequence was that high society balls were mostly attended by married women who (many of them past their prime years) encouraged and were flattered by the attention they received from the young gallants.[100]

Clarinda, however, was determined to defy the conventional 'wisdom' which asserted that young men her age did not have sufficient means to maintain a wife. She wanted to marry a young man whom she genuinely loved regardless of his income; but such sentiments were abnormal in elite society, and she had to fight both family and friends who erected obstacles to her forming serious relationships with young men simply because their small incomes (between £200 and £300 per annum) were unable to rent a large house, keep a carriage, and maintain a family in the style and manner befitting an upper class status complete with an army of servants. Most of these young bachelors, because they were rendered socially ineligible by their limited financial resources and could not afford luxuries, spent the greater part of their time in useless and idle flirtations ('womanizing') or frequenting elite social clubs (social climbing). Yet Clarinda was determined to rock the boat if necessary and marry any young man whom she really loved regardless of his financial position, and to accept, live and work for him. "I will be at the door to welcome and kiss him as he returns from work. House and wife will be kept tidy and I will share in his cares and sorrows . . ."[101] She would demand neither horse nor carriage, as was customary, if they could not afford such luxuries.[102]

Clarinda's stubborn and outspoken idealism was very courageous though by no means revolutionary since she still adhered to the traditional Victorian middle class conceptualization of the woman's role in the family and home. However, in her own limited way she was demanding the freedom for young women to choose whom and when they should marry rather than be constrained by the restrictions of a male dominated society. How representative this position was in late nineteenth century Guyana is not clear. Most certainly there were some loud dissenting voices among her peers who were not quite so willing to defy convention and forego the good life. Jessie, for instance, would never contemplate marrying a fellow worth only £250 a year. She feared that the first six months of honeymooning and love-making would give way to the harsh realities of upper class demands. Could love satiate her hunger or buy her even ordinary calico? Could £250 pay the house rent, servants, washing and all the other trappings of upper class life? And what about providing for children?[103] These were very important considerations for anyone who aspired to or wanted to preserve their social status in the upper echelons of creole society.

Finding a suitable man who could meet those exacting status criteria, however, was not an easy matter, and many young women had to be content with waiting until 'Mr. Right' came along with an offer of marriage. This, however, meant running the risk of being 'left on the shelf'----a prospect too dismal for one or two more enterprising souls who advertised their wants. On the other hand, the 'conditions' of marriage, which often meant marrying an older, albeit fairly financially well-off, man were not always compatible with the woman's happiness; and apparently some women were just as eager to be rid of their husbands as they had been to acquire them in the first place.[104] No doubt many women stuck it out for the material benefits and high status that went along with marriage to a well-to-do man.

In the colonies, no upper class woman worthy of the status (the rare Clarindas excepted) was prepared or expected to perform household chores. The middle class Victorian notion of the genteel elite woman of leisure received its fullest expression in the plantation society of Guyana. "The ladies of the higher classes usually spend their time in reading, and now and again, though only to break the tiresome monotony, in light feminine tasks. The kitchen only knows the lady of the house and her daughters by name, and the remaining cares of a housewife are just as much unknown to the former as to the latter."[105]

The elite male therefore had to be able to afford domestic help and all the other trappings of upper class life which a small salary could not sustain.[106]

Elite gentleman and wife with retinue of servants

RITES OF PASSAGE

Birth

As we noted before, less than half the white population in nineteenth century Guyana were local born (creole). Throughout the postemancipation period creole whites not only numbered less than 45 percent of the total white population, but their numbers remained relatively small and static. Indeed, the creole white population increased by fewer than 500 in the forty years between 1851 and 1891.[107] Births, therefore, were not many or frequent, and consequently the historical records do not reveal much about how they were celebrated. It was, however, customary for the elites to announce the birth of children in the press, e.g., in 1866:

> THOMPSON—On Saturday the 21st ultimo [April],
> the wife of *J. W. Thompson* Esq., of plantation Perseverance,
> Essequibo, of a Son.[108]

or, in 1873

> VYFHUIS—At the Brickdam, on the 1st instant [August],
> MRS. HERMAN VYFHUIS, of a Daughter.[109]

Apart from such public announcements, it would seem that the Euro-elites treated birth as a private matter, and consequently not much is reported about their birth customs. Perhaps a small social gathering of close friends and relatives was held to celebrate the event.

The formal naming of the child took place at the time of his/her initiation into the church by baptism or christening. This was a more elaborate affair. It was held a few weeks or months after birth and involved the attendance of the child's parents, relatives and close friends at church for a special baptismal service. The priest baptised or christened the child by pouring a few drops of previously blessed water on his/her forehead, and 'godparents' were appointed purportedly to ensure the child's Christian upbringing. After the ceremony a typically lavish creole ball was held complete with claret and champagne. In subsequent years each birthday might be celebrated with a daytime party at which neighbouring children of equal social status were invited. These parties were punctuated by 'dinner' at about 2.00 p.m., and tea at about 5.00 p.m., before ending at sundown (about 6.00 p.m.).[110]

The colonial Euro-elites retained certain superstitious ideas brought from Britain about how the child's personality and appearance might be influenced by the day of birth. Normally transmitted in nursery rhyme fashion, it was held that if born on Monday, the child would be fair in face; if on Tuesday, the child would be full of grace; if on Wednesday, it would be sour and sad; on Thursday, merry and glad; on Friday, loving and giving; if born on Saturday, the child would have to work hard for a living; but if on Sunday, it would never want.[111]

Marriage

If birth was treated as a very private affair, marriage on the other hand, although still clearly private, was an occasion for great public display of pomp and affluence. Again, however, they were by no means frequent because of the tendency of white men to import wives from the metropolis. But when marriages were celebrated in the colony, they tended to be clones of the genteel Victorian affair and were attended with maximum extravagance which reflected the status, real or aspiring, of the individuals and families concerned. The wedding of Henry Messervy, manager of Plantation La Bonne Intention, East Coast Demerara, and an upper class white girl at the Pro-Cathedral (Anglican) in Georgetown in January 1889 was a typically high society affair.

The church was decorated with three arches of orange blossoms and green foliage placed at stated distances in the main aisle through which the bride would pass up to the chancel. The pulpit, chancel and altar were similarly decorated. Around the lectern, plants were arranged in flower pots, while from the head of its brazen eagle, hung an arboreous wreath interspersed with orange blossoms (signifying fertility).[112]

> The bridegroom arrived at 2.40 p.m. with his best man, and the bride at 3.00 p.m. She was greeted by the archdeacon, three priests and forty choristers robed in white vestments, who sang a marriage hymn as they proceeded up the aisle. The bride entered leaning on the arm of her father. She wore a dress of thick cord silk, with a front of Limerick lace and a Court train of ivory moiré silk, four or five feet in length, ornamented with orange blossoms and loops of ribbons over a petticoat trimmed with Horton lace, a tulle veil, fastened with a diamond arrow, and sprays of orange blossom. She also wore a gold 'Merry Thought' brooch, and a magnificent diamond bracelet, and carried a bouquet of white roses and myrtle, and a feather lyre fan.[113]

The two pages who upheld the train wore Court suits of apricot green plush with cream moiré waistcoats, each carrying enamelled silver-headed walking-sticks, with their three-cornered hats tucked under their arms. The chief bridesmaid was dressed in a Directoire costume of cream moiré revers and trimmings of apricot green moiré and silver buttons, a large straw hat trimmed with moiré ribbons and bunches of hops, and a diamond and sapphire ring. Two little bridesmaids wore cream, low-necked pongee silks smocked with apricot green, green moiré sashes and loopers, and long cream mittens, cream 'Liberty' bonnets smocked with green and trimmed with green moiré ribbons, and gold bangles.[114]

The ceremony was performed by the bishop, assisted by the arch-deacon, after which the couple proceeded to their carriage around which a crowd of well-wishers gathered to throw flowers on them. All invited guests then proceeded to the Woodbine Hotel, residence of the bride's father, for a sumptuous *déjeuner* (lunch). Thereafter the bride and groom left for the railway station where an express train waited to convey them to Plantation Friendship for the honeymoon. In keeping with the pompous occasion, the gifts were lavish and expensive. They included a complete set of glassware, a pearl horseshoe brooch, silver salt-cellars, a pearl and diamond bracelet, a table gong, a pair of bronze statues, a Worcester China and silver teaset, etc.[115] Bryan notes that upper class weddings in nineteenth century Jamaica were very similar.[116]

Death

As they lived, so did they die----marked by a grand display of opulence and prestige. So although naturally solemn, the funeral was no less a status seeking affair among the creole elites. But their attitude to death was also influenced by their social circumstances in the colony. During slavery when they were few, mainly male, and generally without kith and kin in the colony, almost the whole white community of a district turned out to see a fellow colonist decently and honourably buried *especially if he was a prominent figure.* As marriage became a feature of elite life after emancipation, there were greater kinship links among families who rallied to each other's support in time of sickness and death. However, the custom of a large funeral still persisted if only as a symbol of the high social status of the deceased and his/her family.[117]

Thus when a prominent white resident died, a notice was circulated and "all the world goes to the funeral". If printed, this circular was edged with black and headed *Memento Mori*, and was derived from the early Dutch inhabitants who called it *Doed Briefen*. Funerals took place at 8.00 a.m. and 4.30 p.m. daily. In the absence of refrigeration, if one died before 4.00 p.m., the funeral would be at 8.00 a.m. the next day; if the death occurred after 4.00 p.m., the funeral would be 4.30 p.m. the following day. As many as one hundred carriages might be counted in a funeral *cortège*.[118] The funeral of one Mr. Hunter, a Scotsman, in October 1874, for instance, was attended by a large number of friends. The *cortège* left his residence in Main Street at about 4.00 p.m., and the coffin was borne by some of his workers to St. Andrew's church where the funeral service was held. After that, the procession went to the Le Repentir cemetery where a solemn ceremony of interment took place.[119] Henry Bullock pointed to some very interesting features of elite funerary customs. If a deceased man were unmarried, no matter how old he was, his coffin would be white and the bearers were required to wear white in their hats and white scarves. The coffin was carried by means of three towels passed underneath. Certainly up to the 1860s, palls were not used by the Guyanese elites.[120]

It appears that the elites preserved the British practice of the lyke- or liche-wake over the bodies of departed friends and relatives before burial. This practice of sitting up was, as in the British Isles, done as a social mark of respect for the deceased and his/her relatives. It was undoubtedly conducted with far less noise and theatre than the Afro-Creole wakes which the elites universally condemned (chapter 5).[121]

Summary

With the exception of architecture, both in their material culture and in their social attitudes and values, the cultural elites placed great emphasis on importing their models from middle class Britain. This orientation was very largely bound up with their firm belief that the artifacts, values and symbols of British middle class culture had to be the cornerstone of colonial civilization, and thus anyone with pretensions to elite status was required to demonstrate his/her 'good breeding' and mastery of that imported culture. This outward-looking import mentality, however, stifled any natural creative impulses that may have been extant among them. Even those who were locally born, including the brown-black *évolués*, looked to the 'mother country' for cultural leadership and moral guidance. It was thus only in the field of architecture where perforce of necessity they could not rely entirely on imports, that their creative talents, given full scope for expression, flowered and produced fairly unique and long-lasting styles.

Despite their strong inclinations to replicate metropolitan culture, in many respects the reality of life in a frontier environment where the civilizing influences of family and religion were relatively weak, and where there were several other cultural influences present, produced significant differences in their way of life from the Victorian model which they idealized. So even though towards the end of the nineteenth century the cultural elites appeared, at least at a formal level, to conform more closely to British middle class ideals of Christian morality and manners, it is obvious that sexual promiscuity remained prevalent. Likewise, although public displays of drunken behaviour were no longer commonplace among the upper classes, there is no doubt that, as we shall see, excess drink continued to play a major part in the social activity of the white male.

But as the dominant cultural section, the behaviour, attitudes and values of the elites served as role models for the rest of the society, and this was reinforced by the cultural power at their disposal in a colonial situation. Thus whether for good or ill, their obsession with high social status and the prejudicial attitudes and behaviour which went along with that, their love of pomp and extravagance, and of the pleasures of the flesh, set a tone for all socially aspiring individuals to emulate. The same goes for their material culture which they projected as desirable symbols or objects of civilization and progress regardless of their appropriateness in the colony. They thus used their cultural power in an effort to create a consensus around the notion of the superiority of British Victorian middle class culture.

Aerial view
of
Georgetown,
c.1860 (Water
Street)

The Tower
Hotel,
Georgetown,
c. 1890

ELITE VICTORIAN CULTURE:
Leisure

It would be true to say that the wealthy white residents of Guyana in the nineteenth century were a leisured class. A typical day for the average upper class colonial resident began a little before 6.00 a.m. with 'tea' and toast. "The little black butler brings you upstairs a cup of Berbice coffee . . . Along with coffee is a little bread and butter or a little toasted cassava cake . . ." Thereafter until about 9.30 a.m. they had their baths ("pouring the water over the body with the 'calabash'"), dressed and prepared for breakfast. There was little horse-riding or early walking exercise. Around 9.30 a.m. they had breakfast which was a very substantial meal. "Fish is plentiful, and we have some excellent kinds. The querriman steaks, or gillbacher, or snapper, we can get five mornings out of seven, and at a very reasonable price. To fish we have, as a rule, 'rice' and yam, and cassava, and sweet potato, and plantain." Such elite consumption of Afro-Creole foods cooked by Creole domestics was highly indicative of their creolization. After breakfast, business was conducted with decreasing energy until lunch at about 2.00 p.m. when they had a choice from a wide range of tropical fruit. Thereafter business died away in the course of the afternoon.[1]

In Georgetown, after work at about 5.00 p.m. everyone "with any pretensions at all to culture, position, or outward superiority" (except for the whist and euchre addicts at the elite clubs) took an 'airing', by hurrying off to the promenade—the Sea Wall—"the public place where the whole aristocracy is seen united, though divided by political and domestic differences". Of course, only those with carriages went there.[2]

> He who goes on foot would expose evidence of his poverty, and would accordingly prove 'impossible' in those circles. As a rule, walking is avoided here more than anywhere else and any one enjoying but a fair amount of means keeps his own trap which is very generally a light two-wheeled vehicle called a gig, or at most a phæton. Gigs bring officials to their offices, merchants to their warehouses, physicians to their patients, the world both pretty and ugly to the promenade, to 'the Ring'; then it is that the younger and wealthier ladies mounted on their palfreys and surrounded by equestrian knights and knaves, accompany their mother sitting in her gig or phæton.[3]

The Sea Wall,
Georgetown
(promenade
for urban
elites)

In New Amsterdam and the rural areas, the elites would drive or ride along the coast for their afternoon relaxation. At this time, too, nursery maids took their charges to the public gardens, black boys exercised their masters' dogs, and horsemen rode out to the racecourse. The more athletic minded would play a sport, most likely cricket or lawn tennis.[4]

Dinner was about 7.00 p.m. According to Crookall:

> The usual course is soup—and they [Creole cooks] are excellent soup makers in this country. A good cook will give you a fresh kind of soup every day in the week. 'Foo-foo' soup is a great favourite amongst the people. It is a soup into which they put pounded plantains made into little balls. After soup comes fish, then fowl, or a roast, then pudding, and a cup of tea . . . Of course I have described an ordinary dinner for the middle class. There are those who add to this, and those who have to subtract. Some . . . have to be satisfied with a good dish of foo-foo and vegetables.[5]

Certainly some of the clergy had to be satisfied with less. On successive days in January 1859, for instance, dinners at the Jesuit Presbytery were:

Sunday - soup, cut of leg of boiled mutton, yams, mashed pumpkin, fried pumpkin pudding, cheese and an orange;

Monday - soup, beef which had been boiled for the soup but hashed after it was taken from the soup, yams, fried pumpkin, bread and cheese, and an orange;

Tuesday - soup, hashed pork chops and potatoes, and cheese. Beer and wine were served every day.[6]

What is clear, however, is that the Creoles exercised enormous influence on the eating habits of the white elites. Afro-Creole dishes became an integral part of the elites' normal everyday fare through the black hands of the cooks. This, in the colonial context, was reverse acculturation: the imbibition by whites of Afro-Creole culture with respect to food. But as we shall see later, the fare for formal dinners, though prepared by the same Creole cooks, assumed a more pretentious European form, and from all accounts suffered as a result.

Dinner was followed probably by some music which wound up the day,[7] or by social visits of friends. Those cultural elites who lived *en famille* had each their calling list of friends who could saunter in at any time uninvited. Mutual visits were arranged in an easy fashion. "This night may be the 'at home' [*sic*] of Mr.___; on the next Mrs.___ may receive at her house." In the absence of electricity, little fairy lamps were used to light up the rooms and "an hour or two soon passes spent in whist, billiards, social games, or it may be an impromptu dance; and after light refreshments the guests separate at the gateway, their various paths home perhaps enlightened by the glories of a full moon".[8]

This daily schedule of elite life accords fairly closely to that described in Trinidad by Brereton.[9]

Wherever they went Victorian middle class men took with them their passion for clubs. According to Foley, these had their origins in eighteenth century Britain where informal gatherings at coffee houses evolved into the grand men's institutions of Pall Mall and St. James's. Throughout the empire, as in Britain itself, clubs played a major role in the daily social life of elite males. "In them, protected from the demands of wife, children, and household, a man collected his mail, took his lunch, drowsed in the library, and settled political questions over the billiards table."[10] In Guyana, some clubs were formed to serve various artistic and recreational needs (these will be treated later). But there were three major social clubs, patterned on those 'at home', which catered to the relaxation, class and gender preoccupations of white elite males.

The Georgetown Club, founded in 1858, occupied the bottom storey of the Assembly Rooms (see below). It was "somewhat aristocratic in its pretensions, and exclusive",[11] and earned its highest accolade when in 1878 Governor Kortright became the first chief executive to seek and be granted honorary membership.[12] The leading planters, merchants and government officials belonged to this club, and it was there, no doubt over drinks, that many a business deal was negotiated, and even political/administrative decisions taken. Women, however, were explicitly barred from membership. The Georgetown Club was thus the social centre of the white male aristocracy in the colony; the other clubs being imitations of this pretentious 'blue-blooded' institution.

The British Guiana Club, formed in 1871, was located at New North and Hincks Streets. On the ground floor, there were billiard tables; on the first, dining and coffee rooms, card rooms, a bar and snuggery; and on the upper floor, an extensive suite of bedrooms to accommodate country members and bachelors.[13] Amphlett (1873) stated that: "The British Guiana Club is on the model of an English one, where you can dine or breakfast, as in England; but the other [Georgetown Club] seems to be more of an institution for billiards, cards, liquor, and smoking, mingled with edifying conversation".[14] Yet the B.G. Club was not considered nearly as exclusive as the Georgetown Club as "from the admission of persons of doubtful social position, it has lost character and caste".[15] What that meant was that apparently it admitted less well off whites and a few wealthy Portuguese, who could not gain entry into the Georgetown Club, to membership.

Indeed the new premises at Bentinck and Main Streets (formerly the location of Hamilton's hotel) to which it was removed in 1875 were owned by a Portuguese businessman, M.F. Camacho. These new quarters had spacious airy apartments for dining, billiards and reading in addition to bedrooms.[16] Perhaps as evidence of its lack of aristocratic pedigree, some ten years later the furniture and effects of the club were seized and sold by court order for arrears of rent for the premises.[17]

At the end of 1880 a new elite social club, the Demerara Club, was established at the Caledonia hotel, again with Portuguese involvement. In an effort to promote its credentials as an exclusive club for the cultural elites, membership was restricted in the first instance to members of elite sports clubs like the Georgetown, Essequibo, East Coast, and Belair cricket clubs, and the Rowing, Football and Boxing clubs.[18] For this reason, it did not endear itself to those social aspirants who were excluded from membership. The 'Rambler', a columnist of the *Royal Gazette*, predicted its demise on that basis. With cynicism he stated that: "Their committee are of the stamp of the creole aristocracy; and one who has studied that particular phase of colonial life, knows well enough that that is neither fish, flesh nor red herring; only snobbishness". He thus dismissed the club as "redlegged buchraism".[19] Nevertheless it survived such criticism and found a niche for itself among the upper classes.[20]

While providing facilities for relaxation, these social clubs fitted well with the status preoccupations of their members. As Bryan notes, clubs "can be important instruments of social interaction, and equally, social exclusion. Ostracism in society generally could be reflected in exclusion from a club. As such, the club can serve the function not only of excluding large numbers of potential members, it can also discipline or enforce the conformity of members of the elite group through the fear of ostracism".[21] However, once the social boundaries were adhered to, the clubs, in keeping with white creole custom, were famed for the hospitality of their members, and for their concoction of swizzles. There was an unwritten law that no one in the clubs should drink alone, and so the unwary stranger who was admitted within their sacred portals found himself invited to drink by thirty or forty persons.[22] "It is sufficient if you are acquainted with one member of the Club. Your friend takes you there, places your name in a Visitor's Book, and introduces you all round to those present. Then begins your difficulty and your trial. Every one thinks he has a claim upon you to drink with him; and everyone asks you."[23]

Visitors were not allowed to pay for drinks. Excellent lunches and dinners were served at the clubs; and on occasion, visiting British naval officers were provided food, drinks and accommodation free of charge and could play billiards and cards all day. These clubs were exceedingly well supplied with books, papers, and periodicals, both American and English.[24]

The swizzles of these clubs (known as the 'Trinidad cocktail' in that colony)[25] enhanced their popularity among residents and visitors alike, although in the envious eyes of those excluded from their hallowed portals the sale of alcoholic beverages reduced the clubs to little more than respectable grog shops. The swizzle was a deceptively potent mixture of a delicate pink colour——a distinctly unique creole drink. The recipe was: a small glass of hollands (Dutch gin) or rum, same of water, half a teaspoon of Angostura bitters, a small quantity of syrup or powdered white sugar, and crushed ice. These ingredients were whipped up with a swizzle-stick twirled rapidly between the palms of the hands, until the ice melted. The liquid, like foaming pink cream, had to be swallowed at one draught. Exactitude in proportions was essential to producing a perfect swizzle.[26]

In the elite creole lifestyle, there was no special time for indulging in a swizzle, and as a rule it was accepted whenever offered. "It is taken in the morning to ward off the effect of chill, before breakfast to give a tone to the system, in the middle of the day to fortify against the heat, in the afternoon as a suitable finale to luncheon, and again as a stimulant to euchre, and a solace for your losses. Before dinner it acts as an appetizer, and it is said that when taken before going to bed it assists slumber."[27]

Club life formed an integral part of the colonial elite male's social life. They spent most of their spare time at the club in social intercourse with their peers,[28] gambling, playing euchre, whist and billiards, drinking brandy and water, swizzles etc., smoking cigars and eating meals.[29] Some men, in rather carefree manner, even neglected their domestic responsibilities for the club. One forsaken wife complained that she could not even appear decently dressed in public as her husband preferred to squander his money at the club rather than provide her with money to buy dress, bonnet or boots:

> I do feel at times very sad and low-spirited when having planned to the best of my ability to have something nice for his dinner, he returns from his Club between six and seven o'clock, sulky and morose with not a kind word for me, not even the slightest recognition. He has lost at cards, or something else has made him cross, and I am the victim. He complains that the soup is bad and cold, and I am indirectly abused and spoken at. . . [Later] up jumps my husband; after he has given full vent to his ill-temper, seizes his hat, and off to his Club again, and I am left alone for the weary hours till his return.[30]

This lifestyle was typical among upper class males who frequently made life a misery for their wives. Excess drinking caused many to return home inebriated, "and then what a scene! My heart is like to break, but what can I do——Nothing", pleaded another forlorn wife.[31] But in their quest for individual expression and social intercourse with their peers at the club, the home offered comparatively few comforts and luxuries to the average upper class male.[32] This certainly exempli-

fies the sharp separation in the activities of the two sexes among the
cultural elites----men monopolizing the public sphere (political and
economic life) with these exclusively male clubs providing relaxation;
women confined to the home and perhaps engaged in voluntary activities associated with the church. This was a key feature of Victorian
middle class social life, but was accentuated in colonies like Guyana
where social conditions imposed further restrictions on the roles and
activities of the genteel white elite woman.

Intellectual and Artistic Activities

The attitude of the cultural elites to artistic and intellectual activity
was largely conditioned by three considerations: firstly, their perception of a temporary sojourn in the colony; secondly, their primary
preoccupation with making a fortune; and thirdly, their hunger for
high social status. The first two considerations had a negative effect on
the arts and intellectual activity. "Literature, beyond books of the day,
is not common; medical men, the clergy of the established churches,
and some of the officials, have had an education to enjoy literary
pursuits; but as the generality of Europeans arrive in the colony with
few acquirements beyond those required for their advancement in
wealth, the pursuit of literature must for some time be a secondary
consideration."[33]

Because most of their creative energies were spent fortune-seeking,
there was hardly any incentive to invest in the finer things of life. This
was not unique to Guyana or the Caribbean. Even in a settler society
like the Cape Colony, intellectual and artistic activity was limited, and
for pretty much the same reasons.[34]

On the other hand, anyone with pretensions to high social status
had to at least feign an interest in the arts and intellectual activity, and
this was to some extent encouraged by the need to find things to do to
ease the boredom in one's spare time. The result of these divergent
forces was that a shallow, superficial interest in intellectual and artistic
activity pervaded elite society with greater emphasis on consuming for
reasons of status than on creating out of genuine interest, and this
translated itself in wholesale attempts to copy or import metropolitan
art forms and/or performers. In this sense, the Guyanese elites were
no different from their Cape Colony peers who, according to Bradlow, "did not draw on their culturally diverse society to develop their
own sensibilities, but imported Anglo-Saxon artistic and intellectual
assumptions, as they imported their material requirements".[35] Thus
shortly after emancipation, it was observed that the "higher branches
of literature" were not yet much cultivated in the colony; that there
were no genuine literary or scientific institutions, and any learning

beyond the common was about the growth and culture of the 'mother country' where those intended for "the learned professions" were sent to be educated.[36]

As in the Cape, there was a small minority of elites, mainly in the towns, who were inclined to reading and "mental cultivation" in their spare time, and who possessed a respectable collection of books. A few, no doubt products of the British public schools and universities (Oxbridge), were highly educated—scholars of the classics and mathematics, but they had very little influence, if any, on their peers. During the 1840s, a few institutions were established in Georgetown to stimulate an interest in intellectual activity, some of which were to prove durable. These were a small public library, an Agricultural and Commercial Society, an Astronomical and Meteorological Society, a Society for Natural History and Geology, and a grammar school.[37]

Founded in 1844, the Queen's College was modelled after the English grammar schools and it is not surprising that its curriculum was geared to producing persons who could either fill administrative positions in the Civil Service or go on to specialize for one of the liberal professions befitting an educated English gentleman, e.g., law, medicine, teaching or the priesthood. Indeed the school was administered by the Anglican Church before becoming a government institution in 1876 (the first principal was Bishop William Piercy Austin). There were two academic departments: Modern in which Reading, Writing, English grammar, Arithmetic, Algebra, Euclid, English history, Geography, and Latin were taught; and Classical where to the above subjects were added the Classics (Latin and Greek literature) and French. For the entire period of its existence in the nineteenth century, the student population was very small and very elite, numbering only about seventy up to the 1870s, and increasing to just over 100 by 1900. The masters were all English public school and Oxbridge products.[38]

The Queen's College (elite boys' grammar school), c. 1890

These were small beginnings, and a recognition among some persons that a free society required certain basic intellectual and cultural amenities for the upliftment of its members. But very few people were involved in any of these organizations; and by the end of the century, the absence of a significant literary class (intelligentsia) was still very noticeable. People were more concerned with material matters with a view to accumulating wealth before returning to Britain than with the arts and literature. Kirke explained away this attitude thus: "A few there were who tried to arouse some feeling for the true and the beautiful in art and nature, but the seed fell on barren ground and produced no fruit. But young vigorous communities are too much occupied in providing for the necessities of life to have time for art studies, which must be sought amongst old and somewhat decaying civilizations".[39]

The leading intellectual and cultural institutions were the Royal Agricultural and Commercial Society (R.A.&C.S.), the Berbice Reading Society and the Athenæum Society. The first was established in 1844 with between 200 and 300 members and was later placed under the patronage of the British monarch.[40] Although the first thing it did was to organize a public ball for the social elites,[41] its professed objectives were to promote the improvement and encouragement of agriculture and industry. It also operated an Exchange Room, a Reading Room, Museum and Model Room, and a library for its members.[42] But as late as the 1860s it was very little more than a lending library and reading rooms, and had done precious little to promote either agriculture or industry.[43] During the 1880s, however, it began to publish a periodical called *Timehri* which constituted a major contribution to the intellectual life of the colony. Nevertheless, the fact that membership only reached 487 by 1891[44] (less than 10 percent of the elite population) is indicative of how limited was the interest in intellectual activity within the elite circles.

In 1868 a museum was opened with a local exhibition next door to the R.A.& C.S. Not surprisingly, its inauguration was the occasion for a grand ball at the Assembly Rooms. It was operated by the B.G. Museum Company, a shareholding enterprise, and was open to the public twice per week free of charge. At least in its early days, it attracted many curious visitors.[45]

The Berbice Reading Society was formed in 1843 by subscription for the purchase of books, maps, pamphlets and periodicals for the enlightenment of its members, and was fully incorporated by law in 1852. It proved to be the most durable elite cultural institution in nineteenth century Berbice.[46] It was furnished with a fine reading room on the upper floor of the building, but the lower floor, used as a billiard room, was somewhat dilapidated.[47] Until 1889, no alcoholic beverages were allowed within its precincts.[48] In keeping with the general disinterest in intellectual pursuits among the cultural elites, membership was always small and fluctuated considerably: 46 in 1869, 91 in 1877, 52 in 1885. By the 1880s, however, it had built up a respectable collection of over 4,000 books.[49]

In an admirable attempt to promote the spread of intellectual pursuits to a wider cross-section of society and by implication get around the exclusivity of the Berbice Reading Society, a group of churchmen of different denominations set up a committee in 1888 (the jubilee year of emancipation) to establish a public library in Berbice. Funds were raised for the importation of books and indoor games, and after occupying temporary quarters in an infant schoolroom, the Berbice Public Library was formally opened in October 1892 with about 130 members. Situated on High Street, New Amsterdam, its reading rooms on the third floor were well ventilated and furnished. The recreation rooms on the second floor housed billiard and bagatelle tables, draught and chessboards, and other games.[50] It is interesting to note that the cultural elites always found it necessary to marry intellectual pursuits and entertainment, and indeed one wonders how much emphasis was placed on the former.

The Athenæum Society in Georgetown was founded in 1851 by a group of liberal elites, among them J.T. Gilbert, George Quayle, and the coloured merchant/politician Richard Haynes, all of whom were associated with the movement for political reform of the 1840s and 1850s.[51] The Athenæum Society was intended as an intellectual cum cultural institution with a small library and reading room where young *men* (as opposed to women) who could not gain admission to the senior elite social clubs, could spend their leisure time. Public lectures were organized on different topics from time to time, as well as classes in music, drama, etc. Occasionally the Society's dramatic club staged plays for public audiences. Its main problem, however, was the general apathy of the city's upper and middle class male youths to such intellectual and artistic pursuits. They much preferred spending their spare time after work in athletic exercise or in the pleasures of the flesh.[52] The result was that membership was consistently low: 84 in 1869, 103 in 1879, 75 in 1886.[53]

Beyond those organizations, there was not much more to provide intellectual stimulation among the cultural elites. In 1866, a Literary and Debating Club was formed in Georgetown with only fifteen members. Weekly meetings were planned for debates, lectures, recitations and theatricals, and there were proposals to start a library and reading room.[54] Not surprisingly, this mini-club does not seem to have survived very long.

In the fields of music and drama, a number of societies were formed from time to time. Musical concerts were very popular throughout the postemancipation period. Open air performances were done by the Militia band in the afternoon on the sea wall, and towards the end of the century their moonlight concerts in the Promenade Gardens were well attended. Indoor concerts were organized by private organizations and individuals, and by the churches.[55] The Georgetown Philharmonic Club was fairly active performing at concerts in the Assembly Rooms during the sixties,[56] and their efforts were given a great boost by the erection of a Philharmonic Hall in 1873. This was an impressive building both in terms of size and stage facilities, and the acoustics for concerts and theatricals were much better than the Assembly Rooms. It was very tastefully decorated, and the stage curtain was described as a masterpiece of one of the most famous English scene painters[57] (another British import).

In 1869, a Demerara Musical Institute made its appearance with lectures and musical performances;[58] and in 1874 the Amateur Orchestral Club held a concert at the Philharmonic Hall.[59] Neither of these seemed to have been long-lived, and indeed not much use was made of the Philharmonic Hall until the Demerara Musical Society was formed in 1883. This society survived into the 1890s.[60]

During the 1880s, a new fad took hold of the male elites—— smoking concerts. Audiences were very select, all male, and by invitation only. They gathered, smoked either cigars or pipes, sang ballads, banjo songs, comic songs, Scottish songs, etc. "The comic was the prevailing element throughout." As can be expected this was yet another attempt to copy something that had become fashionable in the metropolis.[61]

Occasionally visiting troupes of performing artistes travelled to the colony to stage operas or concerts, but Guyana was so far off the beaten track of international performers that visits were very irregular.[62] Among the more notable of these visiting artistic groups were the Galli Opera Company of Italy which performed at the Dutch Theatre in 1844;[63] the pianist, Baron de Fleur, who held a recital at the Old Agricultural hall in 1851;[64] the Fabri Troupe who performed a show of song and dance at the Assembly Rooms in 1862;[65] and the Tennessee Jubilee Singers who performed both in Georgetown and New Amsterdam in 1891.[66]

After emancipation, there was such a dearth of theatricals that it was left to the privates of British armed forces stationed in the colony to fill the vacuum during the late forties and fifties.[67] Governor Barkly's wife also tried to stimulate some interest in drama by organizing and even acting in a few skits to very select audiences.[68] But for a long time, very little was done in drama largely from a lack of enthusiasm among the cultural elites, but also because of the absence of a proper theatre in the colony. The Assembly Rooms, although used for such purposes, were not very suitable.[69]

It was only after the mid-sixties that some concerted activity in the field of drama was discernible with the formation of a number of small dramatic clubs, e.g., the Adelphi Theatre, the Berbice (Amateur) Dramatic and Musical Club, the Georgetown Histrionic Club, and the Demerara Dramatic Club.[70] Even so, despite the erection of the Philharmonic Hall, performances continued to be put on only occasionally, for want of genuine interest among the elites. No performance could last for more than a few weeks at a time, and it was very difficult to keep the dramatic clubs going. By 1889, the Berbice club was in grave difficulty of going under. Its sister club in Demerara, however, remained more viable until the end of the century and continued to stage performances. Membership in 1898 fluctuated between 388 and 411, still small but encouraging.[71] Throughout this period plays staged were invariably English dramas or comedies; indeed there is no indication that any local plays were written by the literate elites.

Other forms of entertainment included the occasional visits of circus companies to the colony,[72] fund-raising bazaars and tea meetings usually associated with churches,[73] and local exhibitions of colonial products, e.g., fruit, vegetables, cotton gins and other machinery, books and pamphlets, sugars and rums, ornaments, basketwork, etc. Such exhibitions were held in 1861, 1866, 1868, 1872, 1878, 1879, 1885 and 1891.

During the 1890s, attempts were made to organize 'Fêtes' at the Promenade Gardens in Georgetown. These were variety entertainment shows patterned on those fashionable in Europe at that time; but like most things copied from abroad, these efforts were shortlived. The fêtes featured acts by artistes representing different cultures, e.g., Surinamese dancers, Syrian musicians, costumed Madrasi dancers, and even included 'painted' Amerindians from the interior as a curiosity for the city folk who generally never came into contact with them. For these fêtes, the Gardens were gaily decorated and illuminated.[74]

On the whole, there was very little by way of entertainment in nineteenth century Guyana which perhaps helps to account for the excessive drinking and sexual promiscuity which prevailed among the cultural elites. In so far as they paid attention to cultural matters, their focus was essentially on material culture which reflected their primary economic interest, plantation agriculture. They exhibited very casual or fleeting interest in creative or fine arts, preferring either to import visiting artistes from the metropolis or to copy metropolitan art forms for their own productions. As such although they were responsible for introducing several British art forms, they were not particularly creative and so did not make a significant contribution to the development of the local 'creole' arts.

Dances and Dinners

The cultural elites' love of extravagance and pomp was fully reflected in their dances and dinners. The governors themselves contributed to this by their levees on their assumption of duty or departure from the colony, and by "a more promiscuous ball at Government House on the queen's birthday". The levee was apparently open to most of the elite residents in order to give the governor an opportunity to become acquainted with them. Indeed if they hoped to be invited to the prestigious queen's birthday ball, they had to pay their respects by a formal call on His Excellency soon after their arrival in the colony or by attendance at a levee.[75]

The levee was a rather solemn, formal affair. The status-seeking visitor was met at the threshold of the governor's mansion by an official who took his card and entered his name in the large visitors' book in the entrance hall. That insertion was what entitled the visitor to recognition when gubernatorial entertainments were planned. The visitor's card was then passed on to the governor's private secretary in the anteroom, who led him into the presence chamber and announced him audibly by name. On his entering, the governor greeted him with a warm handshake "as if he had known you from boyhood", and his wife did the same. Thereafter the proceedings turned to farce:

> A remark or two as to the weather and the colony, and you find some of the visitors who have preceded you are retiring. The lady of the establishment then asks if you would like tea or a glass of wine, but you probably refuse, and on the appearance of fresh arrivals again shake hands, and without much ceremonious 'backing out', as when royalty itself is concerned, reach the open air feeling like a fish out of water, till you have got rid of your heavy dress hat and clothes and perspiring kid gloves.[76]

The Assembly Rooms, built in 1858, became the principal venue for 'high society' balls, concerts, meetings, theatricals and other entertainments. Its structure was reportedly of a plain and utilitarian design and, as if ashamed of their failure to ape European architectural styles, the *Royal Gazette* commented: "It is true that when we look upon it we see nothing to remind us of the gorgeous structures, erected for similar purposes . . . in various parts of the world . . . We find the Georgetown Assembly Rooms a plain unassuming building . . ."[77]

Yet to their credit the interior of the building was admirably adapted to the purposes for which it was used. Despite their insecurity which stemmed from a deep-seated colonial mentality, the cultural elites again demonstrated their commonsense ability to construct buildings to suit practical conditions in the tropics. A capacious airy ballroom was on the upper storey, and wide spacious galleries ran along each side where the non-dancing revellers could stroll and flirt. These galleries were open to the breeze which made the auditorium delightfully cool and pleasant.[78] As was customary among the cultural elites, the Assembly Rooms were formally opened on February 12, 1858, with a public subscription ball.[79]

Upper class balls were generally of two kinds: formal and fancy dress. Some were official, i.e., held by the colonial state, others private, held either by social organizations or loose groups of individuals. Official balls and those given by private organizations were generally free of charge, by invitation only. More often than not, those organized by loose groups of individuals, e.g., the bachelors of the city, were subscription balls. These balls normally commenced between 8.30 and 9.00 p.m. and lasted into the wee hours of the morning with a break for supper around midnight. Gentlemen were required to appear in black suits. The ballroom was always well decorated and illuminated by numerous chandeliers. Supper was usually quite lavish, especially on state occasions, with a wide variety of dishes, wines and champagne. No expense was spared to make these affairs extremely enjoyable and memorable—all the more so because they were not held very frequently (half a dozen per year at best). A wide variety of European dances were done: quadrilles, gallopades, galops, waltzes, square and round dances, polkas, mazurkas, imperials, highland schottisches, lanc-

The Assembly
Rooms, c. 1890
(principal venue
of elite cultural
events)

ers, etc. Music was normally provided by bands composed of drafts from the militia band or from one of the bands of the imperial military forces stationed in the colony.[80]

Fancy dress balls were generally held either during or not long after the Christmas/New Year festive season, and always seemed to generate enormous excitement among the cultural elites; yet very few were organized perhaps because more planning, effort and expense were involved. The most colourful of these balls were organized by governors' wives: Mrs. Barkly (1851),[81] Mrs. Wodehouse (1860),[82] and Mrs. Longden (1875).[83] These were very elaborate, expensive and exclusive affairs. One observer estimated the 1875 ball to cost about $30,000 (£6,250).[84] At these balls, the costumes were generally quite varied in design and cost, and portrayed royalty, peasants, and various ethnicities, e.g., Turks, Greeks, Albanians, Russians, Hungarians, Spaniards, Chinese, etc.[85]

Fancy balls enjoyed increased popularity during the late 1870s, when some "gentlemen of quality", recognizing the commercial benefits to be gained, quickly formed the Demerara United Amusement Club to organize such events for its members who were required to subscribe one shilling (24 cents) a week. This entitled them to attend anything organized by the club for a nominal entrance fee of one dollar (4s. 2d.). The club's first fancy dress ball evoked the greatest excitement among the cultural elites, "especially among the gentler sex, as to the selection of costumes and other matters; invitations were sent to the *crème de la crème* of society, but the greatest anxiety to obtain invitations was shown by [elite] society in general, and as much as double the subscription fee was offered for the much coveted card".[86]

Costumes at this ball were extremely colourful and had a 'Royal Flair': there were two queens with maids of honour, a Governor Longden, a Colonel Figyelmesy (the American Consul), a Marquis and Duchess of Lorne, and a Count Bismarck. Others portrayed a more carnivalesque look: a Roman priest, a governor's valet, a flower girl, a Rose of Summer, a Milk Maid, etc.[87]

Dances were also organized by Free Masonry lodges which seemed to be popular among the elite males. These were no less colourful than the fancy dress balls. Decorations were elaborate----flowers, palms, chandeliers, Chinese lamps, drapes, Masonic colours and coats of arms.[88] At the ball of Union Lodge, No. 247 held in April 1871, the Assembly Rooms were enchantingly decorated:

> The broad alternate blue and white bars with which the hall was paled; the grotto at the entrance port, with its three fountains emitting refreshing perfumes, beneath the light of a glittering star; the Master's throne, with its luxury of mirrors and flowers and other accompaniments, surmounted with an ideal painting of the cardinal virtues; and most impressive of all, the masonic emblems everywhere

apparent, and the banners of the Knights hanging gracefully on either side of the hall, some of high pretence, others simple with their single device: all conjoined to produce, to a delicate sense, an air of peace and rest soon to be dispelled with the swell of music and the tread of measures.[89]

Five hundred invitations were issued for this ball, and on the arrival of the governor's party at 9.00 p.m., dancing commenced to the music of the Georgetown Militia Band. At 11.15 p.m. dancing stopped and a large body of Knights Templar clad *cap-a-pied* made an entrance to the music. The Grand Prior of Knights of Malta in the West Indies wore the black cloak and cap of that Order over his surcoat of a templar. Dancing recommenced after this grand display, "and as the dancers mingled in the mazes of a quadrille—the Templars with their snow white cloaks flushed with the red cross, their gaudy tunics; the numberless colours of ladies' dresses, with their pretty trimmings; the uniforms of the Officers of the Garrison, the Regalia of the Brethren—the most splendid kaleidoscopic combinations were produced".[90]

As public entertainment was scarce and irregular, formal dinner parties in the home formed a major part of the socio-cultural activity of the elites. This was yet another opportunity for them to flaunt their wealth and high social status. Formal dinners had to be "elaborate and according to the most approved style and fashion of what is considered *ton*" —in short very Victorian upper middle class in form and style.[91] Mr. Pepps noted in his diary: "My wife and I to dine with a friend where much company and display of plate, with costly wines and dishes, so much so that had I not been better informed I should have thought I had been at the table of one of vast wealth".[92]

But in this *nouveau riche* social milieu, more attention was paid to the copied form than to the quality of the content, with the result that these lavish affairs were on many occasions reduced to farce, "worse than purgatory", and the guests very often subjected to dyspepsia. Most commentators were agreed that, unlike everyday meals which had a distinctly delicious Afro-Creole flavour, the European style cuisine of formal dinners was generally detestable. On such occasions, the unfortunate guest had to endure "the prolonged farce of having placed under your nose and that of your neighbours, entrees and entrements [sic] of unpronounceable and unintelligible names and suspicious ingredients, let alone more solid viands which one might relish were the appetite not gone from its delayed gratification".[93]

The invitation to dinner was generally for 7.30 p.m. "for an earlier hour would be considered vulgar"; but it never began before 8.00 p.m. at the earliest. More often than not the whole affair proved disagreeable. The cook (not the hostess!) had so many (unfamiliar?) dishes to prepare that it was probable that the soup was cold and tasteless when served. Then came the relays of entrées, most likely cold and tasteless as well, followed by a slice of roasted or boiled turkey or mutton equally tasteless and not seldom badly done. "Your appetite is by this time gone and your temper with the pleasantest face you can put on, for two or three hours to this protracted exhibition of a multiplicity of badly cooked dishes, any of which if properly prepared and served up in season, you might have dined upon with great satisfaction."[94] Lavish consumption of poorly prepared food was, however, supplemented by a wide variety of tropical fruit, e.g., oranges, pineapples, bananas, mangoes, sapodillas and star-apples.[95]

The almost universal consensus about the poor, tasteless dishes at private formal dinner parties despite the great expense incurred is food for thought, especially since the persons who prepared them were almost invariably black Creole domestics who had a reputation of being excellent cooks. It would thus seem that they were either unfamiliar with the recipes for the European dishes which they were only rarely required to prepare, or alternatively, they deliberately chose these lavish occasions to embarrass their employers, perhaps in retaliation for the daily humiliations to which they may have been subjected. If the latter, this was a dramatic act of cultural resistance.

Public formal dinners were even more elaborate. One held in 1886 to commemorate the establishment of a new government medical service and resuscitation of the Guyana branch of the British Medical Association was held at the ballroom of the officers mess of the 1st West India Regiment. Among the guests was Governor Irving. The menu was as follows:

Soup:	Mock Turtle - Juliene
Fish:	Querriman[96] boiled - oyster sauce cutlets - tomato sauce
Entrées:	Pigeons complete Potatoes and mushrooms
Joints:	Mutton-saddle. Turkey-roast Veal-fillet. Ham
Second Service:	Duck and olives. Guinea birds Galantine of chickens Pâté de foi gras
Entremets:	Wine jelly. Trifle. Charlotte Russe Iced cabinet puddings. Cheese. Macaroni. Straws
Ices:	Strawberry cream. Pineapple water
Fruit:	Dried and green
Coffee[97]	

Dinner parties were not complete without copious amounts of wine and brandy. The creole elites preferred brandy: ". . . in fact, men here, and women too for all I know, imbibe such an inordinate quantity of brandy that their palates become incapable of appreciating the more delicate juices of the grape".[98] Indeed, brandy, like swizzles, was consumed by some persons at all times of the day: "Some drink brandy at Breakfast and also at Supper . . . and practically an unlimited supply of wine without check upon brandy is permitted throughout the day. . . It is all drinking, drinking—there is little inducement to eat".[99]

Sport and Other Pastimes

In addition to clubs, parties and dinners, sports formed a major part of the leisure activities of the cultural elites and, as in other areas of their lives, duplicated those of England. In the metropolis itself there was literally a sports revolution from the 1860s onwards as both the middle and lower classes began to enjoy more leisure time. Organized sport was one means of putting this spare time to constructive use, and this was undertaken largely under middle class leadership and sponsorship, and promoted mainly by the churches, public schools and universities. Games were standardized by rules and regulations governing not only how they were played, but the conduct and dress of the players; and supreme governing bodies like the Marylebone Cricket Club and the Football Association were set up in all major sports (tennis, hockey, netball, golf, racing, athletics, etc.).[100]

In the late nineteenth century the doctrine of 'muscular Christianity' held sway. According to Sandiford, this revolved "around the basic notion that there [was] something innately good and godly about brute strength and power. Physical weakness [was] unnatural since it [was] only a manifestation of moral and spiritual inadequacy. It could be overcome by prayer, upright living, discipline, and exercise". Sport, especially team sport, was thus good for the body as well as the soul. It was considered a civilizing agent, one that instilled such Victorian middle class social values as teamwork, fair play, self-discipline, respect for the rules, obedience to authority, courage in the face of adversity, and so on. In short, sport was the training ground for life's challenges.[101]

Given the importance which sports assumed in late Victorian British social life, it is not surprising that they should have been taken to the colonies. Benny Green notes that when the British went to the colonies they took with them not only utility items, but an odd assortment of leisure and sporting equipment:

> . . . among the portable writing desks and the canvas camp baths, the shoe-trees and the diamond shirt studs, the sauceboats and the chandeliers, the grand pianos,

ukeleles, monogrammed kerchives, embossed cutlery, soda siphons and bars of Pear's soap, there were some items of a subtly differing nature without which few itineraries would have been considered complete: Billeness and Weeks' Automatic Wicket, 'adapted for ship's deck cricket'; F.H. Ayers' Billiard Tables, 'specially designed for hotels and clubs'; the William Curtis Scoring Tent; Szaley's Pneumatic-Grip Dumb-bells; Vigon's Home Horse Exerciser; and the tennis shirts, croquet hoops, shin guards, hockey sticks, lawn boots, sand boxes, jumping sacks, scoring books, badminton nets, fives gloves, squash racquets, club ties, coloured caps, medals, badges, cups, shields, bowls and vases which distinguished the English from all the other predatory Europeans wandering the surface of the planet in search of either God's work or increased dividends or a happy combination of both.[102]

Holt observes that sports were vital both for the colonial official and colonist. For the former, they "helped both to relieve the tedium of a distant posting and to integrate new arrivals into the small world of colonial society". For the latter, they

> served overwhelmingly to express and enhance the solidarity of colonial society. Providing amusement for those far from home isolated amidst an alien and sometimes hostile population, sport was not so much a luxury as a necessity, a means of maintaining morale and a sense of shared roots, of Britishness, of lawns and tea and things familiar. For the more humble middle class emigrant sports also underlined that transition from a suburban to an essentially landed style, which added to the appeal of the Empire.[103]

But sport was taken to the colonies with all of the class and gender prejudices with which it was characterized in Britain. The British working classes were systematically excluded from middle class sports clubs and associations, and there was a rigid differentiation between amateur and professional players. Self-respecting middle class sportsmen ('gentlemen') clung steadfastly to amateur status and would not defile themselves by playing for money (there were a few notable exceptions, not least of all the great cricketer Dr. W.G. Grace). Pay, it was thought, threatened to transform sport into work, and to undermine the fundamental purpose for participation which was not to win, but rather to foster *esprit de corps* and camaraderie among members of both teams. Hence the saying, "It is not if you win or lose, but how you play the game that matters. Play fair, be a good sport". Payment was for the 'lower orders' who had no independent source of income. Indeed the social stigma that football earned was largely related to the lower class origins of most players, and the fact that that sport became professionalized very early.[104] This class bias, when transferred to colonies in the Caribbean, Africa, Asia and the Pacific was reinforced by racial prejudice; and, as Holt notes for the Caribbean, "racial segregation was built into colonial sport. Many whites simply refused to play in or against teams with black players".[105]

While maintaining *social* distance between white and non-white in the colonial context, sport was at the same time intended to serve as an assimilative *cultural* mechanism in order to promote a consensus of shared values, beliefs and attitudes between rulers and ruled. Stoddart points out that dominant British beliefs as to social behaviour, standards, relations, and conformity were transferred through sport. But it is important to note that British sport, indeed British culture generally, was not imposed formally by the state as was done by the French in their colonies. Sport was acquired by the subordinate population on a voluntary, subconscious basis. In this way, resistance to the values which were part and parcel of the baggage of sport was minimized. This method of transference of sporting traditions and values gave the elites tremendous cultural power in the colonial situation.[106]

British sport was also enveloped by gender bias against female participation. With the strict separation of sex roles in British society and the philosophy of muscular Christianity with which sport was imbued, there was little place for women who were characterized as 'the weaker sex'. According to McCrone, the stylized image of the genteel middle class woman held her as a person "imbued . . . with qualities of mind and body that destined her for specific tasks, such as being man's helpmate, nurturing his children, and protecting the sanctity of his home. [This] ideal woman was antithetical to sport. Passive, gentle, emotional, and delicate, she had neither the strength nor inclination to undertake strenuous exercise and competitive games".[107]

Hence although noblewomen had hunted, hawked and ridden horses ever since the Middle Ages, there was still the popular perception that sport was a male sphere of activity, and 'scientific medical evidence' was employed to 'prove' that strenuous exercise was harmful to women, and especially to their 'primary' child-bearing functions. It was not until the late Victorian period that women gradually, quietly, almost clandestinely, began to participate actively in sports, a process facilitated by the girls' public schools and women's colleges of the 'red brick' universities.[108] One consequence of this was that with few exceptions, female sports developed in a totally separate sphere from that of males, and thus mirrored the gender separation in public and private life.[109] The ideal of the genteel woman attained its highest expression in the colonies where there was an even greater perceived necessity to protect their 'vulnerable' physical beings and honour from 'lusting natives'. In the colonies the lady of high status had to conform to strict social codes governing her deportment and physical activity which consequently ruled out participation in those sports that required 'unlady-like' exertion or 'vulgar' movement.

Because of Guyana's large forest and wild life resources, the British aristocratic sport of hunting could be engaged in. In Britain whereas working class 'blood' sports such as cock and dog fighting were driven underground by the dominant middle class,[110] the aristocracy were able to preserve their own hunt for recreation and middle class aspirants to high social status sought to emulate the aristocracy. Holt asserts, however, that in the colonies hunting was not just a form of amusement. "It was often vital for a man to ride in order to be able to fulfil official functions and the ability to shoot was a useful reminder to subject races of the underlying reality of imperial rule."[111] The demonstration effect of hunting, therefore, added to the cultural power of the elites. In Guyana, hunting excursions deep in the interior of the country were prestigious but expensive pastimes. Only the very rich could afford these. Even a short trip of three or four days would cost a party of four $25 (£5.2) per head.[112]

Hunting was often combined with picnicking behind the canefields of the plantations. This, however, perpetuated the separation of gender activities as the men went hunting in the bush while the women remained safely behind with the children.[113] Premium described a 'marooning' party behind his plantation consisting of planters' families. The term itself is interesting and suggests that it may have originated from the practice of hunting maroons (runaway slaves) in the bush during slavery. As usual the women were left in clearings in the shade with fishing rods and a few black boys to bait their hooks. The men went off hunting with "dogs of all sorts, from the fox-hound and harrier to the small Indian cur-like animal, which generally, thin ('maugre') in its appearance, has a good nose". 'Yagers' (black hired hands) were required to face all the dangers associated with hunting scared wild predators (with venomous snakes about) as they went with the dogs into the places which were to be searched for game (usually abandoned fields), while the 'sportsmen' (whites on horseback) with their guns were safely stationed at different coigns of vantage on the outside. When a dog barked, they followed in that direction to shoot whatever animal sought to escape to safety.[114]

It would be no exaggeration to say that virtually anything that moved in the forest was considered fair *game* to the elite colonial hunters. Game included accouries (a kind of guinea pig), water-dogs (otters), labbas (hollow cheek pacas), deer, wild hogs, mypouris (tapirs), monkeys, sloths, water haas (capybaras), armadillos, snakes, tigers, jaguars, iguanas, manatees (sea cows), etc. Birds were also hunted: maroudies (a kind of wild turkey), pigeons, parrots, cranes, toucans, macaws, muscovy ducks, teal ducks, hoatzin (stinking pheasants), etc.; so too were fish.[115] Premium described a typical hunt:

> There is much excitement, and some little danger, in a waterhunt after deer. The creature swims rapidly, and turns sharply around to evade its pursuers, throwing them out frequently to a great distance. Negroes generally have spears, made of bayonets or cutlasses, fastened at the ends to long poles, on those excursions, which, when the animal takes the water, are very useful, for they launch them with great effect, although, in the excitement of the moment, the thrower is very apt to capsize the unstable, keel-less bateau—an occurrence by no means uncommon.[116]

In Essequibo, picnicking sometimes incorporated horse-racing, cock-fighting, card-playing, drinking, swimming and general 'cooling out' around the small lakes which were surrounded by low sandhills. On the white sand shores of these lakes, some planters erected small wooden shanties with hammocks slung where they could spend the weekends.[117] Excursions from Georgetown to the sandhills in the hinterland were also popular and were organized mainly on public holidays. The steamer would leave early, at about 6.30 a.m. amid the merry streams of music for up-river. At their destination, some of the revellers would disembark and hike into the hills, returning later with ferns and other botanical specimens. Others would remain on board the steamer playing card games or engaged in some other form of pleasure with friends. After lunch a dancing party might commence on the foredeck which would continue until the steamer returned to town in the evening.[118]

Both Demerara and Berbice had rifle clubs. The former was established in 1867 and later placed under the governor's patronage. It lasted beyond the end of the century. The Berbice club was of earlier vintage, but does not seem to have survived very long. These clubs were composed of the leading planters and merchants, and members of all branches of the Militia service. Practice shoots were held weekly. Prize meetings were organized at which money, cup prizes, and medals were awarded; and from time to time teams from similar rifle clubs in neighbouring colonies, as well as visiting warships, competed against the local teams. Very significantly, women were allowed to compete for a special Ladies Purse.[119] This may seem to be a departure from the stylized image of the delicate, defenceless, genteel female; but perhaps it was felt that living amidst 'lusting black and brown savages', not only should the white colonial woman know how to handle firearms in order to protect herself in an emergency, but those natives should be aware of her prowess as well. Rifle shooting, like hunting, therefore, added to the cultural power of the elites through its demonstration effect.

On the other hand, an attempt to promote archery as a sport with the formation in Berbice of the Archery Association in 1865[120] came to nought. With the availability of modern weapons, archery was no more than a quaint elitist pastime of no practical significance in the late nineteenth century empire. As such it did not serve as a social deterrent which could enhance elite cultural power. Besides, the association befell the same fate as so many other sporting organizations in Berbice for the simple reason that there were just not enough whites resident in New Amsterdam to sustain sports clubs on a racially exclusive basis for long.[121]

As in Trinidad and Jamaica, horse-racing was extremely popular among the cultural elites,[122] and soon became a major leisure attraction for large numbers of working class blacks, Indians, Chinese and Portuguese. This represented a good example of the subordinate ethnic groups adopting a cultural pastime of the dominant white minority. But the gambling and heavy drinking traditionally associated with this sport, both in Britain and the colonies, were frowned upon by the churches and the imperial authorities since those side attractions did not accord with the social values which the elites wished to impart to the 'lower orders'.[123] Yet, despite those misgivings, horse-racing enjoyed unflagging elite and official support in Guyana because, like the hunt, it was regarded as an aristocratic sport—'the sport of kings'— which lent an aura of high social status to those who attended the Georgetown race meetings. As such, race day in the city was a red-letter day which provided the cultural elites with a grand opportunity to flaunt their wealth and assert their claims to social ascendancy. Small wonder, therefore, that when in 1878 the Turf Club began to prevent non-members from driving into the premises to the Grand Stand, many elites interpreted this as a grave affront and preferred to stay away rather than suffer such 'indignity'.[124]

During slavery, there were race meetings in different parts of the colony, and it was not until 1829 when Governor D'Urban took the initiative, that a proper racecourse was established just outside the city limits at a cost of 11,580 guilders (approximately £827) and presented to the Turf Club. It was an oval, one mile by 96 yards in circumference, perfectly flat with sharp curves. Two meetings were held annually, in April and November, and about £1,500 in prizes were awarded at each, in addition to the Governor's Cup valued at £50. The first race meeting at the D'Urban Course, as it was called, was held on November 3 and 4, 1829.[125]

Racing at the D'Urban course experienced its ups and downs during the century. Up to 1842, the Combined Court made a grant towards the upkeep of the course and to improve the breed of horses, but the financial crisis of that year prevented the grant being made and temporarily stopped horse-racing there until June 1846. The following year the grant was actually removed amidst growing economic distress in the wake of the 1846 Sugar Duties Act, and as a result there was no racing until November 1850. Although no grant was made in 1851, the usual two race meetings were held, reflecting a return to prosperity for the planters after the depression of the late forties. Small government grants were made after 1853, but because of a paucity of horses no autumn meeting was held in 1859. Horse-racing was adversely affected the next year by the death of a few racing horses which reduced the meetings to just one day, and this was followed by the utter collapse of the sport at D'Urban until 1864. Although resuscitated, it continued to be susceptible to the economic fortunes of the plantation system which determined how many horses could be bred and/or imported for racing. The spring meeting of 1885, for instance, had to be cancelled for want of sufficient horses.[126]

A good country meeting was normally held twice a year at Belfield on the east coast of Demerara,[127] and there was also a racecourse near Capoey Lake in Essequibo where the planters rode their creole ponies and mules in rather less structured and more friendly competition. In 1890, however, the proprietors of the Capoey course closed it and transferred the cash in hand to a new racecourse at Suddie, also in Essequibo.[128] Occasional race meetings were also held at the Hague dam, West Coast Demerara, on Wakenaam Island in the Essequibo river, and at the Long Dam beyond the Canje river in Berbice.[129] Considerable excitement was aroused when horses from Trinidad and Barbados were brought to the colony to compete.[130] But although the bigger race meetings in Georgetown featured some good bloodstock of creole (local) horses, as the stakes increased racehorse owners began to do what came naturally to them, i.e., to import English thoroughbreds on a regular basis to crossbreed with the creole stock. Thus, Kirke was proud to assert that "in the veins of the Creole horses runs some of the best blood of the English turf",[131] a statement that clearly reveals the colonial mentality of the cultural elites who harboured the notion that things British (even livestock) were better than what were available locally.

Although horse-racing was a rich man's sport, it rapidly attracted the interest of the poorer classes regardless of 'race', who looked on from the sidelines and conducted their own off-course betting. Some also participated as jockeys and presumably as grooms. This widening participation was aided and abetted by the fact that it was customary to make a general holiday of race days, so that very few places of business were open on those days.[132] Apart from the excitement of the races themselves, race days offered all classes an opportunity to relax and there was considerable jollity, drinking, gambling, cheating, and even fighting "in a most friendly way".[133] But things occasionally turned sour, as for instance in 1858 at D'Urban, when the elites in the Grand Stand betted large sums on a famous Barbadian pony which lost to the creole favourite (it is not surprising that they should have favoured the foreign horse). The unwillingness of some losers to pay— one man reputedly lost as much as $900—led to a serious disturbance in which several people were injured. Of course, not much was made of this incident since it involved cultural elites.[134]

Horse riding was very popular among the cultural elites throughout the century. Ever since the slave days, the horse rider symbolized power and authority in the plantation system, and this image persisted long after emancipation. Horse riding was thus not merely a form of exercise (sport) or of transportation, but was an important feature of the cultural power of the colonial elites. As Georgetown expanded, however, the number of places where one could ride without hindrances of one sort or another became increasingly fewer. In response to the growing need for a safe venue for equestrianism, the D'Urban racecourse in 1878 began to offer members of the race club a venue to ride horses in a more leisurely way between 5.00 and 9.00 a.m. and 3.00 and 6.30 p.m. for a subscription of $5.00. Other persons introduced by two stewards could pay $8.00 for the same privilege, and could invite guests to ride with them. This was a very effective way of denying access to socially undesirable persons. To further facilitate riding, a new (Vlissengen) road was built from the Thomas lands near the sea wall to the Brickdam adjoining the racecourse.[135]

Golf, reputedly a Scottish invention, was naturally played by the Guyanese elites since many of them hailed from Scotland. In Guyana, however, it was always associated with privilege since it required membership of a club with the necessary amenities and land space. It was thus a sport well suited to preserving social distinctions in the colonial situation. Although women played in England during the 1890s, it is not clear whether this was the case in Guyana. Lawn tennis and cricket, however, were by far the most popular athletic sporting activities in which the cultural elites participated[136] and, like golf, were linked with social privilege. Both sports were played by the more athletically oriented in the afternoons after work, on weekends, and on public holidays especially over the Christmas-New Year season; and were promoted among the boys at the elite grammar school, the Queen's College.[137]

Annual tennis tournaments were organized by the La Penitence Lawn Tennis Club in Georgetown and the Berbice Lawn Tennis Club in New Amsterdam. The latter, however, was defunct by the early 1890s.[138] In addition, elite cricket clubs also had lawn tennis facilities. In Britain, tennis was one of the earliest sports in which women were allowed to participate openly, and in Guyana white female tennis players were actually allowed to join elite sports clubs as "Lady Members". Unlike other sports, tennis offered an opportunity to breach the strict social separation between the sexes. Hence although women's singles matches were played in competition, mixed doubles were socially very popular because they provided an opportunity for unsupervised courtship and flirtation.[139] In this, as in everything else, the Guyanese elites followed the etiquette of their British middle class models.

Of all the sports introduced by the British into their colonies, cricket was taken most seriously, and indeed became the most popular not only among the cultural elites, but also among the subordinate ethnic groups. According to Sandiford, the Victorians glorified cricket "as a perfect system of ethics and morals which embodied all that was most noble in the Anglo-Saxon character". Emanating from the aristocracy, it was adopted by the middle classes with great enthusiasm, as they regarded it as an excellent training ground for military and other purposes. "It taught discipline, self-sacrifice, and loyalty to team and country." All classes were encouraged to play cricket primarily because it was seen as a useful instrument of socialization, although it perpetuated the gap between the classes in British society. Within the wider empire it became a vital part of the white man's burden because it helped to facilitate the process of imperial cultural assimilation.[140] Stoddart thus asserts that "cricket was considered the main vehicle for transferring the appropriate British moral code from the messengers of empire to the local populations".[141] In other words, it was certainly one of the most important mechanisms for enhancing the cultural power of the British colonial elites.

Although it is known that cricket was played in Barbados since the early nineteenth century, one of the earliest documentary references of it in Guyana was a report that when the militia went to drill at the Parade Ground on October 21, 1858, it was already being used by a group of cricketers;[142] and indeed until 1885 that ground remained the principal venue for organized cricket matches in the colony. A makeshift pavilion, cynically referred to by one person as a "stereotype coffee logie", was erected for use by the players,[143] and on big occasions tents covered with the branches of coconut and other trees were set up for the ladies.[144] From very early, therefore, cricket became a very important socio-cultural institution for the colonial elites, both male and female, although considerations of etiquette and decorum restrained the latter from playing.

Founded in 1852, and composed mainly of planters, wealthy merchants and high ranking government officials, the Georgetown Cricket Club (G.C.C.)—now the oldest surviving elite cricket club in the Caribbean—was directly linked with the sport from the moment organized cricket took root in Guyana. Its main rival was the Garrison Club composed of soldiers who were probably responsible for introducing the game in the first place.[145] Indeed the military connection with cricket in the colonial context is very important to any analysis of the cultural power of the colonial elites. Cricket instilled precisely those character-building qualities of discipline, willingness to take orders unquestioningly from the superior officer (captain), courage and determination in the face of adversity, and self-sacrifice for one's fel-

*Elite Victorian
Culture:
Leisure*

The Parade
Ground: site of
ritualistic
military parades

The Parade
Ground: venue
for elite cricket
matches

lows (the team), required for military service. The cricket captain commanding his men on the field of play and devising strategies 'on his feet' in the middle of a match was particularly analagous to the army officer marshalling his troops in combat on the battlefield. These skills, inculcated and honed on the cricket field, were especially vital in colonies where whites were grossly outnumbered by potentially hostile non-whites. Cricket thus enhanced the cultural power of the white colonists in a very practical way; and it is no surprise that the military Parade Ground should have served as the main playing arena of cricket in Guyana for most of the century.

In the later nineteenth century the elite grammar school, the Queen's College (Q.C.), became an important centre for inculcating such character building values and skills in young white boys on the cricket field. This was very much in keeping with the tradition built up in English public and grammar schools on which Q.C. was modelled. The school had good cricket elevens even before it had a ground of its own. Even after playing fields were acquired in the 1880s, the boys were permitted to play matches on the Parade Ground and on the G.C.C.'s new ground at Bourda after that was opened in 1885 (see below). During the 1880s, in fact, the G.C.C. probably played against the College more often than against any other club. Indeed, the links between Q.C. and the G.C.C. were formalized by means of an associate system which gave the older boys the opportunity to practise at Bourda. The school thus served as an important feeder/source of young elite players for both the club and the colony. As in England cricket in particular, and sports in general, were strongly encouraged by the school's masters who, as products of the public school and Oxbridge system, placed a very high social value on athleticism. The games ethic was promoted by two principals in particular, Exley Percival (1877-1893) and J.A. Potbury (1893-1898), who were imbued both with the late Victorian mania of physical fitness and of the importance of sport for empire building and maintenance. The latter was himself a keen all-round cricketer who was a member of the G.C.C. and actually represented Guyana on one occasion (1887).[146]

For a long time the playing members of the G.C.C. were the only persons who composed teams to represent the colony in inter-colonial matches. The first of those seems to have been against a Bermudan team in March 1859.[147] The year 1865 witnessed the first overseas tour by a Guyanese team when, in February, Demerara (i.e., the G.C.C.) visited Barbados. That visit was returned by the Barbadians in September. Both matches resulted in victories for the respective home teams.[148] In 1868, the G.C.C. hosted the first visit by a Trinidadian team, the Sovereign C.C., and returned the visit the following year.[149] In the ensuing years, matches were organized among these three territories in an ad hoc manner, but from 1893 a regular tournament was played by them for a Challenge Cup.[150] Interestingly, the first inter-colonial centurians (players who made 100 runs or more in an innings) were both Guyanese: all-rounder E.F. Wright in 1882 (123 out of a total of 168), and C.H. King in 1895 (135 in a total of 444, with Wright contributing 96), both against Trinidad.[151] Matches were also played against teams composed of officers of visiting warships. The high point was the visit of Lord Hawke's English team in 1897.[152] The G.C.C. were also very prominent in organizing the first 'West Indies' overseas tour––to the United States and Canada in 1886. It was their captain George Wyatt who planned and led the touring party comprising four Guyanese, six Jamaicans and two Barbadians.[153]

While the playing surface was fine, the accommodation at the Parade Ground was decidedly substandard especially for inter-colonial matches; so in 1883 a committee of the G.C.C. was appointed to select a site for a new ground. They chose a piece of government land in Bourda near the botanical gardens, bounded on the north by the Lamaha canal, on the south by Regent Road, on the east by Vlissengen Road, and on the west by New Garden Road. The lease of this land was approved by the Court of Policy (an indication of how important cricket was considered by the colonial legislators) and an estimated $6,000 were raised by the G.C.C. for laying out the new ground. This was completed to permit the first match at Bourda to be played on Boxing day, 1885. Bourda thus became the headquarters of cricket in Guyana and soon boasted "all the paraphernalia of a first-class ground" with fine turf and pavilion.[154] According to Heatley, "With constant watering, the ground looks green as an English lawn . . . "[155] (a critical yardstick of acceptability).

In New Amsterdam, the Berbice Cricket Club was formed with only about twenty members in August 1865,[156] but slipped into decline by the 1890s.[157] This is not to suggest that the Berbicians thought less of cricket, but as with all other sports in that county the small number of whites made it extremely difficult for them to sustain any form of leisure activity on a racially exclusive basis. In the country districts the game was occasionally played by the managers and overseers of estates who later organized themselves as the Essequibo, East Coast, and Belair cricket clubs.[158] What is very striking is the fact that these white clubs played only among themselves, not with non-white clubs.

Both Association football (soccer) and Rugby Union football were played by the cultural elites. The Georgetown Football Club was formed in 1880 amidst doubts about its chances of survival especially in the wake of previous clubs which had failed. The 'doubting Thomases' argued that the recreation savoured too much of hard labour to be pleasant. "Football in the tropics is just a little too much for most men . . . "[159] They were of course wrong. Despite its low social image in Britain in the late nineteenth century, the cultural elites seemed to develop a fairly keen interest in football, and matches were regularly played both at the Parade Ground and at the prestigious G.C.C. Bourda ground.[160] This sport was also promoted among the boys of the elite Queen's College.[161]

Boat racing, another product of the British public school and university system,[162] seemed to be fairly popular among the elites in Berbice. From time to time, rowing matches and regattas were organized,[163] and the Alpha Boating Club was formed in 1864. With a membership of just twenty, however, this was a very exclusive grouping indeed and on account of its smallness very susceptible to extinction.[164] On the other hand, the Demerara Rowing Club, formed in 1873, endured beyond the end of the century. Its boathouse was located at La Penitence on the Demerara river, and from time to time it organized one mile races from the Houston *stelling* (wharf/landing) to the boathouse. These events always generated great interest among the cultural elites.[165]

From the late seventies as ordinary bicycles ('penny-farthings') became popular, and with the subsequent advent of the safety bicycle, the sport of cycling was promoted if only to provide exercise after work. To this end a bicycle club was formed in 1882 with an annual subscription fee of twelve shillings for ordinary members and ten shillings for honorary members. The entrance fee for ordinary members was five shillings.[166] In Britain cycling assumed mania proportions during the 1890s and played a major role in emancipating women both by way of freedom of movement and in forms of dress. According to Bryan the same occurred in Jamaica towards the end of the century.[167] Although the evidence is sparse for Guyana, one might reasonably assume likewise. Indeed, bicycles are still one of the principal means of transport in modern Guyana.

About the late 1870s as well, athletics (i.e., track and field) grew in popularity and the B.G. Athletic Club was formed in 1882.[168] But at first only one serious athletic meeting was held annually and no championship trophy was offered.[169] During the 1890s, however, the Georgetown Cricket Club began to organize athletic meetings at their Bourda ground, including both flat and bicycle races, high jump and tug-o-war competitions. Annual athletic sports were also organized for the boys of the Queen's College where greater emphasis was placed on sports in the late nineteenth century and various games clubs were formed. Athletic events were participated in by the lower classes as well because they did not require any expensive equipment or club facilities.[170] But in Guyana athletics did not attain the same kind of mass popularity as cricket because, since the cultural elites did not attach the same importance to it, recognition and social reward for achievement were not nearly as great as in cricket.

In Britain indoor sports and games like chess, checkers, darts and billiards were also very popular. According to Sandiford, the Victorians "not only modernized these games but they virtually overhauled every card game known to man".[171] Holt asserts that in the colonies indoor games were essential to fill in long evenings where there was little other source of entertainment.[172] In Guyana, card games and billiards were by far the most popular indoor games and were played at all the social clubs and hotels[173] and, as we have seen, they played an integral part in after dinner socializing among elite families. Chess attracted a smaller body of participants, but even so on at least two separate occasions clubs were formed to organize tournaments and give instructions to their members. These were the Georgetown Chess Club in 1864,[174] and the Demerara Chess Association in 1875. The latter was an off-shoot of the R.A. & C.S. and held meetings in its Reading Room.[175] A Chess Club was also established in Berbice, and matches were played between the two clubs.[176] The elite newspapers, the *Royal Gazette*, *Berbice Gazette* and the *Colonist*, regularly featured chess moves in their pages.

As in Jamaica, although the British elites generally engaged in the same socio-cultural pursuits, differences did exist particularly between the English and Scots. The latter, who were quite substantial in number in Guyana, had a reputation for clinging together. Thus the predominantly Scottish membership of the Georgetown Gymnastic Club, formed in 1877, was cause for public concern.[177] Equipped with foils, basket sticks, fencing jackets, boxing gloves, Indian clubs, ladders, gym horses, parallel and horizontal bars, this club aroused the keen interest of an increasingly fitness-conscious elite. The controversy over membership, however, must have been resolved to allow Governor Kortright to open the club formally in November 1878.[178]

One pastime that aroused considerable consternation and concern in the late seventies was gambling which seemed on the increase, particularly among a large circle of young white males working in Georgetown. The hostility to this pastime should not be surprising since it reflected Christian Victorian middle class anti-gambling attitudes imported from Britain. Gambling was not new to the colony: the planters themselves were notorious for indulging in it. What was perhaps new and disconcerting was the fact that this upsurge of gambling was not only done in private coteries, but also in licensed resorts where card playing for excessive stakes was allowed. So much concern did this trend arouse that some of the leading merchants compiled lists of places where gambling was carried on as well as the names of persons who frequented them. This was ostensibly to safeguard themselves against employees who might be tempted by their indebtedness as a result of gaming to be dishonest.[179]

Further social sanctions were imposed by Governor Kortright who in 1878 had the names of habitual gamblers struck off the invitation list to Government House. This, however, was not allowed to go unanswered, because it was publicly noted in the press that practically all the elite males played cards which could be interpreted as gambling, and that to penalize the youngsters so harshly (blackballing, especially by the governor, was a very serious matter) was gross over reaction to a relatively minor social problem.[180]

Summary

The cultural elites harboured the mentality of temporary immigrants in the sense that they regarded Britain as 'home' and aspired to retire there one day. They thus saw Guyana only as place of temporary abode where they would remain just for as long as it would take to make their fortunes. What differentiated them from other categories of immigrants was, firstly, the fact that for the most part they were white, British, the colonizers, and as a consequence at the apex of the colonial society; and, secondly, they considered themselves to be the bearers of 'civilization'. The brown-black *évolués*, though native to the colony, to a considerable degree shared in this cultural anglophilia.

As a result of this perception of temporariness the cultural elites had even less desire to change than their counterparts who migrated to white settler colonies like Australia, New Zealand, Canada, and South Africa. In each case, however, the emphasis in their cultural behaviour was essentially to import whatever they could from home. In Guyana they were responsible for introducing several British cultural institutions, artifacts, customs, and values, but generally lacked both the interest and enthusiasm to create new indigenous cultural expressions. What could not be imported from Britain was not in their estimation worthwhile bothering with. In this sense, they harboured a deepseated colonial mentality which enshrined the notion that things local were intrinsically inferior to those from the metropolis. The result was cultural inertia and sterility among the elites who spent much of their time dissipating themselves in lascivious sexual promiscuity, intemperate imbibition of alcoholic drinks, extravagant over-consumption, pomp, ceremony, and an insatiable craving for high social status.

Therein lay some of the most significant forms of their cultural adaptation to life in the tropical plantation environment. The result was that the manifestations of elite Victorian culture in the colony were somewhat different from the British middle class ideal or model on which they were patterned. For all its vaunted 'superior cultural pedigree', the local variant was influenced not only by the physical and social environment, but also by the wider cultural milieu in which it found itself. Weakness of the white nuclear family (because of the shortage of women) and of the Christian church (because of the shortage of priests) encouraged coarse manners and 'immoral' behaviour. But these were only one facet of the creolization process to which the cultural elites were subjected. The other, far less readily admitted, was the 'baneful' influence which the 'lower social orders', in particular the Creoles with whom they had long been in contact, had on them particularly with respect to food, speech patterns, customs and even superstitions. Despite these obviously creolizing influences, however, it was the imported metropolitan culture forms, accorded premium status, to which they clung in order to underpin their social position at the apex of the society.

That social position was of vital importance in vesting the colonial elites with tremendous cultural power which they could use to transmit their 'superior culture' to the 'inferior races' of plantation and other labourers. In a colonial situation where the cultural elites formed a very tiny minority in a population composed of people of diverse racial and cultural backgrounds, control over the political and economic institutions, over the forces of legitimate violence, and the pursuit of policies designed to divide and rule, were very effective, though *negative*, means of **maintaining** social order and stability; but were nevertheless emphasized and made maximum use of in nineteenth century Guyana.[181] The only *positive* way, however, of **promoting** social stability was to create value consensus. This was not by any means lost on the Guyanese elites who employed a range of tactics to bring this about—force of example, public opinion and propaganda in the press, church and school, invented traditions and symbols, and sport. The extent to which these were successful naturally depended on the receptivity and resistance of the subordinate populations. But while, as we shall see in subsequent chapters, the colonial elites rarely resorted to law or force to promote cultural consensus, they left it in no doubt that social mobility was dependent on cultural assimilation. The subtle use of their cultural power was thus instrumental for laying the groundwork for the evolution of a colonial culture/mentality based on the fundamental premise of the superiority of things British.

Thus at no time in the postemancipation nineteenth century was elite Victorian culture the exclusive possession of the white population. By design, an increasing number of the subordinate populations was exposed to various doses of it. In this sense, therefore, the culture always overlapped the strict racial boundaries of the white section. This meant that the social exclusivity of that section could never have depended simply on the possession of Victorian cultural attributes. For most of the postemancipation period, 'race' was employed as the critical factor for differentiating white from non-white. But towards the end of the century when browns and blacks eventually broke down the political barriers which had theretofore denied them access to political office, the 'racial' card was no longer tenable. Under those changing circumstances, therefore, a higher premium was attached to Victorian culture for the achievement of high social status, and this was emphasized not least of all by those brown-black *évolués* who qualified. In this context, and contrary to the pluralist argument advanced by M.G. Smith et al., culture only began to assume priority as a social determinant under conditions of change from a plural to a class stratified society, when its role was oriented towards integration rather one of emphasizing divergence.

AFRO-CREOLE FOLK CULTURE:
Material and Temporal

Afro-Creole folk culture was the culture of the black and coloured
rural and urban working classes. As we noted in chapter 3, the western
educated coloureds and blacks inculcated and practised in varying degrees very many aspects of elite Victorian culture, and in some cases
even sought to shut out Afro-Creole influences from their way of life.
In most instances, however, this process of cultural self-purging was
never complete; hence even in some of the most anglophile of Creoles,
traces of Afro-Creole folk cultural behaviour, beliefs and values could
be found. These persons thus formed an important cultural bridge
between the two divergent traditions of elite and folk culture which
helped to integrate them into a continuum that could form the basis of
a truly national culture. Likewise, we shall see that even the grassroots
Creole working classes were not wholly African in culture, but shared
many traits and values in common with the cultural elites.

In the struggle for the amelioration of the condition of the slaves
and finally for the abolition of slavery itself, considerable attention
was paid to the physical condition and way of life of the slaves. This
interest persisted long after emancipation as the missionaries and the
imperial government itself, under humanitarian influence and scrutiny, were keen to 'uplift' the moral and spiritual condition of the
ex-slaves, although that interest did not extend to ensuring an improvement in their economic and political status. The result of all this,
however, was a great deal of observation, commentary and reporting
by various individuals and institutions—church, state, press, travellers,
to list a few—with diverse motives, which generated an enormous
amount of data on the cultural life of the ex-slaves. Unfortunately, in
far too many instances the information is flawed by prejudice, inaccu-
racy, incompleteness, and superficiality, and focuses only on certain
aspects of Creole life and culture to the exclusion of others. This
renders reconstruction very difficult and uneven. Nevertheless, for
analytical purposes the data are treated in two chapters: this one focus-

ing on the material and temporal aspects of Afro-Creole life, the next on the spiritual.

Accommodation

As pointed out before, the first decade and a half after the ending of slavery (1838) witnessed very dramatic demographic developments in Guyana marked by the movement of ex-slaves away from the planta- tions onto freehold properties which they bought. New settlements were created not only on the coastal plains and in the towns, but also along the rivers in the immediate hinterland. These represented a de- sire by the ex-slaves to establish a real stake in the soil on which they and their ancestors had toiled unremittingly for centuries, and also to provide a supplementary or alternative economic activity to plantation labour.[1] According to Rodney, by 1848 the number of Creoles resi- dent on the sugar estates had fallen to 19,939 while the villages and settlements housed 44,456 persons;[2] and Adamson points out that the native Negro village population grew by 46 percent in the second half of the nineteenth century.[3] Thus, only a relatively small number of Creoles continued to reside on the plantations in the later nineteenth century, for whom accommodation provided by the management con- tinued to be substandard. According to one source, the houses were generally huddled together in a wretched condition, with mud floors, and very little furniture or conveniences: ". . . everywhere, dirt and filth and neglect: no garden, no comfort. Hogs prowl about, rooting up the drains and devouring the garbage that abounds in rich profu- sion . . . There is no water supply, not an apology for a water closet".[4]

It is not surprising that the majority of Creoles should have sought to escape such primitive living conditions. Where they were able to purchase well-drained land, they did materially improve their residen- tial quarters. The village of Ithaca on the Berbice river provides a good example: "This village is built on three separate properties, and con- tains about 300 houses and 1,300 inhabitants, the roads through it are good: many of the houses are good, and the inhabitants, chiefly black people, seem to live a very easy independent life".[5]

But the move into freehold villages and into towns did not always produce such salutary improvement. The principal enemy was drain- age particularly along the east coast of Demerara where the largest villages were established. As Adamson shows, the main cause of the poor drainage was the formation of great mud banks offshore which prevented the system of gravity drainage from working properly. Lacking the capital required to purchase modern steam powered drain- age pumps and erect proper *kokers* (sluices) and dykes, the villagers were the victims of a hostile environment and were subjected to re-

Typical
flooding in
rural villages
after heavy
rains

peated flooding which often left their lands in a deplorable condition.[6]
Thus in the unsympathetic Eurocentric eyes of Anthony Trollope:

> A negro village . . . is not a picturesque object . . . The cottages, or houses . . .
> stand in extreme disorder, one here and another there . . . There seems to have
> been no attempt at streets or lines of buildings and certainly not at regularity in
> building . . . There are no roads, and hardly a path to each habitat. As the ground
> is not drained in wet weather the whole place is half-drowned.[7]

Many settlements were described as consisting of "small wooden
rattle-trap sheds in a dirty yard or rank half-cultivated garden, un-
drained—a perfect morass in the rainy weather".[8] In some instances
where ex-slaves had purchased whole estates, they could not afford to
maintain the old plantation buildings which soon fell into further
disrepair and were taken over by wild vegetation.[9] Thus the move
away from the estates, while offering greater economic independence,
did not always lead to better living conditions for the Creoles.

Likewise economic conditions materially influenced the types of
houses inhabited by working class Creoles. Most of their homes were
built for function rather than for style or elegance. They were generally made of local hardwoods—wallaba, greenheart or mora. The
frame consisted of squared uprights, 5 to 7 feet apart, morticed into a
sill below, and into the roof-plate above, standing about 10 feet high.
The roof was of ordinary pitch; the sides were boarded round with
white pine or American timber. When the means were available, the
whole building was shingled with splittings from the wallaba tree, and
so was the roof.[10] These houses were generally hardly larger than 10
feet square. There were many window openings, but no glass—

wooden shutters being used. Hewn from the coarsest timber, the doors were rough. The houses generally stood 2 feet or more above ground, on wooden stilts or posts in order to remain dry in the event of flooding. The basement or 'bottom-house' was used to shelter livestock and for storing some household articles. Wooden steps led to the door which was almost invariably in the centre of the building.[11]

The interior of these houses consisted either of just one open room,[12] or two compartments for sleeping and sitting. The sleeping compartment was separated from the sitting room by a pictured or canvass screen, and contained a bed spacious enough for seven since it filled the whole room. In the sitting-room, there were generally one cherished piece of furniture in the shape of a half-polished sideboard, various bits and pieces "from a greasy bent candlestick to a brass thimble", including cups, glasses, tumblers, calabashes and bottles. Just like the houses of the elites, there was no kitchen attached to these wooden buildings in order to minimize the risk of fire. All ordinary cooking was done in the open air on a simple coal-pot. A small garden in the yard provided a variety of plants.[13] A few tubs lay outside, and perhaps a puncheon with a board or dried 'palm-loaf' connected with the roof to collect the rainwater.[14]

Although Creole women generally took great pleasure in keeping their homes clean, and tried to ornament them with glassware, handsome bedsteads, sofas, tables and chairs, the reality of poverty and the need to 'hustle' to make ends meet led in some cases to a neglect of their domestic cares.[15]

In the urban centres, housing for the working class Creoles was generally squalid, particularly the yard ranges, i.e., long, narrow buildings subdivided into self-contained rooms or apartments. Even if the physical condition of these buildings was good (and that was rare), the interior and surroundings were often filthy as a result of overcrowding and poor sanitary facilities. A survey of north and south Cummingsburg, Georgetown, in 1888 revealed the entirely atrocious conditions in which many working class Creoles had to live. In one yard on Carmichael Street, a range of fourteen small rooms, each rented at $2.00 (8s. 4d.) per month, was found "overcrowded in excess". In some rooms, the 'part-off' and bed were the only furnishings, but other dwellers had crowded tables and chairs into their one little room in which an average of five or six persons lived and slept.[16]

Another range of eighteen rooms was so densely overcrowded that the rooms were in a filthy state despite the fairly good physical condition of the building. Yet another yard was described as having no redeeming feature, though it did not suffer from the usual overcrowding. But the buildings were in an inconceivable state of dilapidation. The principal one was an old rotten three-storied structure. Filthy refuse was found around the doors on the ground floor. The staircase was described as "a heap of rotten wood". In one of the first floor rooms which housed a family, the walls were in danger of collapsing— full of cobweb, rotten wood and torn wall paper. The floor had holes over which pieces of tin and wood were laid to keep the occupants from falling through. It leaked badly, and for the privilege of such accommodation ten shillings ($2.40) per month were paid. The top storey of this building was in the same state. These were typical of the sort of accommodation that the urban working class Creoles had to endure.[17]

Creole settlements, whether in the rural or urban areas, and the architecture of their dwellings, were unquestionably the products of the plantation system and the poverty which it produced for those who constituted its dependent labour force. The layout, the structures, and the materials used, were all local.

Afro–Creole Value System

It was the yards and streets of these rural settlements and urban ghettos which formed the breeding ground of a dynamic and vibrant folk culture of the Afro-Creole working people in postemancipation Guyana. Given the lack of physical space in the typical urban or rural house or apartment inhabited by working class Creoles, the yard/street became a natural extension of the home—in a sense the living-room—where they gathered to relax and entertain one another (called *liming* in Trinidad). The community therefore formed one large extended 'family' where the values of survival in a world of disprivilege and poverty were learnt and transmitted.

This socio-cultural milieu fostered both communal cooperation and individual competition. It also bred a strong desire to achieve recognition and respectability both from one's peers and one's social 'betters'. This meant two things: first, a desire to emulate the behaviour of the cultural elites; second, the nurturing of an assertive sense of 'one-up-manship' *vis-à-vis* one's peers. While the first favoured an acceptance of elite Victorian moral values such as modesty, dignity, orderliness, civility, decorum, etc., which signified a desire to accommodate to the dominant social norms, the latter encouraged such counter-values as gregariousness, bravado, loudness, ribaldry, rowdyism, aggression and even coarse vulgarity which formed the basis of Afro-Creole resistance to complete cultural domination. Premium referred to this counter-culture in 1840 when he noted that:

> Scarcely a night passes without some boisterous quarrel, which disturbs the whole plantation, and rouses us from sleep, the mansion-house being only about a couple hundred yards from the Negro village. There is seldom any mischief

Urban ghetto
woman (Tiger Bay,
Georgetown):
personification of
the yard culture

done, for the heroes have all the scolding propensities which we observe in those
of the Iliad, before engaging in battle; but the parallel holds good no farther,
inasmuch as Homer's men proceeded to work in earnest, whilst ours content
themselves with the war of tongues throughout . . . The ladies, in general, are the
firebrands among them.[18]

Physical violence, however, was not unknown; in fact it added theatre to
the war of words. Dalton described a typical 'cuss-out' thus:

The women are notorious quarellers [*sic*] and fighters. The disputants begin
by the interchange of a few unpleasant remarks, generally of a personal
nature; gestures of contempt and defiance follow; the voices are raised to a
very high pitch; invectives, declamations, cutting expressions on the character and quality of their relatives following, and a system of admirable attitu-
denizing and vehement acting follows, which beggars description. Unless
separated by the crowd which instinctively gathers round them, they pro-

ceed from bad to worse, until the war is settled by force of arms. If separated, the excited disputants slowly retire, but keep up a volley of personal
abuse for the length of a street, and when forced to go home, continue
declaiming and posturing for a long time.[19]

These virtuoso performances, called *tracing* in Jamaica, wholly scan-
dalized the cultural elites who recoiled from the venom of the Creole
tongue and the yard values with which they were associated. 'H.R.'
was overawed by the verbal dexterity of working class Creole men and
women. One

> . . . encounters some of the vilest language that ever issued from human lips; for
> genuine, downright swearing puntmen, cartmen and coal women can, I think,
> whip creation; the scientific way in which they commence would create amaze-
> ment, if it did not excite disgust; they will take a preliminary glance at your
> ancestors, then pronounce an eulogium on yourself and immediate relations, and
> conclude by giving a prophesy as to the probable fate of your descendants.[20]

Trotman sees this practice of 'cussing' or 'buseing' both as a revelation of the poverty and deprivation of the participants and as a demonstration of their ability to use words effectively. Both for Creole men
and women it was part of the process of self-affirmation in a situation
of powerlessness.[21]

This yard/street culture, however vulgar it appeared to bourgeois
observers, provided the critical values and tools for resisting white
cultural dominance and fighting back against social injustice and racial
discrimination. But its coexistence with the elite value system was
uneasy and, as we shall see, bred cultural ambivalence among the
Creoles—what Orlando Patterson sees as a love-hate relationship with
elite culture.[22] Thus on one hand, elite culture was considered desirable as the only means of achieving social respectability and mobility
in the colonial society; on the other it was resisted and its bearers and
perpetrators literally abused because it threatened to emasculate the
folk traditions of Afro-Creole culture.

Language

The long contact which blacks had with whites in the plantation
environment resulted in the almost complete loss of their native African languages, with the exception of a few words or phrases used
almost ritualistically. Only the 'liberated' African immigrants were
able in the late nineteenth century to communicate in their native
tongues, and they were an endangered species. According to Bronkhurst, "The Black Creoles never can relish the language of their ancestors, though they hear it spoken in their presence".[23] This seems to
suggest that the Creoles inculcated the devaluation of African languages by the dominant whites. However, in lieu of their native
languages the Creoles developed a new lingua franca, called *Creolese*

(Creole English), which was a linguistic syncretism of African languages and English. This was sufficiently distinctive to be classified as a language in its own right. Several varieties of *Creolese* were spoken depending on the status of the individual. At the lowest level basilectal *Creolese* was used. This could scarcely be understood by English-speaking strangers, and even long resident whites had some difficulty understanding it when spoken: "a clipping of words running one into the other . . ."[24] Rickford argues that in many instances this was a symbol of non-accommodation to enslavement and colonial oppression.[25] Thus far from accepting linguistic inferiority, many Creoles spoke a language which made it possible for them to resist the unwanted cultural impositions—ideas, values, etc.—that often go along with the acquisition of the language of an imperial power.

African immigrants, who spoke their own languages, also had great difficulty communicating in *Creolese*. "By signs and gestures the Africans make themselves understood when they cannot express themselves in the patois of the people."[26] Exposure to formal English education, however, undermined the new language by incorporating more English words, phrases, idioms and grammatical structures, so that Creoles who had been schooled spoke a more standardized English-based form of *Creolese* which was fairly intelligible to English speakers.[27] But as Rickford notes, this also had the effect of increasing the social stigma attached to the less English varieties of *Creolese*.[28]

Richard Schomburgk considered *Creolese* to be "a real 'pidgin' derived from almost all the idioms of Europe and Africa, the indigenous 'Creole-Dutch'".[29] This is typical of the confusion of Europeans in their attempts to explain the linguistic phenomenon of *Creolese*. There were indeed two distinctly different 'Dutch Creoles' developed in earlier times, one in Essequibo, the other in Berbice, which were still in fairly widespread use during the first half of the nineteenth century; but they were gradually replaced by the more English-based *Creolese* which became the lingua franca of the Creole population during the postemancipation period.[30]

Creolese was neither merely a pidgin made up of English and African words as Schomburgk thought, nor a bastardized form of English composed of mispronounced old and new English words, learnt mainly from the Bible, as van Sertima implied.[31] It is true that it contained many West African words and expressions,[32] but its most important inheritance from that source was its basic linguistic structure within which it incorporated many English words. *Creolese* was, therefore, a cultural creation of the Afro-Guyanese, which was in fact acquired and added to not only by the dominant whites, but later on by subsequent immigrant groups. It was used by the Creoles with facility in all forms of communication, including verbal abuse.[33]

The elites, however, used their cultural power to seek to indoctrinate the Creoles into believing that things which they created and employed were of no value, and that the acquisition of English language was essential for social respectability and mobility. Hence, those who were exposed to English education generally sought to exhibit their ability to articulate fluently in that foreign linguistic import. As Bronkhurst noted:

> Among a certain class of educated Creoles there is an impression that unless they could employ long or big words, either in their conversation or in writing, they would not be looked upon as men of education ... Among the working class also a knowledge of long words of late has become quite the fashion ... The Barbadians especially are fond of using long words ... Sometimes, too, words and expressions used by the educated gentlemen acquire a local and temporary popularity.[34]

Examples of this tendency were not difficult to find. According to Hardy: "Among our local brethren we have some well-read, thoughtful, and original preachers. 'We will expounderate de doctrine; argufy de principle; and den, put on de rousements', is not a bad way of treating a text ..."[35] He cited another instance when a minister's horse took ill, and a Creole farrier examined it: "After a long and most careful examination of the horse's tongue, eyes, &c, &c, he turned to the minister, and putting on a very wise look said, 'Well, sah! what is de mattah wid dis hoss is, he be sufferin', sah, wid a complexialry ob billiousry'".[36]

But as Trotman points out, the colonial education system reinforced a penchant for oral dexterity that was inherent in the Creole language. Because the emphasis was on learning by rote, it "encouraged a concentration on and a delight in the sound of words. The sound of the word gave the opportunity for skilled wordsmiths to infuse new meanings into old words. Those who were orally dextrous had in their possession a weapon that could be used to defend themselves against perceived oppression".[37]

Thus the acquired language became a double-edged sword in the mouths of the Creoles, and was as much a tool for achieving social respectability as a weapon of cultural resistance.

Creole pronunciation of some English words, however, could prove quite amusing at times. Many Creole speakers found it difficult to pronounce the '*th*' in some English words. Thus, for instance, "When taking their wedding vows, instead of saying 'Until death us do part', they say, 'Until "debt" [det] us do part', and 'hereby I give thee my "trot"' [i.e., throat] for 'throth'".[38]

Names

After emancipation, among the native born Africans in Guyana several nations or tribes were represented including the Abuna, Akan, Aku (Yoruba), Egba, Effa, Fula (Fulani), Ibo, Ijesa, Kongo, Kru, Ondo

(Doko), Oyeh, and Yagba. Many of these were sub-groups of the Yoruba. These Africans had their own tribal marks and for the most part retained their traditional names: "Some of them are poetical. They are racy of the African soil".[39] The data, however, are extremely sparse. Yoruban names seem to have been relatively commonplace, e.g., Ajimoko (someone who wakes up to work with the hoe), Famayadeh (one who walks majestically with the crown—signifying perhaps nobility), and Olonuraba (we come back to meet God).[40] According to Bronkhurst, the Yoruba also named their children according to the day of birth. Thus if born on Monday, the names given were Quia (m) and Aju-ba (f); on Tuesday, Quarquo (m) and Bamba (f); on Wednesday, Quaminah (m) and Ahwobah (f); on Thursday, Yo-u (m) and Yabah (f); on Friday, Quoffie (m) and Afibah (f); on Saturday, Quamini (m) and Amimbah (f); and on Sunday, Quashie (m) and Quashiba (f).[41] Quite apart from the fact that the Africans' indigenous calendars were different from the European Gregorian calendar, this practice of naming children according to the day of birth was not unique to the Yoruba, but was common among other West African peoples. This probably helps to account for Bronkhurst's inaccuracies (as was so often the case with contemporary European observers). While some of the names which he listed were indeed Yoruban, others were unquestionably Akan in origin, e.g., Quaminah/Ahwobah, Quoffie/Afibah, Quamini/Amimbah, and Quashie/Quashiba.[42]

The vast majority of the black/coloured population in nineteenth century Guyana were Creoles and the same creative dynamism of the yard culture which influenced their language could be seen in the names they gave their children. Ever since the days of slavery the cultural power of the elites had been effective in placing a negative value on African names. Hence, Creoles placed a premium on European words/names though in some instances retaining the African penchant for description, e.g., Belly, Lettice, Bacchus, Creole Johnny, Spadille, Blaize, Codine, Sans Souci; in some cases these were used in combination with genuine African names, e.g., Captain Quashie.[43] Old slave names, European in origin, such as Venus, Adonis, Hercules and Pompey were often used as surnames, e.g., Thomas Hercules, William Adonis, etc. Some Creoles also adopted the surnames of estate proprietors and managers: hence there were several Bascoms, Fields, Russells and Macalmans.[44] This undoubtedly reflected their desire for respectability and a sense of self-esteem, and was also manifested in the liberal use of European titles as popular Creole first names, especially among the women.[45] "We have around us whole families made up of Queens, Princes, Generals, and the like."[46] Ex-Sheriff Kirke was characteristically abusive: "One decidedly plain young woman told me her name was Lovely Venus; whilst another dirty commonplace piece of humanity, after she had kissed the Bible, gave her name as Princess Matilda".[47]

Creoles also adopted English place names as first names, e.g., London Quamina, or Liverpool Prince. In addition, famous Europeans with 'catchy' names were "sure to have their counterparts (in name at least) among the Creole peasantry of Guiana"; for instance, one man gave his name as Wellington Napoleon Hamilton Smith.[48] What is clear, however, is that the naming of children by the Creoles again reflected the influences of both West Africa and Europe, although in the prevailing socio-cultural climate of postemancipation Guyana and the Creole desire for social respectability therein, the bias was clearly towards the latter.

Dress

The dynamism of the yard/street culture was also reflected in the way the Creoles dressed. Their long contact with a dominant white culture in plantation society, and their desire to achieve social respectability, caused them to adopt European forms of dress thus, except for recent African immigrants, leaving little trace of traditional African forms by the time of emancipation: "They have no national or peculiar costume. Every individual who makes any pretension to respectability, attempts to imitate the dress of the white or upper classes".[49] By emancipation, the Creoles could be considered to have fully assimilated western forms of dress. Indeed they had positively developed an appetite for fine expensive European clothes. Parents took great pride in outfitting their children in smart European garments for school and church, even if that meant depriving themselves of certain necessities. On the other hand, these same children might very well be found at home literally "in rags or a state of semi-nudity".[50]

Thus as in other traditional rural societies, the Creoles developed their own pattern of dressing which was as much related to poverty as it was to custom. There were two standards of dress, one for the work place and home which despite the European form bore noticeably African traits; the other for Sundays and special occasions which was strongly European high-fashion oriented. At work and at home, the men dressed in shirt and trousers with or without boots or shoes, while the women dressed in petticoats and frocks, with their heads tied, African-style, with headkerchiefs called 'tie-heads'. "To the black Creole labourers boots and shoes are a perfect nuisance during week days."[51] As in West Africa, the women ordinarily plaited their hair by dividing it into a number of partings running in all directions.[52]

On Sundays, holidays, and special days, however, the Creoles donned their high-fashion European finery with great extravagance:

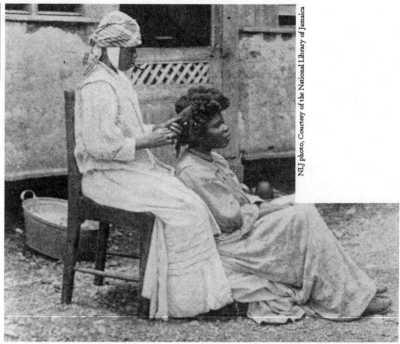

NLJ photo, Courtesy of the National Library of Jamaica

Creole
woman
plaiting hair
in the yard

". . . on those days [they] have really a smart easy air, as if they had
worn buckra clothes of the first fashion always".[53] "In the towns there
is absolute beauism on Sundays, as much as in a European town." The
men wore tight-fitting coats, fine shirts, waist-coats, French hats and
cravats, strapped trousers and glazed boots, complete with watch-
chains.[54] Even towards the end of the century, and as the white men
began to shed the top hat and frock-coat, Creole men ironically held
on steadfastly to those articles of European wear as essential parts of
their formal attire.[55]

The women studied all the fashions in the world (i.e., Britain) and
were "not a whit behind their pale sisters at home". They were "amazingly gay" in light muslins, brilliant shawls, and fashionable bonnets,
"while their hair is cruelly straightened and rolled into as near a resemblance to chignons as wool is capable of assuming". Imitation jewelery
was abundantly worn by both sexes. According to Crookall, "They
have their light muslin dresses of white and pink and skyblue, and pale
green and red and yellow; their dark hair often adorned with sweet-smell-
ing jessamine or a pink rose. In their hands they carry their fan and their
book, whilst their feet are compressed into little high-heeled, patent-
leather shoes, which contrast with the shapely white stockings".[56]

The ladies invariably carried umbrellas over their heads to shelter
from the sun "under which they had been probably working the
whole week".[57] And there was also "a peculiar walk called the Sunday

Everyday dress
of Creole
working class
women

walk, which is very different from the ordinary week day one".[58]
Schomburgk described the dress of Creole men attending a ball: "A
black or blue frock-coat covers the faultless shoulders: a red, yellow,
or sky-blue vest worked in with gold----this is enclosed with a huge
watch-chain and heavy pendant . . . ----covers the powerful chest: the
white dancing pumps neatly laced up to the knees: the silk stockings
and red or yellow shoes".[59]

The reality of economic life in postemancipation Guyana meant
that the Creoles could not support their French fashion tastes on loin
cloth pockets. High taxation, exploitation by Portuguese shopkeepers
and moneylenders, and the failure of the peasant village economy
reduced the vast majority of Creoles to a state of chronic poverty, and
left them with very little to spend on expensive clothes. Thus by the
early 1850s, many of them were generally poorly clad.[60] But they still
made a conscious effort to save for special occasions such as weddings
and balls.

Sunday dress
of Creoles

Wenty Bowen photo. Reproduced from the Collections of the UWI Library (Mona)

If the Creoles were lavish, and in some cases even exquisite, in their tastes for western clothes, adjustment to this standard apparently came slowly and painfully for the African immigrants. Premium, with typical derision, mocked the dress of the unacculturated Africans which produced in his eyes "the most ludicrous exhibitions . . . on the highway while they are crowding to church". One African, he noted, appeared with nothing but a hat "and a fig leaf of modern savage life, a lap [loincloth]". In addition to the loincloth, another African wore a new swallow-tailed coat and gloves: "all the rest was 'birthday suit'".[61] Crookall too commented on the 'funny side' of black dress: "Sometimes you will see an old negress sitting boldly up in front of you with *three* hats on. First a 'kerchief' round the head, worn like a turban, which they call a 'tie head', then an old bonnet on the top of that, and crowning the whole some dinged and cast-off billycock, or 'chimney pot'".[62]

These admittedly amusing anecdotes demonstrate the enormous cultural pressures which Africans and Creoles alike must have encountered to alter their mode of dress in order to conform to the Anglo-elite model. The result was a decided bias toward the latter. What influenced this transformation more than anything else was an overwhelming desire among the lowly placed ex-slaves, after generations of vilification by the elites, to achieve some measure of social respectability for themselves and their families; and that was generally attainable in the colonial society only by adopting the dominant Anglo-Creole culture.

Food

Because they were all built of wood, Guyanese houses whether belonging to the elites or to the working classes had no fireplaces or chimney-pots. The Creoles, therefore, cooked their food in the yard or on the steps near the door on a coal-pot—an iron charcoal stove, shaped somewhat like a huge squat egg cup, with its base open to allow a free draught of air. A little grating divided this cup from the stand, where the fuel (firewood or charcoal) was put. On this was placed a frying-pan or meat pot, and a little fanning did the rest.[63]

The main items of the black Creole diet were beef, veal, mutton, pork, salt meats, dried salt fish, mackerel, herring, salmon, butter, lard, alcohol and malt liquors, wine, biscuits, wheat flour, cheese, tea, cocoa and chocolate. Most of these were imported from Europe and North America, but local food items were also used extensively by the Creoles. A large draught of coffee was drunk early every morning—in fact, coffee was the main beverage consumed. Sugar was also widely used, esti-

The coalpot: stove on which food was cooked

100

Cultural
Power,
Resistance,
and
Pluralism

mated at fifty pounds per capita per annum. Plantains, however, were the staple diet and each person consumed about seventy pounds per week.[64]

For the Creoles, each meal consisted of one dish. Plates and spoons were used by the elders, while the children used their hands. The favourite dish was plantains and salt fish seasoned with hot pepper.[65] The whole was boiled in water until it became thick and was called *Cutty-cutty*. *Foo-foo* soup was another delicacy. It was a typical Afro-Creole meal which derived its name from the plantain which was boiled and pounded or crushed with a greenheart mortar pestle.[66] "The method of pounding—namely, with a long mortar-stick which enables the woman to stand up—is typical Africa . . ." The name itself was African in origin. According to Cruickshank, "'Fu' is white in Yoruba tongue; 'fu-fu' white-white—the [pounded] substance which is white-white": for, as he noted, 'fu-fu' in Yoruba (southern Nigeria) is not made of plantain but of white yam.[67] The soup was made by boiling a few pieces of cassava or plantains in a pot of water until they were soft. They were then crushed and the soup was flavoured with a small piece of pork, salt beef, salt fish, onions, a handful of pepper, and local freshwater fish such as the *patwah*.[68]

Another dish, called *Come Asunder* consisted of rice boiled with salt fish and pork mixed.[69] *Konki* was a preparation of boiled cornmeal and flavoured with pumpkin, a few currants, sugar and black pepper, and wrapped hot in a plantain leaf. It was derived from Guinea and Benin where it was used as bread.[70] Although they did not lose their liking for *konki*, the Creoles, partially acculturated to white eating habits, generally used wheat bread instead, with cassava bread derived from the Amerindians as a substitute.[71]

Pepperpot, adopted from the indigenous Amerindians, became such a favoured meal among the Creoles (and whites as well) that it is now generally regarded as Guyana's national dish. This was made in a large earthenware pot into which was put *cas-*

Ken Morgan photo. Courtesy of ISER Publications (Mona)

Typical Creole method of preparing food by pounding substance in a mortar with a wooden pestle

sareep, a liquid preservative and seasoning made from the juice of the bitter cassava. *Cassareep* is "dark in colour, and of the consistency of molasses". Peppers were added to the pot, and "into this all kinds of flesh, fish or fowl that are not eaten at once are placed, and the pot is set on the fire; with the result that the meat is preserved for an indefinite period, and a most delicious kind of stew is always ready".[72]

The diet of the Barbadian Creoles differed in some respects from the locals. They preferred American breadstuffs, sweet potatoes, yams and eddoes to the local Creole plantain and cassava. *Coo-coo*, made from cornmeal, with herrings and eddoes, was their favourite dish.[73] All Creoles, however, made great use of coconut water as a beverage, although the main source of drinking water was from the rain which was stored in tanks or vats, the taps of which were generally put under lock and key.[74]

Many Creoles believed in taboos relating to food. The term *kenna* was used to refer to these. It is of Bantu origin----called *Tschina* in Loango.[75] This was the belief that certain meats were unwholesome; that the human blood was affected by the kinds of meat consumed; that the blood of each family differed from that of another; that each family had a predisposition to certain diseases which might be developed or suppressed by the use of or abstinence from such meats; and that meats good for one family might be blood poison to another. "The observers therefore of kenna scrupulously abstain from that which they have heard to be the kenna of their family—the forbidden meats unused by their ancestors."[76]

Although there were evidently many African influences in the basic Creole diet, it is very striking that the foods they ate included many ingredients from other cultures, notably Euro-American and Indo-American (Amerindian). In their diet, therefore, the Creoles exhibited the same openness to other influences as they did in other aspects of their culture. Very strikingly, though, the documentary evidence does not reveal any food items in the Creole diet borrowed from the nineteenth century immigrant groups—Portuguese, Indian or Chinese—which did become favourites among the Creoles later on. This might be further indicative of very limited cultural contact and integration among these groups at that time, or just simply another example of uneven recording. Food, however, was one area of their cultural matrix through which the Creoles, as we have seen, significantly influenced the colonial elites----reverse acculturation.

Sex, Morality and Domestic Life

According to Raymond Smith, "the main functioning unit in the Caribbean is the household group".[77] While concurring with this Nancie

102

*Cultural
Power,
Resistance,
and
Pluralism*

Solien distinguishes between the 'household' and the 'family' in black Creole society because some households contain no family: "Many, if not most individuals belong to both a family and to a household. At times the two units coincide, but quite often they do not". She defines the 'family' as "a group of people bound together by that complex set of relationships known as kinship ties, between at least two of whom there exists a conjugal relationship. The conjugal pair, plus their off-spring, forms the nuclear family". There may be extensions of this nuclear type depending on the nature of the relationship between any of the conjugal pair and other members. For Solien, the 'household' implies common residence, economic cooperation, and socialization of children. Hence a household may be bound by kinship relationships, and may or may not contain a family.[78]

Smith states that households are established through the association of males and females in some kind of conjugal relationship.[79] What, therefore, was disparagingly referred to after emancipation as 'concubinage" by the cultural elites is sociologically classifiable as households. This type of domestic unit was common among the Creole population in Guyana after slavery. "Concubinage is the rule rather than the exception";[80] "from the age of puberty to the decline of life, the people are madly under its influence."[81] "No disgrace or shame attends those who live in this immoral state."[82] "The rising generation appear quite indifferent as to whether they are married or not, living together as man and wife without any sanction of the marriage tie is considered by them as no degradation . . . With the African, open and avowed polygamy is one of his characteristics."[83] It was noted in 1850 that at Plantation The Friends in Berbice for instance, out of over fifty Creoles and Africans, "only two couples are married; the rest live in concubinage".[84]

It is interesting to note that most of the criticisms of 'concubinage' among the Creoles emanated from the moral and political guardians of white civilization, i.e., priests/missionaries and government officials, notwithstanding the 'loose' mating patterns of their fellow white residents----estate managers and overseers, merchants, clerks, and even some government officers—who, as we previously saw, practised the same thing on a wide scale. In fact some less biased observers opined that more 'immorality' was practised by the Europeans than by the 'natives'.[85] Be that as it may, the point is that as the norm in creole society (both black and white), these so-called 'concubinage relationships' attain sociological significance as normal conjugal relationships to justify treating them as normal 'households' with or without 'families'. And as Herskovits noted many years ago, some of these non-legal matings can achieve enough stability to receive equal recognition with regularly performed marriages.[86]

The prevalence of 'concubinage', or common-law marriage, to use a less pejorative term, meant that only a very small minority of Creoles was legally married in the postemancipation nineteenth century (less than 1 percent in 1853).[87] Legalized marriage was in effect a Victorian middle class cultural importation which required not only the legal registration of the act, but also the acceptance of the Anglo-Christian ideal of monogamy. It also carried with it an implicit requirement that the European customs and ceremonies associated with a Christian wedding should be adopted. On the other hand, common-law relationships were clearly sanctioned by custom among the Creoles and also reputedly served the purpose of offering the parties an opportunity to "test each other's tempers before they became permanently united".[88] It is obvious though that legal Christian marriage became a desired goal among Creoles seeking social respectability, with common-law unions merely a stage along the way.

Legal marriages thus tended to be chiefly between persons advanced in life or who had cohabited for some time and had children.[89] In other words, family formation preceded legal marriage. It was disapprovingly asserted by a priest in 1886 that not 15 percent of Creole girls would enter wedlock before 'bedlock' and became mothers.[90] "It is seldom that the mother of a family has all her children born in wedlock, or the offspring of one man."[91] Smith has subsequently confirmed this cultural practice.[92]

In fairness, the missionaries and other Victorian prudes regarded common-law marriage, whether practised by the cultural elites or by the Creole working classes, as sexual laxity and moral degradation. But criticism of the Creoles was always rather more trenchant: "Among the mass of people to whom we refer, sensuality is rampant in both sexes, and the prostitution of the female sex commences at that age when children in a civilized country have hardly been detached from their mother's apron strings."[93] "It is rare to meet with a virtuous female after the age of fourteen among the lower classes."[94] This rampant 'sexual degeneration' among the Creoles was attributed to the absence of proper parental guidance since boys and girls were, it was alleged, allowed to run about naked from ten to fourteen years of age.[95]

Intent on imposing their own Victorian middle class cultural ideals on the Creoles, it is not surprising that these critics regarded marriage and family among the Creoles to be inherently unstable. According to Stipendiary Magistrate W.H. Ware, "Marriage as an institution does not exist. Home, with all its humanizing influences, is a word that in the majority of cases conveys no idea to the mind. Affection for wife and family has no force—attentions are transferred from one person to another with disgusting facility".[96] As far as such writers were concerned, even legal marriage was a sham for the Creoles who "in nine

104

*Cultural
Power,
Resistance,
and
Pluralism*

cases out ten" left each other after a short period to cohabit "indis-criminately" with others;[97] and it was not uncommon, they added, for a married man to cohabit with two or three women, or a married woman with the same number of men.[98]

There is no doubt that infidelity was a serious problem which adversely affected the stability of the black family. Many male-female disputes seemed to arise as a consequence of this.[99] Males were apparently more prone to this than women.[100] Stipendiary Magistrate Carbery generalized with considerable prejudice that in many cases a labourer after being married for years with a family of two children, might desert his wife and offspring, settle in another part of the colony and form an 'illicit' connexion with another woman. "His wife has probably outlived his liking, or has got into bad health, and become unable to labour, and the task of supporting her is a duty the performance of which he is anxious to escape."[101]

There may indeed have been several instances of men going off to live with other women. Reports of this are too numerous to ignore, although one can legitimately question the frequency of the occurrence. But to attribute this purely to sexual licentiousness is facile; and more importantly it ignores the economic circumstances which in many instances contributed to it. In this regard, Carbery's comment above is very significant. Survival for the black male after emancipation very often depended on physical mobility in order to maximize his earning capacity. This often meant moving from one district to another in search of work, whether for a short term of weeks or months, or for a longer term of years. This pattern of migration encouraged the contracting of casual sexual relationships with different women. In fact, because men were likely to move on at short notice, young women were reluctant to enter permanent relationships with them. Sexual promiscuity there undoubtedly was, but this was in no small way fostered by economic circumstances, and in this sense much less inexcusable than the gay (no pun intended) sexual adventurism of the roving white bachelor.

Whilst portraying black women as essentially prostitutes who were as attracted to a life of wild sexual abandon as their menfolk, the cultural elites did recognize that the women were the prime victims of black male desertion. Undoubtedly those in their child-bearing period who were consequently most dependent on their 'husbands' were the most vulnerable. If abandoned, these women had to support themselves and their children entirely, while the men reportedly spent lavishly on one or more other women in various parts of the neighborhood.[102] In fact, even when the conjugal pair cohabited, the burden of child rearing and maintenance fell mainly on the woman.[103] It was undoubtedly to ease the burden of deserted women that a law was

passed in 1855 (Ordinance No. 6) to make provision for the maintenance of 'illegitimate' or 'bastard' children.[104] Of course this was en-
acted as much with white men in mind as black; but how effective that
was is open to question.

Within the household, black men were typically portrayed essentially as tyrants over and abusers of their women.

> He contributes just what he chooses to the funds required for supporting his
> family, while she must supply whatever is deficient, or brave his wrath, which is
> vented usually in blows . . .[105]

> So far from making their wives companions at Board, as well as bed, they keep
> them at a great distance, compel them to do all the drudgery of the household,
> weed the provision ground, and in fact treat them more as servants than wives.[106]

> The men often eat at the table alone, while the women sit on the floor, and feed
> out of a calabash.[107]

It was also alleged that black males beat their wives severely on
occasion and in some cases even caused internal and external injury.[108]
The reason proffered was: "If I give my wife orders she must always
have some word to say before she obeys me".[109] Black women were
indeed noted for their independent spirit: "The woman scolds,
screams, and curses her husband in a style quite original";[110] and were
evidently not prepared to play second fiddle to their male partners.
The only way some men felt they could assert their 'manhood' was to
resort to physical violence. Such behaviour, far from being unique to
the Creoles, was shared by their culturally elite 'superiors'. At a superficial glance it would appear that some women internalized this culture of male violence and even *expected* to be beaten as a token of love!
"The black Creole women [feel] that unless their husbands to whom
they are married, or their 'men' with whom they live . . . beat them,
horse-whip or cow-hide them, from time to time in a brutal manner,
they do not show much love or affection to them, the wives or 'keep-
ers'."[111] But to accept that is to trivialize domestic violence. Trotman
pointed to a more fundamental factor when he noted that as many of
these wives, whether legal or common law, were either unemployed
or marginally employed, they often preferred to suffer brutalization in
silence rather than face a life of poverty without the financial support
of some man.[112]

Wife beating was, it seems, accepted as a normal part of working
class black male-female relations in a society which emphasized male
dominance as evidence of manhood. But this coincided with genuine
affection between the partners and does not appear to have threatened
the stability of the family unit. One contemporary marvelled at the
courtesy which black men usually displayed towards their women in
public, while recognizing that in private these same men often casti-
gated their 'wives'. A black man who was complimented for his very

106

*Cultural
Power,
Resistance,
and
Pluralism*
gallant behaviour towards his 'wife' in the public gardens in Georgetown, asserted: "Yes, bos, but when I does get home I does lick she".
The reason given was that the woman often quarrelled when her
'husband' danced with other women. At the same time, however, he
did not allow her to dance with other men: "No, bos, you'self, sir;
how could I allow she to do a ting like dat; impossible, she musn't
dance wid any person 'cept meself". Still it was evident that such
domestic squabbles, accompanied as they might be by male violence,
did not usually affect the stability of the household or the way black
couples related to each other in public.[113]

It also appears that common-law unions were no less stable than
legal marriages. Both were subject to the same economic and cultural
pressures, and if they broke down were normally terminated without
the sanction of law. Separation was very often effected with mutual
cordiality and good humour, and the children went with their
mother.[114] This is a far cry from the capricious desertion which many
elite commentators alleged to be so commonplace.

Although women depended on their men to support the family
financially, the fact that they themselves contributed significantly in
this sphere and worked outside the home to improve the economic
position of the unit evidently gave them a considerable voice in the
management of the household.[115] "The women are quite emancipated
and act independently . . ."[116] Disagreements sometimes led to quarrels
and squabbles between the conjugal pair. "It is a common occurrence
in Demerara to see wives and husbands wrestling, fighting, and per-
petually rowing in the presence of the children and others."[117] The
women were clearly not passive partners in the black household.

According to Bronkhurst, inherent instability of the black household or family unit led to a general laxity in child rearing.[118] Other
cultural elites supported this view claiming that parental affection was
not strong, and that in most cases it was conspicuous by its absence.
They further propounded the view that children were not as properly
cared for after emancipation as before, particularly with respect to
their diets and health. Since infant mortality was very high and mothers
rarely had more than five or six children who survived, it was
(strangely) alleged that black parents were relieved when a child died.[119]

Of course, the general lack of adequate medical facilities particularly in the rural areas was ignored. Although the legislature made
provision for the establishment of village dispensaries in 1854, they
were few, scattered and inefficient.[120] Moreover, living conditions in
the villages, especially along the East Coast of Demerara where the
largest concentrations of the black population were located, were in-
sanitary due to poor drainage. Nevertheless, there is clear evidence
that parents were strongly attached to, and were very protective of,

their children and indeed took great care of them after emancipation.[121]

The cultural elites also criticized black parents for sending their children to school only until they could work and earn their own wages and support themselves. Once they began to earn money, the children were accused of thinking only of themselves, and failing to contribute to the support of their household.[122] Parents were held culpable for this because it was claimed that, with few exceptions, they did not insist on the children's subordination beyond insisting that they did a few domestic chores.[123] Such children were therefore considered most likely to get into "bad company", eat, drink, sing and dance all night, and so pave the way towards living in "concubinage".[124] The use of ribald language by some of the grown children was regarded as a direct consequence of the absence of moral guidance from their parents. According to Stipendiary Magistrate, M.J. Retemeyer: "Family order or discipline, family ties, are hardly known . . . With too many mothers the Principle which I have heard many times is still prevalent: 'true Massa I made the child but not the heart, if God does not keep the heart I cannot keep it'".[125] The result, as Kirke and his fellow elite contemporaries saw it, was the racial stereotypes of the black male as criminal and the black female as whore: "There seems to be a spirit of lawlessness amongst [them], an impatience of control, a thirst for independence and licence . . . The boys are idle and dissolute, the girls dirty, foul-mouthed, and dishonest. At an age so early as to be almost incredible, many of the former become thieves, and the latter prostitutes".[126]

Yet, if anything, some black parents perhaps tried too hard and sometimes used excessive force to instil 'discipline' in their children. Socialized by the brutality of a former slave society, a minority evidently abused their children,[127] e.g., throwing peppered water into the child's eyes, or rubbing crushed pepper and salt into the tender parts of the child's body.[128] In one instance, the neck, arms and back of an eight-year-old girl were reportedly left raw after a beating from her stepmother; in another, it was reported in an unquestionably hyperbolical vein that a man allegedly caught his nephew by his legs and swung him, as he would an axe, crashing his head against the ground![129] In so far as the press reports can be taken as accurate, these were undoubtedly rare aberrations, no more horrifying than similar cases of child abuse frequently reported in Europe and North America even today; but as was customary such exceptions were generalized to become the norm. Thus Schomburgk wrote:

> How often did I draw back with closed eyes and stuffed ears on seeing one of the furies tearing the clothes from off her boy or girl in heedless frenzy, seize it by the hair, throw it on the floor, and then like an enraged beast stamp upon the

108

*Cultural
Power,
Resistance,
and
Pluralism*

writhing and groaning child—or when, after tying hands and feet she hung it up and raving, foaming, and yelling, let out a three or four strand rope, not worrying where the blow fell, till blood flowed from the wounds, mouth and nose.[130]

The tendency of Creole parents to use excessive force in punishing their children was observed in Trinidad by Trotman who explained it as partly an attempt to "restrain them from potential conflict with the ruling class by curbing youthful exuberances", and partly as an unconscious taking out of their own frustrations, created by an oppressive colonial system, on their defenseless children.[131]

During the 1950s Smith noted that motherhood was not only a biological relationship in black society since women often 'mothered' children other than their own——either adopted children or their daughters' children. Hence the family lost its nuclear features and extended matrilineally. He observed, however, that such children were adopted fully and were not regarded as servants or domestic help, but grew up as children of their adopted parents and often inherited property in the same way as if they were natural heirs.[132] At the end of the nineteenth century, however, Kirke painted a rather different, typically prejudiced picture.

> Every black and coloured woman in the country, except the very poorest, has always some girl in her possession whom she . . . 'cares for'; that is, the child works for her all day, sweeps, does errands, and performs all menial offices, in return for which she gets blows and curses, no pay, a pittance of food, a cotton frock, and a pair of drawers, and the bare floor to sleep upon. These girls have been given up by their mothers, who found them an incumbrance, or who were too poor to support them. Of course, when the unfortunate girls reach the age of thirteen they are sold to some Portuguese shopkeeper by their mistress, or else, anticipating matters, they each choose a boy for themselves and go off with him.[133]

The black household or domestic unit in postemancipation Guyana was a uniquely creole product of the plantation environment. Neither African nor European in form or structure, it was evidently nurtured during slavery and persisted as a viable and remarkably stable unit after slavery despite constant denigration by the cultural elites. But relationships within it were not only influenced by socio-cultural conditions of the slave past, but also by poverty spawned by the plantation system long after slavery. Even so, however, the members of these very households were able to create a rich and dynamic folk culture which in many ways belied their lowly material circumstances.

RITES OF PASSAGE

Birth

One might think that with so much attention paid to reporting how Creole children were (or were not) reared, some observation would have been made about their birth customs. This is just another example of how uneven and patchy the historical data are. Peculiarly, the only documentary reference found about Creole birth customs after emancipation relates to death. Rev. Pearson observed that the Creoles did not appear to make much of a fuss over the burial of an infant. After having baptized an infant, he was astonished to learn on enquiring about the baby the next week that it had not only died, but had been buried. Annoyed at not being asked to bury the child, he was told by the father: "Ow parson, you self too, how you think me able for trouble you about that little thing?" The child had been buried nearby without a word to anyone.[134]

This attitude may have been derived from West African tradition (although the evidence does not permit us to determine how closely the Creoles adhered to the traditional African birth rites), and reinforced by the high incidence of infant mortality both during and after slavery in the plantation environment. According to Field though, after the birth of a child in West Africa it is "kept like an egg" indoors for seven days. It is then held to have survived seven dangers and is worthy to be called a person. So on the eighth day it is taken out and the child is acknowledged as a member of the family and is given a name. But if it dies before the eighth day, it is considered as having never been born.[135] In the Guyana case, creolization led to newborn babies being baptized by a Christian priest and named even though they were evidently not considered full persons until after a week.

Marriage

Legal Christian marriage was one of the key ideals of the average Creole in postemancipation Guyanese society. It was a major element in the quest for social respectability. But one of the factors which militated against early legal marriage among Creoles was the great cost incurred in the wedding. In the first instance, marriage licences issued by the government were expensive, being charged with a heavy stamp duty of $20 (or almost seventeen weeks' basic pay at the statutory rate for plantation field workers).[136] In addition, there was the parson's fee for conducting the ceremony.[137] Those, however, were just the tip of the iceberg. The quasi-westernized Creoles held in common with their fellow white colonists the view that an elaborate and extravagant wedding was indispensable. Therefore, until they could afford a lavish display, the legalization of the conjugal unit had to be postponed.

Black weddings thus incorporated many of the ostentatious trappings of their white counterparts----carriages, white satin, extravagant wedding cake, dance, and lavish feast.[138] Outlays on weddings were considerable, not infrequently exceeding $200 (about three and a quarter years, basic pay). Sarcastic elite observers asserted that "the highest ambition of Quashy [was] to have a grand wedding; to strut to church in Frankish garments, looking 'big like Governor self'; to give a day's jollification to his countrymen collected from all the country round! ... That is our fashion".[139]

It was indeed creole 'fashion' which *both* blacks and whites shared in common. Many blacks, however, because of their precarious financial circumstances, were allegedly reduced to a state of bankruptcy after such grand displays, and left without "a penny with which to buy bread, nor . . . a bed to sleep on, nor even common chairs or tables", and were thus obliged to borrow.[140] But this tendency to spend extravagantly on weddings, even to the point of indebtedness, is quite common in traditional societies in several parts of both Africa and Asia.

In the late nineteenth century, religious organizations mounted a campaign to try to encourage poor couples to get married without incurring too much expense. Anglican Archdeacon Farrar, for instance, intimated in 1889 that he would marry without fee all couples who walked to church to have the ceremony performed instead of having gaudy equipages which they could not afford. This practice was begun a few years earlier in Berbice and seemed to have had an impact, some couples even agreeing to get married in their working clothes. But such persons were undoubtedly a minority among working class Creoles.[141]

Typically the parties to be married may have cohabited for as long as twenty years. The bridesmaid was not uncommonly an 'old' married woman of forty selected, Archdeacon Veness derisively claimed, "probably in consequence of her ability to deck herself in glorious apparel and thus shed an air of dignity on the ceremonial". A band of music consisting of a pair of violins, clarionets, triangle and kettle drum, was indispensable.[142]

Led by the band, the marriage procession at one wedding formed in pairs, "each gallant holding an umbrella over his sable partner, in whose attire lace and orange blossoms and the brightest colours figure prominently". They marched "with solemn step and stately mien" to the church, outside which a party awaited to salute them with a *feu de joie* when the rite was accomplished. They then reformed in procession and marched back to the house of the happy man where a bountiful repast was served, "from which ham and suckling pig must on no account be absent". Veness was highly cynical of these affairs:

> The bride looks very uncomfortable in her tightly fitting dress, and very embarrassed as to the manner of manipulating her knife and fork, till some attentive cavalier relieves her by cutting up her food—as we should do for a child. Ordinarily she would dine off an *olla podrida* . . . served in a calabash, without the assistance of our new fangled implements; but this is a grand occasion, and everything—even to speech-making and patent leather boots—must be conducted *à la* Buckra.[143]

Such derisive commentary sought to create the impression that the black Creoles slavishly mimicked their fellow white citizenry. Undoubtedly some elements of European culture were incorporated in these black wedding ceremonies, but they nevertheless remained distinctly Afro-Creole both in form and spirit. More important, however, is the black Creole notion that respectability was given to the proceedings by the inclusion of such European cultural elements. Indeed the very act of getting legally married by Christian rites after many years of stable common-law conjugal relationship was a clear indication that black and coloured Creoles had inculcated the view peddled by the cultural elites that Christian monogamous marriage was an ideal to strive and save for. Thus, when the time was deemed appropriate, they had to celebrate it with similar pomp and extravagance as did the white colonists. This, however, placed a premium on white cultural forms, while Afro-Creole forms (in this case common-law relationships) though practised willingly, openly and without disgrace were nevertheless regarded as inferior.

It indeed became quite evident shortly after emancipation that the ex-slaves regarded legal marriage as a sign of respectability and social prestige. They even referred to one another as "my Lady or my Gentleman" if legally married. Married people apparently considered themselves superior to those who cohabited without the sanction of Christianity and the law, even though it is questionable whether the husbands were more faithful since many continued to keep paramours even after wedlock.[144]

But the adoption of the Euro-Christian wedding occasionally provoked unsolicited humour. Crookall recounted the story of a priest whose groom was getting married. Accustomed to touching his hat when his 'master' spoke to him, he did the same thing as he stood before the altar repeating the marriage service. The minister discreetly leaned towards him and whispered, "Never mind touching your hat, but say, after me . . ." Then, he went on: "Wilt thou have this woman to be thy lawful wedded wife?" Up went the groom's hand to his head, and he loudly exclaimed, "After you, sir" —at which point both minister and congregation burst into loud laughter.[145]

The historical evidence concurs with Raymond Smith's claim that "legal, Christian, monogamous marriage is everywhere accepted as the correct and respectable form of mating relationship . . ." among blacks in the Caribbean. Thus he considers common-law relationships as a "cultural characteristic of the lower class, and can be regarded as a permissive deviation from the norms of the total social system". In short, "there is a moral system within a moral system so to speak".[146]

112

Cultural
Power,
Resistance,
and
Pluralism

Death

As in most cultures, death among the Creoles throughout the Caribbean after emancipation was an occurrence of great significance. But the way in which it was marked embodied a typically creole blending of West African and European culture forms. The central feature of mourning was the wake which in style was derived from West African tradition, although there were several inputs of European origin; in fact, Alleyne notes that they actually bore some resemblance to Irish wakes.[147] The night following the death of an individual was spent by the deceased's relatives and friends (and even friends' friends) in the house or yard in which the body was laid; and the visitors entertained themselves.

> Those who are musically and religiously inclined keep inside the house, or if it be too small for the accommodation of all, some seat themselves on benches near the door, and sing hymns, sometimes with fiddle or clarionette accompaniment, diversifying the music with extempore prayers, recitative and dirge-like. Outside, and farther away in the yard, groups of persons congregate—some playing at forfeits, the proceeds of which are devoted to the purchase of candles, peppermint, and beer. Others are putting riddles to be solved, or narrating 'Anansie Stories'.[148]

Generally the wake portrayed an atmosphere of merriment and even vulgarity to the uninitiated and biased observer. Beginning with the singing of hymns and other religious songs, it eventually gave way "to love and lewd songs, filthy tales, and disgusting conversations, with obscure gestures and dances, gambling, and frequently ending in free fights".[149] According to one writer, between midnight and 4.00 a.m., "the Devil takes possession".[150] A distinctive feature of the wake was the copious consumption of alcohol. This no doubt contributed to the scenes of apparent irreverence which disgusted elite observers. It almost certainly accounts for the proposal of marriage which one widow allegedly received at the wake of her husband, as well as her response to her would-be suitor—that she had already made other arrangements![151] Such scenes were condemned by the cultural elites as an awful mockery of the dead and an affront to Christian morality as they supposedly contrasted starkly with the quiet solemnity with which English people commemorated death: "There is no setting-up, no candle-burning, and no feasting".[152] Brereton found similarly hostile attitudes among the colonial elites to the Afro-Creole wake in Trinidad where too there was a desire to suppress them.[153]

Afro-Creole wakes in Guyana and the rest of the Caribbean were similar to those in West Africa from which they were in part derived. In these societies the wake is considered as the main means by which friends and relatives say goodbye to the deceased and support the bereaved. With reference to West Africa, Field notes that "This indeed is the keynote of all funeral ceremonies. To sever the ties between the living and the dead man without giving offence is the object of most of the rites".[154] All neighbours are expected to be asked to a funeral;[155] and according to Herskovits: "even if the dead had quarrelled with his children, they come to his funeral. Weeping, they beg forgiveness, and it is said the dead hears them, giving recognition by opening his eyes".[156]

Field observed similarly lavish expenditure and merriment at West African wakes. Expenditure is necessary to appease the dead who must be made to feel superior or he would be angry. Stinginess is an insult to the dead. As a sign of veneration, visitors contribute money to his funeral expenses. Although the expense is often beyond their means, a lifetime of debt is preferable to an offended dead relative. "The mourning, wailing, and ceremonial dances give place imperceptibly to cheerful drinking and merrymaking, ostensibly to hearten the bereaved." This is very similar to what took place in postemancipation Guyana. But Field further notes that open house (wake) among the Ga people lasts for over a week.[157] There is no evidence of that in Guyana.

Since the corpse could not be preserved, the burial usually took place on the day following the death. However, if it were possible, a Sunday burial was generally preferable since it allowed all friends and relatives to attend. According to Wallbridge, "The Sunday funeral is a great institution. I have heard of an old man who was likely to die before Sunday. Every effort was made to prolong the old man's life until Saturday".[158]

The burial itself was expensive. Between £4-6 ($20-30) were spent on an ordinary occasion. The coffin and burial fees averaged about 25 shillings ($6.00), and the rest was spent on "other little things".[159] Many villagers, therefore, preferred to bury their dead on their own land in order to save on burial fees.[160]

The funerary customs themselves were evidently derived from West African tradition.

> Before the dead was lifted out [of the house], the little daughter of the deceased man was hoisted over the coffin from one side to the other. This was thought to be a charm for the protection of the child against the interference of evil spirits in general, and the spirit of the dead parent in particular. They then proceeded with the corpse into the street towards the hearse, singing very mournfully.[161]

Mourning continued for some time after the death of a relative, and mourners wore black to symbolize their bereavement. No data have been found to indicate the length of the mourning period but, according to one observer, a woman stopped going out of her house for several weeks after her husband's death. The reason attributed was that she had no "weeds of widowhood" (mourning clothes).[162] This may, however, represent a dilution of an old West African custom which constrains the widow to remain indoors for fifty days.[163] Be that as it may, it is evident that as in other aspects of life, the death and funerary customs of black Guyanese reflected a synthesis of both African and European cultural forms which was uniquely creole. But while in this fusion the African customs remained relatively strong, greater value seemed to be placed on the Euro-Christian forms.

COOPERATIVE ACTIVITY

One of the striking features of the Creole commemoration of their rites of passage was the extent to which they involved the local community. Trotman argues that these occasions, whether of joy or grief, "offered opportunities for the celebrant [or bereaved] to reaffirm kinship and community links".[164] This cooperative spirit extended to the sphere of work as well. Herskovits claimed that the tradition of cooperation in the field of economic behaviour is outstanding in black cultures everywhere: "[Such] cooperation is fundamental in West African agriculture, and in other industries where group labour is required, and has been reported from several parts of the slaving area. This African tradition found a congenial counterpart in the plantation system; and when freedom came, its original form of voluntary cooperation was re-established".[165] One needs, however, to be careful not to create the impression that such cooperation is uniquely African. In fact it appears to be characteristic of cash-poor traditional rural communities universally.

Guyana provided ample evidence of voluntary community cooperative activity in the immediate postemancipation years. The original establishment of communal or joint-stock villages with common village lands for agriculture is proof of this spirit. Likewise the widespread practice among the ex-slaves of working in task gangs as hired labourers is further evidence of economic cooperation.[166]

This spirit was also evident among the new African immigrants who settled together in small communities in different parts of the colony. Among the *Aku* (Yoruba) of Canal No.1 on the banks of the Demerara river, for instance, "It was . . . the custom very often on a Monday for a number of the Aku to go to the farm of one of their number----either an old man or one who was sick----and, working with prodigious energy, weed his farm for him 'done'. Then----preceded by drums and shak-shaks—they would go to the house and wind up with dancing and singing".[167] This resembles the Haitian *combite* (in Trinidad *gayap*, Tobago *len han'*, Jamaica *morning wo'k* and *gi'e-a-day*) and is similar to the Dahomean *dokpwe*.[168]

These cooperativist tendencies received their strongest expression in the establishment of friendly (benevolent) and burial societies and lodges.[169] Bryan notes a similar development in late nineteenth century Jamaica.[170] According to Wallbridge: "The Burial Society is a very favourite institution. The greater the mortality the greater the prosperity. When a member dies the surviving members subscribe. The amount subscribed exceeds the immediate requirements, and the amount in excess is deposited with the treasurer to the credit of the fund".[171]

The friendly and burial societies were often organized in connection with the churches under the supervision of priests.[172] The outward form was European, but the cooperative spirit which made it functional was Afro-Creole. Herskovits claimed that black involvement in friendly societies was a remnant of the traditional African idea of secret societies which in the contact situation of the New World was tangibly expressed in the form of the lodge derived from Europe.[173] Friendly societies were yet another clear example of the process of creolization utilizing syncretized African and European cultural features. But at the same time, in being fundamentally antithetical to the prevailing ethos of individualism which characterized the capitalist plantation system, these cooperative societies represented a form of cultural resistance to the established white dominated colonial order which would have made them, in some respects at least, functionally different from their counterparts in Britain.

Membership of these early societies fluctuated: 2,448 in June 1848, 1,151 in December 1850, 1,629 in December 1854,[174] and embraced not only working class, but also middle class Creoles. But since many Creoles had inculcated the prevailing spirit of individualism, these friendly societies always faced an uphill task to maintain membership levels, funds, and ultimately to stay afloat. Many indeed sank into financial failure amidst recrimination from their members who lost their hard earned savings. That in turn further discouraged other persons from investing their scarce resources in new societies.[175] Nevertheless, a few small societies always continued to exist throughout the postemancipation nineteenth century.[176]

The benevolent society movement received a shot in the arm during the 1870s when the L.M.S. missionary Warder was authorized to open lodges of 'Good Templars' under his Grand Mastership.[177] The regalia of English friendly societies with which the local lodges were affiliated, and the carnivalesque street parades, attracted the interest and enthusiasm of the Creoles. The 1880s thus witnessed a mushrooming of these lodges. By 1883 there were already more than thirty in Georgetown alone.[178] It soon became customary for benefit societies to be formed and then subsequently seek affiliation with British societies.[179] Again this makes it quite evident that the cooperative spirit was generated voluntarily among the people who merely sought to estab-

116

*Cultural
Power,
Resistance,
and
Pluralism*

lish links with British societies as a means of conferring respectability and, of course, to procure the right to wear their gaudy regalia.

As a result of the proliferation of these societies, general legislation was soon considered necessary to incorporate them under law. This was duly done in 1883 (Ordinance No.10). But unlike the English situation, the rules of the local societies had first to be approved by the colonial legislature which, furthermore, determined whether incorporation was expedient. The colonial state thus assumed "the whole moral responsibility of the good government" of these societies.[180]

It was obvious that the objective of such legislation was to control the activities of these societies and to restrict their growth. Without full legal incorporation, members had no protection of their finances in the event of fraud or liquidation procedures. This, therefore, made them increasingly vulnerable to financial loss and had the effect of discouraging them from joining unincorporated societies. The elites thus exploited the desire of the Creoles for legal protection to exercise supervision over what these societies did. This was evidently because they were apprehensive of the possibility of the societies becoming secret political organizations at a time when the Creole middle classes were beginning to agitate more vociferously for political change; and/or of their interfering with the administration of 'justice' by suppressing evidence because their members were bound to secrecy. In this sense it represented the exercise of cultural power by the elites to control and regulate a cultural institution that had grown up among the Creoles which was perceived as a potential threat to the former's hegemony. Consequently, only those societies about which absolutely no doubts were entertained were incorporated, while all other applications were refused.[181] The result was that only five societies were incorporated by 1888 when the process was suspended.[182] In 1893, however, under Colonial Office pressure, a new ordinance was promulgated which brought the law more in line with that in Britain.[183]

As in Jamaica, these societies served very important socio-economic purposes by providing welfare insurance and moneylending services aimed at redressing the tragic deficiency in the existing commercial insurance and banking institutions which were generally hostile to the financial needs of the Creole population. At the very least, they provided welfare assistance in time of sickness, old age and death.[184] Some were more ambitious and provided insurance benefits in the event of accident, unemployment, shipwreck, and fire. A few even offered assistance towards the education of members' children.[185]

Still others provided loans to enable members to embark in small business enterprises, whether of a commercial, agricultural, or mechanical nature. The primary objective of these moneylending societies, however, was to break the commercial dominance of the Portuguese retailing, moneylending, and pawnbroking enterprises.[186]

Finally, some of these societies functioned as tradesmen's associations, e.g., the British Guiana Mechanics Society and the Printers' Benevolent Association, and no doubt sought to address the problems of their specific trades. In this sense, they can legitimately be regarded as forerunners of modern trade unions.[187]

Some of these societies flourished;[188] but for those which were not incorporated under law and whose finances consequently did not enjoy legal protection, the scope for fraud by venal officials encouraged internal dissension which was always liable to threaten their existence. The lodge room of the Workman's Helping Hand Society, for instance, was stormed by irate members in 1885 who demanded the return of their deposits.[189]

These societies also provided social entertainment for their members. Balls and dinners were organized, usually accompanied by grand parades to churches in all the sartorial splendour of lodge uniform.[190] A typical example was the march in 1885 from Alness to Achlyne in Berbice by the members of the Eversham Mutual Aid Society "attired in black and green sash, and neck ribbon of the same colour bearing the insignia of the society".[191] Likewise on New Year's day of the same year, after marching to Trinity Methodist chapel in Georgetown for a service, the members of the Humane Charitable Tobits Society partook of a sumptuous luncheon in the lodge room of the Hand-of-Justice Friendly Society.[192] But undoubtedly the greatest service which these societies provided was to demonstrate tangibly to the Creoles the value of cooperation and combination in order to address, with their own resources, some of the problems arising from the institutionalized inequalities of the colonial system. In this sense, the friendly societies were an important symbol of Creole cultural resistance to the established order.

LEISURE

Music and Dance

We have already had several glimpses of the central place of music and dance in Afro-Creole life and culture. They were very much a part of all Creole rites of passage, and were integral to the activities of the lodges and friendly societies. Music was also used at work (work songs) and, as we shall see in the next chapter, music and dance played a vital role in Afro-Creole religion as well. What is evident, therefore, is that music and dance straddled both the temporal and spiritual spheres of Creole culture, and it is perhaps for this reason, reinforced by cultural prejudices, that the sources written by Eurocentric elites are notoriously unreliable. As far as those observers were concerned, whatever the name, these dances and music all formed part and parcel of the same pagan religious rituals which Creoles and Africans practised from time to time. Bronkhurst, for instance, asserted:

> The Tchibounga, the Comfoo, the Racoon, the Joe and Johnny, the Somma-Somma, the Shilsh, the Shake-shake, the Drupoid, the Water-Mamma or Mermaid, and other dances are all connected with the practice of Obeahism. When a male of the tribe dies, they hold a festival called 'Macquarie', and a dance called 'Mocquarie' for his memorial; and when a female dies, they have a dance called 'Hauyarie'. They have also the dances called 'Bimmuth', the humming-bird dance; 'Hichurie', the turtle dance; and 'Hanorah', the crane or heron dance. But the most immoral and vulgar dance among them is called 'Shah-coco-lih'.[193]

That kind of prejudice and confusion makes it difficult to reconstruct these art forms with accuracy. As we shall see, *Cumfo* and *Watermamma* were one and the same, and Everard Im Thurn, the noted contemporary ethnologist, identified the *Macquarie, Mocquarie,* and *Hauyarie* as Amerindian dances,[194] although the Creoles could have adopted them in the same way they adopted the Amerindian dish 'pepperpot' ever since the period of slavery when there was greater contact between runaway slaves and the indigenous people in the hinterland. Still there is some element of confusion.

What is clear, however, is that both Africans and Creoles were very fond of singing and dancing, particularly on moonlit nights, and formed circles for that purpose despite and in defiance of the denunciations of the cultural elites. Afro-Creole music and dance were demonstrably very important symbols of cultural resistance. A favourite dance was the *racoon*, and the only musical accompaniment was the timeous beating of a drum which provided the rhythm for the chants of dancers and audience. "It is undoubtedly a lively dance and involves great physical exertion."[195] Premium observed that "The sable performers beat the ground with their long heels----the toe is not fantastic with them----and when one man chanted a line of rude verse suitable to the cause of merriment, the rest repeated it in full chorus to a time of their own, till it swelled loud and high, far and wide, over the din of the well-beaten drum".[196] Most elite observers, however, found these dance sessions unpalatable: "A very powerful aroma pervades the atmosphere on such occasions, and . . . a new-comer [is] not [advised] to stand to the leeward of a group of dancers in violent exercise".[197]

Afro-Creole dances of Yoruban origin, often in memory of the dead, were called *S'iku* and were accompanied by songs. J.G. Cruickshank, a keen and unusually unprejudiced observer, pointed out that African dance was not merely, or for that matter even chiefly, physical exercise as most other elites were inclined to think. "The 'ganda' or dance-ring, is really the African theatre. Dramas, comedies and tragedies are all acted there; accompanied by songs in the African tongue which . . . go near to the heart of Negro-land."[198]

The principal instruments of Afro-Creole music were the drum, *shak-shaks*, the tambourine, the triangle, and the violin. The last three are clearly indicative of the acculturative process. As Alleyne found in Jamaica, the drum was generally a barrel (*gumbi/gumby* in Jamaica) or hollow tree-trunk (*gumba/gumbah* in Jamaica) covered with cow, bullock, goat, sheep or deer skin; and was unquestionably the main instrument.[199] Cruickshank quoted a drummer and went on to comment:

> "It don't take no little boy to knock drum. Big big man no able fo' knock um self." Time is everything in these dances, and the drum gives the time. An able drummer will make his drum 'talk'. Some 'Nations'—such as the Ijesa, Oyeh and pure Yoruba—knock the drum standing up, with sticks. Others—such as the Yagba and Abuna—knock the drum sitting down with their hands. It is held between the knees and the energetic drum-man bends over the goat-skin—sometimes with his shirt off, the moon shining on the Black skin—until he is streaming in perspiration.[200]

As in Jamaica and elsewhere, the *shak-shak* was a supportive percussion instrument used particularly by the *Yagba* who, for some strange reason, were reportedly ranked lowest among the Africans in Guyana. The 'superior' tribes or nations, i.e., *Ijesa, Oyeh* and *Yoruba,* never used it. It was a small round or oblong calabash, scooped out. 'Buck shot' (beads or seeds) were put into it, and a stick was run through for a handle. Some *shak-shaks* were painted with figures, the meanings of which were apparently lost even to the actors. "You can play a shak-shak in two ways. Either you pass it rapidly up and down on the palm of the hand—back and forward, back and forward—or you can thump it on the knee. Either way the noise is equally prodigious."[201] What certainly distinguished Afro-Creole music was the rhythm produced

Ken Morgan photo. Courtesy of ISER Publications (Mona)

Creole village
string band

120

*Cultural
Power,
Resistance,
and
Pluralism*

by percussion instruments, of both African and European origin, with comparatively less emphasis being placed on melody than in Euro-Creole music.

Both Africans and Creoles in the rural villages participated in African dances. But the more anglicized Creoles became, particularly those resident in the towns, the more ashamed they were of their ancestral dances which they were indoctrinated to believe were uncivilized. Most of these quasi-westernized urban Creoles were lower class, but nevertheless "are only happy when indulging in [English] country-dances, quadrilles, etc."[202] In January 1859, for instance, the domestics of Georgetown organized a subscription ball at the Assembly Rooms (a very unusual occurrence) which earned plaudits from the press for the decorum with which it was attended. Supper was very tastefully laid out in the upper gallery and dancing lasted until early next morning. Masters were invited as guests by their servants. It was a rare occasion in which the classes of creoledom mixed socially, although the groups maintained their ascribed places—the blacks and browns served, the whites dined and were entertained.[203] Similarly balls were held from time to time by organizations such as the Mechanics Union Society.[204]

These affairs, commonly referred to as 'dances of social decorum', were accorded a high degree of respectability by the Creoles who spent considerable sums to outfit themselves appropriately, i.e., in elegant European finery, for the occasion. As one contemporary observed: "I have frequently recognized from outside men, who all day are content with a costume of rice bags, carefully attired in full evening dress and offering *petits soins* to the ladies accompanying them with an air that would have graced the court of the first gentleman of Europe".[205]

Fancy dress balls were also popular among the Creoles and normally lasted from 8.00 p.m. to about 5.00 a.m. Even the normally abrasive Kirke was forced to admit that "the people behave very well and there is little or no drunkenness". He further observed that the costumes of the black people were usually marvellous, though he could not resist being a wee mischievous:

> At one to which I had been invited, a tall, stout black woman represented Queen Victoria; she had the place of honour on the dais; an obsequious courtier was fanning her, and, seeing that her Majesty was perspiring freely under her robes and crown, suggested a little iced water, but the Queen replied, 'No buddy no waater, me tek' a little able (strong) punch'.[206]

Richard Schomburgk, however, exhibited far less grace:

> [At] the over-done gaudily decorated ball-room of the Creole negroes, where only quadrilles and country dances are fancied, the Paradise of Deities and Heroes is re-enacted save that the Gods and Goddesses appear in other costumes. Silk covers their mortal bodies. Minerva foots the light fantastic in crimson spencer

and white gown before Mars, who is perspiringly anxious about cutting the latest
French capers properly, while Diana, in a sky-blue dress and white spencer, gazes
in the eyes of love-lorn Narcissus.[207]

Far less respectable were the affairs known as 'dignity balls', organized by the lower classes of urban dwellers—"the lowest of the low".
"Each individual who wishes to attend and have a dance in the room
must pay a certain sum at the door."[208] Such dances were apparently
held "almost every night" in certain parts of Georgetown and were
very popular among working class Creoles, i.e., "porters in stores, cart
boys and boat boys, the fair sex being represented by coal women and
domestic servants". They were held in large rooms generally owned by
Portuguese shopkeepers which were kept entirely for hire to Creole
dance organizers.[209] Sometimes, the musicians were members of the
Militia band (whence came the instruments as well) and music, played
loudly, lasted until almost daybreak when the revellers began to dis-
perse—the men amusing themselves "by performing sun-dry fantastic
'steps' on the road, accompanied by the most discordant noises".[210]

These public dances were deplored not only by the whites, but also
by 'respectable', socially aspiring middle class blacks and coloureds
who felt embarrassed by what they considered indecent, immoral, and
rowdy orgies which "were very annoying to well-conducted citizens,
whose industrious habits in the day necessitated rest at night". What
disturbed them most was not merely the loud music into the wee
hours of the morning, or the occasional brawls which did occur, but
"the postures of the dancers [which] were far from delicate"[211]—hence
the label 'orgies'. In short, the dignity balls brought Afro-Creole dance
styles, considered vulgar, into the city (the heart of the European
culture sphere in the colony), and by fusion with European dance
forms transformed ('corrupted') them into wholly new ('debased')
dances (e.g., see 'the chip' below). These dignity balls thus represented
the essence of creolization by incorporating and modifying European
dances:

> Although the position of the frequenters of these entertainments is not lofty, the
> graceful style in which many of them dance would do honour to any ball room,
> their waltzing in particular is excellent; it is an amusing sight to see a boat or cart
> boy and a tie-head lady, both of them bare-footed, gliding round to the strains of
> a waltz, played by a couple of cracked fiddles, as solemnly as if they were in a
> Belgravian drawing-room dancing to the music of the Coote's band.[212]

But the Creoles did not simply ape European dance steps. Instead
they transformed/creolized them to their own fancy. For instance in
1879, they created a totally new dance called the 'chip' which became
very popular, essentially by introducing an extra step in the quadrille.[213] It was this kind of improvization and adaptation, involving a
fusion of African styles and European dance forms (creolization),
which was condemned as vulgar by the cultural elites. Hence, "A

122

Cultural
Power,
Resistance,
and
Pluralism

Demerara dignity dance of the present day has nothing humorous. It is simply an exhibition of brazen, unblushing vice in its most hideous form, vice stripped of its gewgaws and showing itself in all its native ugliness . . . They are simply orgies of the lowest and most degraded description".[214]

The dignity ball was undoubtedly a truly 'creole' popular form of entertainment emanating from among the urban black working classes. But because of its form and clientele it was vigorously attacked by the elites, both white and coloured, who used their cultural power to try to suppress it. Thus, for instance, a clause was inserted in the Tax Ordinance during the 1850s which required persons who organized balls or dances "for money or reward, or by subscription" to obtain a licence for $25 (£5.21). That, however, hardly dampened the enthusiasm of would-be organizers where the demand for cheap entertainment among the working classes existed. Indeed, many 'dignity balls' were held without licence, and the police were frequently deployed to break them up and to arrest both organizers and participants. Punishment could be severe as, for example, when one female reveller charged with disorderly behaviour was sentenced to imprisonment and to have her head shaved. On occasion, some organizers were even forced to flee the country to evade the long arm of the law. But even these actions and the denunciations of the press did not deter working class people from organizing and attending these dances.[215] This provides a good example of cultural resistance by the Creole working classes who refused to be bullied into giving up an integral aspect of their popular culture. But at the same time it should be noted that these same people considered the more sedate European-style ball, requiring expensive European finery or fancy dress, more respectable than their dignity balls.

Whatever their social ranking, or their cultural predilections, whether Afro- or Anglo-Creole in orientation, the black Creoles' and Africans' love of music and dance was proverbial. "Any kind of musical instrument, from a 'jew's harp' upward, is appreciated. And wonderful melody they produce from such simple instruments as the guitar, banjo, mandolin, or even a tin whistle. Many of them have excellent voices, and some may be described as remarkable for height, depth, and fullness."[216] But even such acclaimed musical talent was not good enough for some elite commentators who still stubbornly maintained that "their voices lack the softness and flexibility of those of Europeans".[217]

Unlike Trinidad where under the influence of a dominant Roman Catholic religious tradition the pre-Lent carnival became the major popular festival among working class Creoles, both in Guyana and Jamaica Christmas became the main Afro-Creole festival and was celebrated with tremendous *éclat* in music, dance and feasting. This in itself indicates the extent to which the acculturation process had affected the Creoles. Christmas was as much their religio-cultural festival as it was that of the Europeans, and it was celebrated in public in very much the same way as the Portuguese celebrated Pentecost, or the Indians *tadja*, or the Chinese their lunar New Year.

The whole community was likely to be awakened at any time between midnight and 4.00 a.m. by music and drumming of masquerade bands (*John Canoe* in Jamaica). As in Trinidad, the dancers were of both sexes, and were costumed and masked. "Here and there, about the streets, may be seen some buffoons with costumes a la circus clown, astride stilts, for the people's amusement; and maskers with grotesque habiliments to teach the little ones the excellence of beauty by contrast."[218] The street band was accompanied by a procession of merrymakers:

> Sometimes in concert, oft times in confusion, drum and flute, cornet and clarionette, shac-shac and steel, tom-tom and tambourine, proclaim the happy morn, while high above all, in dismal diapason, *vox humana* dins into the ear such proclamation as this:
> 'Christmas ma'nin come again
> An' I ent get no cawfee wata'.[219]

That was not surprising, of course, because it was said that on Christmas morning no one drank coffee: "they revel in rum". Street revelry continued throughout the day. "Mostly they congregate in the vicinity of the rum shops, the owners of which provide liquor for the 'musicianers', as the common people call them."[220]

Most Creoles, however, in keeping with their desire to appear socially respectable, started the day quietly by attending church services and, masqueraders apart, generally spent Christmas day at home with the family/household, singing and playing music: "In every nook there were the strains of music heard from morning until night, even in the poorest house . . . Apollo found welcome, whether with the refined strains of the schools or the rustic din of the tambourine and triangle and shrill piping of the tin whistle".[221] On the following day, Boxing day, some urban Creoles indulged in outdoor activities. Many others went by rail into the country on picnics. Special railway services were put on for this purpose, and the trains were usually crowded. In Georgetown, the sea wall was the main centre of amusement. Literally thousands congregated there; and, "of course, the usual theatre of ditties and rustic dances was opened . . . on the Wall and largely attended by its votaries. In Bourda, Albert Town, Packwood Dam, Albouy's Town and several other suburban quarters, masquerading, rope-dancing, etc., formed the nucleus of pleasure . . ." Fireworks and the firing of squibs, a practice undoubtedly borrowed from the Portuguese or Chinese, completed the Christmas celebrations.[222]

124

*Cultural
Power,
Resistance,
and
Pluralism*

Artist's
impression of
Masquerade
revellers

Masquerade bands danced through the streets for the entire Christmas-New Year festive season, but were considered a necessary evil by the cultural elites whose ears were 'tortured' by the sounds of the drums, fifes and other 'discordant' instruments. Imagine "a company of men and boys, who for personal appearance could have given points to Falstaff's ragged regiment, marching down Main Street to the inspiriting sounds of a drum and fife band". Not only were these masquerade bands considered a nuisance, but a danger as well: for their appearance and the "horribly discordant sounds" they produced could easily cause any restive horse to take fright. For these reasons, some elites advocated the banning of these bands, just as those in Trinidad did with respect to the carnival bands.[223]

Sport and Other Pastimes

In a society where the missionary influence was so strong, it is not surprising that the church should have played an important part in the socio-cultural leisure activities of the Creoles. Except for the period between 1848 and 1860 when many Creoles were cynical of the institutions of the dominant white culture, churchgoing was a major social activity particularly since it was considered to confer social respectability on the participants (see chapter 6). As a consequence all sorts of activities were organized by local churches, many of them to raise funds while simultaneously providing fun, relaxation and entertainment for the people in a socially and morally acceptable environment. As Bryan found in Jamaica,[224] so too in Guyana concerts and bazaars were commonplace for most of the postemancipation period; but, in addition, there were some rather quaint forms of church entertainment. One was the 'cake walk'. All members of the congregation were invited to purchase tickets costing between a *bitt* (eight cents) and a shilling (twenty-four cents) each. Several cakes were baked (another Creole forte) for the occasion. The subscribers formed a procession in pairs, and a small flag was handed to the leading couple. At the sound of the music, played by an organist with his back to the proceedings, the procession marched around the room in time, singing as they went, and passing the flag from one couple to the next at each stanza of the hymn or song. The couple which held the flag when the music stopped suddenly won a cake. This continued until all the cakes and processionists were exhausted.[225]

A far more pompous affair was the Rally of Tribes. Twelve 'tribes of Israel' were selected, each led by a captain or lieutenant. Each 'tribe' consisted of as many persons as wished to enlist, and each member was given a card on which to record donations: *bitts* by dots, sixpences (twelve cents) by circles, and shillings by stars. On the Sunday of the rally, each 'tribe' was assigned a stall decorated with palms and flowers, and each member wore a band with the name and colour of his/her 'tribe'. The 'tribes' then marched in procession with their banners to the church, singing; and circled the building before entering for the service. Three such services were held during the day, at each of which four 'tribes' participated. When the priest called each 'tribe' by name, they would follow their captain to the front of the church where he reported on the donations collected by his 'tribe'. At the end of the service, the procession reformed and marched from the church to a suitable place for dispersal. These rallies were generally very successful and raised hundreds of dollars for the churches. Women usually played the major role in such fund raising activities even though it seems that it was the men who were appointed leaders of the 'tribes'.[226] Church related cultural activities were a very important means of transmitting Euro-Christian values to the Creoles, who incorporated them in a voluntary manner.

Storytelling was a popular Creole pastime in the villages and at wakes. *Anansi* stories were by far the most favoured. In Afro-Creole folklore, *Anansi* was a spider from which man was thought to have been descended. The *Anansi* of the stories was the half developed man from the spider who, in his transitional state, combined the agility and craftiness of the insect with the intelligence and cunning of man, and was always represented as speaking in a snuffling indistinct manner. In the stories, the animals were made to talk and act as men. They were

126

*Cultural
Power,
Resistance,
and
Pluralism*

often humorous, and though some elite observers considered them simple (childish), they conveyed the morals and values of Afro-Creole society,[227] and provided a very important counter to the many insidious methods employed by the colonial elites to impose their own cultural values on the Creoles.

As in Jamaica 'tea meetings' were quite widespread among the Guyanese Creoles. Bryan states that in Jamaica they were entirely secular affairs,[228] but the evidence for Guyana suggests that at least in their original form they were essentially religious. Yet both in Guyana and Jamaica they aroused the hostility of the cultural elites, especially the missionaries, who regarded them as immoral gatherings. In Guyana the problem stemmed from the apparent creolization of the affair by including elements of Afro-Creole culture. Hence as Rev. Duerwaarder complained, no longer were they "the quiet orderly and Christian meetings which are sometimes held under that designation; these they will not attend:—But, Assemblies, which . . . are scenes of wickedness and abomination".[229]

The 'immorality' of the tea meetings stemmed from the inclusion of music (drums and other percussion instruments) which may have led to dancing and even spirit possession later in the proceedings. Such 'abominable' behaviour would naturally have 'corrupted' the original Christian purpose of these meetings.

> Instrumental music is allowed in these tea meetings; the people sing heartily and lustily enough to the sound of the music. Only sacred . . . music is allowed, and everything goes on well for a time, but by-and-bye, the musicians . . . play a sacred march, and the friends take up the musical strain by keeping time with their feet or by marching round with a limitation of the number of hops in each bar of the music.[230]

There may have been an element of carnivalesque theatre in the tea meeting. Certainly the Creole women went to great expense to prepare elaborate dresses (costumes) for these occasions, with "the individual being but light esteemed who cannot furnish herself with at least two changes of garment during the evening". As in Jamaica these sessions lasted until sunrise the next day, at which time, headed by a band of musicians, the whole company numbering sometimes hundreds, marched through the village singing and dancing. Though this added to the disrepute in which the whole affair was held by the cultural elites, it did not in any way dampen the enthusiasm of the Creoles for this form of recreation[231]----another instance of cultural resistance.

A 'tea-fight' was a rather different affair. "This is generally supposed by the outside world to consist in drinking tea to the sound of slow music . . . but the palm par excellence belongs to the individual who becomes most rapidly oblivious of mundane affairs." It is not clear whether this meant that in reality the tea-fight was simply an 'orgy' (as it was indeed called) of alcoholic drinking until a state of drunken stupor was attained, or if the loss of worldly consciousness implied spirit possession. Certainly the ingredients for the latter were present in the form of a band of drummers "who beat into the 'wee' hours of the morning". If the source can be believed, tea-fights could go on for several days and nights.[232] For all these reasons, these affairs were also deplored by the cultural elites, but to no avail. Afro-Creoles resisted all pressures from above to desist from such practices.

It is not surprising that since the distillation and manufacture of rum was one of the main economic activities in Guyana, the consumption of rum by all classes and races in the society should have been a major pastime. Creoles were no exception and formed the main market for spirituous liquors. This was considerably encouraged by the mushrooming of retail spirit (grog) shops owned by Portuguese immigrants who, despite the legal restrictions and vigilance of district commissioners and the police, sold alcohol all day on Sundays. Most working class male Creoles were reputed to indulge in quaffing. As in Trinidad, alcoholism was thus one of the major social problems among Creole males, and many could be seen in various stages of intoxication on the public streets in both town and country. The formation of temperance societies among church members (mainly women) under missionary guidance, patterned on those in Britain, hardly stemmed this problem. Rum was the social drink of the working man on all occasions.[233]

A very popular Creole pastime was the flying of kites. Easter Monday, a public holiday, was the great kite-flying day on the sea wall in Georgetown and on open lands in the villages. Young and old alike, male and female, appeared to be seized by the kite-flying mania. Easter 1885 serves as a good example: "The appearance of the sky all over Georgetown, but especially towards the Sea Wall, was very striking, the air being thick with kites of all shapes and sizes, covered with gaily coloured paper, all riding bravely on the strong trade wind".[234]

Kite-flying, however, was not as innocent a pastime as one might expect. There was literally a sting in the tail of some kites. Not infrequently the flyers, in a violent effort to give vent to their social frustrations and anger, affixed fragments of glass to the tails of their kites. According to the *Royal Gazette*, "[t] his glass arrangement . . . is for the purpose of performing a kind of aerial warfare between kite-flyers, as it serves the purpose of cutting each other loose".[235] This practice could result in serious injury to unsuspecting persons as occurred, for instance, in 1866 when the tail of a kite got entangled round the neck of a baby and almost strangled the child. In another incident the tail got entangled in a rose-bush of a garden on private premises in Regent

128

Cultural
Power,
Resistance,
and
Pluralism

Street. A child living there went to disentangle it when the kite, becoming suddenly released, made a dash forward and upward. The child's hand was so severely cut by the glass in the tail that he was reported in danger of losing the use of it.[236]

This practice generated elite antagonism towards kite-flying by Creole youths. They complained that the glancing of a kite in front of a horse, or even the humming sound of the kite, could cause the animal to plunge or run away thus causing injury to someone.[237] Indeed in March 1869 a police constable was thrown from horseback and severely injured ostensibly because of the flying of a kite. Not surprisingly, therefore, the elites exercised their cultural power and banned kite-flying in the public streets, and offenders were fined $3.00 (12s.6d.) or sentenced to seven days imprisonment if found guilty.[238] That, however, did not curb the (mal)practice of affixing glass to the tails of kites. The values of the yard/street were fully expressed in the arena of kite-flying.

If kite-flying was cause for concern among the elites, an even greater menace was the 'spring-ball' or 'sling-shot'. This was a sort of crossbow consisting of a crosspiece of wood with a strong elastic band which could propel a pistol ball or small piece of stone a considerable distance and with great force. In 1869 it was reported that a 'gentleman' (i.e., white man) while standing talking to a friend on the east side of Water Street was struck under the eye by a missile from one of these 'weapons' used by a lad on the other side of the street. The injury was so severe that the victim lost blood and suffered great pain.[239] While for the most part used harmlessly, the 'sling-shot' could evidently be employed in an aggressive and violent manner against elite targets; and so, not surprisingly, the cultural elites demanded the outlawing of this 'weapon'.

Although perhaps not as compulsive as the Chinese, gambling was also a very popular pastime among working class Creole males. By the 1860s a number of gambling houses had sprung up in and around Georgetown, and these aroused elite concern not only from a moralistic and religious standpoint, but also because gambling often generated disagreement which brought out the 'worst' yard values even to the point of violence. Creoles betted on anything from dice games to cock fighting and dog racing. Easter Tuesday was the special day for cock fights. Adopted from the English, it was outlawed by the colonial authorities, as indeed it was in England too. So just as in Trinidad, cock fighting was driven underground: urban Creoles had to conduct it clandestinely in the bush on the fringes of the city to avoid detection and arrest by the police; their rural counterparts, however, did not face such vigilance. A good fighting cock was treasured by its owner as a source of income. The urban youth also staged dog races at all times in the public streets.[240]

As Bryan and Trotman found in Jamaica and Trinidad respectively, gambling among working class Creoles was further encouraged by the horse-racing meetings organized by the cultural elites,[241] although on some public holidays villagers organized their own horse races.[242] Horse-racing was one of the British sports adopted by the Creoles with great enthusiasm. Race day was a gala occasion in Georgetown and for all practical purposes was an unofficial holiday since the Creoles were not prepared to go to work. The streets were filled at daybreak as crowds congregated wherever bets could be placed.[243] Obeahmen (see chapter 6) were in high demand as fortune-tellers and sorcerers on race days as they were consulted by bettors to tell them what horses to bet on, and to ensure their winning bets. The jockeys too called on the obeahman for assistance. According to 'Nemo': "The wife of a jockey is said to have implored . . . an obeahman to allow her husband to win at least one race. And it is thought that the man allowed it, or the race would have been lost".[244]

The cultural elites were, however, prepared to defend horse-racing against the charge that it encouraged obeah practices. The sport's promoters disclaimed any responsibility for obeah at the races, and argued that the two grand race meetings each year were a source of great entertainment to all echelons of society. In other words, if obeah were indeed practised, that should not be allowed to detract from the benefits offered by horse-racing.[245] Hence, although horse-racing seemed to encourage yard/street values among the subordinate population (e.g., boisterousness, gambling, cheating, drinking, obeah, cursing and fighting), the elites in this particular instance were determined to use their cultural power to *preserve* it not only because it was one of their major pastimes, but also because its close association with aristocracy ('the sport of kings') satisfied their craving for high social status.

After placing their bets, the Creole racing fans prepared for a full day of fun and excitement at the racecourse: "Rigged out in the most beautiful of the beautiful that his wardrobe comprises, in white trousers, dazzling a long way off, a blue dress coat and glittering vest, with a fuming cigar in one hand and a faultless stick in the other, the negro, full of hope, hastens to the Course".[246] Literally thousands of Creole working people attended the races, although no matter how well dressed, they were not about to be admitted to the grandstand where the cultural elites were assembled. This was a classic example of how the British promoted cultural assimilation through sport while maintaining social distance between themselves and the colonized.

This was even more vivid in the case of cricket which, having been learnt by looking at the whites at play, rapidly became a favourite

130

*Cultural
Power,
Resistance,
and
Pluralism*

pastime among the Creoles. Stoddart argues that more than any other sport, cricket was considered "the main vehicle for transferring the appropriate British moral code from the messengers of empire to the local population".[247] With specific reference to Barbados, he asserts that:

> Through cricket most Barbadians pledged their faith in a social system predicated upon British cultural values, British concepts of social progress, British morality codes, British behavioural standards and British attitudes towards social rankings. In so doing, Barbadians at large accepted the framework of social power elaborated by the dominant culture to replace that lost in 1838.[248]

It may have been no different for the Afro-Creoles in Guyana, some of whom furthermore were Barbadians or had Barbadian ancestry. Cricket was thus an important element of social control in the colonial context. Yet this transference did not occur in a formal manner; like church related cultural activities, it was done subconsciously. Thus, according to Stoddart, "much of the potency of cricket as cultural imperialism came from the sport's voluntary imposition by its new converts rather than from an arbitrary imposition by the imperial masters". What made cricket even more readily assimilable and popular within the Creole folk culture was the social respectability, and indeed fame, which was accorded to those who performed well. But despite its role in promoting common values in support of the existing imperial system, cricket did not promote egalitarianism. There was no pretense at seeking to incorporate the subject peoples as equals in the actual playing of the sport.[249]

In Guyana, therefore, Creole participation in what was regarded as an exclusively elitist sport was at first not welcomed, and as late as 1864 attempts were made to prevent them from playing on the elite Parade Ground unless issued with a red card signed by one of the town councillors. According to the *Colonist*, "It is clear that the only object of the Commissioners in granting tickets is to clear the grounds of a class which as the Police Magistrate so often deplores, infests the seawall also, and renders what might otherwise be a delightful promenade, a horror to respectable families".[250]

Such obstacles, however, did not deter the Creoles who formed their own clubs and organized matches both in town and country.[251] Thus in 1869 one reads about a cricket match on the very same Parade Ground between the 'Black Creoles' and the 'Black Barbadians'.[252] By the late nineteenth century, cricket became extremely popular among the Creoles who reportedly used every available open space of ground to play the game in one form or another. Little boys played on the sides of the streets with an empty kerosene oil tin for wickets and the rib of a palm leaf for a bat.[253] A few were tolerated at the elite clubs to save the white players the trouble of chasing after the balls; but, as Heatley noted, they "probably receive 'more kicks than

Creole children
playing the
imperial game:
cricket

half-pence' for chewing mangoes and gabbling with each other instead of keeping their eyes on the game".[254] By the end of the century, in addition to two major clubs in Georgetown, viz., the B.G. Churchmen's Union C.C. and the Demerara C.C., most villages had their own cricket clubs. These clubs engaged in regular matches among themselves on weekends and holidays. Although scores were generally low, some Creoles became quite proficient at the game.[255]

But the spirit in which some of these matches were played raises very important questions about the extent to which the values in which cricket as an imperial sport was wrapped were inculcated by the Creoles. For instance, in a match at Belfield in 1878 between teams from Victoria and Ann's Grove a bloody fight ensued as a result of disagreement over an umpiring decision. One of the players was so sacrilegious that he even began breaking a bat and destroying the wickets![256] So much for *esprit de corps* and unquestioningly accepting the decisions of the umpires (authority). This incident represented an assertion of the very yard/street values that cricket was supposed to eradicate.

Kirke also cited a match between the Government Secretariat and the Police during which the white Inspector-General put on police constable David to bowl. David was an enormous black man, about 6 feet 6 inches tall, whose run-up to the wicket was estimated at about twenty yards. His fearsome approach was characterized by the whirling of his right arm like a windmill, and when he reached the bowling crease he delivered a terrifically fast underhand grub ball straight on the wicket. This disconcerted the batsmen who were not accustomed

132

*Cultural
Power,
Resistance,
and
Pluralism*

to such a style of bowling.[257] By the late nineteenth century overarm bowling had already become the norm, although underarm bowling was not outlawed. David's bowling thus demonstrated that in their adoption of this British culture form, the Creoles were nevertheless determined to play it in a spirit quite different from the genteel manner in which the elites did. Like the working class professionals in Britain, the Creoles played hard with a view to winning rather than promoting camaraderie. Still, when viewed in conjunction with other borrowed aspects of Afro-Creole culture (e.g., Christianity, legal marriage, British education, etc.), it seems clear that the Creole adoption of cricket signified their acceptance of the superiority of things British as a means of attaining social respectability, although that did not preclude them from creolizing it and transforming it into an important mechanism of resistance against white domination.

Among the Creoles, however, cricket was not just a male pastime. Black working class women, not hampered by the gender restrictions of their 'social betters' with respect to strenuous work and physical exercise, also organized and played their own cricket matches.[258] But in so doing they ran the risk of being vilified as vulgar by the cultural elites who did not approve of such vigorous female activity in what was considered a male sphere—sport. Thus the social obstacles to the development of women's cricket were enormous. Attempts by Creole females to play the game failed to gain recognition and encouragement, and women players certainly were not rewarded with the same respect and honour as their male counterparts. Still, in according high social value to participation in the cricket culture, Creole women shared the perception that things British were desirable.

The efforts by Creoles, male and female, to play cricket met not only with obstacles, but also with scorn and ridicule from some of the cultural elites. The views of the 'venerable' Anglican Archdeacon Ignatius Scoles were laden with derision:

> Our young African then must have his cricket game, because the white man has his. His scanty means, however, make him very independent of London balls and bats and wickets: an old paraffin tin all bruised, battered and just managing to stand, does excellent duty as both bales [sic] and wicket. The red leather ball resigns the honour to some old rags tightly twisted and fairly rounded, or at a great push an oblong mango-stone supplies its place. The bat of course is all in strict keeping, being often the butt-end of a leafless cocoa-nut branch, if perchance a piece of wood has not been fashioned into the conventional, bat-like form, and surely, what more do you want? The noble and scientific game of cricket is carried on with evident satisfaction to the players, and immense amusement to lookers on. It happens often the lively scene of action is close to a wide muddy trench into which the ball goes as often splashing in as not, but in goes the fielder too, enjoying his bath, securing the ball, and scarce wetting his clothes, for he has scarce any clothes to wet! There cannot, we confess, be much interest to solid and sober minds to hear of an honoured game like cricket, spoilt and turned into a mere caricature by the poor Africans in these Western parts ...[259]

(A century later these "poor Africans", under Clive Lloyd, himself a Guyanese, were again being accused of spoiling the game, but for quite different reasons.)

"The poor Africans", however, did not allow such bigoted Europeans to have the last word. Newspaper columnist 'Argus' reported a conversation between two 'tie-head' girls watching a group of white cricketers on the Parade Ground. Said one: "Dem boy can't play cricket; dem is crickets self". Retorted the other: "Yes gal, you is right, dem better go sit on stick and sing, and let nigger boy show dem how foo play".[260] Clive Lloyd and his men certainly did; but it is important to point out that even though some cultural values of British imperialism were indeed inculcated while learning cricket, the Creoles never seemed to accept the idea of their inferiority on a level playing field. If anything sport, and cricket in particular, gave them the opportunity to excel at the white man's game, and to demonstrate that they were just as good, if not better than, their imperial 'masters'. Cricket, the imperial game *par excellence*, was thus transformed by the Creoles into a ritual of resistance, a medium through which they could express in unrestrained manner their continuous struggle for social equality and psychological liberation.

Summary

As an economically and politically disprivileged ethnic group, the largely ex-slave Creole working class population were placed under relentless pressure throughout the postemancipation period to transform themselves culturally by relinquishing their 'barbarous' Afro-Creole beliefs and practices and becoming good, civilized, Christian colonial subjects. This pressure emanated from all sections of the cultural elite, both white and educated brown/black, and was articulated mainly in the press, from the pulpit, and in the schoolroom. Even more insidious was the voluntary inculcation of the Victorian code of ethics especially through sport, and in particular cricket; for since no conscious pressure was exerted, resistance was minimized.

It is also very significant that only very rarely did the cultural elites resort to draconian measures, such as legislation or the use of the police, to stamp their will on the Creoles in matters of culture; and whenever this was done it was to prohibit or control a specific cultural practice or institution rather than to impose an aspect of Victorian culture. But at the same time, they left it in no doubt whatsoever that social mobility and respectability were largely dependent on cultural assimilation. For their part, the Creoles responded as best they could under the circumstances, and creatively, incorporating and transforming elements and symbols of Victorian culture to suit themselves,

134

*Cultural
Power,
Resistance,
and
Pluralism*

while resisting change in certain aspects of their folk traditions. Their willingness to adopt aspects of the dominant Anglo-Creole culture was largely conditioned by their unending quest for social respectability within the colonial context. Resistance, on the other hand, stemmed from the values nurtured and transmitted in the yards and streets of the villages and urban ghettos. Yet even when they opted to conform culturally, they were ridiculed as childish imitators by the white elites. For the idea behind the transmission of elite culture was not to promote social equality. In the British colonial tradition, the encouragement of cultural assimilation and the preservation of social distance went hand in hand. Ridicule was employed as a tool to indicate that no matter how assimilated they became, the Creoles could never be equal.

NLJ photo. Courtesy of the National Library of Jamaica

The Wesleyan
Methodist
church,
Georgetown,
c.1860:
ministered
mainly to the
Creole
population

AFRO-CREOLE FOLK CULTURE: Spiritual

One of the problems of analysing traditional cultures is that it becomes patently clear that the distinction between temporal and spiritual is largely artificial. There is constant overlap between the two spheres, and as far as the Creoles are concerned we have already seen this in relation to music and dance and religion. Nevertheless, in this chapter we shall focus on the 'purely' spiritual aspects of Creole culture.

Religion

Ever since the early nineteenth century, the Guyanese slaves began to come under the influence of white Christian missionaries, and by the time of emancipation most of the slave population had been converted to Christianity, and were very zealous in the worship of their new god. In fact, the ex-slaves strongly believed that their emancipation from slavery was largely the work of the missionaries to whom they were overtly grateful. The missionaries in turn used their enormous influence among the ex-slaves to try to eradicate vestiges of 'barbarous' African religious and secular culture, and must be credited with some measure of success during the nineteenth century. It was they who were mainly responsible for inculcating in the Creoles the idea that things white and British were best (the white bias), while things black and African were uncivilized and worthless.[1]

But in spite of the indefatigable efforts of the missionaries, the Creoles retained significant aspects of culture derived from West African tradition which they adapted, reworked, and syncretized with European culture. Not least of these retentions were West African religious rituals. Their practice of these coexisted with their belief in and practice of Christianity which they generally seemed to accept as superior, while continuing to engage, ofttimes surreptitiously, in Afro-Creole religious rites. But, not unlike the situation in Jamaica in roughly the same period, between 1848 and 1860 Afro-Creole religion

138

*Cultural
Power,
Resistance,
and
Pluralism*

enjoyed a considerable upsurge in popularity while attendance at the Christian churches fell significantly.[2] This was a period of tremendous disillusionment with white civilization in the wake of the failed 1848 labour strike when even the missionaries came out in support of the planter establishment[3], and Afro-Creole religion was an important manifestation of cultural resistance to resurgent white domination.

Retentions of West African beliefs and practices were naturally stronger among more recent African immigrants, and Creoles in areas remote from the contact situation with western Christian influences. As in Jamaica, the 'liberated' African immigrants worshipped their traditional gods: for instance the Kongos worshipped the Bantu gods *Gorgonzambe* and *Jammypoongo* (called *Ganga Zumba* and *Zambiapongo* by their Brazilian countrymen) derived from the original Kongo *Ngana Zumbi* (the Lord God) and *Zambiampungu*. This suggests (although the historical records are silent) that their religious rites must have been similar to the *Kumina* and *Macumba* practised by fellow Bantu groups in Jamaica and Brazil respectively. Even so the influences of Christianity diluted such traditional beliefs and practices into vague memories among the Africans. Crookall observed that by the end of the century, the title *Gorgonzambe* had apparently lost its original meaning and instead Christian priests were being called thus.[4]

As regards Islam, in the absence of hard evidence, one can only speculate about its fate as an active religion among Africans, old and new. It is known that Indian Muslim immigrants were referred to as 'Fulamen' by the Creoles—a reference no doubt to the fact that they worshipped like the Fula (and other African Muslims) who were present in Guyana ever since the period of slavery. This would suggest that the practice of Islam did survive in some form among Africans after emancipation. If so, it might in part help to explain the active interest shown by some Creoles in the Indian (Muslim) *tadja* festival (see chapter 8).

The most popular religious rituals of West African origin, however, were those known as *Cumfo* which were practised on a fairly wide scale by both Africans and Creoles. The word *Cumfo* is derived from the Dahomean *Komfo*, and in Guyana the religious practice was also referred to as *Watermamma* (*Watra-mama* in Surinam) or *Wind* (pronounced 'wine') in honour of the river gods.[5] Worship of river gods forms a very important aspect of most West African religions,[6] and it is very probable that the *Cumfo* rituals were a syncretism of those relating to that common aspect of West African religious belief, and which achieved further relevance and significance to the African slaves and their descendants by virtue of the fact that rivers are so numerous in Guyana. So popular was *Cumfo* after emancipation that religious associations or societies were organized to glorify and worship the

Watermamma. Most of the devotees were members of Christian congregations, but a few not only abandoned Christianity altogether but were very hostile to any missionary who sought to suppress *Cumfo* ceremonies.[7] One gets the impression from the written sources that the 'cult' may have been strongest in Berbice, but it is clear that it was practised all over the country and in particular by 'liberated' Africans (most notably the Kru) at Canal No.1, West Bank Demerara.[8]

Rev. C.D. Dance thought that in Guyana the *Watermamma* worship may have been syncretized with the European mythology of the mermaid (or 'fair-maid' as it is locally called), and that the Creole belief in this being was in part a sexual attraction. According to him, they believed that in the lower part of the rivers and on the coasts, the water spirit attached itself mostly to men, especially if they were married. Thus:

> A young married man is absent for a week or more from his young wife, whom he persuades to believe that he has received a mysterious mandate to go somewhere, which, on pain of death to him, her, and their child or children, he may not neglect: when he returns after his absence, he talks to his wife of heaps of money, for the Water Spirit is liberal with silver; but the wife sees none of it. The young wife must bear her wrongs and her grief in silence, lest evil come to her and her husband and their little ones . . .[9]

Other commentators, building on this mermaid theory, sought to rationalize it by claiming that the *Watermamma* was in fact the *manatee* (water-cow) which inhabited the rivers. They argued that these creatures were of a dark greenish colour with fins which could resemble the human arm, and with hair and breasts like a woman's. Since they sometimes caused death by rushing against small canoes in the rivers, it was thought that the Creoles perceived them to be an embodiment of an evil spirit and thus worshipped them.[10]

Cumfo sessions were generally held when a misfortune had befallen a family or district, or when information was required, e.g., the name of a person suspected of causing someone's illness or death, or disease among stock, and so on. The *Watermamma* was thus normally invoked either to remove evil or to divulge information. In some respects, therefore, there were tenuous links with obeah (sorcery and medicine—see below), and indeed contemporary observers often made no distinction between the two. The *Daily Chronicle*, for instance, claimed that "the object [of *cumfo*] is simply to 'catch some evil spirit' to work obeahism with".[11] Data found by Higman on the slave period in Berbice do suggest that some *cumfo*-men practised obeah as well.[12]

Cumfo ceremonies were usually organized by one or more devotees or mediums in the open air, sometimes at the request of an individual who paid a sum of money for the services of the chief medium or *cumfo*-man and his fellow devotees. On one occasion, as much as $65 (£13 11s.) were paid. Sometimes the rituals were conducted on several consecutive nights, and appeared to vary in form but always consisted of a dance, sometimes called *cabango, cumfo,* or *catamarrha* (it is impossible to attest to the accuracy of this since elite observers were both ignorant and inaccurate about what they saw). In one instance, two empty coffins were placed in a yard around which the devotees were reported to have danced in a semi-nude state "making hideous contortions of the body" (hence the term *wind*).[13] Elite observers were generally outraged at these scenes which they referred to as sexually promiscuous meetings with sensual dances and profligacy of the most atrocious kind.[14]

In one instance, the session began early in the evening with the *Yuroo* and *Dutch Dance*[?], and was gradually transformed by the "small hours of the night" into the *Cumfo* or *Minje-mamma*.[15] "During this dance, the performer throws himself into every possible variety of attitude; tumbles, jumps, and foams at the mouth, while the assembled multitude follow him singing some non-sensical words, understood neither by him nor them."[16]

This was obviously spirit possession. Richard Schomburgk, despite his narrow ethnocentric bias, was able to capture the scene most vividly:

> In measured beat and slow, the ladies, draped in white muslin, and adorned with huge red-coral chains, trip it with the men in circles advancing and retiring: the excitement of the musicians . . . becomes aroused, and proportionately with it the action of the partners. The blows of the drummer fall even quicker and harder on the skin [drum] . . . the dancers are soon transported with wild bacchanalian lust, when with a series of disgusting jerks, 'winds' and contortions they resemble Furies rather than human beings . . . All of a sudden, three or four fresh performers, no longer able to resist their inner impulses and devilish appetites, spring into the exhausted throng. The music now takes a swifter turn, the dance waxes more fast and furious, even more demonical, and the sibylline spirit that grips them, likewise seizes all the onlookers who, with yelling voices and clapping hands goad the waning strength of both partner and musician to further exertions: finally this frenzy has to succumb to absolute lassitude when, bathed in perspiration, foaming at the mouth and faint with exhaustion, the dancers sink to the ground and fresher people take their places.[17]

According to another observer, "The wizard [spirit-medium] on such occasions performs his enchantment; and by these dances secures influence over his deluded, misguided, and superstitious followers".[18]

> When all have, by the physical effects of such gymnastics on their nerves, reached a sufficient degree of frenzy, the special worshippers are beaten with a bush rope, or piece of root, often until the blood flows, to punish them for their neglect of the water mamma worship, or some offence that they have given to her. When this has been sufficiently done to appease the anger of the water mamma, a calabash of water, after certain mumblings, is thrown on them while kneeling, and the performer then informs his dupes that the water mamma's favour has been secured, and that he will meet her alone in the bush and obtain what is wanted; generally, the name of the person who has been the cause of some one's sickness, or some disease among stock, or some death in a family.[19]

Cumfo
drummers

Cumfo worship evidently involved elements of spirit mediumship
and spirit possession. Beattie and Middleton note that the conception
underlying these 'cults' is that there is a distinction between the immediate and ordered realm of the human and social on one hand, and a
realm of the spirit outside and beyond the control and full understanding of men on the other. "In all of them this outside realm is seen
as containing spiritual forces of various kinds, and in many cultures it
is believed that through spirit mediumship men may, for their purposes, enter into relationship with some of these forces."[20]

Firth distinguishes between the phenomena of 'spirit mediumship'
in particular and 'spirit possession' in general. In both cases, a person's

142

*Cultural
Power,
Resistance,
and
Pluralism*

actions are believed to be dictated by a supernatural force which has entered his body or otherwise affected him; and both may often be regarded as instances of multiple personality whereby the individual concerned assumes another identity quite different from his normal self. But in the case of spirit mediumship, the supernatural force within him seeks to communicate with his audience, whereas in spirit possession, the person's behaviour is essentially merely his bodily expression of the spirit's actions.[21]

In the historical descriptions of the *cumfo* rites and practices above, it is evident that both features were present. Consequently, it is very likely that these ceremonies may also have served the main social and psychological purposes identified by anthropologists. These are firstly to allow the possessed individual to cast off socially imposed inhibitions and behave in a way which might not normally be sanctioned by society. Secondly, they may have served as therapy for some mental illnesses and to sooth certain physical ailments. Thirdly, they may have offered a temporary measure of prestige for persons of low status. And finally, they may have functioned to reassure the adherents of their faith and belief in the spirit world, and of the presence and protection of the spirit gods.[22]

Cumfo survived the rigours of slavery and thereafter the hostility and scorn of elite opinion for the simple reasons that it was psychologically functional both at the individual and community levels, and it was also an important symbol of Afro-Creole resistance to white cultural domination in the colonial situation. Even so, and though not subjected to open (legal) repression, the force of elite, particularly missionary but also middle class black/coloured, opinion—a key aspect of their cultural power—was so strong that lower class Creoles were encouraged to believe that the practice of *cumfo* was devilish and inherently barbaric, and thus should be denounced and abandoned if the individual aspired to any measure of social respectability. This attitude promoted cultural ambivalence towards *cumfo*, and relegated its practice to the subterranean as something to be indulged in only very surreptitiously, while Christianity was elevated to being the ideal religion for any self-respecting socially aspiring individual.

Obeah (Magic and Medicine)

Very closely related to Afro-Creole religion was the practice of magic, sorcery and folk medicine or obeah as it was called. It is probable that this practice may have involved an element of witchcraft as well. The very word seems to be derived from African ideas of witchcraft. Medicine-men ('witch-doctors') among the Ga in West Africa use the Twi word *obeye* to describe the *won*-like entity that is within the witch.[23]

"The witch or possessor of this *obeye* is an *obeyefu*."[24] Likewise, the Akan word for witch is *obayifo*.[25] Alleyne describes the functions of the magician in Africa thus:

> The magician protects against sorcerers and invisible evil beings; he cures people, makes women fertile, ensures and protects harvests, wards off destructive forces, provides antidotes, guarantees success in examinations, ensures safe travel, and so on. As a healer, he has expert knowledge of the pharmaceutical and spiritual uses of curative plants. The same person is therefore doctor and magician (whence the term 'witchdoctor').[26]

This trilogy of magic, medicine and sorcery has not always been recognized. For instance, while Curtin considered obeah in Jamaica to be essentially the practice of magic,[27] Patterson accommodated the element of witchcraft/sorcery, but equated it only with 'bad medicine':

> Obeah was essentially a type of sorcery which largely involved harming others at the request of clients, by the use of charms, poisons, and shadow catching. It was an individual practice performed by a professional who was paid by his clients. It is not difficult to see that obeah approximates closely to . . . bad medicine in the West African sense . . . On the other hand, certain elements of witchcraft are also discernible in obeah.[28]

It is clear though that obeah in postemancipation Guyana encompassed all three elements. It was applied "to any or every act of commission or omission which, under the instructions or directions of the obeah-man, [clients] believe will further their interests, favour their desires, or carry out their wishes, good, bad and indifferent".[29] Creoles sought the assistance of the obeahman for various purposes—the cure of disease, discovery of theft, possession of love charms, telling of fortunes, predictions of horse-racing results, gratification of revenge, conciliation of enemies, etc. Abortion was also commonly done by the obeahman.[30] In one instance the operation was itself aborted when the client was found with "a chain attached to her collar bone and hip, winding through her intestines and her foetus, which could only be removed by payment of some [money] to the pious juggler whose prayers and ceremonies were to be efficacious".[31]

The cultural elites, who themselves believed and feared the potency of obeah, claimed that poison was the main tool of the obeahman: "it is upon a secret and skilful use of poison that the peculiar of the system is supposed to depend".[32] This fear was allowed to reach almost paranoid proportions as obeahmen were regarded as infamous for carrying a drop of snake poison under a sharpened fingernail, a scratch from which reputedly meant death.[33] They also allegedly prepared and provided the poisons for various 'evil' purposes. Lethal potions were made from the root of the bitter cassava (*jatropha marrihot*), the nuts of the sandbox tree (*hura crepitans*), the tobacco seed (*nicotiana tobaccum*), physic nut (*jatropha curas*), the root of the granadilla (*passiflora quadrangularis*), a root called *mirabilis jalapa*, a grass named *spigelium*

144

Cultural
Power,
Resistance,
and
Pluralism

anthelmenticum, and *strichnos guianensis* (the *woorali* poison derived from the *nux vomica*). This obsessive emphasis on the preparation of diabolical poisons masks the fact that obeahmen also practised 'good medicine', and exhibited a high degree of skill in the properties of herbs which earned the grudging admiration of some less paranoid elites: one admitted that obeahmen "would astonish men of European education".[34]

Apart from poisons, the obeahman's tools of trade included such 'charms' as toads, cats' ears and claws, teeth, little bits of bone, and dried human blood. These were sold chiefly to persons for purposes of enchantment or bewitchment.[35] The obeahman, however, also served as doctor. People in pain or sickness often believed that someone had 'obeahed' them. Hence the obeahman had to be called to take the 'spell' off for a fee. Not surprisingly, the cultural elites were very cynical about the obeahmen. "These rascals by sleight-of-hand pretend to extract centipedes, scorpions, worms, and other noxious insects from the patient, while all the time they have the reptiles concealed about their persons."[36]

The belief in, and practice of, obeah were very pervasive and deeply rooted within the Creole community, and were even considered to have become more widespread after emancipation, particularly from the late 1840s onwards when there was an upsurge in Afro-Creole folk practices generally paralleling the temporary decline in Euro-Christian influences.[37] Some of this was accredited to the 'baneful' influence of newly arrived Africans, especially the Kru, who were particularly feared because they were attributed with possessing certain mysterious powers which Creoles never had and old Africans, after a long period of residence and acculturation, were presumed to have lost.[38] Thus Creoles suspected almost every African of being an obeahman "especially if he is very old and very ugly, and they do not scruple, on the slightest occasion to beat him, unmercifully if they think it can be done with impunity". This hostility was in part induced by missionary denunciations which instilled in Creoles the idea that the obeahman only had power by his art to destroy persons who were not Christians.[39]

Nevertheless, a strong fear of obeah remained, and no black or coloured person, regardless of class, would openly discuss the subject.[40] Even educated Creoles (and whites as well) believed in the power of obeah. "Many who would be ashamed to acknowledge it publicly, still cling to the belief that there must be something supernatural in it. They cannot shake off the superstition, although their reason tells them that this is contrary to nature, and, is at best a clumsy fraud."[41]

In one case in point, after an obeahman was reputed to have cured a sick man at Mahaicony by removing from him the causes of his illness, viz., a live frog (*crapaud*) and cricket, hairpins, and several other things which were supposed to have entered his body through a bruise, a Christian Creole woman quite candidly indicated that she believed that those items were indeed removed from the man just as much as she believed that Jesus Christ died for her, "thus coupling the Holy name and finished work of the Saviour with the infamous works of the Devil".[42] In fact some obeah practitioners reputedly used portions of scripture and prayers in their ceremonies. For instance, one Sunday in March 1889, in an effort to ascertain who had stolen a man's money while he slept the night before, an obeahman suspended a Bible by a string from a key which was tied to a tree branch. A small crowd, including a policeman, waited for the Bible to swing as they called out the names of suspects. The person whose name was called when the Bible swung was actually arrested and charged by the policeman.[43] This signified the syncretism of European and African beliefs so central to the process of creolization in the plantation environment.

This deep-seated belief in and fear of obeah meant that the practitioner occupied a very special place of great influence among Creoles. This did not go unnoticed by the colonial authorities who feared the potential consequences of such influence. They recalled that during slavery some estate managers were killed by poisons dispensed by obeahmen. And they also had reason to suspect that obeahmen were largely responsible for the effectiveness of the labour strikes of 1842 and 1848. Their influence or 'intimidation' was credited for the binding secrecy to which the strikers were evidently enjoined. "No reward could induce a single individual to betray the leaders in the work."[44] Thus in the acephalous Creole community, the obeahman was a very important symbol of resistance, both cultural and political, to white colonial domination. It is no wonder that with the general upsurge of obeah practices after emancipation, the elites utilized their cultural power to impose draconian legislative measures to suppress the phenomenon.

By Ordinance No.1 of 1855 undefined practices of obeah, which was equated with witchcraft, fortune-telling and confidence trickery, were outlawed on pain of imprisonment for one year with a public whipping for a first offence; for subsequent offences, the penalty was increased to three years' incarceration accompanied by three public floggings. Women were liable to be placed in solitary confinement for one month (first offence) and three months (subsequent offences) in lieu of the public floggings. Clients were liable to one year's imprisonment. In addition, justices of the peace were empowered to search by warrant for phials, images and other articles used for obeah, and to arrest the occupants of the place where they were found.[45] The problem with such loose legislation was that it embraced anything consid-

146

Cultural
Power,
Resistance,
and
Pluralism

ered out of the ordinary including the genuine practice of folk medicine which was widespread among Creoles. This meant that many
innocent persons were liable to be arrested, fined, flogged and/or im-
prisoned under the sweeping powers of the law.

The public floggings, which were often executed in front of the
Stabroek market in the heart of Georgetown, were intended as short
sharp shocks to the practitioners who would, it was hoped, be discred-
ited before a large crowd of potential clients. They were supposed to
offer tangible proof of the obeahman's impotence: "the man who pro-
fesses supernatural power on their behalf, cannot in his own case avoid
detection and conviction, and punishment which is sure to follow".
But such draconian methods were counter-productive. Not infrequently, the obeahmen never cried out under the lash of the cat-o'-
nine-tails. These were extraordinary acts of defiance and resistance
which reinforced the beliefs of the spectators in the power of obeah.
Thus public floggings hardly reduced the incidence of obeah practice,
and many convicted and flogged obeahmen simply returned to their
'trade' after being released from prison. The only significant effect of
the repressive legislation, therefore, was to drive the practice of obeah
underground.[46] Obeah practice was thus a very important symbol of
Afro-Creole cultural resistance to white domination.

One of the problems in dealing with practices like *obeah* by law is
the difficulty in defining the offence.[47] This was certainly the great
weakness of the 1855 ordinance; and though it took twenty-two years
and many convictions and public floggings, it is not surprising that in
1877 the Court of Crown Cases Reserved should have decided that in
the absence of a definition of obeah, a person could only be convicted
for receiving money under false pretences if he or she claimed to be
capable of working charms and so forth. In a desperately hasty attempt to get around this problem, the legislature (Court of Policy)
then passed a new law (Ordinance No.12/1877) which omitted all
reference specifically to the term obeah. This law made anyone practising witchcraft, sorcery, enchantment, conjuration, fortune-telling,
palmistry, etc., aimed at deceiving, punishable under Ordinance 21 of
1856 as a rogue and a vagabond. The Police were also empowered to
seize and destroy articles used for those purposes.[48] That obeah should
have continued to be recognized by law until the late seventies, albeit
in a deliberately undefined manner, instead of being treated simply as a
crime of false pretenses (fraud) as elite commentators persistently
claimed it was,[49] is very significant. One can only suppose that this
was a consequence of the dominant whites' own belief and fear of its
efficacy.

Elite denunciation of obeah as mere superstition was thus premised
on ignorance, arrogance and fear. It was a typically ethnocentric aver-

sion to an Afro-Creole cultural phenomenon which they neither understood nor considered civilized, but nevertheless feared. The belief in and practice of obeah, however, survived repression both during and after slavery largely because it was very functional in providing the Creoles with a potent and feared means of fighting back against a repressive and exploitative colonial system. It also offered them psychological therapy for dealing with stresses and conflicts of day to day living[50] in some measure created by that very colonial system of which they were a part. But as with most aspects of Afro-Creole culture, it encountered ambivalence from its own adherents who were indoctrinated to believe that there was something wrong, immoral, and irreligious about obeah. Because the practitioners could suffer from a loss of social respectability, it was relegated to the dark recesses of their cultural matrix, to be employed only covertly as the occasion arose.

Spirit Belief

[The Creoles] have a great dread of graveyards during the night, and fear much after dusk being near old tombs or ancient tombstones, scattered as they are on all sides, in the house garden or in the adjoining paddock, on the roadside or in the plantation; for in days gone by, men buried their dead friends just where they bury their dead horses now— i.e., just where they liked . . .[51]

Belief in spirits was quite prevalent among the Creoles. This was undoubtedly derived from West African tradition. The local term *jumbi* (also in Trinidad) was used to designate any spirit, although it was evidently derived from the Kongo *zumbi* (also used in Brazil) ----a spirit of the dead, a revenant (*zombi* among the Kumina in Jamaica, *zambi* in Haiti).[52] As do West Africans, so too the Creoles believed that other spirits, vaguely anthropomorphous but without distinct individualities, inhabited the inanimate parts of nature, hills, trees, watercourses, the bush, etc.; and that they could be either good or evil.[53] Hence the *jumbi* were both feared and revered: "He is a great personality and power. Sometimes he is treated as a petted friend, and at others he is shunned as a dreaded enemy".[54]

Special dinners were occasionally provided for the *jumbi*. These were probably more directly related to the appeasement of the spirits of the ever-watchful dead who, according to West African tradition, have the power to bestow either blessing or adversity, even life or death.[55]

When something goes wrong 'Jumbi is no pleased', and so he must be propitiated. A dinner party, or some such thing, must be held in his honour. But only little children must be invited—he is particularly fond of children . . . This party is held in an open field, and boiled rice and chicken without salt is the repast (Jumbi dislikes salt), and the little folks are told that Jumbi is there partaking of the food, and enjoying himself in their midst—though he can be neither seen nor heard.[56]

148

*Cultural
Power,
Resistance,
and
Pluralism*

Spirits were sometimes believed to assume human shapes. For instance, the *Long Bubbies* were supposed to be ghosts of dead women which appeared with the right breast elongated or lengthened at pleasure, with which they threatened certain night walkers and flogged others. There were also the *Cabresses* which were supposed to be spirits of courtesans. These would visit dancehalls and other public places of entertainment and apparently participate and enjoy the amusement. They would attach themselves to 'reckless lovers of pleasure' and lure them to a desolate spot where they would either break their necks or squeeze them to death "in the moments of dalliance".[57] It is evident that though women did not enjoy equality with their men during their temporal lives, they were accorded enormous powers as guardians of morality after death in Afro-Creole folklore.

The *Warning Spirits of Dead Relatives* reputedly intimated the death of those to whom they appeared or warned them against evil committed or permitted by them. On the other hand, the *Adopi* were little superhuman men with extraordinary physical strength. They were black bushmen whom elite commentators likened to the fabled green men or fairies of the North. The *adopi*, however, were not supposed to possess thumbs, and to propitiate them when met in the bush one could not expose one's thumbs to their view, or they would break them off.[58]

Spirits of the dead could also take on animal shapes. The *Rolling Calves*, for instance, were believed to be the furious spirits of bad men who died unpardoned. They reputedly appeared in the form of calves with eyes of fire dragging long chains at night through yards and streets, making hideous noises. They were considered supernatural police to restrain people indoors during 'unseasonable hours', thus discouraging burglary and late-night debauchery.[59]

Trees and plants were also accredited with spiritual qualities. The sand-box tree (*hura crepitans*) was nicknamed the 'Monkey dinner bell tree'. When its seed-vessels (the size and shape of a Spanish onion, but flattened and deeply furrowed) burst with a loud sharp explosive sound, sending their seeds all rattling among the branches and rolling on the ground, the Creoles said they there was going to be a *jumbi* wedding. The seeds were also reputedly used by obeahmen.[60]

The silk-cotton tree (*eriodendron anfractuosus*) was supposed to have supernatural powers. Despite its huge size and outstretching roots, Creoles believed that at dead of night it walked about, and crossed and recrossed wide and deep rivers; but that it was always sufficiently active and sharp to find its way back to its original place before daybreak. Moreover, it always managed to escape detection in its nocturnal perambulations. It was nicknamed the '*jumbi* tree' or 'devil's tree'. Creoles never troubled this tree, and none would ever dare cut it down or otherwise destroy it: "for they all say, the executioner will not long survive the cutting of the tree". Not surprisingly, in keeping with its ascribed supernatural powers, obeahmen were reputed to sit under it to make up their bags of 'goodies'.[61]

The Creoles also applied the term *jumbi* to some plants and other things. For instance, they called the mushroom *'jumbi* cap' or *'jumbi* umbrella'. The smooth-billed Ani (*crotophaga ani*), a black bird with only one white spot was called *'jumbi*-bird'. Creoles were alarmed by its visits "for when he flutters around inhabitable dwellings, it is a sad omen that one among the living will quickly be numbered among the dead".[62]

Animals too were said to be vested with spiritual powers. It was not unusual for people buying *mauby* (a local beverage made from the bark of the Carob tree) to hold it in front of a donkey's nose for a while before drinking it. Creoles believed that the donkey by breathing into the *mauby* bottle would give a long breath to the drinker "for donkeys are considered to have long breaths themselves, and moreover are accredited the power of imparting that long breath to others by breathing into the vessel to be drunk from".[63]

Notwithstanding the ridicule and denunciations of their beliefs in ancestral and other spirits which were interpreted as pagan ancestral worship and superstition by the cultural elites, particularly the missionaries, the Creoles were successfully able to resist such pressures and not only retain their own traditional beliefs, but also incorporate European superstitions into their belief system: hence the superstition of haunted houses. They adopted the belief that certain urban houses and abandoned rural mansions were haunted and were frequented by ghosts, i.e., *jumbi*. These buildings enjoyed "all the special privileges, rights, titles, and immunities of haunted dwellings! Where strange sounds and unearthly noises are heard, where mosquito-curtains shake, and their doors bang".[64]

Another European superstitious belief inculcated by the Creoles was that the horseshoe brought good luck. Hence they frequently nailed horseshoes on the doors of their buildings to prevent attacks of hogs, and to keep off the evil machinations of witchcraft and witches.[65] Spirit beliefs as a whole, incorporating both African and European derived elements, represented another area of culture where the Creoles proved capable of resisting (even if subconsciously) elite cultural power aimed at eradicating same; but the intense desire for social respectability meant that the socially aspiring Creole was strongly influenced to deny, at least in public, an adherence to such 'dark' beliefs.

The practice of witchcraft was widely believed in and feared by Creoles in Guyana. Such beliefs were evidently derived from similar notions held in West Africa and perhaps reinforced by European superstitions on the subject. Parrinder outlines the common features of African witchcraft thus:

> The witch is generally female. She goes out at night and meets in an assembly with other witches. She leaves her body in her hut and flies to the assembly, often as an owl, other bird, or animal. The witch preys on other people and procures a victim for consumption in the assembly. The blood of the victim is sucked or its members eaten. This causes a wasting disease to his physical body, and the victim lingers until the heart, liver, or some other vital organ is eaten. Children are often thought to be eaten by witches. Any disease may be taken as a sign of their evil machinations.[66]

In nineteenth century Guyana, witches were generally believed to be old women and their victims were mainly babies and young children. As in Jamaica, the witch was called *ole haig* (old hag); and in Trinidad, *soucouyant*.

> These old women, by the recitation of some absurd lines, are said to be empowered to take off their skin, which they fold up and hide in a convenient place. They anoint their skinless bodies, and assume superhuman powers. They fly through the air: they enter closed rooms, and suck the life-blood of infants. During the time they remain without their skin, a lurid halo surrounds them.[67]

Field asserts that in West Africa "witchcraft is a bad medicine directed destructively against other people, but its destructive feature is that there is no palpable apparatus connected with it, no rites, no ceremonies, incantations, or invocations that the witch has to perform. It is simply projected at will from the mind of the witch". She notes that witchcraft demands two types of people: those obsessed with the fear that they are being bewitched; and the still more terrified set of neurotics who believe themselves being made witches against their will.[68]

Evidence of the former was not wanting in Guyana. In 1877 a black man from Victoria on the east coast of Demerara went to the front of a woman's house, called her a hag, and shouted to neighbours to assist him in beating her and in taking "the fire from under her arms". He later claimed that the woman's brother had threatened to kill either his child or him, and in fact did kill the infant. According to him, the child was strong and healthy until the day of the threat when he/she "began to grow thin in consequence of the quantity of blood sucked from the body". The child died three days later. So convinced was he that it was witchcraft that although a doctor was within reach he did not call him to attend to the sick child.[69]

According to Nadel, the Nupe believe that when the witch attacks a person at night in his/her sleep, it is always the *rayi* (living state) or *anima* (life soul) she feeds on, thus causing the *naka* (body) to fall ill and waste away. But when the witch takes her victim to the gathering place where all other witches will feast on him/her, it is only the *fifingi* (shadow soul) that is brought along and devoured, not the person in the flesh who remains asleep in his/her house. Likewise, when witches move around at night (flying), they do so not in body, but in soul (their *fifingi*). Hence, it is a shadow feeding on a shadow.[70]

The Creoles, however, evidently believed that the witch simply removed her skin, hid it and flew on her diabolical nocturnal business. Hence if her wrapped-up, hidden skin could be found and pickled while she was skimming the air high overhead or, like a vampire bat, gorging and disgorging infant blood, it ceased to be of use when the hag attempted to replace it because it would burn her skinless body. And since the charm was only for one serial trip each night, the old wretch was bound to be discovered in the morning. Another method of detecting an *ole haig* was to throw down before her skin an odd number of grains of Indian corn (maize) which she was bound to pick up and count before she could put on her skin. But since she could pick them up only in pairs, the last odd one would trouble her, causing her to recount time and again until daylight revealed her to the enraged community.[71]

Such strong belief in witchcraft meant that old women in rural villages were not safe, for any sudden illness of a child was likely to be blamed on the oldest neighbour who would be labelled an *ole haig*. She was then liable to be flogged with calabash switches (since it was believed that hags could feel nothing else) until she restored the child's health or was rescued from her tormentors.[72]

Under missionary influence, Afro-Creole belief in witchcraft was denounced as barbarous superstition of the ignorant and, as was the case with obeah, *cumfo*, and spirit belief, deplored and considered unchristian. Creoles were therefore urged to purge themselves of such superstitions and become good practising, socially respectable, Christians. Yet, that such beliefs were never expurgated from their minds was surely an indication of resistance, however subconscious, to the cultural power of the elites aimed at imposing Victorian cultural ideas.

Summary

In 1838, Creoles were released from bondage but, despite the upward social mobility of a minority of individuals, were to remain, as an ethnic category, at the bottom of the social hierarchy (alongside the Indian and Chinese immigrants) for the rest of the century and beyond. Again, although a small minority did migrate overseas, for the vast majority Guyana was their permanent home. Indeed the Creoles

152

*Cultural
Power,
Resistance,
and
Pluralism*

were the only ethnic category within the plantation environment who consciously perceived their presence in Guyana as permanent. They were the natives of the soil. This perception of permanent residence and the reality of social subordination in no small way moulded their attitudes to life and to the cultural influences around them. Forced ever since the days of slavery to adapt to the social will of the Euro-elite classes, Creoles were left in no uncertain position that social advancement could only be achieved by conforming to the 'civilized' mores, values and customs set by the cultural elites. In particular, it was the Christian missionaries who were charged with the responsibility after emancipation of bringing 'civilization' to the ex-slaves and their descendants, and who in consequence tried to instill Victorian morals and values, and other forms of British middle class culture.

Thus, already by the time of emancipation influenced by ideas of the superiority of British culture, Creoles throughout the remainder of the nineteenth century continued to incorporate British morals and values into their cultural matrix. The result was a continuous process of adaptation and change which characterized the complex fusion of African and European cultural forms that was Afro-Creole folk culture. But although there was always a strong element of the African components which influenced the everyday life of the Creoles, these were persistently under attack from the cultural elites, including middle class assimilated blacks and coloureds (both by force of opinion, secular and religious, and by law in some instances), intent on impressing on working class Creoles the inherent barbarism and inferiority of African derived culture. Afro-Creole folk culture forms and beliefs were thus consistently degraded and devalued. Family life was deplored as non-existent or unstable; expenditure on weddings was rebuked as evidence of inherent improvidence and thriftlessness; Afro-Creole religious rites were dismissed as superstition and fetish; Afro-Creole dance was condemned as sensuous and immoral; wakes as noisy, debauched nuisances; and so on. In other words, Creoles were pressed to believe that there was nothing worthwhile, decent or uplifting in their Afro-Creole cultural heritage. This did not, however, go unchallenged and there were several manifestations of resistance emanating from the yards and streets of rural villages and urban ghettos to this kind of cultural assault, the most important being obeah, *cumfo*, spirit beliefs and witchcraft, music and dance, and the friendly societies.

On the other hand, the desirability of inculcating European cultural values, customs and beliefs was stressed, and the rewards for this would be social respectability and upliftment. The insatiable hunger for those rewards played a critical role in encouraging the Creoles to shun their Afro-Creole cultural heritage. Yet when they did incorporate aspects of Victorian culture, they were ridiculed as childish imitators of their 'betters'. For in the colonial situation cultural assimilation was never intended to produce social equality. Nevertheless such acculturation was encouraged, and it entrenched in the minds of the Creoles the idea of the superiority of British culture. While, therefore, strong manifestations of Afro-Creole culture persisted in their everyday life, a high premium was placed on the acquisition of European forms which became idealized within the Afro-Creole cultural matrix. This (con)fusion of cultures, however, bred apparent contradictions in belief, morality and behaviour. Thus, good Christians who frequented chapels every Sunday continued to practise *cumfo* rites on Saturday night, and to fear, revere and resort to the obeahman. Likewise Creoles embraced the European idea that monogamous marriage was the ideal while continuing to live in common-law units.

Afro-Creole culture was further enriched and made more complex by borrowing (however minimal) from the Amerindians who resided beyond the plantation culture sphere in the hinterland, and with whom there had ever since the days of slavery been very minimal contact; and from the new immigrant cultures which were brought to the colony in the nineteenth century. As will be shown in subsequent chapters, Creoles participated in some of the ethnic festivities of both the Indian and Chinese immigrants. This meant that the Afro-Creole culture was constantly adapting to new influences which in turn rendered it more dynamic and creative. Yet it remained very clearly and identifiably 'Afro-Creole' at base, and provided the Creoles with a way of life that was viable and functionable. It thus had the potential to provide them with a distinct cultural identity as a separate ethnic community in the colonial society if its practitioners regarded it positively and accredited it high status. Unfortunately, it was to some degree devalued by even the most lowly in the social hierarchy, and all too eagerly discarded by upwardly mobile black and coloured individuals who were ashamed of the long shadow of 'disgrace' which they were induced to believe it cast. Thus it was relegated to the status of an undesirable, debased, lower class, 'nigger-yard' sub-culture within a broader creole cultural matrix in which Euro-Creole forms were the dominant ideals to aspire to.

Because of the social stigma with which it was associated, Afro-Creole folk culture did not perform the same unifying role that the immigrant cultures, as we shall see, did. It was in very many respects prevented from promoting black ethnic group consciousness and cohesion. In their ambivalence, Creoles became a disparate ethnic category lacking a strong ideological and cultural identity by which to resist effectively the twin evils of imperialism and racialism. They remained a loose collectivity with differing values, ideals, beliefs, and behavioural patterns. While Afro-Creole culture was closely identified with

154

*Cultural
Power,
Resistance,
and
Pluralism*

the low social status ascribed to the Creoles on the basis of 'race' and colour, the acquisition of British values, customs, beliefs and practices by individual Creoles did not on their own alter that prescribed social status. 'Race' therefore continued to be the primary determinant of the social status of the Creoles for most of the postemancipation period. It was only when the racial barriers began to break down late in the century that culture began to assume greater importance as a social determinant. And then the key criterion for high social status was the assimilation of British culture. Therefore, culture assumed priority as a social determinant, not under conditions of pluralism as M.G. Smith argued, but only when the society was in the process of change from a plural to a class stratified structure.

As regards the theoretical debate on cultural integration versus pluralism, the Creole folk culture by the postemancipation period was inextricably linked in a subordinate manner to the elite Victorian culture. Although there were several cultural institutions, belief systems, behavioural patterns, customs and values that were distinctly Afro-Creole, and which became *foci* of cultural resistance to the dominance of the Anglo-Creole cultural model, the fact remains that the Creoles did share the same *basic* institutions, socio-cultural ideas and values as the elites. In this context, Afro-Creole folk culture formed a subculture of the dominant Victorian culture system. The case of the Afro-Creole folk culture is, therefore, strongly supportive of the integrationist theory as advanced by Braithwaite, R.T. Smith, Hall, et al., and bears very little resemblance to the notion of cultural pluralism propounded by M.G. Smith in particular. Yet, as the numerous instances of resistance seem to demonstrate, even at the end of the nineteenth century the process of cultural assimilation, particularly among the rural Creoles, was by no means complete.

INDIAN BHOJPURI CULTURE:
Material and Temporal

By far the largest body of immigrants who went to Guyana during the nineteenth century were from India. By 1900 some 210,639 Indians had arrived in the colony on contract to work for at least five years on the sugar estates. Most of them, both male and female, were either poor, seeking to make money quickly and return home, or social outcasts seeking to escape ostracism in their home communities.[1] They had their origins in various parts of the vast subcontinent of India, but mainly because of the planters' preferences, an estimated 85 percent came from the north Indian provinces of Bihar and Uttar Pradesh.[2] Vertovec notes, however, that the composition of these immigrants varied from shipment to shipment, and from year to year. The result was that they comprised a disparate and heterogeneous category composed of persons of diverse regional, social, cultural, linguistic, religious, and economic backgrounds.[3]

The Indian community was the subject of considerable curiosity and scrutiny. The sheer size of their number (by the end of the century they constituted over 40 percent of the colony's population) created new social and security problems. Their very introduction as indentured workers was highly controversial: for two-thirds of their passages was paid for by taxing Creole workers, whose wages and ultimately jobs on the estates, were undermined as a result of this large supply of new labour inputs. But quite apart from those issues, to members of the host society the Indians looked different, dressed and behaved 'oddly', spoke an unintelligible 'gibberish', ate strange foods, had 'queer' customs, and believed in and worshipped 'weird' gods. This not only generated enormous curiosity, but also a considerable amount of written commentary by the cultural elites. For analytical purposes, the data have been divided into two chapters, the first treating the material and temporal aspects of Indian culture, the second the spiritual aspects. This division, however, is not altogether precise since

156

*Cultural
Power,
Resistance,
and
Pluralism*

many features of the temporal culture do have strong religious (spiritual) underpinnings.

Accommodation

When the Indian (and other) indentured immigrants came to Guyana they were placed in dwellings on the estates which were invariably located in the old 'Negro yard' where the slaves had formerly lived. Where there were sand reefs, or where dams were convenient, the dwellings were built there since these were higher and drier than the clay flatlands. But in general, they were erected on low land which, if the drainage was bad, suffered from chronic dampness and periodic flooding.[4]

There were several types of estate dwellings, but in almost every case they were quite different from what the immigrants had been accustomed to at home. The most common were long ranges of buildings of two storeys forming barracks, a far cry from the thatched mud huts, however humble, that the Indians had left behind. The barracks were built to accommodate as many labourers as cheaply as possible, although they might have been considered superior to the old slave huts. Each had about thirty rooms, the lower storey with twenty arranged in two rows back to back, with another row of ten on the upper storey. Sometimes the upper storey also carried two rows with a corridor down the middle. It was generally accessed by an external staircase at each end of the building. But since these barracks were built across the path of the prevailing north-easterly winds, those rooms on the leeward side were not well ventilated and were thus hot. The double-tier structure made it difficult to enforce adequate cleanliness since the occupants of the upper storey were in the habit of throwing unwanted items through the windows. In addition, the floors were not water-tight. On both accounts, therefore, frequent quarrels were generated among occupants of the upper and lower floors.[5]

During the 1860s new single row ranges of between 100 and 200 feet long were built with a draught through. The apartments were about ten by twelve or fourteen feet, and the Indian practice of making the floor of hardened mud and smearing it with cow-dung which destroyed vermin was adopted. These buildings were generally built of clapboard, whitewashed inside and roofed with shingles. Sometimes the upper part of the adjoining wall was left open for ventilation, but this encouraged theft.[6] Another storey was added to this style of building during the 1870s and 1880s with each of the ten apartments having its bedroom on the upper level, and a gallery on the leeward side. Each apartment was used to accommodate four single men or one family, and they were in most cases kept clean and tidy.[7]

Type of
imm grant
dwellings on
the estates:
double-storied
ranges

158

*Cultural
Power,
Resistance,
and
Pluralism*

Probably the worst type of estate dwelling was the old coffee logie or storehouse. This was an immense edifice, rigged up inside with "crazy floors and staircases" and inhabited as thickly as an ant's nest. One at Plantation Friendship and Sarah on Wakenaam island, Essequibo, in 1870 had big barrack-rooms each inhabited by between twenty and thirty men and boys with hardly any furniture, and was in a miserable state of disrepair.[8] Such cases of gross overcrowding created enormous problems of cleanliness, privacy, and ventilation, and also with respect to cooking arrangements,[9] which made it almost impossible for the Indians to maintain their caste rituals.

The problem of overcrowding was grave. The colonial authorities tried to absolve the estates of responsibility by claiming that the Indians in particular liked "to pig together" five or six to a room. A visitor asserted that "the Coolies, men and women, appear to crowd together almost indiscriminately". In 1870 a commission appointed to enquire into the causes of a series of disturbances by the Indian immigrants claimed that "it was not the manager's intention, for instance, to put ten or eleven people into an apartment of two rooms, above and below as we found them at Peter's Hall". But thrown together in a strange environment, it was only natural that the immigrants should want to be close to old friends, relatives, and shipmates until they adjusted to life on the estate. Certainly they did not consider this a permanent condition, as their desire for separate cottages which offered privacy and security testifies. Where the estates were clearly at fault was in not catering to the special needs caused by insecurity of newly arrived immigrants. Generally speaking, however, the average accommodation on the estates tended to be one room to a family or to three single men; though placing single men above a family, especially given the chronic shortage of immigrant women, often posed a threat to the family's privacy and security.[10]

There were also ranges of two-tier cottages with double apartments below and single or double apartments above. Like the older barracks, the leeward apartments were poorly ventilated and hot. Double and single room cottages were also present, but were more expensive to build. Yet since their occupants enjoyed more privacy and comfort, they were generally kept in good order.[11]

During the early 1860s, Plantation Diamond pioneered a new structure (as opposed to the ranges). Twenty-seven two family cottages were built on brick pillars two feet high, with shingled roofs. Each cottage was twenty by fourteen feet with a partition in the centre running from the windward to the leeward side so that each apartment could benefit from the prevailing winds. A stairway in each led to the bedroom above. The roof had a pitch of fourteen feet, and projected three feet beyond the wall on the windward side and two feet on the

Type of
immigrant
dwellings on
the estates:
single-storied

Wattle and
daub (*bacca*)
house

160

*Cultural
Power,
Resistance,
and
Pluralism*

leeward. A window in each gable supplied ventilation and light to the bedrooms. A kitchen was erected in the rear for every two cottages, thus serving four families or apartments. It was eighteen by eight feet with the upper part of the walls composed of laths or splits placed at intervals.[12]

Finally, there were wattle and daub cottages which were mostly found on the Berbice estates where a greater effort was evidently made to accommodate Indian tastes and practices. These cottages were generally built by the Indians themselves sometimes at their own cost, although sometimes the materials were provided by the estate. This was precisely the type of house which they built after leaving the estates. Generally the estates did not encourage the erection of private cottages, save as an inducement for the immigrants to reindenture. The planters felt that if the workers were scattered over a larger area, as would be required for extensive cottage accommodation, there would be a greater difficulty in enforcing discipline or turning them out to work.[13] Moreover some of the cottages were not well built since the immigrants were generally too tired after a full day's labour.[14]

These houses were generally small with walls made of wattle and covered on both sides with clay, sand and cow-dung which gave a smooth compact appearance. There was a thick, substantial clay hearth (*choolah*), and the roof was always thatched with palm, coconut or palmyra leaves. The door was low and the shuttered windows small. The rafters, made of bamboo or palmyra, were split to the necessary size and fastened by withes made of the *spatha* (sheath) that encloses the flower of the palm or coconut tree. On either side there might be a small verandah or alcove, made of baked clay, where visitors were entertained. Off the estates, this type of house was surrounded by a fence.[15] These cottages were greatly prized by the Indians for "they have there an opportunity of reproducing as nearly as possible the conditions and circumstances to which they have been accustomed in India; so much so that in visiting these cottages I could almost have fancied I was in an East Indian Village".[16] Bisnauth has indeed observed that these houses "were replicas of those in which poorer Indians lived in their native land. They were obviously modelled on the Hindustani *kacca* house, with the more substantial roofs, doors and windows, adapted to keep the Guianese rains out".[17]

These wattle and daub cottages also offered the occupants considerable privacy and security generally lacking in normal estate accommodation. Caste rituals could also be more strictly adhered to. Where permitted, they were kept clean and the occupants took great pains to supply themselves with such 'luxuries' as furniture and household utensils. This was largely because they conformed more closely to what the Indians were used to; and moreover cooking could be done inside[18] thus ensuring greater adherence to caste requirements.

As a rule, however, cooking arrangements varied considerably on the estates. On some, kitchens were provided a short distance from the dwellings and all cooking was prohibited inside the dwellings. Since such arrangements did not cater for caste proscriptions regarding food, great vigilance had to be exercised to enforce the prohibition. In some of the larger buildings, a gallery on the lower floor (and sometimes on the upper) was provided for cooking. But on a great many estates, cooking was actually done within the apartments, even in those over-crowded logies and barracks. This was, of course, very dangerous to health and safety; and had it not been for the fact that the Indians built clay hearths for cooking and also heavily coated their apartment walls with clay, fires would undoubtedly have been frequent.[19] Bisnauth, however, notes that the clay hearths in the wattle and daub cottages were much more substantial than those in the ranges and signified a sense of permanent residence.[20]

The rudimentary nature of estate accommodation, in addition to the strong inclination of the Indian immigrants to save as much as they could for their return home, led to an almost spartan existence. Their dwellings were plain without any expensive or gaudy furniture. "High tables and chairs, and other necessaries, are not only out of place, but in the way at all times, and many of these, the females think, are a great nuisance and encumbrance."[21] At the same time, their homes were not decorated in accordance with European tastes. Bronkhurst described them as being

> in a state of confusion and disorder, *topsy-turvy*. You will, perhaps, see a bedstead in one corner, on which the husband, wife, and children (if any) sleep . . . In another corner of the house you will find all their kitchen utensils, and not improbably a bundle of grass or a heap or bag of plantain skins to feed their cows with; and in another part of the room you may find all their wearing apparel, either in a trunk or bag, or thrown about formed into a bundle.[22]

Bronkhurst also noted that many Indians made their own cots from pieces of bamboo tied or nailed together. Others, however, simply "spread their mats on the floor, or on the ground, while others again sleep on the bare ground, taking a piece of stone or brick for their pillow. . ."[23] Indians who lived in their own cottages had a little more by way of material possessions. These might include a low wooden four-posted settee or bedstead with a rope or wickerwork bottom which was used to sit on during the day and sleep on at night, a few stools, several earthenware vessels, a loose mat, and a box for clothing, books and ornaments.[24] It is clear, therefore, that although for the most part unable to live in dwellings which suited their cultural tastes and habits, the Indians wherever possible tried to fall back on their

162

*Cultural
Power,
Resistance,
and
Pluralism* traditional cultural practices. There was very little effort to adopt those of the host society.

Language

Communication was one of the first major problems that the Indian immigrants had to deal with in the new environment. Having originated from different parts of India, the immigrants spoke a variety of languages and dialects. According to Vertovec, given the wide catchment area from which they originated, the languages spoken would have included Bengali, Punjabi, Hindi/Urdu, Oriya, Nepali, Gujerati, Teligu, Tamil and several tribal languages. This was to some extent confirmed by the contemporary Josa. But in addition, Vertovec lists a large number of regional dialects of Hindi including Bhojpuri, Magahi, Maithili, Bangaru, Vanga, Eastern and Western Hindi, etc. Sanskrit was a ritual language and was used only in Hindu temples. Very few Hindus knew it, and these were almost invariably pandits (priests).[25]

This wide diversity of spoken tongues meant that communication was at first very difficult among the Indians themselves. But as with other aspects of Indian immigrant culture, a process of homogenization gradually took place leading to the emergence of a koineised or levelled form of Bhojpuri, the Hindi dialect of eastern Bihar, as the lingua franca of the Indian immigrants.[26] When Josa claimed that 75 percent of the Indians spoke 'Hindi', he was no doubt referring to this dialect. This was very similar to what occurred in both Trinidad and Mauritius. Following Chaudhury and Durbin, Vertovec argues that Bhojpuri emerged dominant because while being close to several of the regional and caste languages of northeastern India whence came most of the immigrants, its structure was far less complicated and enabled non-Bhojpuri-speaking people to acquire it relatively easily.[27]

The emergence of Bhojpuri as the lingua franca was in large measure due to the conditions of life and work in which the Indian immigrants found themselves. Literally thrown together in estate dwellings without regard to social, religious or linguistic differences, and more or less isolated from members of the host society, the language of the majority naturally predominated and over time became standardized. This process was to some extent reinforced when the Indians left the estates after the expiration of their indentures and set up ethnic villages. So just as Ramyead observes for Mauritius, "Freed from the restrictions of plantation life, the great majority of immigrants were now receptive to the religious and cultural forms flowing from a rich and resurgent Bhojpuri oral culture".[28] Other Indian languages were still spoken within sub-groups of the Indian population, especially since new immigrants were continuously entering the society.

After some time in the colony, the Indians also acquired an "English patois more or less intelligible".[29] This undoubtedly represented an adoption of *Creolese* essentially for use in places of contact with members of the host society (i.e., at work, in the market-place, etc.). This 'patois', according to Rickford, incorporated many Indian words, idioms and speech patterns.[30] In other words, while forced by conditions of work and life in the plantation environment to acquire *Creolese*, the Indians considerably modified and enriched the local language.

Devonish goes further to argue that since the Indian immigrants spent most of their waking hours at work, *Creolese* "would immediately have become the language they would use most frequently in the course of their lives", and he does provide evidence to indicate that many Indians used the language with native-like competence. But his suggestion that *Creolese* became the main language of the Indians at the expense of Bhojpuri and other Indian languages[31] does not seem plausible for the nineteenth century. So long as fresh batches of immigrants continued to be imported on a regular basis from India, and remained concentrated and relatively isolated on the plantations or in Indian villages, with every intention of returning to India, Bhojpuri was retained as a language of ethnic identification and cultural resistance for normal communication within the home, the wider Indian community, and even at the work place among Indian workers. But Bhojpuri itself would have undergone significant change incorporating words from other Indian languages in the process of homogenization, as well as Creole words. Thus, as in Mauritius, this would have made it significantly different from the parent dialect spoken in India.[32]

Very few Indians acquired standard English in the nineteenth century for the simple reason that they were not exposed in any significant numbers to formal education. As we shall see in chapter 8, despite the passage of a law in 1876 making primary education compulsory for all, enforcement was practically non-existent especially in the rural areas beyond the end of the century, and the planters were notorious for evading their responsibilities to provide school facilities for immigrant children. The Indians themselves were either indifferent or opposed to schooling for religious, cultural and racial reasons. They were opposed to the Euro-Christian religio-cultural content of the curriculum. In this context, the development of Bhojpuri as the Indian ethnic language was an important aspect of their resistance to cultural domination by the Anglo-Victorian elites. Therefore, only a very tiny minority did manage to acquire standard English during the nineteenth century.[33]

On the whole, therefore, the Indians became multilingual in the plantation environment. While Bhojpuri as the lingua franca became

164

*Cultural
Power,
Resistance,
and
Pluralism*

the language of cultural resistance, many other Indian languages continued to be spoken. In addition, *Creolese* was adopted to facilitate
everyday communication with the host society while at work or in
the market place, and a very small number of Indians also acquired
standard English through school.

Dress

The dress of the Indians revealed a very strong identification with
their parent heritage, and only very slowly did they adopt the dress
code of the host society. Hindu men generally wore two pieces of
cotton cloth or calico. The upper part looked like a loose short shirt
with short sleeves and had a piece thrown over the shoulders like a
Roman toga. The lower piece was wrapped around the waist, and
looped and twisted in a way which left the lower leg bare. This was
called a *baba*. Muslim men tended to grow a flowing beard, and generally dressed in turbans of white calico, loose jackets, and flowing trousers of white or multi-coloured muslin or calico. Inside their houses,
Indian men commonly stripped themselves "almost to a state of nu-
dity". Hindu women generally wore gaily coloured clothes: a long
piece of cotton or muslin wrapped round the middle, and falling in
ample and elegant folds below the knees. To this was added a crimson
cotton-velvet *ravukkei* (jacket) with very short or no sleeves which
closely fitted the body and covered, though it did not conceal, the
bust. Above all this was frequently thrown a light scarf which sometimes covered the back of the head also. Muslim women generally
wore a green gauze *burkha* or *mukkadu* (veil) which was simply done
by drawing over the head the upper part of the garment. Young children simply had a "piece of string tied round their waist".[34]

Both Hindu men and women, especially married women, were
fond of jewellery. Gold and silver were their favourites and they had a
seemingly endless variety of chains, bracelets, anklets, necklaces and
rings.[35] The women wore rings all around their ears, not only in the
lobe. Most of them also wore a nosering either through the middle
cartilage or through any side of the nose. Holes were bored during
infancy for such rings, and when they were not wearing them, they
inserted a small wooden or silver stopper in the hole. They also wore
rings on each finger, and around each toe called *minji*, one of which
emitted a tinkling sound when the wearer walked.[36]

Bangles or heavy gold or silver circlets were worn around the ankles, and four or five thick ('massy') silver bands, about ⅜ inch in
diameter were frequently worn around the arms, a little below the
armpit, at the wrist, and around the leg below the knee. It was also
quite common to see men and women wearing gold and silver coins

An Indian
immigrant
family

around the forehead, suspended from the neck, and covering a system
of network, attached to the back of the headdress. The last was done
by high caste women, the gold being worked into the long, glossy,
black hair, and small pendants of it suspended at different distances
throughout, with a circular ornament or brooch to fasten the golden-
worked headband in front.[37]

These ornaments were more especially worn at weddings and other
festive occasions, on Sundays and on holidays. Married Tamil women
also wore the *tali* around the neck. This was either a band of gold
richly chased, or a silk network entwined with a silver cord. But such
lavish jewellery was not intended just for pomp or ostentation. It was,
of course, one method of saving. But both in India and Guyana, the
display of jewellery on women and children was believed to draw off
the 'evil eye' (see chapter 8). Indian women thus indulged more in
jewellery than in clothes.[38]

166

*Cultural
Power,
Resistance,
and
Pluralism*

Typical
dress of an
Indian
woman

The cultural elites, however, considered the way male Indians in particular dressed to be immoral and uncivilized, and urged the government to compel them by law to wear nothing less than a short pair of trousers from waist to knee. "It is time that these planters' babies, now called unruly heathens, should be legally compelled, without infringement, to adopt the civilized mode of dressing . . . and not continue with us any longer, to shock, by their crude and indecent Indian habits, the feelings of every virtuous family residing throughout the country districts."[39]

Change, however, was slow. For the most part the Indians resisted the adoption of western clothing preferring to adhere to their traditional forms of dress. Those who did adopt some form of western dress were mainly the christianized and the local-born. Some of these, both male and female, began to adopt European clothing although it was obvious that they were uncomfortable and awkward for a while. It was not unusual after a while to see some Indians in a soft felt hat, a black coat cut in European style, a dungaree shirt and trousers, and either English boots or perhaps no foot covering at all. But it was noticeable that on special occasions, even these part-creolized Indians reverted to their native dress made only of the finest materials.[40] Traditional dress, therefore, was regarded both as a symbol of cultural resistance to the pressures emanating from the elites, as well as a symbol of Indian ethnicity.[41] Creolization, even where it did take place, was thus very incomplete, to use Brathwaite's notion.[42]

Food

The chief ingredients of Indian foods were white rice, yellow rice, *dholl, churall, gram*, coconut oil, mustard oil, *goorackoo*, tamarinds, *jeera, daneirau*, tumeric, chillies, *gunga*, and *ghee*.[43] The favourite fare was rice and curry together with vegetables, greens, pulse, fish and fruit. Although Hindus were prohibited from eating the flesh of the sacred cow, and all Indians were taught that it was unclean to eat the meat of the hog, vulture and even some kinds of fish, these proscriptions were often broken in Guyana. It is true that many Indians did scrupulously observe them, but some were fond of pork. Most, however, ate mutton, fowls and fish.[44]

Since most of the indentured immigrants were single males, they had to prepare their own meals. But once married, food was generally prepared by the woman of the 'house', though that might just be a barrack-room. When she was in the field with her mate, the meal was cooked by her on their return while the husband slept or visited his *mattis* (friends). If they had a daughter old enough, she would cook while her parents were away. "They take care to have their food cooked clean and nice." The rice was boiled in an earthen vessel, iron pot or saucepan. Mutton, fish or chicken was cooked in another tempered with *ghee* or butter to which was added *masalei* (a mixture of red pepper or chili, coriander, saffron, cumin, garlic, onion and tamarind and made liquid with coconut 'milk' or pure water).[45]

When the meal was ready, the man of the 'house' and his male friends washed their hands and were served. But before eating, he placed a small quantity of the prepared food before the deity of the house to propitiate his favour. He then mixed his rice and curry with his right hand, and rolling a small quantity into a ball, 'tossed' it dexterously into his mouth, taking care that none fell into the dish,

168

*Cultural
Power,
Resistance,
and
Pluralism*

since such a mishap would defile the remaining mass. "Some, however, since their arrival, have learned to use spoons and forks; but in general they have neither knives, forks, nor spoons. Their fingers serve all the purpose for which spoons and forks were invented. As their meat is always cut up in small pieces, or cooked until it is ready to fall to pieces, knives and forks are useless . . ."[46] The women never ate with their husbands, brothers and grown-up sons. They served the men, and after they had eaten, the women regaled themselves with what was left.[47]

Apart from the fact that in their eating practices Indians were very different from the member groups of the host society, it is very significant that the historical records do not suggest any adaptation on their part to include creole dishes as part of their diet. One cannot, of course, dwell too much on that since the records may not be adequate for this purpose; but it does leave one with the distinct impression that in this area there was not much creolization taking place.[48]

Sex, Morality and Domestic Life

The cooking and eating arrangements described above bring into sharp focus the relations between male and female in the Indian immigrant household. Indian emigration overseas, and in particular to the Caribbean, was attended by a gross disproportion between the sexes.[49] In the case of Guyana, between 1838 and 1868 the number of women per hundred men who landed varied considerably from as low as 11.3 in 1851 to 61.5 in 1858, averaging 32.2 during that period.[50] Generally speaking, however, between 1838 and 1900, there was a gradual improvement in the proportion of Indian women resident on the estates. Whereas in 1851 it was just 27.33 women per 100 men, by 1870 it had risen to 36.69, and in the 1890s it remained constant at 41.[51]

This sexual imbalance was much more pronounced among the indentured Indians than among the unindentured. The unindentured males, being longer resident in the colony, generally married local-born Indian girls and those who were brought from India with their parents. Also being financially better off than their indentured counterparts, they were better able to attract and marry most of the single adult female immigrants, and in many instances to commute the latter's terms of indentureship by paying a proportionate part of the indenture fee. Hence there was generally a greater proportion of women among the unindentured Indian population (averaging 54:100 men during the 1890s). Moreover, a higher proportion of women remained in the colony after their indenture was completed.[52] The ratio of Indian women living off the estates was believed to be higher.[53] Yet even among the indentured immigrants, the proportion of women gradually increased, influenced by the Colonial Office stipulations of 1856 and 1868 that for every hundred men recruited there should be thirty-three women (1856) and forty women (1868).[54] Of special importance too was the contribution of female children whose proportion was consistently over eighty per hundred boys.[55] Even so throughout the postemancipation period, there remained an acute disproportion between the sexes within the Indian immigrant population.

This chronic sex imbalance contributed to a radical deviation in mating patterns from what obtained in India. The single woman was reported to have become an 'institution' in the colony, cleverly dispensing her favours "to attract and fleece men and leave them discontented and quarrelsome". The cultural elites disparagingly tried to explain what they perceived as gross immorality among the Indians by observing that many of the women were either prostitutes from Indian bazaars or otherwise disgraced persons who adroitly utilized their sexuality to extract maximum rewards from the men.[56] This oversimplification, however, missed the fundamental point stressed by Mangru that it was the failure to attract sufficient female immigrants which "promoted unsettled habits, lowered the standard of morality, produced unhealthy competition, made seduction more likely and fostered a feeling of jealousy . . ."[57] The fact is that the sexual imbalance which attended this immigration enhanced the power and importance of Indian women *vis-à-vis* their menfolk which they were fully prepared to employ to their individual benefit. Moreover, as in Trinidad, the position of Indian women was further strengthened by the fact that the men felt inhibited from mating with non-Indian women on account of both racial and caste prejudices.[58]

Women were thus able to choose male partners relatively freely, uninhibited by traditional gender restrictions which had broken down in the new environment. Some made maximum use of that new found freedom and were quite unprepared to stay with one man if he were not willing to treat them properly or able to provide them with whatever material and other benefits they demanded. Some women thus reputedly moved from one man to another with impunity, and sometimes returned to one with whom they had previously lived.[59] Even marriages solemnized by Hindu and Muslim rites were no longer regarded as permanent. In 1887, for instance, one woman at Bush Lot in Berbice, Kama Cherry, was said to have been married no less than three times within the year by Hindu rites.[60]

Kama was by no means exceptional. An even more striking example of the desire of Indian women to maximize their new freedom and bargaining power was Mary Ilandun, young, attractive, of medium height and fair complexion. Born to 'Madrasi' parents who went to Guyana in 1846, she grew up on an East Coast estate. In 1864, at age

170

Cultural
Power,
Resistance,
and
Pluralism

sixteen, her parents arranged for her marriage to a relatively well-off, but much older Indian suitor. This is in itself interesting since both she and her parents had to have been converted Christians to arrange for a Christian wedding (conducted by the Methodist missionary Rev. H.V.P. Bronkhurst); and it demonstrates that even they preserved the Indian cultural practice of arranged marriages. But that aspect evidently did not please an independent-minded and ambitious Mary who deserted her husband after four years and eloped to Barbados with a young Creole man, taking about $2,000-$3,000 in cash and jewellery from her husband. In consequence of a lawsuit by her enraged husband, her Creole paramour was deported back to Demerara in 1869 where he stood trial and was convicted to five years imprisonment. Mary, however, managed to evade arrest and was not heard of in Guyana until her return in 1884. It is not clear if she went back to her husband, but certainly after his death in December 1887 she did lay claim to half his property.[61]

In the intervening years (1868-1884), Mary seems to have blazed a trail of infamy and fortune in different parts of the Caribbean. Leaving Barbados, she went to Trinidad where in 1876 she met and married a wealthy Christian Indian merchant, Richard Bunsee, in San Fernando. After two instances of 'marital misconduct', she was again afflicted by the four year itch and absconded with another young coloured man, taking $490 which her husband had entrusted to her to pay his creditors in Port-of-Spain, plus eighty $20 gold pieces, and jewellery worth about $900. After a year in different parts of the island, her paramour died, and Mary returned to and obtained the forgiveness of her husband. But within a year, she again deserted, this time with a young Indian man from Demerara. On this occasion, she took $400 worth of jewellery and about $2,500 in cash which reduced her husband to a state of bankruptcy.

How long Mary remained with her Guyanese Indian lover is not known, but she ended up in Grenada where she eventually married a Chinese merchant. In the interim, her Trinidadian husband re-established himself as a cocoa farmer and, although the connection was not known to him, negotiated an arrangement to market some of his cocoa in Grenada through Mary's new husband. That deal, however, never materialized because Mary once again ran off after helping herself to her Chinese husband's savings. She reportedly migrated to St. Thomas (Danish Virgin Islands) with a black Grenadian shoemaker whom she subsequently ditched to marry a local coloured man. Very probably, the Virgin Islander was her next victim when she decided to return to Guyana in 1884.[62]

The colourful 'career' of Mary Ilandun took a further twist when Richard Bunsee, her Trinidadian husband, on reading of her claim to her first husband's estate, travelled to Guyana to confront her. But she calmly offered to pay his return passage to Trinidad if he would not interfere in her affairs in Guyana. When he presented his marriage certificate to the local authorities, Mary was charged with bigamy.[63]

Mary Ilandun was unique in many ways. Not merely was she very deliberate, perhaps even a trifle callous, in dealing with men, but the wide range of her activities took her to several Caribbean islands. Secondly, unlike many of her compatriots, she evidently harboured no racial prejudice and was prepared to sleep with black/coloured and Chinese men as well as Indians so long as they served her purpose. Finally, as a Christian she would have been regarded as an outcast in the Indian community, and this perhaps made her more daring than she might otherwise have been. It certainly gave her more flexibility as regards the choice of mates within the Caribbean. Her story vividly demonstrates how some Indian women were able to capitalize on the shortage of females within their ethnic community.

The behaviour of these women should not be adjudged as immoral. They were merely intent on making full use of their new freedom of action provided by circumstances within the social milieu of the plantation, and they seemed especially keen to throw off the yoke of male hegemony to which their gender had been subjected for centuries. In Guyana they found themselves in a position where they could assert their independence from that age old dominance, and could even manipulate and exploit men for personal gain and material advancement. Men, therefore, continued to play a crucial role in the search for independence and self-improvement by Indian women. This contradiction, however, meant that gender relations became increasingly volatile as mating relationships lacked stability.

These circumstances produced several variations in the form of domestic arrangements and in the attitudes of the conjugal partners. Although monogamy continued to be the ideal form, given the acute shortage of women, polyandry, not unknown in India itself, became an increasingly attractive and acceptable alternative among the Indian immigrants. Thus as in Fiji, it was reportedly not uncommon for one woman to cohabit with three or four men, though Shepherd claims that in Jamaica polyandry was rare.[64] Because women became highly valued as sex partners, it was also claimed that some men exploited their wives by hiring out "the[ir] partial use" to other men.[65] This, however, was a high risk venture which could result in the permanent loss of their 'spousal' assets. Mangru also asserts that some parents "*sold* [my emphasis] their young daughters to men old enough to be their fathers and grandfathers".[66] This practice was observed in Fiji by Gillion who stated that money might even be extracted from several successive suitors or 'husbands' and the betrothals repudiated.[67] This

172

*Cultural
Power,
Resistance,
and
Pluralism*

demonstrates that among some Indians, marriage in the plantation environment came to be regarded largely as a business proposition rather than as the foundation of the family. Since the migration was conceived as a temporary short-term phenomenon, every opportunity was seized upon to amass as much money as possible with which to return home, and marriage was no exception. This applied to both men and women, although the latter evidently had greater opportunities and motivation to treat marriage as a business venture. And it does make one wonder if, while preserving Indian cultural traditions such as arranged marriages, Christian converts like the Illanduns also 'sold' their Marys (daughters) to financially acceptable, though no doubt Christian, suitors.

If in the politics of sex Indian men suffered from insecurity of 'tenure' in the marriage, the women were always vulnerable to physical abuse by the men. This was very often the main male recourse to ensure female fidelity—a course of action which could extend in desperation to almost ritualistic murder sanctioned by religion. Both Brereton and Dodd observe that in a situation where women were scarce, a wife was an important symbol of status and male self-esteem particularly on the estates which no man could easily afford to lose.[68] Female infidelity, seriously disapproved of in India, was regarded as intolerable abroad. Consequently some of the most gruesome assaults and murders of women were committed as a result of male jealousy and loss of self-esteem.[69] Between 1859 and 1870, thirty-four women were brutally killed by their ex-paramours; and between 1872 and 1890 another seventy-nine women suffered the same fate.[70] Wood, Reddock, Brereton, Trotman and Hoefte all note that this phenomenon was evident in Trinidad and Surinam as well.[71]

In almost every case the crime was committed by indentured men, generally early in their period of service; and it was usually provoked by the absconding of their women to men who were resident in the colony longer and who were thus in a better financial position to woo the women with lavish presents including jewellery.[72] In an effort to curb this practice, section 11 of the 1860 Heathen Marriage Ordinance made the enticing away of the wife of an immigrant a criminal offence; but this charge was virtually impossible to prove.[73] In 1887 the prohibition was made more stringent by adding the words 'cohabits' and 'harbours', but still to little avail[74] because the fundamental causal factor, shortage of women, was not effectively addressed.

As we have seen wife murder was not unique to Guyana; it was committed in other plantation colonies to which Indians migrated and in India itself. But figures produced by Mangru indicate that the incidence of such crimes of passion was higher in the plantation environment where the shortage of Indian women was acute, even though they were generally less than 1 percent of the Indian immigrant population.[75] Yet it was clearly ingrained in Indian religio-cultural tradition. Because the tenets of Hinduism did not sanction divorce, the husband of a disgraced wife could only repudiate her in order to preserve himself from contamination. But he was still obliged to maintain her even though she was socially ostracized. The laws of *Manu*, however, sanctioned the punishment of adultery by death.[76] Yet, however divinely inspired, those religious laws were written by men with the clear objective of rendering women subordinate to men; and it was very noticeable that they were applied only to women. Almost invariably, therefore, it was only the women who were killed, and very rarely their male lovers.[77] Even more rarely did the aggrieved husband commit suicide.[78]

The instability of the conjugal unit caused by the shortage of women may have militated against legal marriage. The Immigration Agent General opined in 1885 that as most of the women were in his biased estimation of dubious character and background,[79] marriage was regarded as hazardous and objectionable and the men preferred to live with them in 'concubinage' unfettered by bonds of legal union. If this is indeed so, it would appear on the surface to suggest a convergence with the Creole model. But this would be erroneous because both the structure and relationships between the conjugal pair within the Indian unit were fundamentally different from the Creole common-law unit.

It is not clear how prevalent even common-law marriages were among the Indians. For all marriages not solemnized by Christian rites or registered under the Heathen Marriage Ordinance of 1860 were not recognized by law.[80] Thus most bona fide Hindu and Muslim marriages were branded as 'concubinage', and the children of those unions were considered illegitimate and could not inherit property. It was not until 1894 that marriage conducted "according to the religion and personal law" of the Indians was recognized as legal, and even then as Mangru points out, such recognition was circumscribed by restrictive conditions.[81] This meant that although the immigrants did celebrate marriage according to their own customs and regarded it as more valid and binding than any other form,[82] no proper recognition was accorded them for most of the century. Guyana was by no means unique in this regard. Hoefte and Brereton note that similar non-recognition of Indian marriages obtained in both Surinam and Trinidad until well into this century.[83]

In Guyana the Heathen Marriage Ordinance (1860) divided Indian marriages into two categories. Firstly, the marriages of immigrants who arrived in the colony as husband and wife were recognized under section 2. These numbered 8,054 between 1860 and 1893 (an average of

174

*Cultural
Power,
Resistance,
and
Pluralism*

237 per annum). Secondly, there were those persons who were married after a period of residence in the colony under section 3 who numbered just 1,900 in the same period (an average of 56 per annum). These statistics do not include a small number of marriages celebrated by Christian priests which were not reported to the Immigration Department.[84]

The small number of legal marriages under section 3 was in part due to weaknesses in the law itself. In the first place, the absence of all ceremony in the civil registration was unappealing to the Indians and lacked the binding force and sanction of religious rituals. It also was costly and inconvenient to travel to the Immigration Department in Georgetown for such a meaningless process.[85] Secondly, many Indian men did not think that legal marriage offered them any greater security in an environment where female infidelity was so rife. For the law embodied no provisions to punish those women nor to annul the marriage and allow the aggrieved man to recover either his presents to the woman or damages from the successful suitor who harboured his wife.[86] Such omissions were serious, in particular with respect to the presents which represented the hard earned savings of the man. It was not until 1887 that the law instituted procedures for divorce and division of property.[87] Until then, therefore, the only legal recourse was to prosecute the wife and her lover, but that was too costly for most indentured immigrants who had not been long resident in the colony.[88]

Most Indian men thus regarded legal marriage as useless and not binding, and further changes in the law hardly altered this attitude.[89] Incorporating the 1887 reforms relating to divorce and division of property, the 1891 Immigration Ordinance made it possible for district magistrates to conduct civil marriages, free of cost, thus obviating the necessity for the parties to travel to Georgetown. It also recognized marriages conducted by Hindu and Muslim priests on condition that a certificate of clearance was obtained in advance from the Immigration Department, and that within a week after the marriage the district immigration agent was furnished with a certificate of the deed.[90]

Under this law, the number of civil marriages of Indian immigrants between 1894 (when it took effect) and 1900[91] was 1,165 (233 per annum), a noticeable increase; but the number of registered traditional marriages celebrated "according to religion and personal law" was remarkably low—only 138 between 1895 and 1900 (excluding 1898). In fact the number decreased sharply from 69 in 1895-96 to just 18 in 1897-98 and 19 in 1899-1900.[92]

This was officially attributed largely to the fact that marriages conducted by the district magistrates were free; but that explanation is not convincing. Mangru thinks that the legal conditions imposed on customary marriages, relating to clearance and registration, were encumbrances to legal marriage. These requirements were "needless obstacles" which tended to deter registration and promoted the contracting of invalid marriages.[93] No less important was the enormous cost of customary marriages which could hardly be afforded on the pittances paid indentured workers. Many Indians undoubtedly had to postpone marriage until they could save sufficient money to celebrate in a manner that accorded with their religio-cultural tradition. Bisnauth, however, is of the view that the Indian immigrants simply placed no value on legal recognition of their marriages: ". . . they did not see the necessity of having those unions recognised by the law of the colony. In their native village, such a course was unknown". Thus, in his opinion, legal marriage was generally only resorted to by persons who for one reason or another could not prudently undergo a traditional religious ceremony, e.g., those who had previously been married with due ceremony but were separated, those seeking to marry across religious lines (i.e., Hindu-Muslim), a woman who had become pregnant before getting married, or a person seeking to protect his or her property by law. He further notes that females who migrated alone for whatever reason, being generally between ages twenty and thirty, would probably have been previously married in accordance with Indian custom and thus disqualified from remarriage; those recruited from Indian bazaars were similarly ritually disqualified from religious marriage.[94] In any event such women were very independent in spirit and were probably quite unwilling to subordinate themselves to the absolute will of their menfolk.

In India, female subordination is largely enforced by the religious ideology, social institutions, and sanctions of a strongly viricentric society; but these underwent significant modification in Guyana which weakened their efficacy. The reality of acute female shortage fundamentally altered the power equation between Indian men and women. According to Mangru, "This . . . seemed to unsettle the traditional submissive role of Indian women as they began to adopt roles which gave them greater prominence in the immigrant community".[95] No longer was a woman dependent on the support of any one man. Moreover since women earned their own wages as estate workers, it further enhanced their independence of the man or husband. This undoubtedly had its effect not just on the stability of the marital unit and on the relationships between the parties, but on the desire of women to contract legal marriage in the first place. The simple fact is that marriage meant compulsory subordination to the husband. Single women who had emancipated themselves by the courageous act of migrating overseas as individuals, and who in the colony enjoyed the benefits of their new freedom, were not likely to relinquish that for a

176

*Cultural
Power,
Resistance,
and
Pluralism*

life of subservience to any man. This perhaps played a very important role in militating against legal marriage among the Indians.

Even so the Indian immigrants tried as far as possible to preserve traditional marriage customs. One of these was the practice of 'child marriage'. It was customary for fathers to arrange the marriage of their daughters at an early age, in some cases even before puberty and, as one writer put it, to men "twice, three or four times older than themselves". In India, while such a disparity in age is not unknown, it is more normal for both parties of an arranged marriage to be equally young. But the shortage of females in Guyana undoubtedly led to the normalization of a cultural aberration. Under the 1860 law, the legal age of consent was fixed at fifteen years for males and twelve for females. The latter was raised to thirteen in 1891.[96]

The above aberration may have led to further adjustments both culturally and physically. For, according to Attorney-General Haynes-Smith, in cases where the bride-to-be was under fourteen years of age, the parents laboriously enlarged her sex organs by mechanical means until she was ready for the "aged purchaser". However, no corroborative evidence of this alleged practice has been found either in Guyana or elsewhere. What is clear though is that in the more permissive social environment of Guyana, where many equally young suitors were available, it was very difficult for an older man to retain the fidelity of his young wife once she had grown up and her sexual desires were stimulated.[97] In other words, the attempt to adhere to tradition made the problem of adultery worse in the world of the plantation.

Traditional Hinduism enjoins upon the wife the duty of effacing herself completely for her husband. A wife is expected to regard her husband almost as her deity.[98] Even in India, however, this does not hold absolutely true. Though the husband is acknowledged as superior, he is never a completely dominant, authoritarian and patriarchal figure.[99] In Guyana, however, the woman was considerably liberated from that traditional role. For the man to have expected his wife to be totally obedient, subservient and unwaveringly faithful, as many undoubtedly did,[100] was at best unrealistic in the altered circumstances in which they found themselves.

The men, however, did not depart from tradition without a struggle, and tried even by use of physical violence to reimpose their authoritarian will and notions of supremacy on their women/wives. Wife-murder was undoubtedly the most brutal form of that struggle. But male supremacy was manifested in many other ways. It was asserted (though not without considerable prejudice, and certainly without reference to how normal it is in many traditional societies worldwide, and not least of all in Europe) that as a rule the men ate first and only when satisfied did they "throw down the saucepan to the woman . . . in many instances, with not as much grace as we give food to our dogs! Woman is a mere chattel".[101] Similarly, women could not walk alongside their men/husbands, but behind them; nor did they call them by their first names.[102]

Socialized into a highly viricentric culture, the Indian women in Guyana put up with this behaviour but only until the promise/hope of something better seemed to present itself in the form of another partner. Changing partners and refusing to get married were thus key mechanisms in augmenting the freedom of action of Indian women in nineteenth century Guyana; but these were only successful to a point since the vast majority of Indian men held the same views on gender which were greatly at variance with the altered expectations of the Indian women in the alien environment. The males retained and sought to uphold the traditional ideal of male supremacy, and consequently felt that women had to be forced to accept their dominance. If all else failed then wife-murder was the final resort; and since it was sanctioned by religious law, it could be employed with a strong sense of moral justification.

Changing partners, therefore, could not in the final analysis provide Indian women with permanent or long term equality with their menfolk. If they were to achieve any lasting measure of individual freedom, one option would have been to seek partners *outside* of the Indian community, not necessarily as permanent mates, but certainly to indicate to Indian men that they had no natural right to or over them. (Ironically, this was the way out for the men as well—to seek partners outside of the Indian community, which would have lessened their need for Indian female mates.) This is precisely what Mary Ilandun did, which made her unique. But with their options restricted on account of racial and other considerations, the use of force by the men gradually proved effective, and eventually the women were forced to resubmit to male hegemony and authority. Ultimately their exercise of real power in the household was gradually reduced once again to the traditional spheres—over their children and daughters-in-law.[103]

But although eventually forced, literally on pain of death, to recognize her husband's authority, the Indian woman in Guyana by no means became totally self-effacing. She was a true helpmate to her husband, and their property (livestock, etc.) might even be held in her name. That is one reason why Indian men considered desertion such a *grave* matter, literally and figuratively. In Guyana, the Indian man generally did not enjoy any luxury in which his wife did not share, nor did he think of buying, selling or transacting any business without first consulting her. She also played a major role in selecting marriage partners for their daughters and sons[104] even, as we have seen, to the

178

*Cultural
Power,
Resistance,
and
Pluralism*

point of 'selling' their daughters for cash and kind. So, while acknowledging her husband's dominance, the Indian wife in Guyana was by
no means relegated to abject subservience in the household. On the
contrary, her authority was considerably enhanced.

Living conditions on the estates made it extremely difficult to re-establish the traditional Indian joint family. Speckmann has speculated
that in Surinam since the age of marriage of boys and girls was low, it
was impossible for newly-weds to set up house by themselves. Hence
the joint family, characterized by virilocality (i.e., the sons and their
wives living in the same house or compound and sharing the same
kitchen as the father's family) was reverted to whenever possible.[105]
But as we have already seen, many marriages took place between
young girls and adult men who would have been allotted their own
quarters on the estates: indeed this would have been the case provided
both parties were of the age of consent and were working and earning
in their own right.[106] Only if children were betrothed before the age of
consent would they necessarily have continued to reside in their respective parents' quarters until old enough to set out on their own.[107]
In estate barracks, in particular, it is difficult to see how sons could
have added their wives to their father's households.

If a joint family structure, whether akin to the traditional model or
modified as a consequence of local environmental and economic circumstances, were indeed established, the most propitious time would
have been when an immigrant obtained a cottage of his own on the
estate probably as a reward for good service, or if he left the estate
altogether and settled elsewhere. Particularly in the latter case, the
wife and children would have become more dependent on the hus-
band/father. Thus the termination of the system of reindenturing immigrants and the establishment of Indian village settlements off the
estates from the 1870s onwards would have been very important to
any efforts to re-establish the patrifocal joint family structure. Certainly it would appear that by the end of the nineteenth century, a
new Indian family unit resembling the traditional joint structure was
fairly well established in Guyana.[108] In this regard, the Guyanese situation seems to have evolved faster than in Trinidad where, according
to Brereton, the joint family structure was not established in the later
nineteenth century: instead "The nuclear family and its interests took
precedence over the extended family".[109]

Vertovec, however, has raised important questions about this idea
of a new Indian 'joint' family based on the pre-migration model
emerging in the Caribbean. He does not concur with those scholars
who claim that the emergent Indian family unit was the consequence
of environmental and economic factors. Instead, following Solien as
we have done with respect to the Creoles, he considers it important to

distinguish between family structure and domestic organization. Thus

he persuasively argues that the new family structure and domestic organization are the result both of the persistence of traditional values as well as of local socio-economic circumstances:

> The structures, among Indians in Trinidad and elsewhere overseas, will exhibit certain variations from those found in different places in India; these are open to the effects of changing socio-economic conditions through history and within the life of a single family. The varieties of organization among families . . . are aspects of value systems which do not change so readily with contextual changes. On the one hand, the meanings, rules, and roles ordering Indian families in Trinidad are drawn from cultural models (and embodied in sacred texts and popular films); on the other, the size and distribution of families in Trinidad are alterable, as they always have been in India.[110]

What clearly emerges from the foregoing analysis, however, is that as regards their mating patterns and family structures, the Indian immigrants strongly resisted elite pressures to conform to the Anglo-Creole model. Despite physical and social conditions which wrought major changes in their sexual behaviour and family life, every effort was made to preserve the essence of the traditional forms of male-female relationships even in the face of laws and regulations which made that extremely difficult. This aspect of their social life in the colony represents a classic example of resistance to the cultural power of the elites.

RITES OF PASSAGE

Birth Customs

One might logically expect that in a situation where women were so scarce, and where men were prepared to pay to have them as wives, the birth of girls would be highly prized among the Indian immigrants. If so, however, this would have been a major departure from Indian tradition in which the premium is on male children. While there appears to be some evidence that such a departure did occur in Trinidad,[111] the documentary sources do not indicate a similar pattern in Guyana where instead the ideal of having male children seems to have been preserved despite the altered social circumstances. According to Bronkhurst, "The birth of a son causes immense joy, and that of a daughter deep sorrow and misery".[112] In some extreme cases, the father of a baby girl in his disappointment might refuse to speak to the mother or even see his child; and their friends, relatives and neighbours, not least of all the females, were as likely to upbraid the wife and condole the husband as if he had been cruelly treated by his spouse.[113] Craving for a son was considered virtuous in Indian tradition, while the birth of a daughter was decried, and this has been clearly revealed in folksongs of the Indian immigrants in Guyana.[114]

180

*Cultural
Power,
Resistance,
and
Pluralism*

One reason why female children were traditionally not much favoured by Indian parents was the cost incurred in celebrating marriage.[115] Besides, a girl was considered more or less a guest of the
family who would belong to someone else after marriage because by
custom she would be required to move into her husband's family's
residence. She would, therefore, be of no help to her parents in their
old age. On the other hand, only a son could continue the family line
and appease the gods on behalf of the ancestors. On the whole, it was
felt that the birth of a girl was not beneficial. She had to be cared for
and protected until the age of maturity; and even after marriage, her
parents still had to worry about her treatment in her new home.[116]
Girls were, therefore, an unending source of trouble. Whether this is
the reason why their lives had to be one of entire subordination as
Josa stated is, however, another matter. According to him, a girl was
regarded as ignorant and was purposely kept so; for the Indians considered it immoral for females to be literate. And when the time of
marriage came, the girl was expected to ask no questions, but instead
was required to marry the person chosen by her parents.[117] Such ideas,
however, were clearly hangovers from the Indian 'ideal' and hardly
related to the actual situation on the plantations in Guyana where
women were far more independent. Old ideas die hard, however, and
it is probable that such sentiments may have persisted despite a reluctant recognition of the increased value of women; but it is also very
probable that the old traditional ideas may have reasserted themselves
as more Indians established residence off the estates towards the end of
the century, which once again made women more dependent on their
menfolk.

Soon after the birth of a child, the Indian immigrants gave him/her
a drop of honey, syrup or sugar in accordance with Indian tradition.
According to Bronkhurst, this rite was prescribed by the *Shastras* (religious books) and was done both by Hindus and Muslims. Priests and
astrologers (*jyotisi*) were consulted by the parents to ascertain under
which planet the child was born, the nature and quality of the day and
hour of birth, and the good or ill luck attending the child's entry into
the world in order that they could choose an appropriate name.[118]

The naming ceremony normally took place on the tenth or twelfth
day after birth, which is at about the same time as in Rampur in
Northern India, Mauritius (*sanskara/nam sunskar*) and Trinidad
(*barachi*) when mother and baby are bathed and purified. According to
Benedict, the period before the naming ceremony represents a period
of withholding social recognition of the child's arrival.[119] This is not
dissimilar to the West African/Creole practice, and is particularly significant in countries with high infant mortality. It demonstrates the
extent to which the environment determined similar beliefs in cultures

as diverse as these two. In Indian tradition, the child is not regarded as a separate being distinct from its mother for the first five to twelve days. During that time both are considered to be polluted and are kept in isolation. Should the child die before being named, it would not have become a social personality.[120]

At the naming ceremony, a *pujari* officiated. Before him were placed a *chembu* (copper pot) of water, a large quantity of rice and other presents. Parents, relatives and friends sat around him, and after repeating a few *mantras* (prayers) invoking the blessing and guidance of God, he named the child. He then asked the father to open the *olei* book (made of palmyra leaves) which he held in his hands with a piece of string attached to it. Then he proceeded to read aloud everything good and bad on that page concerning the infant. The relatives were expected to give a coin, silver bangle, clothes, etc. The rest of the day and night was spent feasting.[121]

According to Bronkhurst, the Indians held some superstitious beliefs regarding which day of the week a child was born. Children born on Monday were considered jealous; on Tuesday, honest; on Wednesday, quick-tempered but easily placated; on Thursday, mild; on Friday, talkative; on Saturday, hot tempered and quarrelsome; and if born on Sunday, they were considered parsimonious.[122]

No documentary data exist about whether the 'planet name' of the baby was kept secret as it is in Trinidad in order to prevent its use by enemies to cause injury to the child, or whether as in Mauritius its knowledge was confined to the immediate family and used only for rituals.[123] What is known is that a second Hindu name was given which was used publicly. In Guyana, this seemed to have been marked by another ceremony which took place when the child was about a year old at which friends and relatives were again gathered.[124] This is in keeping with upper caste Hindu tradition in some parts of North India; but in some places it coincides with the hair shaving ceremony within the first month of birth.[125] Bronkhurst, however, noted that in Guyana the Hindu hair shaving ceremony took place when boys were three years old. He also observed that the names given usually related to some peculiarity in the child, e.g., Punchy if he were small, Kalu if dark skinned, Locoo if large. Other names were added, e.g., Appo if the child was of good caste, or a name derived from the occupation of the father or the place of abode, etc. In any event, it seems that the Indians believed that an unnamed child was more liable to misfortune than one who was named.[126] The absence of data about the naming of girls is perhaps indicative of their low status.

The Muslim birth rites apparently differed only slightly from those of the Hindus. Muslim women were purified soon after birth (most likely about the sixth day thereafter in keeping with ancient tradition),

182

Cultural
Power,
Resistance,
and
Pluralism

and again at the end of forty days' seclusion before resuming their household duties. The child's head would no doubt have been shaved at the first purification ceremony as in Trinidad, or on the next day as in India, since Muslims consider the presence of hair at birth to be unclean. At this ceremony (*chhatti/catthi/catee*), two male goats were sacrificed for a boy, and one for a girl,[127] again signifying the greater importance attached to boys among Muslim Indians. Like Hindus, Muslims named their children on the tenth or twelfth day after birth.[128] At this ceremony (*hakika*), the *Azan* (a prayer) would, in keeping with tradition, have been recited in the child's ear, and then a 'good' name chosen from the Koran.[129]

Bronkhurst observed that when naming their male children, Muslims generally joined the name of the divine being to one of his (not her) attributes or to some other word: e.g., Abd Allah meaning servant of God or Ameer ed Deen, faithful in religion. They were also reputed to name their children according to the day of birth. Thus when a child was born on Sunday, he might be called Duad or Ibrahim; on Monday, Ahmad or Muhammed; on Tuesday, Ismael or Ishaq; on Wednesday, Ali or Hussein; on Thursday, Jusuf or Mustapha; on Friday (the Muslim Sabbath), Adam or Esa; and on Saturday, Abd-ul-qadir or Nizam-u-din, and so on.[130] No data, unfortunately, have been found about the naming of girls.

Nevertheless, the foregoing clearly demonstrates that the accent in Indian cultural behaviour during the nineteenth century was on preservation of traditional birth rites and practices with a view to retaining their authenticity. Their birth customs reveal no evidence of cultural borrowing from the host society, and despite minor alterations they remained for all practical purposes faithful to Indian tradition, both Hindu and Muslim. Such changes as did occur were more related to a gradual process of syncretism among the variants derived from different parts of India, except where religion emphasized differences. Here too, therefore, the Indians were successfully able to resist conforming to the dominant norms and customs of the cultural elites.

Marriage Customs

One reason why marriage is so important among Hindus is because it gives special emphasis to the continuity of the family. According to Bronkhurst, a typical nuptial congratulation went as follows: "May you both spread wide as the branches of a banion tree; put forth roots as diffuse as a creeping stem of the areegam-gram . . ."[131] Marriage was not complete until a child, preferably a son even in Guyana, was born to the young couple: "Indian tradition considered it a religious and social duty for a man to father a child. The belief that through one's children one reincarnates [one's] self and thus secures immortality and salvation is commonly expressed in Indian traditional literature . . . After marriage, the woman is shown to be dissatisfied until she becomes pregnant". Vatuk has observed that this theme is recurrent in Guyanese Indian folksongs.[132] But this has to be balanced against the fact that as we have seen in Guyana marriage came to be regarded by some Indians as a business venture.

Under normal circumstances, however, failure to have progeny was disastrous although, according to Bronkhurst, the Tamil immigrants could partially circumvent such tragedy by surrogate parenthood whereby the sterile husband would lend his wife to a trusted kinsman or other person of the same caste for purposes of procreation. Such a course would, even under normal circumstances, have been a high risk venture, let alone in a situation of acute female shortage. The child of such circumstance was termed a *Cshe Trajah* derived from two Sanskrit roots meaning a 'field' and 'born', signifying that the offspring resembled the produce of a field which belonged to the owner of the soil, not to the casual cultivator. Sometimes by special agreement between the parties, the two fathers had joint right to the son who was then referred to by a term meaning 'the son of the wife having two fathers'. In that case he could inherit the estate of each father.[133]

Speckmann notes that "this strong stress on procreation for the purpose of continuing the family line explains why selection of a mate and marriage cannot be left to the individual".[134] Marriage was thus contracted at an early age as an obligation of religion. It was the prime duty of parents to get their daughters married. Courtship, however, was regarded with horror.[135]

But as Brereton notes, since Indian immigration to the Caribbean did not generally involve families, but rather individuals,[136] negotiations for marriage could not always follow 'the book', i.e., between the fathers of the two parties. Instead there had to have been considerable direct 'negotiations' between individual men and women, or perhaps between individual men and the fathers of young girls. This would have been an important adaptation to suit the peculiar local circumstances. However negotiated, after a suitable partner was chosen for a girl, the date of the wedding was set by a *jyotisi* or family astrologer.[137] On this occasion, the 'gods of the house' were consulted sometimes by sticking wet flower petals on the cheeks and breast of the divine image, accompanied by a short prayer asking that the right-side petals fall first if the union was auspicious.[138]

Among high caste Hindus, the girl presents a dowry to the boy at the *tilak* (betrothal ceremony) which is held about a week before the wedding.[139] Among the lower and pariah castes, as well as the Muslims, however, it is the reverse: the boy gives a dowry to the girl.[140] In

184

*Cultural
Power,
Resistance,
and
Pluralism*

nineteenth century Guyana (as well as in Trinidad, Jamaica and Surinam), the acute shortage of women so enhanced their position that Hindu men of *all* castes were forced to adopt the lower caste tradition and offer a dowry if they hoped to win a spouse.[141] This was a further indication of the dissolution of caste practices in the plantation environment, but also of the impact of the acute female shortage in the Indian immigrant community. This certainly enhanced the value of girls, though not necessarily to the point of eclipsing the traditional preference or bias for boys.

Some contemporary commentators considered the dowry offer as bride purchase, and claimed that a young girl could be bought "for so many dollars and cents, or pounds, shillings and pence".[142] While, as we have seen, marriage was regarded as a business venture by some Indians, it is difficult to determine how pervasive that attitude was. Certainly the dowry payments did occasionally cause friction and misunderstanding between the parties. For instance, in 1888 one man who had been cohabiting with a young woman for a long time, arranged with her consent (since she was ill) to seek her parents' permission to marry her younger sister. The parents agreed, the dowry was paid and the wedding took place. But the girl with whom the groom had lived broke down during the proceedings and aroused her parents' sympathy. Thus when the groom called for his new bride and the parents refused to give her up, he demanded a refund of his dowry; and on failing to get it, he threatened to take legal action.[143]

Preparations for one wedding in 1881 went on all week at the bride's relatives' house in New Amsterdam. Between 6.00 p.m. and 7.00 p.m. on the wedding day, many guests of both sexes, went decorously clad to Sheet Anchor where the groom resided and formed a marriage procession. At about 8.00 p.m., sounds of music and drums proclaimed the approach of the groom. He was attractively apparelled in red and blue with bells and trinkets pendant, and was seated veiled on a pony with an umbrella, spotted with gold and silver paper and continuously twirling around, held over his head. During the course of this procession, several stoppages were made and fireworks exploded. Women sang to beating drums and other instruments. Arriving at the bride's house, the groom was lifted from his horse and supported by an attendant on his side, while a number of the bride's relatives, sent from within, performed the rite of throwing some sweets on and around him, and uttered some pleasantries. He was then taken into a pavilion made of coconut branches and entertained with music, dancing and acrobatic feats.[144]

There seems to have been some flexibility in deciding the location of the wedding. The one above took place at the bride's home which is the traditional Hindu custom.[145] But some were held at the grooms' homes as well. At Tamil weddings, a large *pandal* or nuptial shed (*maro* or *manro*) was built in the yard and decorated with flowers and other things. A large *medei*, a square seat made of hardened clay, was erected and placed in the centre of the *pandal* and adorned with flowers, and gold and silver leaves, and tinted yellow with a solution of saffron water. A small image of the deity (*Pulleiyar Swamey*), made of cow-dung and clay with a few pieces of grass and some flowers in its head or hand, was placed in one corner of the *medei*.[146]

At one such wedding (Tamil Hindu), the ceremony was conducted by a priest (*Velan Andi*) who was paid, at least in part, by offerings of money and other articles from the guests. The bride and groom, dressed in silks and satin, and attended by friends, came out of the house in procession, and approached the *medei*. After prostrating themselves before an image of the god, they went around the *medei* in regular procession about ten times, each time invoking the god to be favourable to them and to bless their union. When this was done, the priest, who had theretofore been sitting beside the divine image, ordered the bride and groom to mount the *medei* and pray or, as one contemporary writer would have it, "to worship the god and himself". They were then reported to have washed the feet of the priest, kissed them, and then tasted the water as a mark of respect and religious honour. While bowing, the couple were blessed by the priest with a solution of saffron water. On rising they circumambulated the *medei* about six times, before the groom tied the *tali* (marriage knot) around the neck of his bride, whereupon the drums, timbrels and tambourines began to play. Amid the general stir, the happy couple retired to the house with the blessings of their friends. The feast which ensued lasted for two days.[147]

Most of the Indian immigrants originated from the Bhojpuri culture sphere of northeastern India, and it seems that their wedding ceremonies differed considerably from those of the Tamils described above.[148] One important difference was that instead of tying the *tali* around the neck of the bride, the marriage was solemnized by the groom impressing upon the forehead of the bride a straight line with vermilion or red ochre.[149]

Generally the wedding ceremony of the Bhojpuri immigrants began by worshipping Ganesha (the elephant-headed god) who was invoked at the commencement of every action since this was believed to ward off obstacles by which all undertakings were liable to be thwarted by the malice of evil spirits. After all the gifts were presented, there was the *saptapadi* when the bride and groom followed the pandit around the sacred fire each time in seven steps (*hawan*). The groom then made an offering of *loma* (burnt oblation) comprised of ghee, flower petals and water to the sacred fire, and also a little parched rice (*lawa*).[150]

186

*Cultural
Power,
Resistance,
and
Pluralism*

This was followed by the exchange of vows and the binding to-gether of the bride and groom symbolized by each of them putting on the *hasli* (a gold or silver necklace), which they borrowed if they were poor. After the pandit's speech, the groom's sash was knotted to the end of the bride's *sari*, and the couple circled the sacred fire seven times throwing a little *lawa* into it each time. For the first four times, the bride would lead the groom, and then the order was reversed for the remainder. In keeping with tradition, the bride would sit on her husband's left on resuming their seats. After the ceremony the bride was taken to the groom's father's house and put under the care of his mother.[151]

As far as the Muslims were concerned, marriage was solemnized, after the customary interchange of presents, by reading the first chapter of the *Koran*, the *Fatiha*. But as there were very few copies of the holy book in the colony, a substitute often had to be found by the priests. At this ceremony (*Shaddi* or *Nikka*), the groom repeated 'certain formulae' with the five creeds, the articles of belief, and the prayer of praise. Thereafter he joined hands with the proxy bride (*vakil*) since the presence of the real bride in person contravened Islamic notions of delicacy. Their faith was plighted in a 'prescribed formula'. Prayers were then offered by the priest who concluded by sending some sugar candy to the bride with a message that she was married to such a person. Only then was she conducted by her female companions and friends to her future home.[152]

Indian weddings were very expensive affairs. All the guests present gave a nuptial gift (*parisam* or *sparida*) to the newly married couple. It was also customary for the *tambulam* (plate) to be put in a conspicuous place or to be handed around by an appointed person. Soon it would be heaped with a large sum of money, often between $300 and $400, which was given to the couple.[153] The fathers of both parties also incurred enormous expense for the wedding.[154] Josa claimed that no respectable marriage could be celebrated at a smaller cost than $2,500 and in rare instances expenditure was said to exceed $60,000.[155] These figures seem extraordinarily exorbitant and quite out of the reach of the average Indian family. More realistic are the figures provided by thirteen Indian petitioners in 1896 who stated that generally between $300 and $500 were spent on weddings.[156] Even so this represented a relatively large sum of money, and one can agree with Josa that the savings of years were often exhausted in a few days of extravagance, and that families which were in reasonably comfortable circumstances were plunged into poverty and debt by the wedding of one of their members.[157]

Yet although the number of guests was usually large——in the case of the well-to-do Mr. Parahoo of New Amsterdam, the guests to his thirteen-year-old daughter's wedding in 1871 numbered over 500[158]----most of the money was reputedly not spent in food and drink or in giving presents to the bride, "but [in] the giving of presents or garments and money to the guests, feeing the Brahmins, processions, and fireworks".[159] More recently Smith and Jayawardena noted that for the parents, the staging of their children's weddings is a most important event in their lives. Furthermore, the lavish expenditure and extravagant display are a means of demonstrating the families' prestige and respectability, as well as of repaying the hospitality they have enjoyed at other weddings.[160]

Even private ceremonies and celebrations like weddings were not exempt from official harrassment by the cultural elites, and were consequently liable to interference from the police. One of the key musical instruments used on such occasions was the *dholuk*, a small drum. Since the wedding ceremonies continued through the night, the beating of this drum annoyed those cultural elites resident nearby. In 1893, therefore, the law (Ordinance No. 21, sec. 172) required the permission of a magistrate or police officer for the *dholuk* to be used at Indian weddings after 10.00 p.m.—permission which in practice was invariably withheld. This effectively contradicted the 1891 Immigration Ordinance which allowed the Indians to contract marriages according to their religion and personal law. Where they attempted to do so by beating the *dholuk* after 10.00 p.m. without the required permission, the police would intervene and break up the festivities. Although compensation might eventually be obtained through the Immigration Office, it was usually far from adequate. Following two petitions from some Indians in 1896, however, the colonial authorities removed this unfair restriction.[161]

It is appropriate to note that the marriage customs of the Indians remained in their entirety Hindu or Muslim, as the case may be, and that there was virtually no cultural borrowing from the host society. Yet changes did occur, some related to local circumstances, especially in relation to the shortage of women which caused a change in the dowry arrangement among high-caste Hindus and altered attitudes, both male and female, towards the institution of marriage. The Indians also had to contend with the cultural power of the elites through use of the law which had an impact on the conduct of wedding celebrations. But no less important were the changes which occurred over time to narrow differences in practices derived from different parts of India. These enabled the Indians in Guyana to evolve a fairly homogenized system of marriage customs which enabled them to resist the cultural power of the elites and at the same time distinguished them from all other ethnic groups in the society.

188

Cultural
Power,
Resistance,
and
Pluralism

Death Customs

Among the Tamil immigrants, when a man was considered to be at the point of death, it was customary for a goat to be brought to his bedside. The man would place his right hand on the goat's head, and his sins were duly recounted by the *pujari*. The goat was let loose and was never touched or killed by the relatives of the dying man. It thus became the scapegoat or the goat of dismissal (*azazel*).[162]

By the 1880s, the Indians would, as in Trinidad, hold a wake on the night on which a death occurred.[163] This custom was obviously borrowed from the Creoles, because it is foreign to Indian tradition. According to Bronkhurst, both Hindus and Muslims had such abhorrence for dead bodies that they would not suffer them to remain in their house longer than could be helped. The wakes resembled those of the Creoles in some respects, particularly as regards the gambling[164] and the consumption of rum. But a description by a Presbyterian missionary, George Ross, of a Siva Narayani (Sieunaraini) wake indicates that the Hindus called on their own religious traditions:

> Before dark all arrangements have been made. Candles and incense are at hand. Rum, too, is provided and shortly after darkness settles down the Hindu wake is in full swing. Instruments, anything but musical, jingle and clang accompanied by the most mournful and monotonous of dirge and wail. The Mahant [religious leader] presides. Camphor incense is burned at intervals . . . and throughout the night the dismal requiem is heard. At five o'clock the estate bell sounds its rousing alarm. The wake ends.[165]

Beyond that, however, the Indians seemed to adopt traditional funerary customs which to some extent dovetailed with local customs. When someone died, the corpse was at once bathed and shrouded, and the funeral ceremonies or obsequies performed as soon as possible. Mourning women beat their breasts in sorrow, putting their arms on one another's shoulders, drooped their heads in the centre and wept. The relatives and friends gathered in the deceased's house were forbidden to eat or bathe as long as the corpse was lying there. When the funeral procession left the house, no one presumed to walk in front of the corpse. That space was reserved for the ancestral spirits (Bronkhurst said "angels") to escort it to its final resting place.[166]

More elaborate efforts were evidently made for the funerals of prominent Indians. In one instance, on the death of a priest who was visiting the estate, the immigrants at Plantation Versailles, West Bank Demerara, quickly collected subscriptions ranging between $5-$10 for the funeral. The coffin was elaborately dressed and ornamented with gold and silver leaves, and a large body of mourners escorted the corpse to its burial place. Eight priests participated and the funeral procession included eight singers and eight drummers. Incense was used, and lavish use was also made of perfume not only for the dead, but for those in the procession. Money was thrown into the grave, and considerable amounts of beer and alcoholic spirits were consumed by the mourners.[167] According to Ruhoman, lighted camphor was also placed at the four corners of the grave and the body lowered into it with the head to the north. Klass claims that the burning of the camphor symbolizes cremation.[168]

Although cremation was the most common method of disposing of the dead among Vaishnavite Hindus in nineteenth century India, burial was practised by the Kabir Panthi and Ramanandi sects, by Shivites such as the Sannyasi Brahmins and the Siva Narayani (Sieunaraini), and by Muslims. While not expressly forbidden by law, it is probable that the Vaishnavite custom of cremation of the dead body on a pyre before disposing the ashes into flowing rivers or the sea was discouraged by the estates' management who did not want to encourage incendiary practices on their properties. Thus Bisnauth notes that the estates encouraged burial by providing specially designated cemeteries, and in some instances even provided coffins for the immigrants.[169] Not only in Guyana, but also in other colonies, e.g., Jamaica, Trinidad, and Fiji, the Hindus adopted the practice of burying their dead.[170] While this caused them to alter their funerary practices to suit the cultural demands of the elites, it does seem that they adapted by falling back on their own cultural traditions rather than borrowing from the Creoles. For some of their burial customs outlined above, e.g., the careful preparation of the deceased's body, and offerings including lighted camphor lamps, incense, drink and money, resemble in part those of the Sannyasi Brahmanic tradition described by Dubois at the beginning of the nineteenth century.[171] This, therefore, is more in accord with the process of Brahmanization which Veer and Vertovec observe than creolization as Rodney suggested.[172] Such issues did not pose a problem for the Muslims who traditionally buried their dead.

After the burial they returned to their dwellings and performed the necessary ablutions to purify themselves and their garments contaminated by the touch of the deceased, or by mixing with those who were polluted. Special purificatory rites, Brahmanic in origin, were held on the third, eighth or tenth, and thirteenth days after death. In keeping with Indian traditions, those of the third day (*dudh mukhi*), signifying the return to earth of the departed soul and its assumption of a new form, would have involved the cleansing of the house, washing of all household linen and clothes, and the throwing away of all earthenware used for cooking and storing water. Immigrants belonging to the Siva Narayani (Sieunaraini) sect held a special wake on this occasion. According to Ross: "When midnight is passed the Mahant takes some very fine ashes, sprinkles them over a small space on the floor and covers it over with a basket-like awning . . . At five o'clock the

190

*Cultural
Power,
Resistance,
and
Pluralism*

Mahant arouses them. With great solemnity he lifts the awning . . . Whatever marks are visible give indication as to the form which the transmigrated spirit will take".[173]

On the eighth or tenth day, flowers and jewels were removed from the bereaved. The widow's jacket was forcibly torn at the back. The *tali*, in the case of Tamils, was severed from her neck and from thereon she was recognized as a widow. After this, oil was rubbed on the heads of all the mourners to purify them before eating. Public mourning terminated with a feast to friends and relatives in the name of the dead. Life was restored to normalcy after the final purificatory rite on the thirteenth day.[174]

In India the tombs of some Sannyasi Brahmins were visited by pilgrims from different parts of the country who brought offerings and made sacrifices.[175] There is some evidence of a similar phenomenon in Guyana where in 1888, for instance, it was reported that Indians from all parts of the country queued on Sundays on the sideline between Plantations Providence and Herstelling on the east bank of Demerara to visit the tomb of an Indian man, Syne Babboo, who had been dead for many years and was buried at Herstelling. Because he was reputed to have lived a very devout life, the Indians put great faith in him and went to ask his spirit to do something for them. One Sunday, a grand feast was held at the graveside by an Indian couple in honour of their infant whom they named after Babboo.[176]

As in India, the immigrants practised ancestor veneration. On certain days, in order to appease the spirits of the dead, they would send in the name of the deceased large quantities of cooked rice and other food to all their friends and neighbours, no matter how numerous, and make presents to the poor.[177] They also sprinkled rum about the graves of their dead relatives, although in his usual scoffing manner Scoles asserted that ". . . as a rule the coolie prefers to use his rum more to excite the *living* than to pacify the *dead*".[178] Dube notes that in India during the *Petramasa* fortnight, water is offered to the ancestor spirits.[179] In Guyana rum was evidently substituted for water and may, to some extent, have represented a cultural borrowing from the Creoles who also tended to sprinkle rum on the ground in reverence of ancestral spirits (*jumbi*). For the most part, however, the Indians adhered to traditional cultural beliefs and practices related to death, even though some elements of Creole culture, in particular the wake, were incorporated. But the Creole wake was the last thing the cultural elites would have wanted the Indians to adopt. Thus even in the process of acculturation, there was a strong orientation towards cultural resistance to the dominant Anglo-Creole norm.

Social Organization

Already several references have been made to caste considerations as
they affected the cultural behaviour of the Indian immigrants. Given
the diverse regional and social backgrounds of the immigrants, it is not
surprising that they represented a vast array of caste groups at different
levels of the Indian caste hierarchy. According to Smith, 13.6 percent
were Brahmins and other high castes, 30.1 percent were from agricultural castes, 8.7 percent from artisan castes, and 31.1 percent low castes
and outcastes. There were also 16.3 percent Muslims and 0.1 percent
Christians.[180] Because they had been introduced to be agricultural labourers on the plantations, it was in the interest of the planters to
recruit people who were suited to the onerous tasks characteristic of
plantation labour. By a process of trial and error, the planters were
able to determine the suitability of Indian labourers along caste lines.

It was generally thought that the low castes and outcastes (pariahs)
produced the best plantation labourers, while the artisan and cultivator castes provided moderately good labourers. On the other hand,
high-caste people were considered the worst labourers. Indeed as late
as 1894, the Executive Council of the colony opined that high caste
labourers were not desirable. There were, however, some exceptions
to these general categorizations. For instance, several people from artisan, cultivator and other so-called 'middle-caste' groups made either
excellent labourers, e.g., the *Kewat (Keot)* and *Kori (Koree)*; or alternatively, poor labourers, e.g., the *Dhuniya (Dhooniah)*. Some low-caste
groups also furnished poor labourers, e.g., the *Dhobi* (washermen).
Likewise, high-caste men sometimes proved to be good labourers, e.g.,
the *Tiwari (Tewor)* and the *Rajwar (Rajowar)*.[181]

There is no doubt that the idea of caste was retained by the Indian
immigrants in the completely different social environment of plantation Guyana during the nineteenth century, though it is evident that it
lost its apparent rigidity. One contemporary writer, E.A.V. Abraham,
claimed that "The new Coolie believes in caste and pretentiously sticks
to its tenets for his first years in the Colony . . . But after residing for a
time, he sees here that caste only means,—'That man is a Chumar, and
therefore I am a better man because I am a Brahmin'".[182]

The conditions which allowed the evolution and perpetuation of
the caste system in India did not exist in Guyana. The very act of
leaving India meant a loss of caste, although this could be regained if
on their return the emigrants underwent a purification ceremony
which involved the *panchgavya*----the five products of the sacred cow: a
mixture of milk, clarified butter, curds, urine and dung.[183] Moreover,
no effort was made to preserve caste distinctions either at the emigration depots in Calcutta and Madras, or on board ship during the

192

*Cultural
Power,
Resistance,
and
Pluralism*

voyage. All the immigrants were huddled together and were forced to partake of the same food and drink irrespective of caste.[184]

Similarly, in the colony itself, no recognition was accorded to caste prescriptions and proscriptions either by the host society in general or by the estates' management in particular. The immigrants were housed in barracks without reference to caste affiliation and had to use the same cooking and eating facilities. The organization of labour on the estates in gangs composed of individuals from different castes further prevented caste segregation and also prevented occupational segregation by caste as was customary in India. It was not in the interest of the plantations to foster the re-establishment of caste groupings, if only to forestall the possibility of easy combinations among the immigrants. Proprietors and managers deliberately chose men speaking three or four different languages from different areas and caste groups to prevent any such combination.[185]

Such conditions which fostered interaction across caste boundaries would have implied an abrogation of caste concepts governing pollution. According to Schwartz, most of these concepts are included in proscriptive regulations based on commensal, sexual and physical interaction. These regulations and their proscriptive counterparts serve to isolate the different caste groups from each other as well as to insulate these groups from excessive interaction.[186] Similarly, Dube notes that the *jatis*, which are the real units or groupings of the caste system, do not dine together, whilst intermarriage between them is prohibited. Each *jati* is subdivided into several 'sub-castes' which are endogamous and are, for all practical purposes, independent groups by themselves. Consequently, there is a permanent social distance between these 'sub-castes'.[187]

Conditions in the plantation environment, however, did not permit such clear-cut separation of individuals from different castes either for purposes of labour, residence, or for cooking and eating. On the contrary, local conditions were more conducive to a dissolution of the idea of caste, even in terms of sexual relations and intermarriage. Hence, people of different castes could be seen side by side in a railway carriage "enjoying the comfort and economy of this mode of travelling to different sugar estates without offence to their conscience". Similarly, "Leila, who belongs to [the *Dhobie* (washerman)] caste, actually refuses to wash and iron the clothes of his fellow country people".[188] Superficially it seemed that the Indian immigrants mixed without distinction, ate and drank freely together, and intermarried and cohabited across caste boundaries without regard to rank. Indeed in a few rare instances they even married across racial boundaries, to Negroes, Chinese and Portuguese.[189] "They live to learn that in Rome one must do as the Romans do."[190]

It would be erroneous, however, to suggest that, since local conditions seemed to foster a dissolution, caste lost its significance and meaning to the Indian immigrants. It is true that the system of employment, promotion, and reward on the plantations further compromised the traditional prestige notions of caste. For the former were made largely on the basis of merit and/or patronage, and generally without reference to caste considerations. But the importance of caste as a status demarcator was reflected in the reluctance of high-caste Indians to take orders from their lower-caste 'inferiors' who might occupy supervisory positions such as 'drivers' (work-gang foremen) on the plantations. The plantations' management themselves were not unaware of the importance of caste among the Indian labourers, though they tried to avoid adhering to it. Yet by their tendency to favour the employment of low-caste Indians in preference to their 'superiors' they lent credibility to the idea of caste, albeit in an inverse and perverse manner. Quite apart from the reputation of low-caste Indians as better labourers, they were preferred because of management's fear of the leadership potential of high-caste men. This is a clear indication of the continued importance of caste status in the alien social environment. Surgeon-General Comins noted: "As a general rule, in all strikes involving insubordination or threatened disturbances, the instigators are coolies of high caste who, however, do not appear prominently in the matter, other immigrants being put forward and made to figure as leaders".[191] One clear instance of the continued influence of high-caste people over their fellows was the determination displayed by the Indians of Plantation Skeldon in Berbice in March 1875 to prevent a high-caste man from being flogged in fulfilment of his sentence by the court for assaulting the head overseer. Armed police had to be dispatched to ensure that the man was punished.[192] Similarly, as in Trinidad, Brahmins could abstain from work and obtain the performance of their tasks by their 'god-children'. They were also reputedly supported by contributions from their fellow immigrants.[193] One suspects, however, that not all Brahmins were accorded that kind of reverence and deference, but only the religious officials (*pandits* and *gurus*).

Intermarriage and cohabitation across caste boundaries were rendered virtually unavoidable and commonplace by the severe shortage of women among the Indian immigrants. As we have seen, polyandry was prevalent, and women could change mating partners freely.[194] In such circumstances, proscriptions against sexual intercourse and intermarriage across caste boundaries were blatantly ignored as men tried to secure whichever female they could.

Notwithstanding such permissive sexual behaviour in the plantation environment, caste prohibitions against these practices were not

194

Cultural
Power,
Resistance,
and
Pluralism

completely forgotten. Such inter-caste marriages and sexual unions apparently held good only for as long as the parties were in the colony, but were said to terminate on their return home: "The women go one way, and the men another way".[195] Some Indians avoided this by leaving their wives in the colony and returning home alone. One man was reported to have said: "I cannot take my wife home for they will not receive her as she is a Chamar, and I am a Brahmin. Let her remain here, and when I come back I will live with her again".[196] One wonders, however, if given the greater degree of freedom which Indian women enjoyed in the colony, the decision to remain was not in many instances theirs rather than their husbands.

Even in the permissive environment of Guyana there was a minority of Indians who tried to adhere strictly to caste regulations against interaction in those aspects of life in which this was possible. There was a fine example in a law case before a magistrate in 1876 when an Indian man objected to the idea of legal dispensation for his daughter to marry a low-caste fellow. According to the father: "He is a low fellow and not fit to be married to the girl, he is a Doberwallah [washerman] . . . and I am a cowminder which is far higher than him----he shall not have her".[197] The old man was no doubt not simply objecting to the idea of inter-caste marriage, but more importantly to the idea of his daughter marrying 'down' (hypogamy), a feature which is strictly prohibited even in parts of India where intermarriage is permitted.[198] How representative this man was of the Guyanese Indians, however, is not known, but Vertovec notes that hypogamy and hypergamy (marrying 'up') became widespread in Trinidad, though the source he cites suggests that it was essentially male hypogamy.[199]

There has been a lively debate among sociologists as to whether the Indian immigrants attempted to upgrade themselves by 'passing' for higher caste people. It is argued that since they emigrated largely as individuals, and not as groups or families, it was relatively easy to 'up-caste' themselves without being found out. Smith and Jayawardena point out that those who dared to do so, even if their contemporaries disbelieved them, had only to weather some sneering and gossip which decreased with the passage of time.[200] Klass, however, doubts whether caste passing was done since it would have been quite difficult for such persons to get away with it----to behave consistently like a man of a higher caste to which he did not belong without being discovered.[201]

These sociological speculations lack the benefit of historical perception and evidence. Most Indian immigrants in the nineteenth century migrated on a temporary basis with the objective of returning home after accumulating sufficient savings to justify their voluntary exile. To people who thus intended to return to their families, relatives and friends in the not-too-distant future, the idea of 'up-casting' themselves was quite meaningless regardless of whether or not they could avoid detection. 'Passing' would have benefitted only those who decided to settle permanently and wished to upgrade their status within the immigrant community. Such a decision would have to have been made prior to, or very soon after, arrival. Very few immigrants would have been prepared to do so at that stage. At the same time, however, one must acknowledge that the individual nature of immigration did present scope for 'passing', which by the disparate nature of the caste categories in the new environment and the laxity of social sanctions would have rendered it not too difficult to get away with it even if detected. But the immigrants' perception of a temporary sojourn away from home was a critical factor which would have restricted the extent to which caste 'passing' would be practised.

Although it is quite clear that caste practices and the adherence to caste regulations and taboos were adversely affected in the plantation environment, the idea of caste was kept alive by the steady influx of fresh immigrants from India. There is no doubt that first-generation immigrants never forgot caste though they may have been lax in their observance of its prescriptions and proscriptions. But Comins may have been correct in his view that if immigration were stopped the idea of caste would either be dissolved within fifty years or radically altered from its parent tradition. Indeed as he wrote (1890-91), the alterations were already patently obvious. Second generation Indians did not seem to pay much attention to caste observances, while even adult immigrants after a long period in the colony showed significant changes in their behaviour.[202]

Notwithstanding such apparent modifications and relaxations in caste practices, the idea of caste distinctions still persisted. Bronkhurst observed that: "One of the Hindu labourers in this colony, belonging to the Vellalan caste, nearly lost everything he possessed for losing his caste by eating in a Pariah-man's house, but money alone enabled him to regain it".[203] This represented a significant watering down of the penance required for regaining caste, but it demonstrated how important the idea of caste still was. This was endorsed by Josa who pointed out that "The fear of losing caste is the greatest deterrent to the Hindu joining Christianity. He would have to lose all".[204] The idea of caste, diluted as it may have been, evidently remained a key mechanism for enforcing ethnic group cohesion and solidarity in the alien plantation environment. It seems obvious that an informal redefinition of caste regulations had taken place which was fully recognized and enforced by the majority of Hindus. Any one who transgressed those ran the risk of being ostracized in the Indian community.

Such a redefinition of caste regulations would necessarily have entailed a modification or simplification of the ranking system of the

196

*Cultural
Power,
Resistance,
and
Pluralism*

caste hierarchy itself to make it relevant to the new environmental situation. But making such a modification acceptable to the majority of Hindus from different geographic and linguistic regions of India would not have been easy. The practice of mixing people from different regions and caste backgrounds undoubtedly made caste regroupings somewhat difficult.

Since, however, conditions in the colony led to a breakdown in pollution proscriptions governing commensality and intermarriage among persons of different castes, it is most likely that caste regroupings were facilitated to some extent by the fact that *jatis* of comparable status in different regions of India often share a common generic name and title.[205] Consequently, although in the home environment there is no intermarriage or dining together among these *jatis* or their subdivisions (sub-castes), a modified version of caste categories could be established in Guyana based on the coming together of people from *jatis* of similar status and title. Indeed, in Trinidad, Niehoff has found a ranking system of castes which reflects that of North India quite well.[206] Klass similarly observes that "whatever opinions might be held in India on the subject, the Kahar of Amity [in Trinidad] considers himself a member of the Kahar 'nation' of Trinidad as a whole, which in turn he considers part of the Kahar 'nation' of India".[207]

The retention of the idea of caste among the Indian immigrants did not, however, signify a retention of the functional aspects of caste in traditional Indian terms in so far as they related to corporate groupings characterized by residential segregation, occupational specialization, economic interdependence, caste endogamy, and regulations governing purity and pollution; but rather a retention of the notion of status, prestige and hierarchy derived from Indian caste. According to Klass, "Prestige, ceremonial rights, the criteria of the ranking system— all derive primarily from India".[208] Caste could not be retained with its traditional ramifications in the plantation environment. The restoration of the concept of caste in the colony was clearly not an attempt to reconstitute Indian social structure in Guyana. Rather caste was used as a frame of reference for the social reorganization of the Indian immigrant community. Writing for Surinam, Speckmann asserts that:

> The basis for a restoration of the caste structure was the fact that every immigrant knew his own caste, and sometimes even claimed to belong to a higher one. Since the people came from different districts, not every caste name possessed significance for the whole group. The caste hierarchy, which gradually reformed, based itself on a few important caste groups . . . But it was no longer possible to speak of the existence of castes in the native sense . . . The fact that the caste system in India functioned as a point of reference did not make its restoration in the new country any less incomplete and defective.[209]

The most feasible and commonly acceptable method of re-establishing a ranking system of the modified caste categories in the plantation environment was no doubt with reference to the *varna* system. Hindu society in India is popularly divided into a fivefold hierarchy of *varna* in the following order: *Brahmins* (priests), *Kshatriyas* (warriors), *Vaishyas* (traders), *Shrudras* or *Sudras* (servants and labourers), and *Untouchables* (pariahs or outcastes). The first three are the 'twice-born' and are alone entitled to undergo the ceremony of *upanayana* which constitutes spiritual rebirth, to study the *Vedas* (scripture), and to perform the Vedic ritual on certain occasions. Although, as Srinivas notes, the *varna* classification is an imprecise one for a clear understanding of the Indian caste system, it does furnish an all-India framework for arranging the *jatis*, and it represents a scale of values for the *jatis* which facilitates the spread of a uniform Hindu culture.[210] Fox further observes that this uniformity emerges from the common ideological acceptance and mechanical duplication of the *varna* models in different regions.[211]

This all-India framework provided the basis on which the modified local caste categories could achieve a uniform and traditionally sanctioned status system whereby old ideas of prestige and rank derived from traditional caste affiliation could attain significance within the immigrant community in Guyana. Speckmann agrees that though the caste system proper did not survive the migration, "the status differentiation in the new country was nevertheless founded on the basic [*varna*] pattern of caste system in India".[212] This meant that ideological concepts of status and hierarchy were retained: Brahmins were still acknowledged as the leaders of Hindu society and Chamars and others were at the other end of the scale.[213]

Although the concept of caste was denounced by the cultural elites of the host society, that society itself had been structured with certain caste-like features, not based on socio-religious ideology as in India, but on principles of 'race' and colour. The structure of the host society was essentially a graduated hierarchy premised on the twin myths of white superiority and black inferiority, which accordingly placed whites at the apex and blacks at the base, with an intermediate mixed or coloured category. According to Berreman, a caste system is "a hierarchy of endogamous divisions in which membership is hereditary and permanent". It is characterized by inequality both in status and in access to goods and services, interdependence of the subdivisions, restricted contacts among them, occupational specialization, and a degree of cultural distinctiveness.[214] These characteristics were very much present in the creole society of Guyana after emancipation, although it was by no means as rigid as Indian caste society.

This meant that the Indian immigrants left one type of caste society and entered another, albeit with a different ideological basis. In fact, the myth of racial superiority which underlined the Creole social hier-

198

*Cultural
Power,
Resistance,
and
Pluralism*

archy was not unknown in Indian castedom. Ghurye notes that there exists a rough correlation in Uttar Pradesh between social gradation and physical differentiation. The Brahmins are said to have retained close similarity with the ancient Aryans who were characterized as being 'long-headed' and 'fine-nosed'. At the other end of the scale, the *Chamar* and *Pasi* are said to resemble the aboriginal peoples whose chief characteristic was a broad nose.[215] These features have a striking similarity to the physical characteristics of the whites and blacks respectively in Guyanese and Caribbean society. It is also significant that the majority of the Indian immigrants had their origins in Uttar Pradesh.

Similarly, Béteille has subdivided South Indian society into three segments: the Brahmins, non-Brahmins, and Adi-Dravidas (untouchables). He points out the striking physical differences which relate to status:

> In the popular image the Brahmin is regarded not only as fair, but also sharp-nosed, and as possessing, in general, more refined features. Although some non-Brahmins also have features of this kind, they are rare among the cultivating and artisan castes who constitute the bulk of non-Brahmins in Sripuram [a South Indian village]. Among the Adi-Dravidas fair skin-color is so conspicuous by its absence that normally a Brahmin would be mistaken for a Palla or a Paraiya. These differences are of significance because fair skin-color and features of a certain type have a high social value not only in Sripuram, but in Tamil society in general, as indeed in the whole of India. The Brahmins are extremely conscious of their fair appearance and often contrast it with the 'black' skin color of the Kallas, or the Adi-Dravidas.[216]

Hindus were also influenced by the popular religious epics, especially the *Ramayana,* in which demons (*Rawan,* et al.) were dark-skinned, short, and with 'negroid' or Dravidian features.[217]

This social background undoubtedly assisted the Indian immigrants to adjust to the social colour hierarchy of the host society. This adjustment, however, had to be rationalized in their minds by reference to the notions of caste status with which they were familiar. The pale-faced, thin-nosed, dominant white element of creole society was labelled by the same term applied to the British ruling 'caste' in India—*Jati-heen,* persons void of caste. The broad-nosed, black-skinned Negroes were regarded as *Kale* or *Karroon jat*—persons of the lowest or most degraded caste, not fit to be associated with, i.e., akin to the Untouchables. "They belong to 'Ibliss'."[218]

The caste system was not transmitted to, and retained, in the local plantation environment with its traditional authenticity in terms of strict adherence to the elaborate rules and regulations governing the interrelations between caste groups and the ritual practices associated with caste ideology. Rather in the alien environment, the retention of caste notions centred around traditional concepts of prestige and status. A modified version of caste categories was established with a ranking system derived from the *varna* scheme which fostered a uniform ideological and socio-religious base understood by, and acceptable to, Indian immigrants in general. The concept of caste served as a reference point for the social reorganization of the Indian immigrant community in Guyana. But it also provided a mechanism for adjustment on a 'rational' basis to the existing framework of the host society. It did not facilitate the integration of the Indians within the hierarchical system of creole society, but provided them with a comprehensible criterion for defining their place as a separate ethnic group in relation to the traditional elements of creole society. The retention of the idea of caste was thus vital for fostering a sense of corporate Indian identity within the colonial society, and furnished the Indian immigrants with an ideological and structural framework for resisting the cultural power of the social elites.

Leisure

Leisure time is directly related to work. For the whole of the postemancipation nineteenth century, most Indian immigrants were indentured or contract labourers on the plantations. This meant that by law they were required to work for five days a week failing which they were liable to be charged with a *criminal* offence. In theory this implied that the two days of the weekend were theirs to do as they wished. In addition, the immigrants were given a choice of whether or not to accept the time-off offered by the colonial public holidays— New Year's day, Easter Monday, Whit Monday, Emancipation Monday, Christmas and Boxing days. Work on those days was purely voluntary; but since most of those were *Euro-Creole* religious holidays they represented a meaningless cultural imposition to the Indians which they resisted by opting to work to increase their earnings.[219] In practice, leisure time was far more restricted, and further circumscribed by pass laws which sought to prevent the unauthorized movement of the immigrants more than two miles from their estate. Since the indentured workers were legally required to complete five undefined tasks per week, several (particularly the weaker and incapacitated) found themselves working very long hours each day and into the weekend as well.

In addition, the estates themselves controlled the amount of spare time the immigrants had. The 1870 commission of inquiry observed that instead of paying the workers on Saturday morning which would leave them the rest of the day free, it gradually became the practice for some estates to pay them on Saturday evening which severely curtailed their free time.[220] It was even worse during the grinding season when workers employed in the factory averaged fifteen hours a day (instead

200

*Cultural
Power,
Resistance,
and
Pluralism*

Indian
musicians

of the statutory ten), and occasionally could be called on to work
continuously for as long as eighteen or even twenty hours in extreme
cases.[221] There was in such circumstances hardly any time for sleep, let
alone for leisure. It was only when the Indians left the estates and became self-employed that they could regulate their time to allow for
leisure. The system of indenture, therefore, legally vested the planters
with the cultural power to control and regulate the leisure time of
the immigrants.

Short though their leisure time was, the Indians engaged in a variety
of recreative pastimes. They generally found great pleasure in congre-
gating round a *Pandit* (or *Mullah* in the case of Muslims) to listen to
the tales or sacred books read by him. For the majority Hindus, this
was very much in keeping with growing ascendancy of the Vaishnavite *bhakti* variant of Hinduism[222] in the colony. Some Indians en-

gaged in athletic exercises, dancing, singing, and playing musical instruments such as the flute, *saranga* (Indian guitar), drums, etc.[223] As a rule, music formed an integral part of all Hindu cultural activities whether solemn or gay, and was often a key feature of entertainment in the evenings after work. To the Euro-Creole ear, the number of tunes played seemed limited and characterized by a constant repetition of the same notes, and the beat of the drum seemed to stand out: ". . . one that is dinging in your ear . . . the tom-tom".[224]

As in Fiji and Trinidad, *Ramlila (Ramleela)* theatrical performances were held especially on special occasions such as weddings and birth ceremonies. These were "very effective . . . representing various episodes in the ancient history of India".[225] Religious themes formed a major part of these performances. All the deeds of Krishna, Ram, Siva, Durga and other Hindu deities were portrayed on stage. These performances were held after work (or on weekends) at night and often continued until early morning. The spectators were fully involved in the proceedings and reacted visibly with grief or joy according to the drama. They usually demonstrated their pleasure with the performance by generously recompensing the *maistry* (producer) for his efforts.[226] These performances provide further evidence of the consolidation and homogenization of Hinduism in Guyana around the Vaishnavite *bhakti* tradition.

On Sundays, visits were exchanged between those living on different estates, and dinners were frequently hosted by the more wealthy immigrants at which from 100 to 150 persons could be present. Seated in the yard, they would be served with rice and curry on plantain leaves.[227] But the feast put on by Ghoolmahumad Khan, the head of the Muslim community in Georgetown, in October 1898, for the poor people of all ethnic groups in a building adjoining the Queenstown mosque, was undoubtedly exceptional. About 800-900 people were present, the vast majority (about 700) being Indians, both Muslim and Hindu. The feast began at 11.00 a.m. and lasted until 6.00 p.m. during which the gathering was regaled with baked *ghee pourri* (Indian bread) and curry. One Punjabi immigrant is reported to have amazingly consumed fifty-five *pourris*, equivalent to about 120 pounds of flour, and six pounds of curry![228]

Fortune-telling was very popular among the Indian immigrants especially on Sunday mornings. Indian fortune-tellers could be seen parading the streets and visiting different houses of their countrymen with bags hanging down their shoulders in which the presents were put. They had *kudu-kei* (small drums) in their hands, which were beaten with thumb and forefinger "to keep time whilst [in the view of one cynical observer] their imagination is busy with the invention of some foolish and taking falsehood".[229]

202

*Cultural
Power,
Resistance,
and
Pluralism*

The Anglo-Creole passion for horse-racing was readily adopted by the Indians. "Race days afford great enjoyment, and they flock to the course in great numbers." Such days were practically holidays for those residing on or near the sugar estates in the vicinity of the race-course. Very significantly, race days permitted light-hearted interaction with people of other ethnic groups, especially Creoles, which aided the process of integration made easier by a liberal consumption of alcohol and excessive gambling. Likewise young local-born (creole) Indian boys learnt, and became very fond of, the imperial sport of cricket (and creole games like 'tip-cat' and 'marbles') by playing in the plantation 'negro yard' with Creole and Chinese children.[230] Comins reported in 1892 that about fifteen or sixteen creole Indian youths at Plantation Port Mourant, Corentyne, asked for a pass to plant rice on their lands, but instead spent the time playing cricket matches. When fined $3.00 or seven days' imprisonment, they opted for the latter. But by the 1890s, "many of the sons of East Indians born in the colony play cricket regularly. On Saturday afternoon on most estates a game can be seen going on, the players being partly Creole cooly boys and partly 'black', and the game is played with great spirit. Many managers encourage them to play, and some even get up rival matches with neighbouring estates".[231]

Cricket was also one of the principal sporting activities, along with horse-racing and athletics (walking and running races, and high-jumping) organized by the estates' management to treat their workers (of all ethnic groups) to dinner in order to celebrate the success of the sugar harvest. Usually a day was set aside after the grinding season (sometime in January or February), and the most industrious and well-behaved workers were rewarded with medals and gifts of sugar, rum, rice, etc. Still, a day of relaxation for the workers, even with a cricket match on hand, did not imply a relaxation of social barriers as white estate personnel often remained aloof and played cricket matches among themselves.[232]

Thus while cricket did promote a measure of social and cultural integration between Indians and other subordinate ethnic groups, its integrative role was hampered by white (racial) resistance. Specifically among the Indians, in the absence of any desire on their part to acquire British culture via colonial education or Christianity (see chapter 8), their voluntary participation in cricket offered the best chance of assimilating the dominant elite cultural values. But there is no evidence that cricket did promote value consensus among them based on the idea of the superiority of British culture, for they did not adopt British sports with a view to achieving social respectability or mobility within the colonial social fabric to which they were marginal. Yet, as it was for the Creoles, for the young Indian male, too, cricket (the white

man's game) provided a golden opportunity to prove a vital point.
Not only was it a means of entertainment, but also it allowed unfettered self-expression through which the Indian could exhibit his prowess and natural ability free from the artificial constraints imposed on
him in everyday life by the indenture system. He could demonstrate
that he was as good as, if not better than, any other man (whether
white or black) on the cricket field. This was a major attraction of the
game; and he played it without seeking social rewards in the form of
respectability from, or incorporation in, the alien colonial society.

Race days were not the only times that the Indians indulged in
potent alcoholic drinks, narcotics, and gambling. From as early as the
1850s there were frequent complaints about their increasing addiction
to alcohol and resultant intoxication, as well as to gaming and gambling mainly in the form of cock-fighting and the 'three-card trick'.[233]
Indian immigrants were frequently seen, especially in the rural areas
on Saturday nights and Sundays, staggering from one side of the road
to the other, and yelling, or lying like logs by the road side in various
stages of drunkenness.[234] These 'vices' might be interpreted as evidence
of creolization. The use of alcoholic beverages, for instance, is prohibited by both Hinduism and Islam. But even if it was too much to
expect the immigrants working hard, long hours on estates where rum
was manufactured, and living in close proximity to Portuguese rum
shops illegally open on Sundays,[235] to resist the temptation to indulge
in some rum drinking, the use (and abuse) of alcohol was by no means
novel to them; and likewise one wonders about gaming and gambling.

The Indians in fact took their own techniques of alcohol manufacture to the colony. Coconut toddy was obtained from the long,
sheathed flower bud of the coconut tree. The bud was tied in three
places soon after it appeared in order to prevent it expanding, and its
tip/point was cut off. It was then beaten with a hard wooden mallet to
crush the flowers inside the *spatha* (sheath) and to promote a flow of
sap before being bent downwards and fixed in that position. After a
few days a round earthen vessel or calabash was suspended underneath
to catch the liquid as it exuded from the bud as a thin slice was cut off
the point each day. A good tree could yield from four to five pints
daily. After a few months the drawing was stopped since it exhausted
the tree. For teetotallers, the best time to drink toddy was said to be
early morning before it fermented and became intoxicating. Its taste
was described as 'peculiar' and no doubt according to the state of
fermentation was compared to milk, cider and champagne.[236]

Although in India, toddy manufacture was the preserve of the Sha-
nar caste, in Guyana the immigrants hardly paid any attention to such
restrictive caste specializations[237] especially since the sale of toddy was
lucrative. The colonial authorities, however, considered toddy a dan-

204

*Cultural
Power,
Resistance,
and
Pluralism*

gerous drink, although very oddly rum manufacture did not arouse similar concerns. Licences were thus imposed with expressed intention of *restricting* its sale.[238] This differs significantly from the licences imposed on the retail of spirits generally (rum, wines, etc.) which were primarily *revenue raising* taxes rather than attempts to reduce the amount of alcohol sold. Those retail spirit licences were also designed to preserve the stranglehold of Portuguese traders on this highly lucrative economic sector. The official attitude to the sale of coconut toddy thus smacks of hypocrisy, and no doubt the toddy licences were likewise aimed at preserving the near monopoly of the Portuguese over the sale of alcoholic beverages.

Perhaps a more serious indulgence was the use and abuse of narcotics especially *ganja/ganga* (*marijuana*). Some Indians also used opium,[239] but this was far more commonplace among the Chinese. The abuse of *ganja* was thought to have resulted in several cases of insanity, violence and even death, although some persons recognized that it was less harmful than rum.[240] Large quantities were imported from Britain, the United States, India and occasionally from Trinidad and Surinam (some was re-exported). These imports increased by nearly 900 percent from 2,456 pounds in 1860 to 21,760 pounds by 1883.[241] Although given the size of the Indian population, the consumption per capita was by no means high,[242] it did cause official concern. Thus as early as 1861 strict regulations were imposed to control its sale and use (along with opium), and these were made even more stringent in 1880 and 1889.[243] In addition the import duty which was fixed at eight cents per pound in the early 1850s was dramatically increased to $3.00, and again to $4.00 during the 1880s.[244] This caused a sharp reduction in the importation of *ganja* (and a loss of revenue for the government!). Between 1884 and 1891, a total of just 84,237½ pounds were imported.[245] But by then *ganja* was being grown by the Indians in the colony,[246] and there is some evidence of smuggling from abroad as well. Indeed a few enterprising Indians were prepared to go wherever good *ganja* could be obtained. In 1898, for instance, Abdool Simud was arrested and charged with smuggling nine pounds of *ganja* from Jamaica in a trunk with a false bottom. His objective was to see how it would fare in the local market with "the better prepared article from India". He was eventually discharged by the courts.[247]

It is evident that the Indians in their few hours of leisure and relaxation tried to recreate a lifestyle as nearly traditionally Indian as was possible within the plantation environment of Guyana. But as usual they had to contend not only with altered conditions in the colony, but also with the attitude of the elites who were prepared to use their cultural power to curb certain practices. Both of these factors influenced modifications in the cultural behaviour of the Indians. It is also very noticeable that since leisure activities were far less restricted by ethnic proscriptions than other areas of cultural life, there was greater scope in this sphere for adopting *creole* cultural practices and behaviour. The extent to which this was possible was of course conditioned by the amount of social contact between the Indians and members of the host society. But in so far as it did occur it did foster their cultural integration, though it is important to stress that this was rather peripheral to the core of Indian immigrant culture.

Summary

The transition from India to Guyana was difficult for the Indian immigrants both on account of the physical environment and the attitude of all sections of the host society. Living conditions on the estates under indenture were not only harsh (though perhaps no more so than in rural India), but also made it virtually impossible for the immigrants to organize themselves in accordance with the rules of their traditional caste system. The numerical disparity between the sexes played havoc with mating patterns and the institution of Indian marriage and family life. In addition, the immigrants found it extremely difficult to communicate with the locals and had to learn a new language to make themselves understood. On top of all this, as a subordinate ethnic group literally on the margins of the host society, they had to deal with the cultural power of the elites some of whom were intent on impressing on the Indians the need to change their ways and become 'civilized'.

Try as they did, therefore, to recreate a traditional way of life at a personal, familial and community level, circumstances under indenture wrought substantial cultural change. But that change essentially entailed a redefinition and reorganization of their traditional institutions and customs to produce a homogenized *Bhojpuri*-based culture, a process which was in fact to some extent accelerated with their establishment of free village settlements in the late nineteenth century. For the most part the Indians were successfully able to resist the cultural power exerted by the elites, while their limited contact with the Creole population minimized cultural assimilation at that level. Thus although British sports were adopted, particularly by the local-born Indians, and did encourage their social integration, such leisure activity did not promote value consensus around the idea of the superiority of white culture since they were not seeking social respectability as defined by the host society. For the most part, therefore, the Indians maintained their traditional value system and cultural patterns.

206

*Cultural
Power,
Resistance,
and
Pluralism*

A typical
East Indian
village

INDIAN BHOJPURI CULTURE:
Spiritual

While the focus of the previous chapter was on the temporal aspects of
Indian culture in Guyana, it was quite evident that there were very
many links with the spiritual aspects. Religion lay at the heart of
Indian culture. It sanctified everything in the individual's life from the
womb to the tomb, it regulated his or her day to day activities, it
sanctioned the gender roles laid down by society, and it underscored
the hierarchical social organization of the caste system by which everyone in the society knew their place and occupation in life. In this
chapter we shall focus on the Indian religious and other spiritual beliefs and practices, and on how they may have been altered in the new
environment which did not recognize some of the key social indices
that made them so omnipotent in India. Attention will also be paid to
the functions which they played in the new social context.

Religion

Coming from a vast geographical 'catchment' area within India, the
Hindu immigrants brought with them a wide variety of religious beliefs and practices. The minority Muslim immigrants were divided into
two major sects: *Sunnis* who, according to Bronkhurst, formed the
majority; and *Shiites*.[1] On the other hand, the majority Hindus were
divided into a large number of differing sects. According to Vertovec,
within the principal regions of North India alone from which most
originated were to be found several different strands of Hinduism.
Bengal, Bihar and Orissa were dominated by Shaktism, whose sects are
devoted to the Mother Goddess; eastern and western Uttar Pradesh by
Vaishnavism, whose sects are devoted to *Vishnu;* and centres like
Benares where Shivism, devoted to *Shiva,* is predominant.[2]

   According to Bronkhurst, nearly one third of the immigrants from
the Bengal Presidency and a few from the Madras Presidency were
Vaishnavites, while the rest (i.e., the majority) were Shivites. This

208

Cultural
Power,
Resistance,
and
Pluralism

would accord with Bisnauth who claims that Shivism, in the form of the Siva Narayani (Sieunaraini) sect, was by far the most popular religious expression of Hinduism among the Indian immigrants up to about 1917. This, he claims, is not only because many of its Chamar adherents went to Guyana, but because of all the variants of Hinduism in the colony, it was the best equipped to survive the shock of transplantation overseas. "This *bhakti* movement was tied to neither shrine nor holy place in India itself"—hence it could survive anywhere.[3] While there has been no reference to the presence of Shaktism in the colony, sociological research has revealed that Vaishnavism is most popular among the Indians in modern Guyana. Whether this means that Bronkhurst and Bisnauth are inaccurate, or that Vaishnavism later emerged as the dominant form of Hinduism, is not clear.

Part of the problem seems to lie in the fact that both the Vaishnavite and Shivite orientations of Hinduism had their own *bhakti* sects. This has enabled Vertovec to argue with equal persuasion as Bisnauth that it was Vaishnavism through its *bhakti* sects which became the dominant variant of Hinduism at an early stage throughout the southern Caribbean. There is no doubt though that *bhaktism*, whatever its affiliation, was indeed ideally suited for overseas Indians. This is because the *bhakti* ideals favoured egalitarianism, inter-caste fraternization and collective activity which, with the breakdown of traditional family and caste structures in the plantation environment, assumed tremendous significance to the immigrants. *Bhakti*-centred Hinduism, because of its ecumenical tendencies, transcended geographical and caste differences and provided the immigrants with a unified, homogenized religion in which they could all participate as equals.[4] These qualities accounted for its tremendous appeal in Guyana and elsewhere. But the problem still remains as to why, if Shivites were a numerical majority among the immigrants, Vaishnavism should have become dominant, whether before or after 1917. Further detailed research is required to resolve this issue.

What is clear is that Vaishnavism was an integral part of the homogenization of Hinduism in Guyana. But such religious homogenization did not occur without dissension. Bronkhurst alluded to rivalry between the Vaishnavites and Shivites who claimed supreme divinity for each deity.[5] In 1880, for instance, a dispute between two members of the *Kabir* and *Siva Narayani* ('Sieunarini' or 'Sir Narain' as it was reported in the local press) sects in Leguan broadened to involve the other members and their leaders.[6] Among the Vaishnavites themselves there were squabbles, quarrels, and even fights among different sects.[7] For as long as these sects remained vibrant, they would undoubtedly have delayed the "redefinition of Hinduism as one religion common to all Indians" of which Jayawardena has spoken,[8] despite the threat which (as we shall see) emanated from the activities of the Christian missionaries. It appears that the Muslims too remained divided for some time.[9]

Both *Vishnu* and *Siva* belong to the classical pantheon of Hindu deities. Among the Vaishnavites, *Vishnu* is worshipped in his *avatars* (incarnations) as *Ram* and *Krishna*.[10] In Guyana, as in India, sacrifice and prayer formed an essential part of Hindu worship.[11] Just as in Mauritius, much of Hindu worship took place at home and every Hindu family had a deity either in the front or back yard, or situated in a separate corner or room of their dwelling place. The early Hindu immigrants worshipped some gods or goddesses of their personal choice and pertaining to their own religious groups.[12] Community worship by Hindus is done in temples, while Muslims worship in mosques. It was some time, however, before permanent structures were erected for religious purposes. In 1870 there were only two buildings in Guyana which were readily identified as Hindu temples, one at Wakenaam island on the Essequibo river, the other on the Berbice river; and there was no mention of mosques at all. This did not mean that the Indian immigrants had abandoned all outward observance of their religions as some persons thought.[13] Rather, until they contemplated settling permanently in the colony, they built temporary structures, some roofless (*medeis*), others in the form of hut-temples (called *kutiyas* in Trinidad) on the plantations. Even so, as Vertovec observes, "this represented the growing establishment and consolidation of Hinduism" in the colony.[14]

The *medeis* were 'high places' or artificial mounds with 'altars' of brickwork around them. The insides were filled with pure earth. On this a sacred tree or grove and an image of the deity were placed. The *kutiyas* were very small and not designed to accommodate worshippers, who were required to congregate in an area just outside the entrance. The priest was generally the only person who entered the temple to perform his religious duties in the presence of the deity whose image stood at the lower end of the door in full view of the worshippers outside. There was generally no window for light or air, which meant that it was always dark except for the low light emitted from a small oil lamp placed before the image of the deity. Beyond those, there was just enough space to accommodate the temple utensils, the offerings and the officiating priest.[15]

The floor of the temple was always conspicuously clean. Indeed these hut-temples were considered so sacred by the Hindus that no unclean person could enter them without the preparatory ablutions. No sandals or boots were allowed either by priest or visitor. If any impurity were found, it was quickly removed by smearing the floor with a solution of cow-dung. Those proscriptions, however, did not

210

*Cultural
Power,
Resistance,
and
Pluralism*

A Hindu
temple
(Albouystown)

An Islamic
mosque
(Queenstown)

deter the arrogant Methodist missionary Bronkhurst from violating
the sanctity of the temples. He reported with pride in 1861 that he
went into one at Plantation Montrose on the east coast of Demerara
"without taking off my boots, and destroy[ed] an idol set up in the
lower end of the door".[16] This abuse of elite cultural power was something which the Indians had constantly to contend with and resist.

When Indian settlement began to assume a more permanent form,
larger temples and mosques were built either by individuals or by the
subscriptions of groups of immigrants. But since the colonial elites
regarded the Indian religions as pagan, they used their cultural power
to deny the immigrants any form of assistance to facilitate their traditional worship. Thus, for instance, when in 1886 some Muslims peti-
tioned the legislature (Court of Policy) for financial aid to erect a
mosque, they were refused although the Christian denominations
were supported out of the public revenues to which the Indians also
contributed as taxpayers. This setback did not deter the immigrants
who completed the construction of that mosque with their own resources in 1890.[17] With similar determination, other groups of Indians
in different parts of the colony were able to overcome such artificial
obstacles erected by the elites to build thirty-three temples and twenty-
nine mosques by 1893.[18] The comparatively high number of religious
places built by the minority Muslims signifies a greater degree of organization among them than the Hindus.

Ramdin observes that in Mauritius Hindu temples are quite different from those in India in the sense that they are seldom if ever
dedicated to one particular deity. The same seems to have been the
case in Guyana where Hindu temples were filled with many divine
images of various gods and goddesses made of brass, terracotta, or
painted by hand. Those which could stand it were washed morning
and evening, and decked with flowers. The most popular divine images were those of *Ganesh* with extended stomach, four arms, and
elephant's head; *Hanuman,* represented by a monkey holding its tail,
smeared with vermilion; and *Kali,* the female counterpart of *Siva,*
again with four arms holding *inter alia* a sword and a bleeding head,
and wearing a necklace of skulls.[19] These along with *Ram, Durga,
Krishna, Surya* and *Satyanarine* formed the pantheon of 'higher' gods.
But, as Josa noted, there were numerous lesser gods as well, no doubt
of a regional nature—testifying to diverse backgrounds of the immigrants. It is evident from the description of the popular divine images
above, however, that the religious traditions associated with the myr-
iad of lesser localized deities declined in favour of a smaller pantheon
of Sanskritic gods as the process of homogenization unfolded.[20]

Daily worship at the temple was performed by a solitary priest.[21]
On one occasion, his only congregation was his little girl. He was on

212

*Cultural
Power,
Resistance,
and
Pluralism*

his knees when the observer arrived, with his face down, uttering *mantras* (prayers) very rapidly. He had marked his body and forehead with a preparation of cow-dung and water. After a time, he rose and blew a shell horn whereupon the child brought a bowl of milk which he presented to the deity. Then he prostrated himself again uttering more prayers. When he rose and blew the horn again, the girl brought a bowl of flower petals which he also presented to the deity. Prostrating himself once more, he prayed while the child beat a gong. Then the service was concluded.[22]

Muslim worship at the mosques was naturally quite different: "They have their Imam who reads the prayers; the Khuteeb, who preaches the sermon or delivers an oration; and the Muezzin, who calls to prayer the 'faithful' followers of the Prophet".[23] Gillion makes the important observation that since Islam is less dependent than Hinduism on a particular social context, Muslim customs suffered less disruption through transplantation overseas. Thus in Fiji, as was undoubtedly the case in Guyana, "most of the religious duties and festivals were maintained, except for the *namaz* (prayers fives times a day), *pardah* (the seclusion of women), and the full observance of the fast of Ramazan"[24]—none of which the work regimen on the plantations would have permitted.

As a rule, when a Hindu appeared in public he bore on his forehead and arms symbols of his faith. When he passed a temple or a *guru*, expressions of reverence were seldom forgotten. The ceremonial of the morning was scrupulously practised and he omitted no part of the long routine of observances.[25] Prayer was an essential part of a Hindu's religious duties, and they were fond of saying their *mantras*.[26] Brahmins prayed at least twice daily. Hindu beggars continuously repeated the names of gods in the belief that they would gain merit.[27] Other acts of religious observance by Hindus were to plant poles with white calico flags in the ground and to place coconuts on the ground at night.[28]

Fasting was another important Hindu practice in Guyana. According to Bronkhurst, some fasted every Sunday and worshipped the deity *Surya;* others, to fulfil a vow, fasted on Monday and worshipped *Siva;* and so on. Still others might fast twice in the same week, or even on behalf of another person. In a Hindu fast, the person usually abstained for three days from anointing himself with oil, from sexual intercourse, from fish, everything 'fired', and ate only once a day. This must have significantly affected their ability to perform the strenuous tasks associated with plantation labour. The traditional religious custom/duty of giving food and raiment to the hungry and naked, and other benevolent acts such as building or endowing temples, were very much alive among the Hindus of Guyana. And there were also many professional mendicants among the immigrants who moved from house to house on the different estates.[29]

Perhaps the most painful acts of the Hinduism taken to Guyana by the Indians were those of *Krya Sutra* to propitiate *Siva*. The most notable form was the *charak puja*, the hook swinging ceremony which was held on the first Sunday of Aries.[30] This practice was widespread on Guyanese estates (though not in Trinidad[31]) during the early 1850s. A *chedil* was erected for this purpose. It consisted of a beam about forty or fifty feet high in an erect position, across the top of which was placed a transverse pole of smaller size. To each end of that was tied a rope which trailed to the ground on one side. To the shorter rope on the other side were attached two sturdy, smoothly pounded, sharp pointed hooks.[32]

The devotees were retained in a building nearby before being led out by *pujaries*, musicians, drummers, relatives and friends. Upon reaching the *chedil*, the devotee was put to lie, face down, while the hooks were thrust under the flesh on either side of the vertebrae below the shoulder blade. He was then suspended in mid-air where he swung round and round for as long as his strength would permit or his vow made necessary—roughly between ten and thirty times. After the ceremony the devotee retired and remained at home for days as further penance, and many valuable presents were given to him by his friends.[33] As many as ten or twelve might undergo this ceremony in one day. Not only did this practice disrupt the work routine on the plantations when individuals stayed away from work, but it also jarred the religious sensibilities of the cultural elites, in particular the missionaries. Besides, the social value embodied in this religious ritual—that of stoic endurance of pain and suffering for one's beliefs, no matter how vilified—ran counter to that of submission and subordination which the cultural elites sought to inculcate in the immigrants. There was quite clearly no way of instilling fear in a people who would voluntarily undergo and withstand such gruelling, self-inflicted pain. Consequently the elites used their cultural power to ban the ritual in 1853 on the grounds that it was "calculated greatly to blunt their [the Hindus'] feelings, and strengthen them in vice".[34]

It was the Christian missionaries who were in the vanguard of the assault by the cultural elites on Indian culture. Ironically the planters, who were very dependent on Indian labour, were not eager to displease their workers by prohibiting their religious practices, however abhorrent they considered them.[35] In any event the British Indian government exercised vigilance to ensure that the emigrants were allowed to practise their religions. But the Indian religions were constantly under attack from the missionaries, though they encountered resolute resistance from the immigrants. Frustrated missionaries per-

214

Cultural
Power,
Resistance,
and
Pluralism

petually complained about the Indians' unyielding adherence to their religious beliefs.[36] One Indian told Bronkhurst: "You are a great deceiver, you come here and tell the people that our religion is a false religion, etc. . . . It is not so, our religion is the only true religion and yours a false one. Our religion has always been accounted to be true, in all ages . . ."[37] Sacred books such as the *Vedas, Puranas, Ramayana* and *Koran* were imported from India by local booksellers and sold to the Indians. But this hardly accounts for the tenacity of Hinduism and Islam among them, since most were illiterate both in English and in their native languages.[38]

It was mainly the Hindu and Muslim priests who were instrumental in countering the missionary assault and preserving the traditional faiths. Muslim *imams* went further and even tried to convert Hindus and Creoles; and if Bronkhurst can be believed, they were successful.[39] (It is probable that there may have been some lapsed Muslims among the Africans whose faith may have been revived by the Indian *imams*.) The social reality of indentureship did not make them feel in any way inferior to the white man. The *imam* was supremely self-confident and walked with pride and dignity, even arrogance. A white voluminous turban enveloped his head, a long thin white close-fitting coat his body, continuations of the same material fitting close around the ankles completed his outfit, with the exception of his loosely fitting leather slippers or sandals. He preferred to live in a detached wattle cottage in a secluded spot on the estate, and was reputed to hold women in 'beautiful scorn'.[40]

Among the Hindus the task of organizing cultural resistance to the missionaries and maintaining a flourishing religion was performed by so-called 'Coolie Parsons' (*pandits*) and *gurus*. At first *pandits* were not restricted to the Brahmin caste; indeed Bronkhurst observed a considerable amount of rivalry among priests from different sects,[41] and as both Speckmann and Jayawardena found in Surinam and Fiji, Brahmin *pandits* would have been initially reluctant to perform rites for immigrants of the lower castes. But they soon changed their attitude and catered to needs of the entire Hindu immigrant community.[42] Robert Moore notes that by the mid-1870s more Brahmins were going to Guyana, pushed largely by bad harvests in India. This enabled them to consolidate both Hinduism and their own position at the apex of the religious hierarchy;[43] and that in turn promoted what Veer and Vertovec call the 'Brahmanization process' through which "Brahmans and Brahmanic ideas have come to have exclusive dominance over [Hindu] ritual activity in the Caribbean . . ."[44] Thus by the late nineteenth century Brahmin *pandits* were regarded as the Hindu high priests; and no matter how poor, their Hindu clientele willingly supported them.[45]

Veer and Vertovec thus note that the Brahmin *pandit* began to function like a Christian parish priest, visiting homes, providing religious instruction, settling disputes, etc.[46] All marriage ceremonies and other religious duties were performed by him. The documentary sources do not make it clear if in Guyana the same Brahmin served both as *pandit* and *guru* as occurred in some parts of Trinidad. In any event, the *guru* was looked upon as the father of the people and especially of his disciples. They in turn were regarded as his own children. On his death, these 'children' were considered orphans. The *guru* was venerated by his followers. Without his presence and advice nothing could be done. As in Fiji, *gurus* paid periodical visits to different estates and Indian villages to perform certain religious ceremonies or offer sacrifices for which they were reputed to receive large sums of money and other presents from the people whom they visited. Vertovec points out, however, that this was an appreciative offering (*dakshina*) rather than mere 'payment', and could range from foodstuff and clothing to even a cow or land. Disciples sometimes sent presents to their *gurus'* homes. No one dared to offend or insult a *guru* who, in turn, imposed penances for all kinds of transgressions. Some Hindu holy men were known as *swamyars* and their duties were reading and learning, teaching, sacrificing, ordering things to be offered, bestowing and receiving alms. Still others were called *Maraj* and *Pujari.*[47]

Like their Muslim counterparts, Hindu holy men were scorned by the cultural elites. Rev. J.G. Pearson could not be bothered to conceal his racism in describing them:

> He wears clothing if he thinks of it, and then it is only a long piece of calico about a yard wide varying from a quarter to half an inch thick with cocoanut oil and dirt according to the time he has had it. He does not trim his beard or cut his hair, not does he comb it . . . He is spare, not to say meagre, but he is as much alive as an old cheese. He is seldom seen without a brass vessel from which alone he will drink. This walking museum of entomological tribes, this offensive upright column of stench, will not deign to drink from another person's cup. He would lose caste . . . He is pharisaical or nothing, only he is usually more ascetic . . . His creed is not so actively damnatory of everybody else but himself, hence he does not appear so intolerant of others . . . [He] jabbers in Sanskrit, but does not understand it . . .[48]

Apart from such obvious racial prejudices, there were very practical reasons why Hindu and Muslim priests were disliked by the cultural elites. Estate personnel considered them a nuisance and a bad influence on the Indian workers. "His finger, a large one too, is in every pie of mischief among the coolies, and he is adept at deceit, subterfuge and hypocrisy of every sort." "His real forte is in hatching plots" and in inciting the Indians successfully to strike. "He does not appear on these occasions, except perhaps as spokesman, when the coolies go to town, at the Immigration Office."[49] Besides, the holy men set a 'bad example' since they were reluctant to do work on the estates.[50] Even-

216

*Cultural
Power,
Resistance,
and
Pluralism*

tually, as Robert Moore points out, the management had to compromise by giving them light work in order to enlist their support of the
social system.[51] And, of course, the missionaries disliked them because
of the considerable sway they held over their comrades and the role
which they played in obstructing Christian indoctrination.[52]

In the final analysis, the Indians were highly successful in countering the cultural power of the elites and preserving their traditional
religions, Hinduism and Islam, in the new social environment to
which they were transplanted. Conditions in the colony and the attitude of the cultural elites did force certain alterations in the way in
which they were able to maintain some of their religious practices, but
they made no apparent modifications to the fundamental tenets of
their religious beliefs which remained faithful to the parent religions.
The religions as reorganized in the colony thus formed the corner-
stones of Indian cultural resistance to the pressures emanating from
the host society to effect their religious and cultural subordination.

Religious Festivals

An integral part of these religions were festivals which were celebrated
with considerable pageantry. But as we have already noted, the system
of indentureship placed enormous cultural power in the hands of the
elites by way of control over the leisure time allowed to the immigrants. This imposed severe limitations on Indian religious celebrations as the planters granted only between two and five days off,
generally early in the calendar year, for immigrant festivities.[53] This, as
we shall see, led to some radical modifications in the forms of celebration of the great Hindu and Muslim religious festivals. Such changes
represented attempts by the Indian immigrants to come to terms with
their altered circumstances in a strange environment by restructuring
their festivities while still seeking to preserve their authenticity with a
view to maintaining a sense of ethnic distinctiveness.

In May 1882, it was reported in the press that an Indian named
Marhajah, nicknamed 'Bishop', had held a series of services in his
village for a few days towards the end of April. The nickname 'Bishop'
was perhaps a designation in *Creolese* to denote his status among
Hindu priests, and while clearly indicative of cultural borrowing,
Marhajah's religious activities were unquestionably Hindu. His temple
was tastefully decorated with paintings in lively colours, flowers and
bright coloured cloth and paper, and the floor was strewn with dried
plantain leaves. Services had been held at intervals during the night
and day, and were attended by large numbers of Indians from neighbouring estates. These lasted until the end of April when the proceedings were terminated with a great feast.[54]

This religious activity seems to have been connected with the Hindu festival of *Rama Navami (Ram Noumi)* which is celebrated on the ninth day of the Hindu month of *Chaitra (Cet)*, around March-April. In India, this festival is observed only by Brahmins, *Komtis*, and a few other upper caste enthusiasts. Its celebration in Guyana and Trinidad[55] must have been part of the Brahmanization process which Hinduism underwent in the new social environment.

Diwali (Deepavali or *Divali)* or the festival of lights is the jewel in the crown of Hindu festivals. It is in honour both of the goddess *Lakshmi* and of *Lord Rama*'s return from the forest. In Guyana, as in Rampur (northern India) and Trinidad, it was celebrated on the thirteenth day *(Amavas)* in the month of *Katik (Kartik)*, i.e., October-November. On *Divali* morning, Hindus took a sieve or winnowing basket and beat it in every corner of the house while exclaiming in Hindi (or Bhojpuri) "*Ishvar paittho Daridar, niklo*", or in Tamil "*Ishvar irruka daridram parakka*" which, according to Bronkhurst, means "God be present, and poverty depart". The basket was then carried outside the house or village, generally towards the east or north-east, and then thrown away: for it was believed to bear the poverty and distress of the people. Sometimes instead of beating a sieve, the Hindus brushed the house, and carried out the dirt in a basket. This corresponds closely to the patterns in India and Trinidad. An integral part of this festival is the lighting of lamps or *diyas* at night----small shallow clay cups containing cotton wicks and filled with coconut oil.[56] What is evident, however, is that in the plantation environment of nineteenth century Guyana this festival lost its prominence among the Hindu immigrants mainly because it is centered around the family which was very weak, but also because the estates did not grant a holiday to celebrate. Consequently celebrations were relatively low key until after the immigrants began to settle off the estates late in the century and the traditional Indian family began to be reconstructed.

The *Dasserah (Durga Puja)*, another major Hindu religious festival, was observed for nine days in honour of the victory gained by *Durga*, the wife of *Siva*, over the giant *Maghisan*. In preparation for this festival, a large *pandal* or shrine was erected, decorated beautifully with flowers, and fenced around with coconut *tatties* (mats). At one end of the *pandal* stood a small temple in which was placed a large, gorgeously dressed image of the goddess *Durga*. This was made of straw and clay and represented her as having ten arms, each grasping a weapon, with one foot on a lion and the other on the prostrate giant. As the *Dasserah* is traditionally a non-vegetarian feast when meats are consumed, several men slew and cut up the sheep for cooking by women who also prepared rice and other meals for the large number of celebrants who were scheduled to arrive later in procession. In India

218

Cultural
Power,
Resistance,
and
Pluralism

the Brahmins worship *shami* leaves and the goddess *Durga* at the shrine, after which the other people snatch the leaves and exchange them with a friendly embrace. Perhaps in Guyana the celebrations took on a more egalitarian character, and they culminated in a procession to the river or sea wherein the divine image was ceremoniously cast to the joyful embraces of the celebrants.[57]

There is, however, considerable confusion in the historical documents with respect to the celebration of the *Dasserah*, and two other Indian religious festivals, *Holi* and *Mohurrum*. Traditionally the *Dasserah* is celebrated on the tenth day of *Ashvina* (i.e., in September-October).[58] Another great Hindu festival, *Holi (Phagwah)*, is celebrated in the month of *Pagun/Phalguna* (February-March).[59] But unlike Fiji, for example, there is no documentary record of the celebration of *Holi* in nineteenth century Guyana. In fact, the 1870 commission of inquiry categorically stated that this festival had not been introduced into the colony.[60] The features of *Holi* are so distinctive that it is very unlikely that its celebration could have gone unnoticed. The only credible explanation of this mystery, therefore, is that in Guyana the Hindus collapsed these two great festivals into one major public celebration. The reason for this would no doubt be related to the fact that the estates only allowed the Indians between two and five days off per year for religious festivities which they referred to as the *tadja*.

This *Dasserah-Holi* festive period, roughly extending from the last quarter of one calendar year through the first quarter of the next, also coincides with the celebration of the great Muslim festival of *Mohurrum (Hosein/Hose* in Trinidad, *Hosay* in Jamaica, *Yamseh* in Mauritius) which is itself very variable in terms of timing.[61] Since the Indians on a given plantation, regardless of their religious persuasion, were given the same time frame within which to commemorate their festivals, both Hindus and Muslims had to stage their public celebrations simultaneously. Geoghegan, the Calcutta emigration agent, tried to explain the apparent absence of *Holi* in Guyana by suggesting that it may have been merged with the *Mohurrum* festival.[62] But instead it seems more credible that the Hindus, anxious not to be upstaged by their traditional Muslim rivals, would have sought to incorporate the more elaborate carnivalesque features of the *Dasserah* into the *Holi* celebrations----in other words a *Dasserah-Holi* merger. To the uninitiated and/or ignorant European observer, there would have been very little difference between a procession of Hindus carrying a 'temple' with an image of *Durga* and another of Muslims carrying a *tazzia* with the coffins of *Hassan* and *Hussein* (see below).

This is not to suggest that Hindus did not participate in the Muslim festivities and vice versa. But the reason why the majority Hindus should have *routinely* (sub)merged their own religious celebrations

into those of the minority Muslim rivals as has been suggested by
some writers, even given the tendency within the Indian immigrant
community to 'collapse' cultural differences, has not been adequately
explained. Kelvin Singh argues that "as a pantheistic people, Hindus
had little difficulty in identifying with other people's religious beliefs
and practices without abandoning their own . . ." Wood, too, while
asserting that the *Mohurrum* could hold little spiritual significance for
the Hindus, observes that their religion tends to overlap tolerantly
into the preserves of others, and cites a few examples of Hindu participation in Muslim festivities in India itself.[63] But in their *janmabhumi*
(motherland) Hindus also celebrated their *own* festivals at the appropriate times and were not constrained as in Guyana, Trinidad, Fiji or
Mauritius to just a few allotted days a year. So it was never a case of
celebrating a Muslim festival **instead of** a major Hindu one. Given
such circumstances in the colonies, it seems, they would have been
more anxious to put on their own 'show' wherever practicable rather
than simply join ranks with their Muslim compatriots and rivals.

Singh further argues that "some Hindus took the religious significance of *Muharram* [*sic*] seriously enough to make vows and offerings
during its observance, and Hindus participated in the construction of
the *tazzias,* the processions, the drumming and the ritual mock battles,
which occasionally turned out to be serious". At the same time, he
observes that the celebration seems to have contained elements of the
Hindu *Krishnalila* in India.[64] These explanations, while credible
enough, probably do not tell the whole story, and much has to do
with the imprecise and patchy nature of the documentary evidence
which historians have to use. What Singh identifies as elements of
Hinduism in the *Mohurrum* festivities were very probably in several
instances actual Hindu celebrations quite *independent* of the *Mohurrum*, and those 'ritual' mock battles that occasionally turned sour were
quite likely communal clashes between rival Hindu and Muslim processions.

In reality, therefore, it appears that a radical transformation in the
religious culture of the Indian immigrant community may have taken
place in the plantation environment of both Guyana and Trinidad,
although this did not signify creolization. Sometime within the period
extending from the last quarter of one calendar year to the first quarter
of the next year two great religious celebrations----one Hindu, the
other Muslim—were held, and simultaneously, because estate management made no differentiation between them. Where perhaps Muslims
were very few, a Hindu *Dasserah-Holi* celebration took place. Where
Muslims were in sufficient numbers to seize the initiative, then the
Mohurrum celebrations were mounted with Hindu participation. Further proof of the existence of a Hindu celebration quite separate from

220

*Cultural
Power,
Resistance,
and
Pluralism*

the Muslim *Mohurrum* festival comes from a most unlikely source----a black Creole who, as a participant in one of the so-called *tadja* processions in 1878, proclaimed that he had given up Christianity to become, not a Muslim, *but a Hindu.* His face and arms were studded with needles and pins,[65] a further manifestation of Hindu asceticism. Again, when the Creoles at Pouderoyen, West Bank Demerara, staged their *tadja* in 1876, they wore chains around their waist and painted their naked bodies.[66] The absence of details leads one to wonder if the paint was not *abir* (see below) traditionally used in the *Holi* festival, thus suggestive that their *tadja* was patterned after a Hindu celebration.

It is thus reasonable to postulate that *Holi* was indeed celebrated in nineteenth century Guyana, but not in a traditional manner. There may not have been the usual bonfires as in India to commemorate the burning of *Kamadeva*, the god of love; or much of the traditional horseplay involving the throwing of water on one another and the rubbing of *abir/gugal* (red oxide) on each other's faces that later became a hallmark of *Holi/Phagwah* in both Guyana and Trinidad,[67] although as we have seen above this may well have been done but in a somewhat different format which incorporated the more carnivalesque features of the *Dasserah.* That would have been the only way that the Hindu majority could rival the very colourful *Mohurrum* celebrations of the Muslim minority. Indeed because of their vast majority within the Indian population, it seems very probable that the *tadja* processions may have been more often than was generally realized Hindu *Dasserah/Holi* bands rather than Muslim *Mohurrum* bands. The most knowledgeable elite contemporary observer, Bronkhurst, did in fact point out that what appeared to be the *Dasserah* was indeed held about the same time as the *Mohurrum* festival, and Bisnauth concurs that the two celebrations, though held simultaneously, were indeed quite separate.[68]

Religious rivalry between Hindus and Muslims on the estates even became violent from time to time. But the inability of most European observers to distinguish between the Hindu and Muslim processions meant that when such clashes occurred, they were treated as if they were all simply *tadja* bands from different estates rather than factional clashes between rival Hindu and Muslim bands. Only Bronkhurst seemed to recognize that some of these were indeed clashes between Hindu and Muslim processions; and Bisnauth has also identified them as such.[69] The violence was so intense on occasion that it resulted in the killing of the protagonists.[70]

As in the case of the *Dasserah/Holi*, the *Mohurrum* festivities had to conform to the work schedule of the sugar estates. Thus even if the month of *Mohurrum* fell outside of the first quarter of the calendar year, the local celebrations had to be held during that period. This was the case, for instance, in 1868 when the first *Mohurrum* fell as late as

May 16. Likewise in the following year celebrations were held in the month of *Zilkad,* and sometimes they were held in the month of *Ramozan.*[71]

The *Mohurrum* festival commemorates the martyrdom of *Hassan* and *Hussein,* the two sons of *Ali* and the prophet's daughter, *Fatima,* in the forty-sixth year of the *Hirjah* (the flight of the prophet). The festival is observed by devout fasting for thirteen days during which the Muslims, especially the *Shiites,* are required to abstain from all work. It is doubtful, however, that this could be strictly adhered to in the plantation environment of Guyana. But the Muslims could abstain from strong drink and nuptial festivities, and some even denied themselves the use of bed, and the consumption of meat and fish, while devoting themselves to building the *tazzias.*[72]

The *tazzia* (called a *gouhn* in Mauritius) was a sort of miniature mosque about twenty feet high and constructed with great skill and nicety. It was built of very light and pliable materials: the framework of slight bamboo strips ingeniously tied together, wickerwork style, and the whole covered with multi-coloured paper, most neatly cut and ornamented with gold and silver gilt trimmings. Within the *tazzia,* two small coffins, representing the remains of *Hassan* and *Hussein,* were placed covered with black cloth.[73] *Hussein's* coffin contained the *Ullams* (his standards), the *Nal* (his horse's shoe), the *Nisa* on which his head was borne by his enemies, the *Rast-hath* (his severed right hand), and the *Parmesht reg* (handful of sand representing the grave). The completed *tazzia* was attached to two long poles extending from front to rear and borne by four or more men (depending on its size—in some cases it could be as many as fifteen or twenty bearers) who considered it a great honour to perform this duty, and it was taken three times around the 'plain of Kerbala', a raised mound representing the scene of Hussein's fall. They then rested for over an hour while a priest said prayers (*fatiha*) and performed other ceremonies. Several worshippers sat around and wept embracing one another by placing the head on the right shoulder of the other and then on the left. Cakes, sugar, milk, money, etc., were offered on *Kerbala,* and *ghee* lamps were lit by female participants. None but Muslims was supposed to witness this scene.[74]

Thereafter the *tazzia* was again borne shoulder-high and carried in procession (called *penk* in Mauritius) with repeated shouts of "*Shah Hassan! Shah Hussein! Dholla! Dholla* [bridegroom]! *Hoce Dwast* [alas my friend]! *Rhuerho* [stop]!" According to Edun, the idea behind the *penk* was to revive and enact the fight at *Kerbala.*[75] The procession stopped periodically to allow the worshippers to dance around the *tazzia.* Some of the male dancers, called *Puli Vesham,* dressed as tigers; others engaged in ritual fencing (*gatka* in Mauritius);[76] still others did

222

*Cultural
Power,
Resistance,
and
Pluralism*

aerobatics (probably including what was known as *ratiffe* in Mauritius involving self-flagellation with swords and knives without inflicting serious wounds)[77] and magical feats. For example, on one occasion a performer reputedly passed a sharp pointed cutlass on a long stick down his throat, and later put a thread through his nose and brought it out of his mouth.[78] The women engaged in ritual mourning by beating their breasts and tearing their clothes while shouting lamentations. As in India, at the end of the procession the coffins were stripped of their fineries and thrown into a river or the sea.[79]

The failure of contemporary observers to differentiate clearly between Muslim and Hindu celebrations necessitates the use here of the term *tadja* to refer to these festivities when no distinction can be made. The cost of building the *tadja* was very high and imposed a heavy tax on the Indian workers, each of whom was expected to contribute no less than 48 cents (equivalent to two days' earnings). On one estate over $200 were collected, although only $75 were reported to have been spent on the construction of the *tadja*. The rest was probably spent on costumes, food, drink, etc., although a cynical white commentator preferred to think that it was misappropriated by the Indian drivers. If a worker refused to contribute, the driver could punish him by assigning him difficult tasks and claiming that they were badly done[80]----a criminal offence under the indenture labour laws. This element of coercion would have made possible the widest participation of Indians; and, in particular, it again seems to demonstrate that the Hindus must have had their own celebrations, for it is unlikely that the predominantly Hindu drivers would have tried to extract money contributions from unwilling Hindu workers for an essentially Muslim festival. In any event the extent of the use of coercion to ensure participation is open to question since most tadja participants did so voluntarily even after leaving the plantations. Indeed some of the largest and most elaborate *tadjas* were made by free Indian villagers.[81]

By the 1880s, there was a discernible decline in the *tadja* festivals. In 1879 one observer noted that on two estates on the east coast of Demerara, the Indians had no *tadja* for years; and at Plantation Enmore, despite the existence of two places of worship which made it a principal venue for the *Mohurrum* celebrations, the Muslims were reportedly 'too busy' to make a *tazzia* for themselves. Instead they bought one from their mates on Plantation Enterprise.[82] (This again suggests that reports of friction between Indians from different estates were exaggerated; instead the rivalry must have been between Hindu *Dasserah-Holi* and Muslim *Mohurrum* groups.) In 1882, four east coast estates and Plantation Providence on the east bank of Demerara had no *tadja*, while Plantation Nonpareil had a very lacklustre festival.[83] In 1883, one of the foremost *tadja* builders said that that was the last time he would be participating in the festival because he was convinced that

Indian Bhojpuri Culture: Spiritual

there was nothing more in it than a waste of money.[84] And in 1885, no festivities were held on the entire Essequibo coast,[85] while the only Indians on the west bank of Demerara to hold any were those at Plantation La Grange.[86]

This decline in the participation by Indians may be attributed to a number of factors. Some may indeed have considered it a waste of money, especially if there was an element of compulsion involved which also allowed venal drivers to cheat the workers of their earnings. Many also felt that these festivities had degenerated into mere drunken revelry and saturnalia, and could no longer be regarded as religious affairs.[87] But one very important factor was undoubtedly the increasing Creole involvement.

Just as in Trinidad and Mauritius, the Guyanese Creoles became involved as bearers of the *tadjas* from very early on. By 1860 it was noted that the juvenile Creole population amused themselves in the festivities and in throwing away the *tadjas* "in imitation of the Coolies".[88] The Creoles reportedly joined "with heart, branch, and voice" in the *tadja* festival. "They marched along with them [Indians] in procession, assisted them to carry their gods, beat their breasts in the same manner, uttered with them the same words and helped to swell the demonlike yells of those poor idolatrous."[89]

During the 1870s and 1880s, the Creole participation increased considerably,[90] and even seemed to be taking over the festivities. The *Argosy* in 1880 stated that although Indian participation was dwindling, the festivals might remain a local institution owing to the Creoles.[91] And although Governor Wodehouse in 1860 had boldly asserted that "the Creole laborers may remain very loose Christians, but they will not turn into Hindoos or Mahometans",[92] as we have already seen in 1878 there was a Creole 'reveller' claiming to have given up Christianity to become a Hindu. Yet if even there were others like him, the evidence does support Wodehouse's view that no large-scale conversions were likely to, or did, take place. At the same time, without firm empirical evidence, it might nevertheless not be unreasonable to speculate that some Black participation in the *tadja* might have been out of genuine religious interest; for it is very probable that the small minority of surviving *African Muslims* (e.g., the Fula) and their children may have embraced the Indian Muslim festival as a means of shoring up their resistance against elite cultural dominance.

In 1873, there had been an all-Creole *tadja* on the Essequibo coast.[93] And in 1877, Creole villagers held a procession at Mahaica where a molten image of a god was clearly identified, and "before the altar of this 'unknown god', there . . . goggled the sons of the soil whose creed from childhood was Christianity, and whose parents were followers

224

*Cultural
Power,
Resistance,
and
Pluralism*

and leading members of the two churches only a hundred roods away".[94] This reference to the image of a god is further proof that the *tadjas* which the Creoles copied were indeed Hindu and that these might in fact have been the majority. Such Creole adoption of Indian cultural practices was explained away by the cultural elites in stereotyped racist terms. "You have only to beat a drum on the village dam, and a crowd [of Creole youths] will soon assemble; if you can add a little display of swordsmanship or any exhibition whereby his vanity may be gratified, he is at the height of his ambition."[95]

This growing Creole participation in the *tadja* festivals can be interpreted as evidence of cultural borrowing. But it did not stop there. As Robert Moore notes, the Creoles began to creolize *tadja* by incorporating African features.[96] Thus, for instance, a "Privileged Spectator" observed that a Creole *tadja* at Sisters Village, West Bank Demerara resembled a masquerade band as the revellers marched "with a martial tread", and about one hundred women brought up the rear "contorting themselves in the eternal cake walk".[97] The occasional Portuguese also became involved as, for instance, at Daniel's Town on Good Friday, 1873, when the *tazzia* was built for the Creoles by a Portuguese artist.[98] That Good Friday was chosen by the Creoles on this occasion to stage their *tadja* is indicative of a syncretic blending of eastern and western religious practices in Afro-Creole culture. How widespread this was is difficult to ascertain.

What is no less significant, however, was the inverse relationship between Creole and Indian participation; for as the former increased, there was a corresponding decrease in the latter.[99] The increasing level of Creole participation in what had come to be regarded as the greatest Indian religio-ethnic festivity was evidently perceived as a cultural threat by both Muslims and Hindus. And indeed their initial reaction was to attack the Creole *tadjas* physically. In one such clash at Plantation Leonora in 1873, the Indians broke up the procession, destroyed the *tadja* and chased away the Creole revellers.[100] When such hostility failed to dampen Creole enthusiasm for the revelry, the Indians decided to retreat. This attitude to cultural integration is very interesting. It is very understandable for the Indians to have sought to resist absorbing significant elements or aspects of the host culture, in particular Christianity, which could lead to cultural emasculation; it is quite another matter for them to have resisted Creole assimilaton of Indian culture. But it is quite probable that they were striking out against what they may have interpreted as a desecration of their religions by the Creoles.

Another very important factor which partially explains the declining interest of the Indians was the decidedly hostile attitude of the cultural elites, both white and coloured. They considered these processions 'intolerable nuisances', and strongly demanded their prohibition.[101] They were also revolted by the violence which frequently occurred when rival processions clashed leading occasionally to deaths. For instance, in 1867 two revellers were killed by gunshots in a clash on the east bank of Demerara, and several others were seriously wounded.[102] It was bad enough when the Indians themselves were involved, but on many occasions innocent passers-by were insulted and assaulted for defiling or polluting the shrine by passing too closely. For instance, in 1853 two whites at Mahaica who tried to pass a procession in their carriage were severely beaten; and in 1870 a white couple had their carriage overturned on the east coast of Demerara.[103]

There were, however, more sinister reasons why some of the cultural elites wanted these public processions prohibited. The growing Creole participation was a matter of grave concern. Great consternation was expressed over the 'pernicious' effects which the 'heathen' immigrants were having on the Creoles who, it was argued, were being led astray from their Christian beliefs and were not heeding the preaching of their (white) priests.[104]

But the source of real anxiety lay deeper. As in Trinidad, the *tadja*, at least for a period, was actually forging cooperation and cultural understanding between Creoles and Indian immigrants, the two largest subordinate sections in the country.[105] Such cultural links threatened to transcend the primary racial divisions upon which the whites had placed so much emphasis on preserving the status quo. A security threat was thus in the making. "As it is, we hear complaints made that the Coolies are becoming more and more riotous during the celebration of their annual festival, but matters will be worse if, through any motive, they can get the blacks or any other class of laborers to act with them."[106]

Singh found the same attitude in Trinidad, and in both colonies there was a concerted campaign among the cultural elites for the *tadja* celebrations to be curbed.[107] They acted with more alacrity in Guyana where in 1869 an ordinance (No.16) was passed to regulate the processions; this in fact became the blueprint for similar legislation in Trinidad in 1882. It gave the governor power to make regulations defining routes, etc., and made the contravention of them a *criminal* offence. Indians had to apply to a magistrate to obtain permission to hold processions.[108] By these means, the cultural elites were able to control the festivities; and no doubt the circumscriptions and proscriptions[109] helped to dissuade the immigrants from applying for permission. By forbidding the processions to leave the estates, the regulations provided no opportunity for public display so vital and integral to these street festivals; and as the great street processions were more or less outlawed, some Indians lost interest.[110] If they attempted to breach the

226

*Cultural
Power,
Resistance,
and
Pluralism*

regulations they were prosecuted and convicted as **criminals.** Similarly, Creole involvement was curbed by seizing their drums and charging those who participated with disorderly conduct.[111] Despite these restrictions, however, the *tadja* celebrations still remained an important Indian ethnic festival, albeit on a reduced scale, on individual estates until the end of the century and beyond.[112] It is very likely though that as the public *tadja* festivities declined, the more orthodox *Holi* celebrations were revived, freed from their previous envelopment in the trappings of either the *Dasserah* or *Mohurrum* festivals.

By 1884 when the Trinidad authorities overreacted by shooting and killing at least sixteen Indians in a *tadja* disturbance,[113] the Guyanese cultural elites could openly criticize them for committing "a great error of tact, and exhibit[ing] an utter want of the true spirit of management",[114] because public celebration of most of the festivals in Guyana had already been effectively brought under their control.

The great religious festivals enabled the Indians to extol and glorify openly and publicly their religious beliefs, and also served as important and visible symbols of Indian resistance to the cultural power of the colonial elites. But in the alien environment, they were forced to make significant modifications in the forms of these celebrations largely in response to the exercise of such power which was aimed at restricting them. Yet, although not welcomed by the cultural elites, the festivals provided a window to members of the host society through which to view and indeed participate in an integral aspect of Indian religious and cultural life. In that sense it offered enormous potential for integrating the Indians both culturally and socially. But on the other hand, in their desire to retain their cultural autonomy as part of a broader strategy of resistance to cultural domination by the elites, many Indians withdrew when it appeared that that autonomy was being threatened by Creole participation. This counteracted and retarded the integrative process.

Christianity and Missionaries

It was the work of Christian missionaries which posed the greatest challenge to the Indians in their efforts to retain cultural autonomy in Guyana. Yet missionary activity amidst them was far less intensive than among the Creoles. In the first place estate proprietors and managers, while not directly opposed to mission work, did not generally positively assist it.[115] As in Fiji, employers seemed to think that restlessness, conceit, and hypocrisy as a general rule followed the conversion of 'pagans' to Christianity, and that the instruction which they received did more harm than good to the character of the labourers.[116]

In any event, at first while their numbers were small and they posed no threat politically (security) or culturally, no church organization seemed particularly interested in the Indians. The London Missionary Society, though, was openly hostile to their introduction, considering such 'idolatrous' immigrants a corrupting influence on the Creoles.[117]

The Wesleyan Methodists did make an early attempt to minister to the Indian immigrants when Rev. A. Williams arrived in 1852,[118] but he died in 1855. Thereafter Rev. Shrewsbury tried to work among them in Essequibo, but being unfamiliar with their languages, had very little success.[119] It was not until December 1860 that Rev. H.V.P. Bronkhurst, an Anglo-Indian, was appointed full-time Methodist missionary to Indians.[120] The Anglican (established) church was quietly inactive during the 1850s, but in 1862 appointed Rev. Ebenezer Bhalanath Bhose, a native Indian, to assume full time duty among the Indians. Such missionary endeavours were further subsidized out of the colonial revenues by an annual sum of $2,000-$3,000.[121] Two missionaries, however, could hardly suffice for an immigrant population of thousands which was being increased continuously by new arrivals; and as Bhose later admitted, "We have long felt the want of men, not only to carry on the work beyond its present limits, but also to watch over our new converts who would otherwise . . . relapse into the heathenism from which they have so recently escaped".[122]

During the 1870s the Anglican church began to intensify its efforts to reach the mass of Indians who by then had begun to show signs of settling permanently. In 1873 Quintin Hogg, proprietor of Plantation Bel Air, proposed to the Anglican bishop the establishment of a 'Coolie Mission' on his estate and offered to pay half the stipend of the missionary for five years and to provide him with a residence. A committee of management was appointed with the title of the 'Bel Air Coolie Mission' under the charge of Rev. S.C. Hore. Its object was the "christianization of Hindu, Tamil, and Chinese Immigrants in British Guiana". Although Bel Air was the headquarters, the five adjoining estates were included in the mission district. The mission conducted visits to and instruction in schools and hospitals, church services, training of catechists and interpreters, adult classes for Christian instruction, and the employment and superintendence of catechists.[123]

It was not before the late 1860s that the Presbyterian Missionary Society (Church of Scotland) did anything about the large immigrant presence, and then they merely had a catechist at Anna Regina in Essequibo. In 1885 Rev. John Gibson was appointed full-time missionary but he died three years later. After retiring from mainstream church duties, Rev. James Slater ran a small mission for about forty Indian children at Plantation Better Hope, East Coast Demerara. When he gave up in 1896, the proprietors, the Crum-Ewings, asked

228

*Cultural
Power,
Resistance,
and
Pluralism*

the Canadian Presbyterians who were already operating successfully in Trinidad to take over the mission. They appointed Rev. J.B. Cropper who was to distinguish himself as an indefatigable worker both as a missionary and an educator among the Indians in the early twentieth century.[124] There was, therefore, nothing in Guyana during the nineteenth century akin to the concerted missionary and educational activity of the Canadian Presbyterian Mission in Trinidad, and consequently very few Indians were affected.

The white missionaries were 'assisted' in the task of proselytizing the Indian immigrants by independent Creole preachers. How many of these there were will always be a mystery, but Hardy recalled one who, with the permission of the planter, apparently conducted a service on one of the Berbice sugar estates every Sunday night for Indian children and any others who cared to attend. The service was held in one of the estate buildings, and according to the preacher was well attended.[125]

The Indian response to missionary proselytization was in general one of resolute resistance, and both Hindus and Muslims greeted the missionaries with a mixture of cold indifference and open opposition. Considering themselves as the possessors of a monopoly of divine truth, Christian missionaries displayed gross naïvety, arrogance and prejudice in bringing their message to the Indians. Starting from a position that the immigrants were sunk in ignorance and superstition, low and degraded, and "the worst of their brethren in India",[126] they claimed that "Deceit, gambling, adultery, theft, and violence, are . . . too common amongst them";[127] and that "They glory in drunkenness—and other awful and most degrading crimes. They are a 'sinful nation, a people laden with iniquity, a seed of evil doers, children that are corrupters'—a set of hardened sinners 'who provoke the Holy One of Israel unto Anger—who steadfastly resist the Holy Spirit of God".[128]

At first, the missionaries were optimistic about the prospects of converting the Indians. They thought that the Indians might be more accessible in Guyana than in India because living among people of a different and 'better' religion, they would be well disposed towards Christianity;[129] and at first they were encouraged by the attendance of curious Indian women at missionary meetings[130] (another sign of how independently those women behaved). By the 1860s, however, a different tale was being told and the Indian women were now very much in the vanguard building resistance to missionary proselytization.[131] Bronkhurst stated that "It is no easy task to try to convince a Hindu of the error of his way".[132] Bhose too observed: "We have as yet only touched the surface; beneath it there is an amount of ignorance, vice, prejudice, and apathy which, while it is appalling to contemplate, would seem to require, if we would successfully cope with it, much patient and persevering labour . . ."[133] After another decade of unsuccessful toil a dejected Bronkhurst seemed ready to give up:

> I have often been tempted to retire from it . . . No sympathy, no help, and no one here seems to understand, or to have the least idea of the uphill nature of the work in which I am engaged. It is indeed very trying to my body and mind. The long walks I have to take under the burning sun, and so little or no success resulting from constant but truthful discharge of my duty are indeed very trying.[134]

The resistance of most Indians to missionary proselytization was stubborn. As in Fiji, many did listen out of curiosity, but that was as far as they went.[135] "They remain quite unaffected, even on the most solemn occasions."[136] Some simply refused even to listen to the missionaries and treated them as imposters; for in their opinion a real parson should have holes in his nose and ears, a red mark on his forehead, and should wear his hair long.[137] Resistance was sometimes more forceful. On one estate a few Indians asked Bronkhurst if he could find nothing else to do than preach about "this rubbish religion called Christianity".[138] On another occasion a woman told him that Christianity was false religion; that hers was true, and neither he nor any other *padree* (parson) could turn her from her religion.[139] One man asked him,

> Who is the lost sheep, you or we. We are not the lost sheep, for we belong to the true fold, and our religion is much older than yours. It is as old as the world. You and all the christians are the lost sheep, for you have all left the oldest religion and taken upon yourselves a religion which only dates from the birth of Jesus Christ.[140]

On yet another occasion while preaching to a group of Indians, two *Rajputs* threatened to assault Bronkhurst and told their peers not to listen to the deceiver and liar.[141] On a visit to Plantation Enmore in 1867, a man approached him and said, "Sir, if you will preach about Jesus Christ to the Coolies on this estate I will break your legs with this stick" (which he had in hand).[142]

Resistance, however, was not uniform. Hindus seemed deceptively less hostile than Muslims. They generally said but little in defence of their religion and contented themselves with asserting that they worshipped the same God as Christians.[143] For them, "the pure and sublime doctrines of Christianity have no attractions". They simply looked upon the missionary as an agent of the colonial government to effect their religious subjugation.[144] The Muslims, however, were decidedly intolerant. They would hardly condescend to hear the missionary. Priding themselves on having received a more perfect revelation than the Gospel they could seldom be persuaded to give a patient and unprejudiced hearing.[145]

The prospect of returning to India at the end of their indentures was a major factor for resisting Christian indoctrination;[146] indeed the Indians regarded the missionary as the bearer of the tools designed to

230

*Cultural
Power,
Resistance,
and
Pluralism*

prevent them from returning home.[147] In particular, the fear of losing caste served as a very powerful inhibitor to the Indians becoming Christians,[148] for violators were utterly condemned and ostracized, if not in danger of physical harm. "An instance of a man having his tongue burnt with a gold pin or pen for losing his caste, may be mentioned . . ."[149] The average Hindu thought he would be drawing the curse of heaven upon his head for abandoning his ancestral faith for that of a foreign people.[150] The force of familial and communal opinion was extremely powerful. As soon as a missionary left an estate, his listeners were sternly rebuked by their fellow caste members, friends and relatives.[151] Yet in total disregard of Indian sensibilities, the missionaries deliberately attacked the very idea of caste.[152] The result of such arrogance/ignorance was that conversions were hard to come by.

To cite a few instances of communal and familial opposition would be apposite. In 1861, the conversion of an Indian man caused such anguish among his relatives and friends that although they were doing well in Georgetown, they decided to sell their cows and other possessions and move to Berbice, away they hoped from Christian influences. Before leaving, they visited Bronkhurst and abused him. The young man's mother, however, fell on her knees and kissed Bronkhurst's feet, beseeching him not to indoctrinate her son.[153] Likewise, in 1878 the desire of Gocool, an eighteen-year-old Hindu lad, to be baptized so upset his parents that they vowed to go on a hunger protest until Gocool's name was deleted from the baptismal register. This threat of suicide caused considerable unrest among the immigrants on Plantation Port Mourant where his father was a leading Hindu; and when, after three days, the 'buckra parson' seemed unmoved by a plea from the boy's parents that their son should be allowed to wait until he was at least of age, the pragmatic estate manager thought it prudent to intervene and urge the priest to soften his attitude.[154]

The great multiplicity of Indian languages presented a serious obstacle to the missionaries. Since very few of them spoke any of these languages, very little effective proselytization could be done.[155] This problem was compounded by the fact that most of the Indians were illiterate in their own languages, and so could not read tracts even when translated.[156] But it was among the more highly educated Indians from whom the greatest opposition emanated, and they used their subtle intellect to influence their less literate fellows.[157] In many instances these men were Brahmins, *Imams* and other priests who had a vested interest in preserving their traditional faiths. "These Brahmins of course do not exercise any authority over the people in a public manner, but they have a way of keeping them down, and preventing them, from attending service in the school house or open air."[158]

The success of Indian resistance to missionary endeavours was further aided and abetted by local circumstances. They were located in large numbers on plantations, and given the reluctance of the planters generally to interfere in their cultural behaviour, were able to develop a distinct sense of separate ethnicity within the multi-ethnic plantation environment in which religion played a central and distinguishing role. Indeed the strong desire to preserve their traditional religious beliefs and practices and to resist the alien religion of the host society typified their whole attitude towards the host culture in general, and served to reinforce the ethnic boundaries which separated them from the rest of the society. As Robert Moore put it, their religions "not only provided a framework of unity within the plantations but equally unified the race beyond the plantations".[159]

Although the vast majority of Indian immigrants remained faithful to their traditional religions, missionary work did bring about a few conversions. Hence the Indian missions were augmented annually by a small number of baptisms.[160] But no mission in Guyana was nearly as successful as the Canadian Presbyterians in Trinidad who committed far more human and financial resources in the field. The Guyanese missions did, however, try their best to cater to the tastes of their converts, even conducting baptismal services as far as possible in Hindi (or Bhojpuri).[161] Although converts were given English (so-called 'Christian') names on baptism, care was taken to select names that sounded like their Indian names. Hence, for example, 'Sepdial' was converted to 'Septimus', 'Jehoiada' became 'Johanna', 'Ramoia'—'Ramsay', and 'Sonie'—'Sophia'. On rare occasions, however, they were allowed to have Indian names so long as in translation they reflected their new faith, e.g., 'Yaguim Masih' meaning 'believer in God' or 'Masih Dass'—'servant of God'.[162]

The missionaries were never sure about their 'converts'. Some admittedly held fast to their new belief and were even prepared to stand up to the admonitions of Brahmins, *Imams*, and the wider Indian community.[163] Others, less strong, were only prepared to attest to their new faith in secret.[164] Still others while not ashamed to be known as Christians, nevertheless continued to participate in Hindu and Muslim festivals.[165] Some, however, were very pragmatic about becoming Christians. If it meant giving up usurious practices (lending money to compatriots at exorbitant rates of interest), then Christianity went through the window. One Indian priest was only prepared to convert if he could be guaranteed a salary.[166] Several Indians in fact manipulated the tag of Christianity for their own benefit. As one stated quite candidly, "while I am here I get employment easily as a christian; but with my people in India, I am a Brahmin".[167] Experienced men in the field like Bronkhurst were thus highly skeptical

232

*Cultural
Power,
Resistance,
and
Pluralism*

about those missionaries who published impressive statistics of converts: "What sort of converts are they? how are they made?" "Dependence upon mere number of supposed converts is not always a conclusive or satisfactory evidence of success in Missionary or Evangelizing work among Hindu coolies . . ."[168]

Although not very active among the Indians, the Roman Catholic church seemed to be attractive to them. Bronkhurst attributed this to the fact that Catholic churches were much more ornate than the Protestant churches with their bare walls and benches, empty altar/table or pulpit with just a Bible. But although they went to the former in relatively significant numbers, he claimed that "they do not become members of the Romish persuasion, but simply attend that church on account of the gaudy, ritualistic ceremonies which are so much like their own religious services". Roman Catholic church documents have not revealed much by way of recognition of this phenomenon. Yet the Indians did borrow some religious customs from the Catholic Portuguese. For instance, when an Indian wanted to make a ceremony or transact some business with his peers, he sometimes carried a few candles and incense to the Catholic church, burned the incense and lit the candles before one of the icons[169] (see chapter 9 for the Portuguese origins of this custom).

As early as 1864 some Indian converts sought their own Methodist chapel and contributed $134 towards its construction. But since the fund fell far short of the required $960, nothing came of it.[170] Likewise in 1876, Rev. Bhose raised over $300 from Indian Christians in Berbice to build an Anglican chapel in New Amsterdam. Again that sum was too small for anything concrete to materialize.[171] In the same year, however, the Indians at Plantation Enterprise built a **temple** for their *tadja* celebrations (again indicative of a *Hindu* celebration) which was used thereafter by the Brahmins for worship. Since in the following year the *tadja* was built elsewhere, the temple seemed to have fallen into disuse by the Hindus and was thus gradually transformed into a chapel by two Indian Christian families who had shares in it. (This indicates that some Indian converts did not forego Hindu and Muslim festivities.) Eventually they acquired the shares of the other Indians before adding a small chancel. The *Royal Gazette* reported:

> Of course, the exterior has the appearance of nothing else than a Coolie hut. The interior, however, is both neat and very clean. At the east there is a text of scripture with the words 'Holy, Holy, Holy' in Hindi; on each side of the chancel there is a flag, one with the Lord's Prayer in rhyme, the other with the Creed. There are other texts in the church, gaudy in appearance so as to meet the Hindu eyes.

This was syncretism at its best: a converted temple retaining its basic Hindu architecture, Hindu-type flag, gaudy inscriptions, and the use of Bhojpuri/Hindi. Services, held every Sunday morning at nine, attracted between fifteen and sixty persons.[172]

On the whole, however, Indian converts to Christianity were few. The Indian immigrant community as a body remained faithful to their traditional religions and, with some support from the plantocracy, staunchly resisted the efforts of the Christian missionaries to impose their religion. Hinduism and Islam thus became important symbols of Indian resistance to cultural power of the elites, and of their ethnic identity in Guyana.

Western Education

In nineteenth century Guyana, although the state exercised supervision over education and contributed financially towards the maintenance of schools and the payment of teachers, primary responsiblity for day to day administration and teaching lay in the hands of the churches. Education, therefore, was transmitted with a heavy overlay of Christian dogma—it was hardly secular. Western education and Christianity went hand in hand. Indeed the term *religious education* would be most appropriate to describe the content (see below). For this reason, it is apposite to treat the schooling of Indian children in this chapter on spiritual matters.

Just as the cultural elites were divided on the issue of proselytizing the Indians, so too they were on education for immigrants. While it was promoted by the churches, missionary organizations and the colonial government as an agent of cultural assimilation, it was like missionary activity by and large opposed by the plantocracy. In addition, the Indians themselves resisted western education. Hence for all practical purposes, the schooling of Indian children in the nineteenth century was more an idea than a reality.

In 1846 just after the commencement of large-scale Indian immigration, the need to establish educational facilities for immigrant children was mooted.[173] In 1850 a Georgetown Coolie Infant School Institution was started by the Anglican church to proselytize Indian children.[174] In 1860 the (Anglican) Guiana Diocesan Church Society (G.D.C.S.) made grants to six Coolie schools at Plantations Blairmont, Bath, Adelphi, Rose Hall, Eliza & Mary, and Port Mourant, all in Berbice. Another school was kept in a room at Plantation Albion with an attendance of thirty pupils, almost all Indian.[175] Yet in that very year the Inspector of Schools, George Dennis, expressed his dismay over the fact that the vast majority of immigrant children were totally without schooling.[176] Although the Planters' Returns submitted to the 1870 Commission of Inquiry claimed that there were fifty schools on the estates with 1,053 Indian and 63 Chinese children, while another

234

*Cultural
Power,
Resistance,
and
Pluralism*

192 Asian children attended village schools, Rev. Bhose's report to the G.D.C.S. in 1869 noted only nineteen Coolie schools in operation. Of these, fourteen were in Demerara, two in Essequibo and three in Berbice. A few immigrant children in Georgetown attended the St. George's and Albert Town schools.[177]

The criticisms of the 1870 commission on this apparent neglect of the education of immigrant children had very little effect. Twenty years later, of 102 estates in the colony, there were 43 still without schools; and even in some instances where a schoolroom was provided, there was no equipment.[178] This state of affairs existed despite a stipulation in the 1873 immigration ordinance (sec. 52) that minors between ages ten and fifteen must not be indentured unless the employer had previously made arrangements for their education; and also despite the passage in 1876 of a law making education compulsory. This required estate managers to obtain a proficiency certificate from the teacher ascertaining the regular attendance at school the previous week of a minor between ten and twelve years of age before he could employ the child; and, furthermore, the law prohibited the employment of all children under nine years old. But the planters had no intention of encouraging immigrant children to go to school because it deprived them of a valuable source of cheap labour. As the 1870 commission observed, "the gentlemen in charge of estates, having other things to engage their whole attention, find it impossible to cooperate with the missionaries".[179] Hence not only did they criticize the 1876 law, but the planters prevented its enforcement on their estates.[180] Because the provision of educational facilities ran counter to the production regime of the plantations therefore, it generated a split among the cultural elites by pitting the powerful planting interests against the churches and the government, thus weakening their power in imposing British culture on the immigrants through this vital instrument.

The Indian immigrants themselves exhibited very little interest in western education and resisted it for various reasons. Disinterest stemmed in part from a more general Indian resistance to British institutions, and their abhorrence of Christianity.[181] Indeed many parents feared that their children would be indoctrinated with Christian doctrine at school.[182] Opposition was thus strong among many on ideological and religious grounds. Others, however, were less dogmatic in their opposition to western education, notwithstanding their fear of Christian proselytization in school.[183] It was of little use to a people who were merely intent on making as much money in the shortest time possible before returning home. Some asked, "Why should I send my children to school as I intend to return home and carry my family and they will not then be benefitted by English institutions?" (a view held although India was a British possession).[184] Many thus tended to be indifferent to the idea of education, feeling that schooling would do no good nor would it improve their children in any way.[185]

Still others adopted a more pragmatic approach to the whole issue arguing that there was nothing fundamentally wrong with their children learning to read and write if the manager allowed them to attend school *and* if it did not affect their earning capacity. If, however, the child was not earning his or her bitt (eight cents), the excuse was that "the children have no rice, no cloth[es] and cannot go". Similarly, if the manager wished to keep them all day at work, their parents would not insist on their attendance at school.[186]

Many Indians, therefore, were prepared to exploit the estates' demand for cheap child labour in order to avail themselves of the earnings of their children and thus supplement their meagre earnings.[187] Money came first; education, not considered necessary or even desirable, could either be fitted in as the occasion arose or ignored altogether. "To the field he must go as soon almost as he can earn a sixpence (twelve cents)—books are laid aside and never often touched from the fact that even the simple act of reading is too laborious, uninteresting and useless to him."[188] Many Indians thus regarded compulsory education under the 1876 law as a nuisance which merely created hardship by depriving them of the earnings of their children.[189] For them education conferred no benefits since they were not seeking the advantages it offered for social advancement in the colonial society.

Although western education was considered of little value by the Indians, it is quite evident that the negative attitude of estate managers helped to reinforce their resistance to it. Were managers more favourable to the idea of immigrant education, Indian resistance would have been more difficult to sustain in the face of the former's enormous power. It was indeed very noticeable that wherever a manager did actively encourage education, Indian resistance weakened so as not to incur his wrath. As the Immigration Agent General stated in 1882, "He is the true *Deus ex machina* . . . It is only where the manager takes an interest in his school that the attendance bears any considerable proportion to the number of children on the roll. When the children are left to themselves, the attendance invariably falls off".[190]

That minority of Indian children who did manage to get an education proved to be intelligent and sharp. Although they worked during the day, some tried to study at night. But in the process several inculcated the values of the host society and sought advancement within it. They wanted to become lawyers' clerks, postmasters, telegraph clerks, interpreters, dispensers, and so on. Just a few, however, realized their ambitions during the nineteenth century.[191] But western education did precisely what many Indian parents feared most. The children were indoctrinated with Christian doctrine—the Catechism, the Command-

236

*Cultural
Power,
Resistance,
and
Pluralism*

ments, the New Testament. School generally began with a hymn and prayers.[192] Bronkhurst was proud that two Indian pupils of his could repeat the Lord's Prayer by heart in English. "They receive the good seed of God's Holy Word into their youthful hearts, which in God's own good time, will spring up and bear fruit . . ."[193] The medium of instruction was English, and not their own languages. Bhojpuri, spoken by the majority, was not taught or used.[194]

The products of this kind of educational process were considerably de-Indianized, and assimilated elite culture. According to Bronkhurst: "These Indian children have no desire or intention whatever to go to India with their parents when it is time for them to claim a return passage . . . They adopt the European style of dress, and speak more freely and readily the English than the language of their parents".[195] And "They do not like the term 'Coolie' or 'Sammy' [Swamy], applied to them, as they do not claim India for their native or birth place [as if that were the reason]. They all speak English well, and are great readers of our daily and weekly journals, and can be reached by the missionary, and through them reach the parents also".[196] Comins, too, noticed the difference: "The children born in the colony of Indian parents revert to a higher type of civilization, and in appearance, manners and intelligence are so much superior to their parents that it is difficult to believe they belong to the same family".[197]

Cultural alienation was the end result of this process of education. The children were taught to despise their parents' culture, and were weaned away from their families and ethnic community. But as Look Lai noted, "the loss of certain aspects of their traditional lifestyle did not mean the loss of tradition altogether".[198] Thus Bronkhurst observed that even when they adopted the elite culture, there was still a tendency to revert to Indian tradition on occasion in order to remain acceptable to their friends and relatives:

> The children in our public schools make good use of the opportunity afforded to them; they are not idle scholars. They have an aptitude for learning which is astonishing . . . They see how people live. They watch them narrowly. Though they do not try to ape as some people do, they strive to imitate them in their dress and manners, desire to do what is right, and try to be respectable in their own way, as far as means will allow them to do . . . They see how their parents live and act; they feel ashamed of their heathenish ways, and yet they lack the moral courage and strength to break away from their influence.[199]

Cultural assimilation in those circumstances was by no means complete. The majority, however, with the support of the planters themselves, successfully resisted the attempts to assimilate them through western education.

Magic and Witchcraft

[In India, the] belief in ghosts and spirits is universal. They are feared and propitiated. Strange mystical power pervading certain objects is recognized, and fetishes and amulets are eagerly sought. Witchcraft is often suspected and three or four people in the community are believed to possess magical powers.[200]

The Indian immigrants brought these beliefs and fears with them and maintained them. They were regarded as superstitious, and believed in lucky and unlucky days and hours, as well as in the power of ghosts, goblins, demons, phantoms, and fiends.[201] Their most deep-seated fear was that of the 'evil eye', the malice of enemies. This is 'bad magic' (called *maljo* in Trinidad), and can be caused intentionally or unintentionally.[202] Against this, countless charms and counter-charms were used by them. Hindus of every sect provided charms for themselves, their children, houses, livestock and gardens. Amulets, generally made with the *rupee* (Indian coin) or a piece of silver, were hung around the neck or hidden in the bosom; and their dwellings and gardens had 'mysterious' signs drawn upon them not only to guard against the proverbial 'evil eye', but also to avert evils, sickness, and accidents. The forehead was sometimes marked with the *tikho* or curdled milk as a propitious omen on beginning a journey.[203]

Other methods were also used to ward off the 'evil eye'. The ashes of the sacred cow-dung were used in various forms. One was *Chhattur*, the covering or cake of cow-dung placed on a heap of winnowed corn. When their children played with other children or were sent to visit, the Indians always placed upon their (the children's) cheeks or foreheads, a black spot (*pottu*) which was thought to have the power of preventing the effects of any expression of admiration.[204]

The Indians were thought to have adopted the Creole practice of, and belief in, obeah; but this is highly debatable.[205] The traditional Indian practice of magic was in many respects similar to obeah both for good and for evil. According to Dubois, Indian practitioners of magic were fortune-tellers, medicine-men, and sorcerers, among other things. This was not unlike the obeahman, and they also employed similar tools and techniques, e.g., bones of animals, potions, poisons, charms, plants roots, etc.[206] It is thus understandable that the casual observer should have thought that the Indians adopted obeah from the Creoles. In one reported instance of Indian magic, sometime between the first and fourth of September 1858, a woman living on Plantation Bochfour on the east coast of Demerara had stillborn twins who were buried at Plantation Hope. On the fifth, the coffin was found violated with its contents missing. The manager of Hope offered a reward of $5.00 for the discovery of the body snatchers. An Indian informant claimed to have seen four other Indians remove the heads and intes-

238

Cultural
Power,
Resistance,
and
Pluralism

tines of the dead babies in a calabash. However, two skulls, a parcel of bones, and two vials of strange looking liquid were later found in his house.[207] A similar incident occurred in 1877 when two Indians were found exhuming the remains of a dead body at Enmore burial ground. The *Colonist* supposed "that the skull, and other parts of human limbs are in the possession of some other coolies on the Enmore estate, and that the exhumation was prompted by a superstitious belief in obeahism".[208] But it is very likely that these, and other such occurrences among the Indians, were their own traditional practice of magic, rather than the adoption of obeah. The problem here is one of identification, the tendency being to label any practice which smacked of witchcraft or magic, regardless of the practitioners, as obeah.

What is clear, however, is that the Indian immigrants successfully resisted the entreaties and denunciations of the cultural elites, especially the missionaries, and preserved their traditional beliefs and practices of magic and witchcraft which, not unlike the great religions, thereby served as significant symbols of Indian cultural resistance.

Summary

The cultural history of the Indian immigrants during the nineteenth century reveals a strong retention of traditional cultural forms, ideas, beliefs, values, customs, etc. Life in the alien plantation environment undoubtedly forced some modification and redefinition, but these never really threatened to undermine their distinctive ethnicity fundamentally. A number of factors accounted for their ability to preserve their cultural traditions. In the first instance, the overwhelming majority went to Guyana with a perception that their sojourn was temporary, and this was to a considerable extent reinforced by the knowledge that they were entitled to a return passage payable in part by the colonial government. There was therefore no need to adopt the alien culture of the host society when there was no intention to remain permanently.

In addition, they were located in large numbers on plantations, more or less isolated residentially and occupationally from the members of the host society, and thus could form large viable self-contained communities in which they could regenerate their cultural institutions in the new environment. This process was further aided by fresh reinforcements of new arrivals from India on a regular basis. 'Mother India', therefore, was never too far away culturally. Even after leaving plantation residence, there was a very strong tendency to establish ethnic village settlements which even more closely resembled Indian rural communities, and which allowed them to revive many aspects of their religious and secular traditions that were either warped or suspended while resident in estate barracks. Hence they never perceived elite Victorian culture as conferring social respectability on them.

In their desire to obtain and keep their Indian workers relatively contented, the planters made very little effort to interfere with their cultural practices so long as they did not adversely affect the work routine and productivity. In fact the planters were not too enthusiastic about the activities of Christian missionaries whose attempts to convert the Indians were a source of unrest. The missionaries, who could have been much more troublesome if the planters were more amenable, were in any event far too few to minister to the perceived spiritual needs of the large immigrant population spread throughout the coastal belt of the colony. This combination of local factors played a very important role in preserving a strong sense of Indian ethnicity.

But the ability of the Indians to preserve their cultural traditions was not wholly dependent on such fortuitous circumstances. The Indians themselves played a very conscious and positive role in resisting the cultural impositions of the host society. In this respect, their continued adherence to the idea of caste status and to their religious beliefs and practices was vital, reinforced by the presence of racial antagonism in the local society. Both with respect to caste and religion, however, they were forced to make changes to suit the altered conditions in the plantation environment; but these changes were primarily with a view to redefining and consolidating their ethnicity by reducing cultural differences among themselves within a pan-Indian framework understood and adhered to by all. This promoted ethnic group consciousness and cohesion, and enabled them to develop a very distinct ethnic identity.

For most of the nineteenth century, therefore, the emphasis of the Indians was on resistance to the cultural power of the elites which threatened to submerge them culturally in the colonial society. This did not necessarily mean resistance to cultural integration. They brought with them new cultural institutions, beliefs and practices which other ethnic groups could adopt if they so chose, so long as they did not defile them; and indeed there is evidence that some of this did take place, particularly in the *tadja* festivities, though the Indians put up the shutters when they thought that the Creoles were beginning to desecrate the celebrations by adding Afro-Creole elements. The Indians themselves acquired *Creolese* (along with its rich lexicon of abusive words) largely for communication at work and in the 'market-place', and adopted such creole pastimes as prodigious rum drinking, gambling (mainly betting on horse races and cock-fights), playing cricket, marbles, etc., while a few even converted to Christianity.

But they refused to allow themselves as an ethnic group to be submerged by the dominant culture of the host society. At no time did

240

*Cultural
Power,
Resistance,
and
Pluralism*

they as a community evince a desire to acquire any aspects of that culture as a means of social advancement, and certainly they never perceived their own religious and secular culture as being in any way inferior. Unlike the situation in Trinidad where the Canadian Presbyterian Mission was quite successful in transmitting Christianity and western culture to a significant minority of Indians through both their missionary and educational work, no such major programme was mounted in Guyana during the nineteenth century. The number of westernized or christianized Indians by the end of the century was insignificant, and even fewer achieved any degree of prominence before 1900, e.g., Joseph Ruhoman (journalist), the Luckhoo brothers—Edward Alfred and Joseph Alexander—(both lawyers), and Rev. Benjamin Masih Das (first local-born Indian deacon).

As a community, therefore, the Guyanese Indians continued beyond the end of the century to adhere closely to their traditional culture and value system as a valuable and no less valid and worthwhile way of life than any other in the colony, and this enabled them to stand proud as a people in a racially hostile social environment. The Indian *Bhojpuri* culture thus performed a very important role of heightening their sense of ethnic consciousness and solidarity within the predetermined ethnic boundaries that separated them from the other groups. In this case, 'race' and culture were virtually coterminous in defining and determining the social position and status of the Indian immigrants. But for a very tiny minority, they shared no cultural institutions or values in common with the rest of the society, and one can only conclude that their cultural integration was minimal by the end of the nineteenth century. The case of the Indians thus clearly supports the concept of cultural pluralism as propounded by M.G. Smith, Despres, van Lier, van den Berghe, et al.

PORTUGUESE LATIN
CULTURE

Portuguese immigration into British Guiana began in 1835 and lasted through to 1882. In that space of time, 30,633 persons were introduced, mainly from the island of Madeira. Menezes notes that most of these were economic refugees fleeing hardship consequent on the decline of the two major industries, sugar and viniculture.[1] Thus despite very high mortality rates due mainly to malaria and yellow fever which threatened to put an end to government sponsorship of this immigration, the Madeirans were prepared to take the risk rather than remain at home.[2] Very strikingly, unlike other ethnic groups who migrated to Guyana in the nineteenth century, Portuguese women were also willing to take their chances alongside their menfolk. Laurence points out that from the early 1840s Portuguese immigration was characterized by a high proportion of women and children.[3] The proportion of women to men among the Portuguese in Guyana was consequently always high, moving from 1:1.5 in 1851 to a position of parity by the end of the century.[4]

This had very important ramifications for the transference to, and preservation of Portuguese culture in the colony. In the first place, traditional family life with the father as head remained intact and the Portuguese were able to reconstitute a relatively stable ethnic community very shortly after arrival in the colony despite, as we shall see, the absence of the moral and organizational influence of the Roman Catholic church. The presence of women within the family ensured too that Portuguese customs and values were transferred to the children, especially those born in the colony. On the other side of the coin, the high ratio of women to men meant that there was little need for the latter to seek mates outside the Portuguese community which minimized intimate social contact with members of other ethnic groups. This not only had bearing on race relations in the multiracial society, but also on their process of acculturation. On the other hand, the fact that so many Portuguese became involved in the retail trade

242

*Cultural
Power,
Resistance,
and
Pluralism*

Ken Morgan photo. Reproduced courtesy of Prof. Mary Noel Menezes (Guyana)

A Portuguese
immigrant
family

(groceries, dry goods, and liquors) provided a basis to bring them into
direct day to day contact with members of the host society which
promoted inter-culturation. One clear example of this was language
since they had to acquire *Creolese* in order to conduct their businesses
efficiently. But, as we shall see, language was to become a major issue
in the struggle to preserve a distinct sense of Portuguese ethnicity later
in the century.

Some of the early Portuguese immigrants were contracted to work on
the sugar estates after emancipation, and consequently lived in huts and
barrack-rooms in the 'negro yard' amidst the ex-slaves. This was an important sphere of culture contact although the role of Portuguese workers
as strike breakers during the ex-slaves' strikes in 1842 and 1848 certainly

strained relations between the two groups. In any event, most Portuguese immigrants either did not work on the estates at all or worked for a very short period (months rather than years), and consequently did not undergo what Rodney called "the indigenization process" of the plantation experience.[5]

Thus from the outset, or very soon thereafter, most of these immigrants lived in working class urban and rural communities, in small wooden houses and yards very similar to the Creoles. Bronkhurst in fact noted that the living conditions of poor Portuguese were no different from those of similarly circumstanced Creoles. They both had few material possessions (a few pieces of furniture, calabash, coalpot and saucepan) and their small quarters tended to be overcrowded with food items such as potatoes, plantains, and saltfish, and even in some cases with livestock (pigs, goats, fowls, etc.).[6] Several Portuguese rented or leased houses built by Creoles and converted them into shops,[7] reserving one or two rooms either above or behind in which to live until they became sufficiently wealthy to afford separate and better homes elsewhere. By the end of the nineteenth century affluent Portuguese families owned and occupied some of the finest mansions in upper-class white areas of the cities.

This growing oppulence was also reflected in their attire and means of transportation. As early as 1842 Governor Light commented that ". . . women who are remembered to be formerly filthy as newcomers, are decked out in shawls or nets and silks on Sundays, with their husbands and their companions in fine broadcloth suits, gloves and beaver hats in full enjoyment of the fruits of their industry".[8] Five years later he not only observed how well the Portuguese looked— "like lower-class Irish" and as clean as the Creoles; but noted as well that many had horses, gigs and chaises.[9] There was essentially nothing in their physical appearance (i.e., dress) that distinguished the Portuguese from the members of the host society.

The Portuguese brought and were able to preserve their own culinary treats largely on account of the regular traffic they maintained between the colony and Madeira. According to Bronkhurst, "the Portuguese likes his mess of cabbage, pumpkin, potatoes, cornmeal, pork and saltfish . . ."[10] At a glance this would appear to be ordinary creole fare, but Menezes lists each of those items as being integral to traditional Portuguese dishes, e.g., cabbage and pumpkin soup, pumpkin fritters, *milho* (cornmeal), *carne de alho* (garlic pork), and *bacelhau* (saltfish). These and other dishes which they introduced were supplemented by local vegetables, ground provisions, and meats which some of them, as farmers, cultivated and reared. No Portuguese table was complete without Madeiran wines which were imported by the Portuguese merchants themselves.[11] Though making good use of local food-

244

*Cultural
Power,
Resistance,
and
Pluralism*

stuffs, their cuisine remained distinctly Madeiran and aided in fostering a sense of Portuguese ethnicity.

Religion

In all Latin civilizations, whether in southern Europe or Latin America, the family and the church are the twin pillars on which the culture
is built. When the Portuguese migrated to Guyana in the nineteenth
century, they took this heritage with them. Thus, as Menezes has
observed, the cultural behaviour and customs of the Portuguese immigrants were closely related to their Roman Catholic religious beliefs
and practices derived from their native Madeira.[12] From the beginning
of their immigration into the colony, therefore, concern was expressed
about their religious education and the shortage of Catholic priests
who could speak Portuguese. Yet despite the considerable inflow of
Portuguese during the 1840s, and strong advocacy by both Governor
Light and Secretary of State Stanley, the planters were unwilling to
increase the government's financial contribution to the Roman Catholic church to provide salaries for additional priests to cater to the
spiritual needs of a small minority simply because it would increase
public expenditure.[13] Of course, they chose to ignore the fact that the
Portuguese immigrants were contributing to the colonial revenues
through taxation. Catholic sympathizers of the Portuguese immigrants
were not slow to point out this injustice, and in a petition to the
Governor and Combined Court in 1845 they requested a grant to
cover salaries for Portuguese priests as well as to build and maintain
suitable Catholic churches/chapels for use by the immigrants.[14] This
was supported by firm representation by Dr. Hynes, the Catholic
bishop, and resulted in the provision in 1846 of $933 for the salary of a
Portuguese speaking priest.[15] Similarly, in 1849, in response to six
petitions from the Catholics of different districts, as well as representation from the Portuguese government, a stipend for a second
Portuguese priest was provided.[16]

Two priestly positions funded by the government were hardly sufficient to serve a community of 7,928 in 1851,[17] who were scattered all
over the country. The Catholic church, in recognition of this, quite
independently recruited a priest from Lisbon in 1845. According to
Menezes, Fr. Joaquim Antonio Correa de Natividade was particularly
well received by the Portuguese, who for the first time were able to
have their services conducted in Portuguese and in a familiar format.
But the daunting task of ministering to so widely dispersed a community discouraged Fr. Correa who requested to return to Portugal.[18]
Effectively, therefore, a large proportion of these immigrants was left
unattended in their religious cares. By the 1850s, the Portuguese

formed the vast majority of Catholics in the colony. It was estimated that in 1858 they amounted to about 5,000 of the approximately 6,000 Catholics in Georgetown and its environs (especially along the east bank of Demerara), while most of the 800 Catholics in New Amsterdam were likewise Portuguese. There were still others dispersed throughout the rural districts.[19]

The absence of a strong Portuguese-speaking Roman Catholic priestly presence to service the spiritual needs of the Portuguese immigrants left a religious vacuum which some ambitious Protestant missionaries were all too eager to fill. This was to some extent encouraged by some Portuguese themselves who, in order to continue worshipping as Christians, attended Protestant chapels. This tendency was furthered if the priests could speak the Portuguese language; but more often than not, the English Protestant priests were ignorant of any other language and thus could not communicate with the Portuguese. Their attendance at Protestant chapels encouraged vain hopes of conversion, but those were quickly dashed. Even though a few of those who could afford it rented pews in Protestant chapels,[20] not a single case of any having apostatized was known; and this was not for want of trying, even to the point where one Protestant church in Georgetown was decorated to resemble a Catholic one in order to attract Portuguese worshippers.[21] The Portuguese evidently regarded their continued affiliation to Roman Catholicism, however nominal, to be one of the major pillars upon which their identity as a distinct ethnic group in Guyana was based and were not prepared to compromise that despite the subtle efforts of the Anglo-Creole elites to entice them to assimilate.

The want of adequate priestly guidance may have contributed in no small way to lapses in their moral and religious behaviour. But the attitude of the Anglo-Creole elites, particularly the English Catholic priests, towards Portuguese morality was reminiscent of the way they viewed other subordinate ethnic groups. They regarded the Portuguese as an ignorant, insolent and wicked people. They condemned the apparent prevalence of 'concubinage' among them, and accused some of the most wealthy and respectable Portuguese of living unmarried with one or more companions, thus encouraging illegitimacy.[22] The elites were thus prepared to use their cultural power by way of criticism and ridicule to pressure the Portuguese to conform to the ideals of Victorian morality.

Even though the Portuguese continued to go to church on special occasions such as baptisms, marriages and funerals, and paid their *Jura* (tithes) well and readily, general attendance at church on Sundays declined considerably, and they hardly went to confession.[23] This was no doubt due to the fact that they were unfamiliar with the form of

246

*Cultural
Power,
Resistance,
and
Pluralism*

service performed by the English clergy in a language which they could not understand, while they themselves were not understood by the priests. It was not unusual, therefore, even during the Lenten season, to see some of the most influential Portuguese spending their sabbaths picnicking on cattle farms—shooting, dancing and singing—instead of fasting and going to church as was their tradition.[24]

So disillusioned with the English-led Roman Catholic church did some Portuguese become that they lost all respect for the English clergy. For instance, after a baptism in 1859, a Portuguese watchman, the infant's godfather, pointed to his common-law wife, the godmother, and said aloud: "I shall have a baptism soon!" Considering this an act of gross immorality, the English priest took the man 'paternally' by the whiskers and told him that he should prepare for his confession. The man responded, however, by grabbing the priest firmly by his cassock. Considering this an assault, the priest threatened his assailant with excommunication. When that failed to produce the desired effect, the priest boxed the man's ears. Still unable to free himself from the man's grip, the priest then "gave him one home under the chin which sent him down the steps and sprawling in the mire". The 'wife' thereupon seized 'Father' by his hair and pulled him down, while one man held his legs and another hit him about the face and head, before depositing him in the mud. The holy man was naturally greatly disturbed by this outrage to his sacerdotal dignity.[25] This was a very dramatic act of resistance against an attempt by an 'alien' to impose Victorian morality on the Portuguese.

The Portuguese were generally quite unconcerned about what the English priests, symbolizing the cultural power of the colonial elites, thought of them. They argued with great logic that they could not be as bad as the priests made them out because God blessed them with plenty.[26] But although their outward religious behaviour (church attendance and morality) might have been modified in their adaptation to the new (alien) physical and socio-cultural environment, they remained at heart loyal Roman Catholics who insisted on preserving their Madeiran traditions, customs and language with a view to resisting the cultural impositions of the dominant Anglo-Creole elites.

By the 1850s, therefore, it was obvious that additional priests fluent in the Portuguese language were necessary to meet the spiritual and cultural needs of the Portuguese immigrants. As none was forthcoming from Portugal itself, the new Roman Catholic bishop James Etheridge, himself a Jesuit, decided to introduce eight Jesuit missionaries from Italy who spoke Portuguese.[27] Thus until the late nineteenth century, the Portuguese congregation were served mainly by Italian clergy who conducted their services and preaching in the Portuguese language.[28] This had a significant impact on the Portuguese immigrants who once again began to flock to the Roman Catholic churches in large numbers.[29]

The most notable of these Jesuits was Father Benedict Schembri who arrived in the colony in November 1857 after a short period in Algeria. Schembri spent his first two weeks among the Amerindians at Moruca in the interior of Essequibo before dedicating himself to full-time missionary work among the Portuguese, especially those in the Georgetown area and along the east bank of Demerara. He acquainted himself with them and their culture and behaviour in every part of the city, and played a significant part in aiding them to retain their Madeiran religious customs in the face of intense opposition from the English Roman Catholic clergy.[30]

As part of the colonial elite cultural establishment, the English Roman Catholic clergy were intent on using their cultural power to press the Portuguese to adopt English religious rituals. As far as they were concerned, the Portuguese were too inflexible in their ardent attachment to their Madeiran religious customs and did "not quite understand why Roman Catholicity in its accidental details is not exactly the same in every place". Of course, since the Portuguese formed the vast majority of the Roman Catholic congregation, it is evident that it was the English clergy who were being arrogantly inflexible. The Portuguese willingly participated in religious ceremonies, "but are rather disposed on such occasions to dictate or take matters into their own hands".[31]

The Brickdam Roman Catholic Cathedral, Georgetown, c.1860

248

Cultural
Power,
Resistance,
and
Pluralism

Schembri appreciated the strong attachment of the Portuguese to their traditional customs. But as there was up to the late 1850s only one small Roman Catholic church in Georgetown, located in the Brickdam, where all the sermons and instructions were conducted in English, the Portuguese tended to stay away. Schembri, however, was able to win their confidence by holding separate Portuguese language services and they soon began to flock to church. That, however, merely set in train a bitter rivalry between Schembri and the Italian Jesuits on one hand, and the English clergy on the other, especially over which group should claim preference of the 11.00 a.m. Sunday mass.[32]

This rivalry seemed to have the makings of a schism within the local Roman Catholic communion. The English clergy felt that Schembri was challenging their hegemony by building a religious empire around the Portuguese. Schembri indeed worked almost exclusively among the Portuguese and allegedly refused to undertake any general ministerial duties.[33] He was even accused of discountenancing the Portuguese from joining Roman Catholic confraternities except those formed exclusively for Portuguese. He held separate devotions for them, and while he may not have actively prevented anyone else from participating in these, he apparently did not invite or encourage any other ethnic group to do so. Several among the English Roman Catholic clergy felt strongly that Schembri would never permit non-Portuguese Roman Catholics to enrol in his associations.[34] Whether this was ever put to the test is not known.

By 1859, just two years after Schembri's arrival, schism seemed very probable. There were two distinct devotional altars in the Brickdam church for use almost exclusively by the Portuguese. Even more ominously, Schembri began to collect funds for the establishment of an exclusively Portuguese church in which there would be no English language services.[35] Schembri went even farther in his pro-Portuguese position. He allegedly discouraged the Portuguese from sending their children to general Roman Catholic schools. So in spite of the fact that a boys' school existed near the presbytery and a girls' school was conducted by the nuns of the Ursuline Convent, there was a number of small schools in the city catering exclusively to Portuguese children.[36] Those who were sent to the two Roman Catholic schools were actually withdrawn by Schembri for separate devotions in the church. The girls were most affected as the convent was some distance from the church; and since Schembri insisted on holding a day of special devotion for the Portuguese pupils at the church instead of allowing the girls to receive the sacraments at the convent, their classes had to be truncated on that day.[37] In addition, on Sundays at 3.00 p.m. he rang the church bell and held a small Sunday school for about forty to sixty Portuguese children.[38] This attracted hostile criticism from the English clergy who felt that if he had his way entirely, "he would scarcely allow the Portuguese children to learn English, in order that they might keep up their own language and traditions, and for fear of their reading bad English books, or becoming corrupted and losing their religion".[39]

If these criticisms were valid, one would have to conclude that Schembri's dedication to the Portuguese while very admirable in one sense, might have been divisive not only within the Roman Catholic communion, but also within the society at large. It was one thing to uphold the religious and cultural identity of the Portuguese immigrants, but to have actively encouraged their isolation within the host society must be highly questionable. The desire to adhere to their Madeiran religious traditions and customs should not have meant excluding others from participating, nor should the preservation of the Portuguese language (or the Madeiran dialect) have meant discouraging the Portuguese from learning English as Schembri was accused of doing. In other words, the retention of a distinct Madeiran ethnic identity should not have been regarded as being incompatible with the integration of the Portuguese immigrants into the host society and their assimilation of that minimum of the host culture which would have facilitated that process.

Having said that, however, it is understandable that both the Portuguese and Schembri should have sought to use the Madeiran religious culture not just to promote a distinct ethnic identity, but also to resist the cultural power of the dominant British section in the society, and to foster group solidarity in a social environment that was decidedly hostile towards them. This hostility emanated mainly from the Creole population; and it attained its worst expression in anti-Portuguese riots on three occasions during the nineteenth century: 1848, 1856 and 1889. Under those circumstances, the preservation of the Madeiran culture was considered critical by the Portuguese and their Jesuit benefactors in order to mould ethnic group cohesion, and to forge a sense of dignity and self-worth to counteract the pariah status with which they were tainted by members of the host society as a result of their economic role as traders.

The ethnocentric arrogance of the English Roman Catholic clergy contributed in no small way towards the desire for ethnic exclusivism which the Portuguese immigrants seemed to crave. They continuously denounced Madeiran Roman Catholic customs as "far from perfection in many ways" (perfection no doubt being equated with English customs). As far as they were concerned, the Portuguese "don't deserve to be humoured"; "we ought to be fatherly but firm with them". While their fears of a schism may have been justified because of the extrem-

250

*Cultural
Power,
Resistance,
and
Pluralism*

Ken Morgan photo. Reproduced courtesy of Prof. Mary Noel Menezes (Guyana)

The Sacred
Heart Roman
Catholic
church

ism of some Portuguese,[40] it is clear that this situation of mutual antagonism was to a large extent provoked by their own narrow-minded ethnocentrism and hostility to the genuine needs and concerns of the Portuguese majority in the colonial Roman Catholic church.

Portuguese resistance to the cultural power of the English Roman Catholic clerical establishment culminated in the establishment of a separate Portuguese church in Main Street, Georgetown, in 1861.[41] Bishop Etheridge supported the scheme as the only prudent solution. For in his view, the Portuguese: "*must be, can only be* [sic] kept, in any sort of a way, to the Church and their duty, by ceremonies and practices something like what they have been accustomed to in Madeira . . . Had we not some Portuguese attractions as well as the Portuguese language to work for us, the Churches would be empty as we found them and the Sacraments except Baptism nearly out of use".[42]

The land was bought for $1,800 and the building was erected at a cost of $12,000.[43] The Church of the Sacred Heart, as it was called, was built in the form of a Latin Cross. Its dedication in honour of the Sacred Heart was due to Father Schembri's ardent devotion, and to the promise which he made to the Blessed Margaret Mary Alacoque to whose care he had committed the success of his apostolic work.[44] With subsequent decorations, this church presented a picturesque sight by the turn of the century:

> The church itself is quite in the Italian style, brilliant in colour, with a wax image of St. Philomena, an object of great devotion, and figure of Our Lord under the high altar, the arms of which can be extended so as to fix it in a cross. At present

there is a most elaborate 'Crib', crowded with figures of all kinds, a landscape, town and running water. On occasion, the whole moves by electricity, and a little automaton in the foreground presents a box for alms.[45]

In spite of the fact that the *Eclesia pro Lusitanis* was a *fait accompli* after 1861, Schembri was firmly opposed by Vicar General Walker.[46] But there was no altering the ethnic exclusivity of the Portuguese church. By 1864 the non-Portuguese congregation were a minority of 2:7 in the Roman Catholic communion. This was just as important a reason for the opposition of the English clergy to the establishment of a separate Portuguese church as the issue of religious culture. For once the Portuguese congregation withdrew to Main Street, the Brickdam church stood to lose revenue which was substantial since by then many Portuguese were quite wealthy. In the end, however, the Roman Catholic communion had to settle for the coexistence of two separate congregations adhering to a common faith, but employing different cultural styles and languages[47]—cultural heterogeneity, in M.G. Smith's conceptualization.

Notwithstanding the tremendous contribution which Schembri and the Italian Jesuits made to the preservation of a distinct Portuguese religio-cultural identity, and despite the long residence of many Portuguese in the colony, they began to press during the 1880s for the establishment of a new church under priests of their own nationality. They claimed that the Italians had but an imperfect knowledge of their language/dialect and so were unable to preach eloquently and to make themselves fully understood. In addition, they claimed that the education of their children in the Portuguese language was to some extent neglected, although education in English left little to be desired.[48] This controversy was eventually settled when on the representation of the Portuguese government, the Vatican authorized the recruitment of priests of any order than the Jesuits for work in the colony. This facilitated the recruitment in 1883 of three Portuguese priests of the Order of St. Peter.[49]

It can be argued that far from being an indication of ingratitude on the part of the Portuguese, their desire for Portuguese priests was justifiable. In the first place, the Italians spoke grammatical Portuguese with an accent, whereas the Madeiran immigrants spoke a dialect of standard Portuguese.[50] Hence it was difficult to understand the Italians. In the second place, to a people so very concerned with resisting the culture of the host society and preserving their ethnic identity, it must have been a matter of grave concern to observe that by the 1880s the majority of Portuguese children and young people not only did not know the Portuguese language[51] but, even worse, apparently did not care to learn it, preferring instead to converse in *Creolese*[52] and becoming fully versed in its rich range of abusive terms: "as to the use

252

*Cultural
Power,
Resistance,
and
Pluralism*

of obscene language, the degree of height cannot be excelled by any other people".[53]

This situation undoubtedly arose from the spread of English education to embrace Portuguese children in the later nineteenth century. Most of the original Portuguese immigrants were illiterate even in the Portuguese language,[54] and remained so despite their accumulation of substantial wealth. "They even ask what is the good of education, when they can grow rich without it." As a result, children were either not sent to school[55] or, if so, the preference was to send them the Portuguese language schools which mushroomed about the city. At the best of times, these small private schools could not accommodate the growing number of Portuguese children, and the introduction of compulsory education in 1876[56] (in so far as it was enforceable) undoubtedly made matters worse as regards the preservation of the Portuguese language. More and more Portuguese children, particularly in the urban centres, were thus forced to attend public schools, preferably Roman Catholic, where instruction was in English.[57] This witnessed a dramatic decline in the use of the Portuguese language among the young which no doubt helps to explain the desire to recruit Portuguese priests in hope of reviving the use of the language at least for formal and ritualistic purposes within the ethnic community.

It is evident that certainly among the first generation Portuguese immigrants the emphasis was on retention, in as pure a form as possible, of their Madeiran religious culture, and the Portuguese language. To do this they had to take on the English hierarchy of the Roman Catholic church who were intent, it seems, on eradicating all traces of Madeiran religious customs and practices. Their resolute resistance to this exercise of cultural power, even to the point of the threat of schism, ensured the survival of their religious traditions. But their success was built around separate ethnic institutions which fostered their socio-cultural isolation from the host society as a whole, thus retarding whatever tendencies towards cultural integration were at work. Indeed for most of the postemancipation nineteenth century they displayed very little inclination to become assimilated into the colonial society and clung steadfastly to their Madeiran traditions. This was vividly demonstrated at an exhibition and concert in 1872 by the young pupils of one of the small Portuguese schools run by one Mrs. Carvalho when the performance began with their recitation of the Portuguese national anthem.[58] Roman Catholicism (Madeiran style) and all the rituals and festivities associated with it, as we shall see, became the principal manifestations of a distinct Portuguese ethnic identity around which they could build a strong sense of group cohesion in hostile social environment. Still they had to make some concessions to the secular forces of creolization which were most manifest in

the sphere of language. By the end of the century, *Creolese* was beginning to break down the barriers which had for so long protected the
bastion of Portuguese cultural exclusivity.

Rituals, festivities and Celebrations

The central role of the Roman Catholic church in the lives of the
Portuguese immigrants is reflected in their faithful adherence to traditional religious rituals and festivals. They planned their leisure around
Roman Catholic festive days even when they were not colonial holidays. One of their principal devotions was the *Novena* of the *Missa de
Parto* nine days preceding Christmas (*Natal*). Respectable offerings
were made by the promoters of the feast (*festereiros*) to the pastor for
the due celebration of this as for other feasts. For nine days before
Christmas, the *Missa Cantata* was sung and a sermon delivered between 4.00 and 5.00 a.m. which was well attended regardless of the
weather.[59] During the mass, a Portuguese hymn to the Blessed Lady
(the Virgin Mary) was sung and at the end there was the Benediction
of the Blessed Sacrament.[60] Since this was not an English custom, it
attracted criticism from the cultural elites especially since it involved
the use of drums and trumpets "to the annoyance of certain respectable neighbours".[61]

Christmas was a great religious festival for the Portuguese and generally began with large attendances at midnight mass as in Madeira.[62]
Immediately before the mass commenced, the priest and his acolytes
would go to the door of the church where children dressed in gala
Madeiran fashion were assembled. They then proceeded in proces-
sional order, headed by a violin prayer, to the sanctuary singing the
Bemdita Sejaes. Each child presented a gift in honour of the infant Jesus
while a strophe was sung to commemorate the kind of offering made;
and the Grace was asked of the Saviour. The gifts generally consisted
of cakes, candles, eggs, fruit, flowers, lamb or goat decorated with
garlands.[63]

The women spent most of Christmas day preparing meals for entertainment on Boxing day (December 26), while the men masqueraded
around their district, firing off guns and exploded fireworks and squibs
as they would in Madeira. Every man discharged his lot independently
of his neighbour thus giving a general appearance of an 'illumination'
nightly during the Christmas season. Music accompanied these celebrations, and a cacophony of sound would often be produced by
several masquerading bands playing simultaneously in the same district. However the cultural elites disapproved, particularly of the fireworks and gunfire, and used the sanction of law to curb these practices
leading on occasion to the arrest of several Portuguese revellers.[64]

254

*Cultural
Power,
Resistance,
and
Pluralism*

Boxing day was generally a 'visiting' day for the Portuguese, and every table, even of the poorest home, was loaded with immense joints of cooked meat, brandy, rum and wine.[65]

Another major festival was the feast of the Assumption of the Blessed Virgin Mary, *Nossa Senhora do Monte* or *Nostia Signora da Monti*, in August. To the Portuguese, like all devout Roman Catholics, the Blessed Virgin (the *Madonna*) was of very special importance as the mother of Christ, and they had the greatest veneration for her image. They made many vows, and some even made pilgrimages to Madeira in her honour; and it was a sore point if their church did not house a copy of her image. In 1859, the Vicar General found it necessary to have one installed over the high altar of the Berbice chapel which the Portuguese decorated with a quantity of silver lace and pure silver fringe.[66] Every year a number of Portuguese pilgrims would go to the little Church of the Assumption of Our Lady in Glasgow, Berbice, for mass.[67] Before this feast, *Novena* devotions were held after the mass each morning, and services were held each evening for nine days before the feast. The Assumption was normally portrayed in the form of a mountain-like cloud ascending to heaven.[68]

Although the facilities were not available in Guyana to make as grand a display as in Madeira, it was evident that the enthusiasm was not wanting. In Georgetown, the whole facade of the Sacred Heart church was beautifully illuminated for the feast of the Assumption, while little pillars connected to one another by graceful flower festoons, each supporting vases filled with flame, stood like burning sentinels in various parts of the church and at its entrance. "The effect was really beautiful, and especially the brilliant diamond-like effect of the Cross . . ."[69] Likewise, the church of the Ascension in New Amsterdam had its tower illuminated each evening of service before the feast; and on the feast day itself it was decorated with a great display of bunting, from the tower and across the street in front of the church, together with the illuminations at the evening service.[70] Services of the day commenced with a communion mass at 7.30 a.m., followed by a high mass at 11.00 a.m. and devotions and sermons at 3.00 p.m.[71] All Portuguese shops were closed from 9.00 a.m. to noon so that high mass could be attended.[72]

On the secular side, this festival was celebrated as in Madeira with great merriment. For instance in New Amsterdam, they erected tents and pavilions on the chapel grounds which they occupied in between church services while being entertained by a Portuguese brass band.[73] Some Portuguese from Georgetown normally travelled by train for a day's festivity to one of the East Coast villages where they would also attend a church service.[74]

The feast of the Holy Ghost on Pentecost or Whit Sunday was celebrated fifty days after Easter. The Portuguese brought with them the Madeiran custom of *Spiritu Sancto* whereby the *festereiros* for several Sundays before Pentecost stood around the altar within the sanctuary at mass. This brought the Portuguese into direct conflict with the English clergy who objected to this practice largely because many of these *festereiros* lived in 'concubinage', and felt that they desecrated the church by being placed in positions of such prominence. Indeed the Roman Catholic bishop prohibited the practice unless such 'scandalous' men were removed.[75] This was an exercise of cultural power by the church hierarchy on moral grounds, and the Portuguese were forced to comply in order to preserve an ethnic religious custom. At this festival, Roman Catholic churches which Portuguese frequented were elaborately decorated with festoons and flags, and were illuminated.[76]

Menezes observes that nine days before the feast "the *emperador* [chief *festereiro*] visited all the Roman Catholic homes of the poor and the sick in his parish/village carrying with him a dove, representative of the Holy Spirit, and crown in which people placed their gift to be used in the celebration of the feast".[77] One of the highlights of the Pentecost celebrations was the Madeiran custom of feeding the poor. After the church service, a procession led by twelve of the most indigent Portuguese who had confessed and received communion, marched to a predetermined place for an elaborate dinner. The chosen were symbolic of the twelve apostles, but were either male or female. They were supplied with suitable apparel for the occasion, the females being given white dresses and white head-kerchiefs. The banquet hall was gaily decorated with flowers, fruit, coconut palms and flags. The twelve paupers sat first and ate as much food as they could which was served by wealthy *festereiros*. The food generally consisted of bread and cheese, wine, cakes, fruit, ham, beef, etc. When they were finished, other less fortunate paupers in the almshouse or lunatic asylum were given rations of food. In New Amsterdam in 1880, about 150 poor persons were supplied at the Pentecost. There was always music provided by a Portuguese brass band.[78]

The secular aspects of the Pentecost celebrations seemed far less orderly and sober. Sometimes, in typical Madeiran fashion, rejoicing began after midnight with the firing of guns and processions of men with flags and poles with lanterns attached.[79] For instance, in 1875, Pouderoyen with its substantial Portuguese community, was reported to be very gay with gaudy displays, noise and confusion as from the Saturday afternoon until the Sunday night, large numbers of gaily dressed people from all parts of the country, together with a band of musicians from Georgetown, rolled in by carriages of all descriptions.

256

*Cultural
Power,
Resistance,
and
Pluralism*

A large logie was hired to form the centre of activities, and was gaily decorated with flags, flowers and gaudy ornaments. These celebrations, however, were disapproved by the cultural elites who complained about the "noisy laughter and wanton shrieks" of dancing men and women, the gun-firing, and "general debauchery and profligacy everywhere observable . . . like hell let loose".[80] They were convinced that the Holy Ghost was not in the hearts of the Portuguese revellers.[81] Again this was another clear example of 'what is not English is not good'.

The feast of St. Joseph, in honour of the father of Jesus Christ, was usually celebrated sometime after Easter and was observed at various churches at different times roughly between March and September. It was celebrated with the same fervour as the other festivals—pontifical high mass at 11.00 a.m. with the bishop and several priests officiating. The high point of the festivities was a grand public procession in the evening. In Georgetown, the Sacred Heart church was usually decorated outside with flags, banners, and hosts of small coloured glass lamps hung on lines; inside the walls were adorned with rich, beautiful banners and drapery, while the high altar was ablaze with candles, and the candelabra and gas jets were also lit. A procession was held after vespers. In this, members of the Society of St. Joseph (male) dressed in their white gowns and blue capes, were joined by the Society of the Blessed Virgin (female) dressed in red gowns and white capes. Each processionist carried a lit torchstick. They were preceded by the Portuguese *Primeiro de Dezembro* (First of December) brass band, the bishop in full ceremonial attire complete with mitre and staff, robed priests, the little girls of the Infant Jesus Society attired in white with floral crowns and wings and carrying bouquets, and the little boys of the Sons of Mary Society in neat uniform. Displaying banners and images of St. Joseph and the angels, this colourful procession went along both sides of Main Street before returning to the church for the bishop's sermon and the benediction of the Blessed Sacrament which brought the festivities to an end.[82]

The feast of St. Peter in honour of the fisherman disciple of Christ who is the acknowledged founder of the Roman Catholic church was celebrated by high mass, followed by feasting where large quantities of strong drink (not just Madeiran wines, but local rum as well) were often imbibed.[83] Menezes notes that one distinctive feature of this festival was a procession of singing celebrants carrying small boats.[84]

As in Madeira, Good Friday and Easter were also major religious occasions for the Portuguese, commemorating the crucifixion and resurrection of Christ. The Portuguese reportedly marked Good Friday with intense emotional feeling, loud shrieking, screaming, and fainting of women at the service. On that night a *Tenebra* service was held to commemorate Christ's presence in the sepulchre during which all ornaments and decorations in the sanctuary were removed. All lights in the church were extinguished to symbolize the plain emptiness and darkness of the tomb.[85]

The feast of St. Anthony was held on June 13. According to Menezes, St. Anthony was "the saint, *par excellence* of Portuguese devotions both in Portugal and Madeira and transferred to Guyana". The main feature of this feast was the distribution of loaves of bread topped with a cross to the poor.[86] The nativity of St. John the Baptist was also celebrated by the Portuguese. On its eve, large bonfires were lit at their doors over which they jumped.[87] Menezes also indicates that they also engaged in fortune-telling by breaking eggs in glasses of water to find out their destiny, the latter being determined by the shape of the egg in the glass, e.g., a church meant marriage; a ship, travel; a star, success.[88]

Numerous other religious festivals in relation to Roman Catholic saints were celebrated by the Portuguese with characteristic church services, processions, and noisy feasting including the use of fireworks. Among these were the feast of the Sacred Heart of Jesus initiated by St. Margaret Mary Alacoque and held in June;[89] the feast of *Corpus Christi* in honour of the doctrine of transubstantiation (the real presence of Christ in the Eucharist) and the adoration of the Host, which was observed on the Thursday after Trinity Sunday;[90] that of the Lady of the Rosary;[91] and of St. Aloysius, an Iberian saint.[92]

Associated with the church, papal jubilees were cause for celebration—in 1871, that of Pope Pius IX (1846-1878); in 1888 and in 1893, those of Pope Leo XIII (1878-1903). If Pius's jubilee was celebrated quietly with special church services, those of Leo XIII were marked by lavish celebrations. On both occasions several churches, and in particular the Roman Catholic cathedral in Brickdam and the Sacred Heart church in Main Street, were elaborately decorated and illuminated, and the poor were treated to sumptuous dinners.[93]

The 1893 celebrations surpassed all others in splendour and seemed to signify a new sense of achievement and confidence among the Portuguese, more than just religious zeal. It was thus as much a celebration of their wealth and success as it was a church festival, and this was vividly demonstrated by their use of electric power to illuminate the Sacred Heart church in addition to the normal lanterns and candles. This was unquestionably one of the grandest illuminations witnessed in nineteenth century Guyana. Beginning with the lighting of about 2,000 multi-coloured fairy lamps at about 7.00 p.m., some 400 Chinese lanterns of different shades hung between the church building and the perimeter fence were lit at 8.00 p.m.; finally at 9.00 p.m. the electric light of 400 incandescent bulbs was switched on to the awe and admi-

258

*Cultural
Power,
Resistance,
and
Pluralism*

ration of all those gathered: "The light bursting forth like the different colours of the rainbow cast a hue along Main Street, that is rarely witnessed in the tropics, and as it died away towards midnight it left behind it the impression that the Portuguese Community of George-town had celebrated the fête in a style which reflected the highest credit on them".[94] In a real sense, it demonstrated their position as a prominent, wealthy, successful and influential ethnic community in Guyanese society.

The feast of the Portuguese Benevolent Society (P.B.S.) was more obviously secular than the others. It was held annually on the anniver-sary of the establishment of the society in 1872, i.e., on the Sunday nearest February 16th.[95] The P.B.S. was actually modelled on similar societies in Madeira and was intended to aid poor Portuguese members in time of need, illness and death within the family.[96] However, it was dissolved in 1888 largely as a result of internal dissensions.[97] During its existence, the annual celebrations were marked with typical Portu-guese extravagance and sumptuous dinners for the poor after high mass.[98] Another purely secular annual celebration was the birthday of the monarch of Portugal which signified the close national and senti-mental links which the Portuguese retained with the fatherland, and which set them apart as a distinct ethnic and national group from the rest of the society. This was usually marked by fireworks displays and parades by the Portuguese band.[99]

At the familial level, marriage occasioned the greatest celebration among the Portuguese. Like other ethnic groups in the society, they spent lavishly, particularly on fashionable clothes for the wedding.[100] The wealthier Portuguese, in particular, celebrated in a manner very similar to the colonial elites. For instance, the wedding of timber merchant Antonio Gonsalves and Miss Fernandes in April 1883 at the Roman Catholic cathedral was officiated by the bishop and five priests, and included pontifical high mass. The bride wore a white silk dress trimmed with silver spangles and lace, orange blossoms and white veil, while the bridesmaids were all elegantly dressed in pink silk dresses. A lavish reception was held after the wedding.[101] Likewise, the wedding celebrations of Albino Fernandes and Maria Adelaide Car-reiro ten years later were equally elaborate. The bride wore a beautiful silk dress with orange blossoms and a diamond brooch. There was a sumptuous *déjeuner* at the groom's house after the ceremony, followed in the evening by a grand ball.[102]

For the most part, however, it would appear that the Portuguese remained entirely faithful to their religious and secular traditions and made no concessions to those of the host society. All their festivities were decidedly Madeiran in form, style and content, mainly centred around the Roman Catholic church and secular Portuguese national-ism. Even so, one cannot but observe that the open display of lavish and conspicuous consumption and the boisterous behaviour on these festive occasions, though in many respects rooted in Madeiran peasant culture, blended very well with, and were reinforced by, typical working class creole ways. In like fashion, though, they had to withstand stern criticism both from the English clergy within the church and the elites on the outside who used their cultural power in an attempt to restrict the Portuguese celebrations.

Minor Religious Customs

Despite the disapproval of the English Roman Catholic clergy, the Portuguese preserved many Madeiran customs, several of a religious character, which differentiated them even from other Roman Catholics and other whites in the colony. They were reputed to do many pious things. For instance, they would stop working and take off their hat at the sound of the *Angelus*. This is a devotion in memory of the Incarnation of Christ. It consists of three *Ave Marias* with vesicles and a collect. It is recited thrice daily at 6.00 a.m., 12.00 noon, and 6.00 p.m., when the *Angelus* bell is rung—three short strokes, one long, and three short ones again on each occasion.[103] They also removed their hats on passing a church, or when one spoke of *Santissimo Sacramento* (Holy Eucharist). They were very fond of buying candles for the altar and sweet oil for the sanctuary lamp before the Blessed Sacrament. Many presents came as thanksgiving offerings after sickness. Sometimes on bringing oil they would insist on putting some of it themselves into the sanctuary lamp. And if ceremonies were not performed in the same way as in Madeira, they suspected that something was wrong.[104]

In the same vein, they attended to baptism with pious zeal. Most of them had biblical names. 'Marie de Jesus' was a typical name for women, and children in the colony were named in very much the same way as in Madeira. On asking for the godmother when about to baptize a child, a priest was told: "Oh, the Blessed Virgin Mary stands godmother".[105]

The Portuguese were also fond of making *promessas* (religious vows). One who had charge of a shop of his employer and fellow Portuguese (who had gone to Madeira for six months), wishing him to find everything in order on his return, made a promise that if the employer should be pleased he would make the church a present of a candlestick and shade for each of the stations of the Cross. He duly fulfilled his promise when his employer expressed satisfaction on his return. When all the candles were fixed, he begged leave to light them all himself the following Saturday evening and was greatly delighted

260

*Cultural
Power,
Resistance,
and
Pluralism*

when he had finished.[106] Another man wished to marry a certain young lady, but there were some difficulties since she was a ward of Chancery. So he made a promise to the church of $21 for masses for souls in Purgatory, 21 packs of candles, and 21 bottles of oil if he succeeded. He was probably 21 years old. When he did get the court's permission to marry, he made good his promise to the church. The custom of vowing a *missa d'esmolas* (mass of alms) for the souls in Purgatory was very common among the Portuguese immigrants. By this they bound themselves to go round to their friends and raise subscriptions of sixpences and shillings, so as to make up the required amount. Normally no one would refuse to give.[107] Cutileiro notes that in rural Portugal what is promised to the saint as payment for his favour is never confided to others before the vow is fulfilled because this would render it ineffectual. Outsiders learn about them when they hear that a mass has been celebrated as payment for a vow or by some other act. He further observes that women make vows far more often than men, and that when the latter do so, it is often at the behest of their womenfolk.[108]

The preservation of these quaint Madeiran religious customs in the face of criticism from the Anglo-Creole clergy signified an act of resistance against the exercise of elite cultural power. Small and insignificant as they might on the surface appear, these customs symbolized the importance which the Portuguese attached to their native culture for fostering a sense of ethnic group identity in the hostile social environment of nineteenth century Guyana.

Pastimes

At least on the surface, the Portuguese seemed to display a similar love for clubs or social associations as the cultural elites. But whereas among the latter clubs were essentially secular, most Portuguese associations were religiously oriented or at least organized in connection with the Roman Catholic church. Indeed all Roman Catholic churches had a number of societies catering to their members, both adults and children, but mainly along gender specific lines.

Apart from the Portuguese Benevolent Society which existed between 1872 and 1888,[109] there were the Dona Maria Society and the Society of St. Vincent de Paul which like the P.B.S. provided relief for the poor; the Catholic Glee Club, the Catholic Reading and Recreation Club, the Portuguese Recreative Dramatic Club, the Portuguese Union Club established in 1865, the St. Joseph's Society formed in 1884, the Catholic Men's Guild in 1886, the *Club Lusitano* in 1890,[110] and several others.

Some of these societies organized theatricals and musical concerts, and from time to time performances were staged by visiting Portuguese artistes.[111] The Portuguse established their own philharmonic club and a brass band good enough to perform publicly. This is not surprising because the average Portuguese immigrant seemed to have musical skills, and on Sundays several went along the public roads singing and dancing to the guitar however rudely played.[112] Thus as early as 1849, one finds reference to a Portuguese band which actually played at a ball in honour of Mrs. Walker, wife of the acting governor.[113] But the first Portuguese brass band to have had a lasting impact was the *Primeiro de Dezembro Band*, established in 1876. This soon earned a reputation for its fine performances and on occasion performed very creditably alongside the Militia Band. The former was always in great demand at Portuguese festivals, and indeed the celebration of its own anniversary became a major event in the Portuguese cultural calendar. This was usually marked by a public concert which attracted several hundred people.[114] Smaller and shorter-lived Portuguese brass bands were formed at New Amsterdam and Plaisance.[115] It is important to observe, however, that while these bands did, for the most part, play at Portuguese ethnic festivities, their performances were not confined exclusively to those but extended on occasion to mixed audiences. This favoured cultural integration through an assimilation by the host society of an aspect of Portuguese culture.

During the 1890s a string band, the *Estudianius Restauracao de Demerara* was formed.[116] Whether this was reorganized as the *Estudiantina Band* in 1898 is not clear, but the latter was likewise composed mainly of stringed instruments including mandolins, *braggas* (small Portuguese guitars), standard guitars and the cello, with the flute being the only reed instrument. This band was composed of about twenty musicians.[117]

For the most part, the Portuguese strove to remain culturally exclusive, and organized clubs and societies (largely in connection with their wing of the Roman Catholic church) to promote this and to mould a distinct ethnic identity. This emphasis naturally retarded their cultural assimilation in the host society, though it did not wholly prevent the process of integration from taking place. Thus, for instance, the Portuguese adopted and learned the British imperial game of cricket, and a few played with players of other ethnic groups especially in the rural areas[118] where some Portuguese shopkeepers also helped financially to equip village teams. Sport thus served as an important racial and cultural bridge at a time when the state of race relations especially between the Portuguese and the Creoles were strained to the point of violence on occasion. But organized cricket was a different matter, and the Portuguese (especially in the towns)

262

Cultural
Power,
Resistance,
and
Pluralism

like the other ethnic groups found it desirable, indeed necessary since access to the elite clubs was not yet open to them, to form their own cricket clubs.[119] This reflected the continued importance of ethnicity in the society at large, and among the Portuguese in particular, even though some measure of social integration was promoted by playing matches against non-Portuguese teams.

Summary

The Portuguese shared one important attribute with all other immigrant groups in Guyana, including the dominant British whites: a perception that their sojourn in the colony was temporary. One day, after amassing great wealth, they would return to Madeira. This meant that they felt precious little incentive to adapt culturally, and indeed they maintained very close cultural, familial, and commercial contacts with Madeira, and insisted on retaining their Portuguese nationality throughout the nineteenth century. Very few opted to become naturalized British subjects. Within the colony the Portuguese found themselves in an invidious position of being social pariahs, isolated socially, despite (perhaps because of) their rapidly growing opulence. Consequently, they found themselves the targets of repeated attacks by the working people who felt cheated by the unsavoury commercial behaviour of many of them. This, however, merely added to the fears and insecurity of the Portuguese who felt inhibited from associating socially with other ethnic categories, as well as from integrating culturally.

The result was a strong desire to preserve their traditional Madeiran culture and identity centred as these were around their belief in and practice of Roman Catholicism, their language and their Portuguese nationality. The Roman Catholic church played a crucial role in re-constituting the Latin culture of the Portuguese in Guyana. This, however, was not accomplished without a struggle, for the dominant English hierarchy within that institution utilized their cultural power with the intention of pressing the Portuguese majority to conform to English religious practices. But even at the risk of schism, the Portuguese resisted that pressure and insisted on preserving the form, style and language of their religious rituals brought from Madeira; and, with the assistance of Italian Jesuits, they were eventually able to establish their own Portuguese language churches. In other words, despite their common historico-cultural antiquity with the British elites, the Portuguese immigrants were not prepared to see their culture subordinated to and submerged beneath the dominant British variant, and were successfully able to assert their own cultural dominance within the Roman Catholic communion.

However their strong emphasis on ethnic exclusivism was indicative of an active resistance to cultural integration within the host society with which they were constantly at odds. The Madeiran Latin culture was regarded as vital for unifying them as an ethnic category in a socially hostile environment, and this is why they placed such great stress on preserving it whole and 'unblemished' by external influences. They no doubt felt that they were sufficiently numerous and wealthy to ensure this. Their culture, therefore, served to reinforce the racial boundaries which differentiated them from the non-white ethnic groups, as well as the class boundaries which separated them from the British elites. Nevertheless, perhaps mainly on account of the high degree of physical contact with other ethnic groups essentially in the market-place (commerce), some measure of cultural integration was virtually inevitable. The most important area was language, but it also extended to general demeanour and behaviour, sport, music and other pastimes. The Portuguese also acquired a belief in and fear of obeah.[120] Thus by the end of the century, many older Portuguese were desperately fighting a rearguard battle against the slow but seemingly inexorable progress of creolization.

The almost coterminous correlation between 'race'/class and culture in the case of the Portuguese after emancipation underwent change towards the end of the century. But because of the persistent animosity directed against them largely on account of the unsavoury commercial practices of several Portuguese shopkeepers, the socio-racial boundaries separating them from other ethnic groups endured. From the standpoint of their institutions and practices, the Portuguese remained culturally distinctive, enveloped in their own ethnic brand of Roman Catholicism as an act of resistance against the cultural domination of the British elites. They never shared the view being peddled by the cultural elites that British culture was superior to theirs, and thus were not integrated with the host society around that critical value system. For most of the period under review, therefore, Portuguese Latin culture reinforced the differences of race and class separating them from the other social groups.

But those differences masked a convergence of other values between the Portuguese and the dominant British elites stemming from a common Greco-Roman antiquity, a common adherence to Christian civilization, a common commitment to western capitalism, and shared notions of racial superiority. On the other hand, the slow advance of creolization tempered their cultural differences from the host society. But the process of creolization was not by the end of the nineteenth century sufficiently advanced for them to be considered culturally *integrated* within the host society, thereby transforming their culture (like that of the Creoles) into a subculture of the elite Victorian model.

264

*Cultural
Power,
Resistance,
and
Pluralism*

The Portuguese remained a distinct ethnic category while sharing some *basic* institutions with the constituent categories of the host society. Their traditional cultural institutions and values remained very potent elements of Portuguese ethnicity. This is not, however, supportive of the idea of cultural pluralism. In fact even M.G. Smith would have regarded their incorporation into Guyanese society in the same way as he viewed that of Greeks, Italians or the Irish in American society, i.e., as indicative of cultural *heterogeneity* rather than pluralism.[121] Thus the case of the Portuguese does not fit either the concept of cultural integration or of pluralism.

CHAPTER
TEN

CHINESE HUA-QIAO[1]
CULTURE

Although most of the Chinese came from the southern provinces of
Fujian (Fukien) and Guangdong (Kwangtung), they were not a homo-
geneous group. They were mainly composed of two mutually antago-
nistic ethno-linguistic categories, *Punti* (Cantonese) and *Hakka*.[2] But
interethnic strife between these two groups in which whole villages in
Guangdong were destroyed (1854-1868), coupled with the bombard-
ment of Chinese port cities by the western imperial powers during the
1840s and 1850s and the outbreak of the anti-Manchu *T'ai P'ing* rebellion (1851-1864), undoubtedly contributed political and economic
refugees to the pool of migrants.[3] Although Levy notes that many of
the original immigrants from Guangdong were farmers or sons of
farmers which made them very suitable for agricultural work in the
Caribbean, Look Lai points out that the Cantonese (who formed the
majority of the Chinese immigrants) were mainly urban artisan and
déclassé elements[4] (i.e., social outcasts reputedly either on account of
indigence or opium addiction, who were thus not particularly adaptable to the regimented life of plantation labour).

One of the striking features of Chinese emigration overseas,
whether to the Americas, the Antipodes (Australia and New Zealand),
or Southeast Asia, was the shortage of women.[5] Guyana was no exception, although Look Lai notes that it fared better in this respect than
Chinese migrations to other parts of their diaspora. This was because
the British authorities made use of voluntary recruiting agencies like
European missionaries operating in China who made a special effort to
encourage whole families to emigrate. Yet even during the peak of the
Chinese migration to Guyana (1859-1866), only 17 percent of the immigrants were females[6]—less than among the Indian immigrants. And
even though the ratio of resident females improved slightly to 25.7 per
100 men by 1880, it was far from adequate. Even then it was just 4:100
among the Chinese indentured workers on the plantations.[7] As late as
1891, there were only 1,131 women out of a total Chinese population

266

Cultural
Power,
Resistance,
and
Pluralism

of 3,714 (i.e., 30.5 percent).[8] This generally low proportion of females was a major factor for the inability of the Chinese community to recreate the traditional family unit or to sustain its size by natural increase in the late nineteenth century.

As in other parts of the Chinese diaspora, the paucity of women among the Chinese immigrants was in large part attributable to their idea of impermanent residence overseas which obviated the need to uproot their families. According to Crissman,

> They did not set out adventurously to begin a new life abroad, but were pushed out of their homes by economic necessity, the unwilling victims of pressure on the land and lack of local opportunities for earning a living. Leaving home was not thought to be permanent but, on the contrary, was seen as a temporary expedient that would allow them to earn enough to live, support their families, and eventually return home as wealthy men . . . emigrants [generally] left China expecting to return home in due time, and leaving in no way cut them off from their families and natal villages. No matter how long they were away they were still considered by themselves and by those who stayed at home to be members in good standing of their home communities.

Cronin further asserts that single women were enmeshed within their family unit and were consequently unable to leave. No female with any sense of propriety or modesty could consent to quit her native home.[9]

The recruiting agents, however, attributed the shortage of women migrants to female infanticide and to the custom of crippling the feet of women to make them unfit for agricultural labour and for locomotion.[10] Ly-Tio-Fane Pineo notes that this custom arose out of an æsthetic premium placed on small feet (called 'golden lotus') as symbols of beauty and of noble birth which dated back to the eleventh century. Hence women of all classes, except the *Hakka*, submitted themselves to this custom despite the pain. It certainly did inhibit movement and "Chinese women with bound feet usually walked by supporting themselves on the shoulders of young servants . . ."[11] It is debatable, however, how many peasant women were affected by this custom.

Chinese men were also very wary about taking their wives and families overseas where they would be subject to racial hostility and prejudice in the host society.[12] And even if they were inclined to embark on the next best option, i.e., import girls and young women from China either as concubines or prostitutes as was indeed done in Southeast Asia and western North America,[13] the great distance and cost of travel from China to the Caribbean effectively ruled that out. Thus in Guyana, as elsewhere in the Chinese diaspora, the Chinese migrant community (*hua-qiao/hua-ch'iao*) in the nineteenth century was essentially composed of single males.

Since the Chinese migrated to Guyana as contract workers, they were arbitrarily allocated to those estates requiring their labour and provided the same type of accommodation as other indentured immigrants. This meant, of course, the rudimentary barracks and cottages in the 'Negro yard'. Although it was claimed that they were "much more anxious to have comfortable homes and their ideas of living are far in advance of Indian notions",[14] perhaps because of the extreme shortage of Chinese women which more or less precluded family life, they preferred barrack accommodation to separate cottages; and as a rule their barracks were generally in capital repair. In their rooms, there were sometimes pictures on the walls and "hangings" on the beds. Of course, being considerably smaller in number, they would not have suffered to the same degree from overcrowding and its attendant problems. They did not share the cultural predilection of the Indians for mud floors smeared with their compost of cow-dung, nor apparently did they favour wooden floors as was the local custom. According to the 1870 commission of inquiry, "they invariably pull up a plank in the floor, and make a mixen [*sic*] in the foundations".[15] Presumably this 'mixen' was the traditional pressed earth floor that was typical of village houses in rural China. Hence although assigned accommodation in buildings which were radically different from what they were accustomed at home, the Chinese adjusted by adapting these to suit their own cultural notions. This is one example of the sort of selective cultural adaptation which characterized the Chinese immigrants throughout the nineteenth century.

Although their material wants were as simple as those of the Indians, the Chinese were very different in some respects. For instance, they demanded a constant supply of pure water, and consequently went to great lengths to get a puncheon to hold rainwater: ". . . they will have it, if permitted, standing in their rooms, and will put up with its leakage, and the leakage through the roof, rather than go without it". Their hearths were a trifle more elaborate than those of the Indians, and "kitchens in general are not thrown away upon them". In the larger barracks on some estates, the Chinese set up a 'club-room' where opium-smokers and gamblers gathered to play cards and dominoes.[16]

After they left the estates those who engaged as peasant farmers or charcoal manufacturers, particularly at Camoenie Creek on the Demerara river where the largest free Chinese settlement was formed in 1865, built thatched roofed houses which were enclosed with 'palm boards' (the spines of palm branches). The spaces between the boards were not usually filled, and indeed the Chinese did not seem to bother whether or not they were. These huts were quite comfortable, certainly with more space than the barrack-rooms or huts on the estates, so much so that they could even offer accommodation to young Chinese lodgers desirous of setting out on their own after leaving the estates.[17]

268

*Cultural
Power,
Resistance,
and
Pluralism*

Despite their traditional ethnic differences and hostilities, survival in the alien environment forced the Chinese, as it did the Indians, to close ranks in the interest of promoting ethnic solidarity. This would not have been easy given the history of antagonism between the *Punti* and *Hakka* which had not infrequently even led to violence on board ship to the colony. Cultural differences, however, had to be minimized in the interest of creating a homogenized culture which could provide a common reference point to all, and around which they could mould a strong sense of group identity. Given the sparsity of data, it is not quite clear how this was achieved though it appears that it entailed both a retention of those aspects of traditional Chinese culture shared by both groups and, curiously, the adoption of the alien Christianity as an 'ethnic' religion. The resulting homogenized Chinese *hua-qiao* culture, therefore, involved both cultural resistance and selective adaptation to the host culture.

Dress, as an aspect of traditional culture shared by both groups of Chinese immigrants, played an important part in the process of cultural homogenization and the moulding of ethnic identity in the colonial society. The Chinese were readily identifiable by their distinctive dress styles which generally consisted of a loose jacket and blue cotton trousers for both males and females. The female trousers, however, were cut differently from the men's. They looked like a divided skirt since they were very wide and had a length a little lower down than the calf of the leg. Over that they wore a silk tunic on special occasions. The women also wore chignons as headgear, while the men wreathed their 'pigtails' (plaited hair) round their heads and wore hats of their own making. Females generally whitened their faces with cosmetics to enhance their beauty in accordance with Chinese aesthetic standards. Some brides continued to keep their faces whitened for a long time after marriage, but respectable widows never used cosmetics whatever their age. The women were also fond of plaiting their hair, and adorned their heads with flowers and various kinds or ornaments. They often wore between six and a dozen kinds of ornamental jewellery on their hands, necks and arms.[18] It is evident that the Chinese made very little effort during the nineteenth century to adopt western styles of dress, preferring to preserve their own cultural styles. Traditional dress forms were thus for the Chinese as important a symbol of ethnic identity and cultural resistance as they were for the Indian immigrants.

As with other aspects of Chinese cultural life, the historical records reveal precious little about their cuisine and eating habits, though it is evident that these were another aspect of shared traditions which promoted cultural homogenization and ethnic identity. This was perhaps most vividly symbolized by their unwavering use of chopsticks[19] in-

Chinese
immigrants

stead of adopting European cutlery. Unlike the Indian immigrants, the
Chinese were not inclined to hoard their earnings, although that does
not mean that they were improvident. Hence they were reputed to
have a very decided relish for the good things of life, and were quite
prepared to spend money to enjoy them.[20]

The Chinese were, therefore, not averse to spending liberally on
items of foodstuff and eating well. Kirke reported being entertained to
a four-course dinner, complete with *Hennessy's XXX* brandy, by a
Chinese family at Camoenie.[21] While this suggests an element of acculturation, for the most part the Chinese cuisine remained very distinct.
They earned a reputation for being epicurean in taste because of their
love of exotic meats of a gamey flavour. Among these were fricasseed

270

*Cultural
Power,
Resistance,
and
Pluralism*

rats, sheep's entrails, and the flesh of young donkeys,[22] items that had no place in either the Creole or Euro-elite diet. Kirke was treated to roast capon for dinner by his Chinese hosts; on another occasion while in the bush, a Chinese companion prepared fish with a 'peculiar sauce'; "it was like clear melted butter, flavoured with some pungent herb. On inquiry I found it was an oil made by melting down the fat which lies like blubber between the skin and the flesh of the great water camoudie or python . . . [boa constrictor]".

Some Chinese, however, were very sensitive to the widespread perception that they ate dogs. This perception was symbolic of the host society's revulsion of Chinese dietary habits, and the elites employed subtle pressure techniques to urge change. Kirke, for instance, teased his (first mentioned) Chinese host, suggesting that he would like to try roasted dog on his next visit. This had the desired effect of embarrassing his host into the angry response: "No good Chinee eat bow-wow; bad Chineeman, he eat bow-wow".[23] Quite evidently for some the pressures were too much to bear. But the majority seemed quite unmoved even though their penchant for exotic wild meats occasionally proved their undoing in an alien physical environment where the toxins contained in the various forms of wildlife were not known. Thus in one tragic instance, a Chinese worker at Plantation La Grange was reported to have died after eating a *crapaud* (frog) which he had caught in a nearby trench.[24]

The Chinese were also very fond of tea (*sou-chong*) which they prepared in a special way and drank plain without adding sugar and milk. The only additives which they sometimes used to flavour tea were a little salt, ginger, or both.[25] It is clear, therefore, that most Chinese made very little effort to adopt local dietary habits, but instead preserved as far as possible their own traditional culinary styles and eating implements. For them, therefore, food was an important symbol of cultural resistance and aided in maintaining their ethnic identity in the alien society.

Sex, Morality and Domestic Life

Because of the acute shortage of females, these immigrants could not easily reconstitute the traditional Chinese family in Guyana. And unlike their compatriots who migrated to Southeast Asia and North America, distance from China and high costs of passages forestalled any ideas of importing Chinese girls for concubinage or prostitution. Even there, Freedman states, "Marriage and family for them were largely matters pertaining to the homeland rather than their life overseas; many had married in China and left their wives there".[26] Because of its proximity to South China, there developed a pattern in Manila whereby Chinese men would return home, get married, and then go back to Manila leaving their wives behind in the protection of their parents.[27] In Guyana such options were not open to them, and in the absence of sufficient women there was very little prospect of recreating the Chinese family unit on a wide scale. Not surprisingly, the number of Chinese children was small,[28] and indeed the Chinese community could not maintain its numerical size during the nineteenth century. From just over 10,000 at the peak of Chinese immigration into Guyana in 1866, their population declined to a mere 2,118 in 1910. But it is important to point out this was not only due to natural decrease, but also to out-migration which seems to have been quite significant in the last three decades of the century.[29]

Nevertheless, for those who migrated as families or who were lucky to marry the few Chinese women in the colony and start a family, domestic life was reputedly characterized by a sense of decorum and good breeding in familial relations. For instance, no one ate meals before all were ready, and food was divided equally.[30] Even so ideas of male dominance brought from China were reinforced in the plantation environment, and this resulted in the occasional 'wife bashing'.[31] But despite an even more acute situation of female shortage among the Chinese, there was significantly none of the wife murders that were so prevalent among the Indian immigrants. This is related not only to the absence of any religious sanctions either in their traditional cultures or their adopted Christianity for such behaviour, but also to their being less disinclined to mating with Creole women than the Indian immigrants (see below).

Their homes were generally regarded as models of cleanliness and comfort. They always hung curtains in their rooms, and decorated them with looking-glasses, little pictures and other things. Their beds were made of a kind of cane-work by themselves[32] (the cane evidently serving as a substitute for bamboo to which they were accustomed). In the home every member of the household was expected and was duty-bound to perform some of the "sub-divided industries peculiar to Chinese housekeeping". Children of about eight to ten years old assisted in many of the domestic duties such as fetching water for the plants, and collecting food for the pigs which received very close attention. Apart from pure domestic chores, the women also worked in the gardens preparing the ground and planting various vegetable plants.[33] It is quite evident from the foregoing that the Chinese made every effort to preserve important elements of domestic relationships and lifestyle in keeping with their own cultural perceptions. This tended to distinguish them as a separate cultural group from any other in the society. Even so, however, they had to make selective adjustments to take into account local conditions.

272

*Cultural
Power,
Resistance,
and
Pluralism*

Towards the end of the century, with two-thirds of the ever-declining Chinese community still foreign-born, and with women composing only 30 percent of its members,[34] the Guyanese Chinese were fast becoming an endangered species. A half-century later, Fried found that pure Chinese were indeed a rarity[35] despite the arrival of small numbers of new Chinese immigrants during that period. Yet, as was the case in Mauritius, despite the acute shortage of women the Chinese initially showed little inclination to mate with Creole or Indian women, though there were a few rare instances of intermarriage. In 1861, for instance, the first two marriages between Chinese men and Creole women were observed, though in one case the woman was soon 'sent away'. Lieutenant-Governor Walker claimed that the Chinese male was averse to marrying black women because he possessed "a feeling which he in a great measure shares with the Caucasian race, accustomed to look upon all coloured races as barbarians who possess neither refinement nor education".[36] In reality the Chinese considered whites as well to be barbarians. Even so, they were less prejudiced where interracial mating was concerned than the Indians who were largely inhibited by caste proscriptions.[37] But because they also had to overcome the prejudices of Creole women who up to the early 1870s were reportedly unwilling to form unions with them,[38] there was very little miscegenation between the two groups and the Chinese community remained as racially 'pure' as when they first arrived.[39]

However, this negative attitude underwent significant change later in the century as they began to recognize that, far from being temporary sojourners, their destiny resided in Guyana; and also as Creole women began to consider Chinese men desirable 'marriage' partners particularly when they set up lucrative retail shops in Creole urban neighbourhoods and villages. What Ly-Tio-Fane Pineo found in Mauritius was equally true for Guyana:

> . . . the 'bachelor' shopkeeper acquires a new social status as he is considered financially better off than most of the inhabitants. He mixes freely with the local society and is eagerly courted by local beauties. Parents usually offer little opposition to the courtship, for a shopkeeper is usually considered a good match for a country girl, although the union is not always legalized before the civil status officer.[40]

Kirke in 1897 observed a similar willingness by the Chinese men in Guyana to mix and mate with Creole women: "As Chinese women are scarce, the Chinaman has always a coloured woman as a concubine; and they generally manage to get the best-looking girls in the place".[41] The result of such miscegenation was that by the mid-twentieth century, 80 percent of the local-born (*t'usheng*) scarcely looked Chinese. According to Fried, "Some of them have few of the phenotypic characters of Mongoloids".[42] Chinese men also cohabited with

Indian women, and in a few instances those women even accompanied their 'husbands' back to China.[43]

Both in Southeast Asia and the Indian Ocean, it has been found that although some Chinese were married before migrating, several started second families overseas with local women. This 'double family' phenomenon did not pose a moral or emotional dilemma since the two wives (and families) were thousands of miles apart and were both supported.[44] Look Lai observes that such mating patterns were indeed extant among the Chinese in the West Indies and Latin America,[45] and the practice is confirmed by the case of the Christian missionary, Wu Tai Kam, whose wife and family had been left behind in Singapore, but who lived with a Creole woman. His 'disgrace' was only on account of the fact that the position to which he had been entrusted by the cultural elites, as custodian of Christian moral values among the Chinese converts, was severely compromised when the woman's pregnancy brought his little secret into the full glare of daylight.[46] Thus even among the most 'respectable' of the Chinese, there was resistance to the Victorian morality espoused by the cultural elites.

The strong propensity for 'herding' together in estate barracks raises another question about the sexual practices of these male Chinese immigrants. Hyam notes that while female prostitution was to be found in most Chinese overseas communities, the Chinese did not suffer from sexual 'hang-ups' as did the Victorians: hence homosexual activity was not stigmatized. Indeed Chinese immigrants to the Witwatersrand in South Africa at the turn of the century were widely accused of sodomy, not merely among themselves, but with the Africans as well. Many of these charges were no doubt born out of racial prejudice and were grossly exaggerated, but Hyam estimates that about 6 or 7 percent of the Chinese were indeed 'buggerboys'.[47] Likewise, Cronin observes that in Victoria, Australia, some Chinese men formed homosexual liaisons.[48] There is no hard evidence to suggest that the Chinese immigrants in Guyana practised homosexuality though, if as in Trinidad most of them remained permanent bachelors, and if they operated as secretly as they did in South Africa (in disused mine shafts),[49] then it is no wonder, especially given their small numbers, that the historical records are silent.

Community Organization

The scantiness of historical data makes it extremely difficult to reconstruct the socio-cultural organization of the Chinese community *(huaqiao)* in Guyana during the nineteenth century. But it is known that wherever Chinese migrated they formed voluntary or clan organizations *(huiguans)* and secret societies. According to Tsai, a *huiguan* was

274

*Cultural
Power,
Resistance,
and
Pluralism*

a traditional and lawful association of fellow-provincials away from home, either visiting or on business.[50] It was based on kinship (usually reflected in common surnames), geographical or dialect ties, and sometimes occupations. It was patterned on those of the regions from which most of the immigrants emanated, mainly Fujian and Guangdong in south China where agnatic lineage very often coincided with local community. In fact, according to Freedman, "both free choice and the policies of labour recruiters in the latter half of the nineteenth century led to there being small groups of men (overseas) who were members of single lineages at home". Thus in Guyana, as elsewhere, people of like agnatic descent and from the same small locality in China must have clustered together although they could not reconstitute lineages.[51] Look Lai does indeed point to the existence of Chinese district associations in the Caribbean catering to those who came from particular areas of the Cantonese region around the Pearl river delta.[52]

Many clan organizations were composed of persons who were bonded by a common surname and were from the same region or shared the same dialect. Since there are only a few hundred surnames in common use in China, and they are inherited patrilineally, persons with the same surname know that they are descended from a common distant ancestor. This provides a good basis for bonding especially in an alien society though, as Crissman points out, not on its own. Overseas the surname principle was usually combined with some other criterion such as locality or dialect.[53] Tsai notes that the first thing a new immigrant did on arrival in the United States was to seek people who spoke his dialect, and this accounted for the proliferation of *huiguans* in Chinese communities.[54] According to Ching-Hwang, the clan was an important source of assistance beyond the family in time of need, and this function assumed even more importance overseas where the immigrants found themselves among strange people speaking unintelligible languages. Moreover, the clans played a central role in helping Chinese immigrants to observe traditional Chinese customs such as ancestral worship and festivals. They also served to satisfy the desire of clan leaders for status and influence within the Chinese communities.[55] Although the data for Guyana are sparse, there can be no doubt that *huiguans* along the lines described above must have been formed by the Chinese immigrants; but given the fact that as indentured immigrants they had no choice over their location and were indeed scattered in small numbers all over the plantation belt, it is very likely that those organizations would not have been particularly strong. On the other hand, the formation of *huiguans* would have been aided by the fact that the sources of the majority Cantonese immigrants were just about a dozen locations in an area no greater than 7,000 square miles.[56]

In Southeast Asia, however, although clans played an important part in the corporate organization of the Chinese immigrants, they were secondary to the secret societies until the latter's suppression during the 1890s. The secret society, known as the *Triad* or *Hong* ('Heaven and Earth' League; called *Tong* in the United States), used some of the same criteria for recruitment as the clans, most notably dialect and occupation, although significantly not surname. While therefore not a kinship organization, it emphasized a bond of brotherhood that was supposed to transcend all others.[57] According to Tsai, secret societies were in some ways like Freemasonry, professing such aims as obeying heaven and acting righteously.[58] Indeed in 1907 some Guyanese Chinese formed the Silent Temple Lodge and followed the example of their Australian fellows who in the later nineteenth century had had their Ghee Hing society incorporated into the international Masonic Brotherhood and legitimized as 'Chinese Masons'.[59] In China the secret societies were decidedly anti-Qing (Manchu) both politically and culturally, and were very much part of the T'ai P'ing rebellion of the 1850s and 1860s. Cronin observes that many of the first immigrants to the gold-fields of Victoria, Australia, were secret society members.[60] Since Chinese migration to Guyana took place at precisely the same time and from the same regions, it is reasonable to assume that some of those migrants were also secret society members.

Overseas these societies tried to maintain their anti-dynastic activities, and raised funds for the struggle against the Qing regime. But far removed from the political front lines, they evolved other functions in their new environments. Many became communal administrative and benevolent societies aimed at regulating the behaviour of their members, adjudicating internal disputes, helping members to cope with pressures (mainly racial, economic, and police) emanating from the outside (host societies), and rendering financial and other material assistance in time of need. According to Tsai, "Emphasizing fraternity and mutual assistance, the secret society had a three-point code: secrecy, help in time of trouble, and respect for one another's womenfolk". Cronin stresses the voluntary nature of these organizations: "No one was required to join but, as membership carried many practical benefits, few Chinese neglected to subscribe". But in addition to their communal 'protective' functions, wherever they were established, whether in Singapore, Malaya, Indonesia, Australia, or the United States, they took on an essentially criminal, mafia-type, character and were involved largely in intimidation, violence, robbery, extortion, gambling, prostitution, drug trafficking and smuggling.[61]

In Guyana the Chinese immigrants were known to organize themselves in criminal gangs during the 1850s and 1860s and engaged in armed robbery (essentially prædial larceny). Perhaps to supplement

276

*Cultural
Power,
Resistance,
and
Pluralism*

their meagre rations while indentured on the plantations, these bands of Chinese workers armed with cutlasses fastened to long sticks roamed the countryside at night, both on the plantations themselves and in neighbouring villages, ravaging stockyards and provision grounds. Numbering in some cases between twenty and fifty, these marauding gangs terrorized plantation watchmen and villagers by the viciousness of their attacks in which several persons were killed. This in fact forced the plantations in 1861 to arm their watchmen.[62] It is probable that these were the outward manifestations of the existence of secret societies. But for the same reasons that the *huiguans* would have been weak organizations, i.e., small numbers and the scattered nature of the Chinese population, so too secret societies would not have been particularly strong although their criminal activities certainly gave them some measure of potency. What is clear is that these gangs not only helped to mould ethnic solidarity among the Chinese immigrants, but their attacks on plantation stores were an attempt to strike against the daily injustices to which they were subjected as indentured workers. In like manner, attacks against Creole villages were a way of redressing the racial abuse to which they were subjected. The gangs were thus symbolic of Chinese resistance to the pressures, cultural and otherwise, emanating from the host society.

An important function of the secret societies in Southeast Asia, North America and Australia was the operation of gambling and opium dens.[63] Such dens were also very much present in Guyana among the Chinese immigrants both on and off the plantations, and were known as 'Chinese Hells'.[64] Until the 1880s when they were opened to the general public, they remained secret and confined mainly (with few exceptions) to the Chinese. As Heatley noted, "Try and get into their dens and you will be met with the decided rejoinder: 'No public massa', for the white man is considered a spy".[65] But since gambling was not only considered immoral, but was illegal, the elites used their cultural power to suppress the dens by prosecuting the operators, even though it was highly questionable whether the law against "keeping and maintaining a common gaming house for lucre and gain" could be applied to the 'Chinese Hells' with equity.[66] That the dens continued to thrive is testimony to the cultural resistance of the Chinese in seeking to preserve one of their traditional cultural institutions in the alien environment.

The documentary evidence on the Chinese in Guyana tends to focus on the more negative aspects of Chinese gang activity. Hence it does not provide any information on how the gangs or secret societies were structured. Apart from the criminal and economic functions which some of them evidently performed, they seemed to provide the immigrants with corporate organization and leadership, transcending tribal differences, in order to build a cohesive ethnic community in a racially hostile environment. But because the Chinese were numerically small, they lacked political significance; consequently, there was no need for the colonial administration to enlist the support of the 'secret societies' or gangs to maintain peace and order within the Chinese community as, for instance, the Dutch did in Indonesia through the *Kapitan* system.[67] On the contrary, the colonial elites in Guyana were distinctly hostile to these organized Chinese gangs and used their cultural power ruthlessly in an effort to suppress them. Special laws were thus passed in 1862 and again in 1865 to curb the Chinese gangs. Convicted offenders were liable to a public flogging of up to thirty-nine lashes. The problem, however, was to apprehend them, which was particularly difficult precisely because they moved in such large numbers. Even so these repressive measures contributed to the eventual decline in frequency and intensity of the gang raids which petered out during the 1870s.[68] As we shall see later, another contributory factor was the mass conversion of the Chinese to Christianity during the late sixties and seventies. Thus despite the great efforts which the Chinese made to preserve an important feature of their socio-cultural organization, local conditions and circumstances made that very difficult and eventually, because the authorities moved to suppress them, the gangs disintegrated and the Chinese were forced to conform, in this respect at least, to the norms of the host society.

Religion

One of the factors which affected the ability of the Chinese immigrants to preserve their traditional culture in Guyana was the influence of Christianity. Euro-Christian ideology and dogma, disseminated in both church and school, were an integral part of the cultural power of the colonial elites who employed them as a mechanism of social control. They were intended, *inter alia*, to instil notions of white superiority and to inculcate attitudes of deference and obedience to the white ruling minority. Specifically in relation to the Chinese, the proselytization of Christianity was also expressly calculated to curb the growth and influence of secret societies among them.[69]

According to Tsai, traditional Chinese religious concepts pictured the universe as a trinity of heaven, earth and man: "Heaven directs, earth produces, and man cooperates. When man cooperates, he prospers; on the other hand, if man does not cooperate, he destroys the harmonious arrangements of the universe and suffers the consequences in the form of natural disasters, such as floods, droughts, and famines".

This is a very environment-friendly religious philosophy with heaven replacing the Judeo-Christian notion of 'God'. Confucianism

278

*Cultural
Power,
Resistance,
and
Pluralism*

was the most believed of China's religions. Its flexible tenets permitted the practitioner to worship a variety of deities, and allowed the widest individual discretion in matters of personal belief. Two other great religions were represented in China, viz., Taoism and Buddhism. Tsai notes that it was quite possible for a single individual to be an adherent of all three religions. "The Chinese call this the harmony of the Three Teachings; they developed a classical, syncretic religious tradition. Many Chinese therefore had a Confucian cap, wore a Taoist robe, and put on a Buddhist sandal."[70] This religious trinity was taken overseas as part of the cultural baggage of the Chinese emigrants, and was undoubtedly represented among the early Chinese in Guyana.

But some of the Chinese immigrants were either already Christians or had been exposed to Christian proselytization before they first set foot in Guyana.[71] By the 1850s and 1860s, Christian evangelization was already well advanced in China and missionaries had moved from the treaty ports into the interior. Look Lai notes that the British emigration agency enlisted the assistance of European missionaries in China to recruit immigrants. Not least among these was the German missionary, Rev. William Lobscheid, who recruited several distressed Chinese families among whom he had worked. He actually visited Guyana and Trinidad in 1861-62, and made several policy proposals to the colonial authorities including the usefulness of proselytizing and educating the Chinese immigrants.[72] Thus on arrival in the colony the christianized Chinese were keen to attend chapels while others were curious. Just a fortnight after the arrival of the first Chinese immigrants in 1853, about thirty of them who were located on the west coast of Demerara went to the Ebenezer (L.M.S.) chapel and, "Without the least appearance of shyness they walked into the Chapel, and leisurely surveyed the interior. One of them quickly made his way up the stair to the bell tower and was about to pull the rope, when one of the deacons motioned to him to forbear".[73]

Some of these early Chinese immigrants frequented the chapels on Sunday in different parts of the colony and seemed to go through the service as if they understood it, kneeling, sitting or standing with the rest of the congregations; and they eagerly accepted religious tracts in their own languages which they read aloud.[74] Hence by the time of the big wave of Chinese immigrants in the early 1860s, great hope was entertained that through the judicious use of elite cultural power, they could be induced to give up their traditional religions and become Christians.[75] It was at the recommendation of the German missionary, Lobscheid, that several of these Chinese Christians were located at contiguous plantations on the Corentyne coast of Berbice (Skeldon and Eliza & Mary) precisely in order to facilitate their worship as a separate congregation in their own languages.[76]

In 1864 Wu Tai Kam, a Chinese Anglican missionary, arrived from Singapore and commenced proselytization among the Chinese immigrants. His efforts were highly successful and considerably advanced the process of conversion.[77] In 1866 he was officially appointed Missionary to the Chinese immigrants on a government stipend of £300 per annum, and was instrumental in obtaining a grant of Crown land from the government for a Chinese settlement at Camoenie Creek off the Demerara river (called Hopetown).[78] It was, significantly, mainly the Chinese Christians from the Corentyne who formed the nucleus of the early Hopetown settlers.[79] By 1867 when Wu left the colony, the groundwork had been firmly laid for the large-scale conversion of the Chinese immigrants.[80] And by the 1880s, there were very few Chinese who were *not* Christians, mainly Anglicans.[81] This differs only very slightly from the situation in Trinidad where a great many of the Chinese became Roman Catholics.[82]

The apparent willingness and ease with which the majority of Chinese were prepared to give up their ancestral religions in the British Caribbean is not only puzzling, but also contrasts starkly with their counterparts who migrated to other parts of the world. Both in Australia and the United States, for instance, where they were subjected to intense Christian proselytization, there was marked resistance by the Chinese. Cronin notes that in Victoria, Australia, the Christian missionaries were ignored, rebuked and insulted. "Chinese fiercely defended and practised their 'pagan' traditions. They would hear no criticism of ancestor worship, to do so implied disrespect for their parents who were so far away." The missionaries thus found their task slow and unrewarding. Converts there were, but they were very few, accounting for just 17 percent of the Chinese community in Victoria by 1891.[83] In the United States, by 1892 Chinese had become members of eleven Christian denominations and had established ten independent congregations in thirty-one states. But, as Tsai points out, these not only represented a very small portion of the Chinese population, but many of these Christians in fact held syncretic religious views. Thus they continued to practise ancestor worship, followed traditional Chinese wedding and funeral rituals, and paid occasional respect to Taoist gods in Chinese temples.[84]

Why then were those in Guyana so different? Clearly Look Lai's view that their "nonreligious pragmatism and secular Confucianism rendered them more open to persuasion from Western religious preaching"[85] falls short of plausibility. The answer seems to lie partially in the smallness of their numbers which after the mid-1860s was in constant decline. Scattered over the length of the inhabited coast, it was very difficult for them to build the sort of self-contained communal social organization which the Indians did in order to withstand the

280

*Cultural
Power,
Resistance,
and
Pluralism*

cultural power of the elites. This power was used very selectively by way of favours (including the grant of land at Camoenie Creek) shown to those who were Christians, both on and off the estates, as opposed to the hostility displayed towards the gangs or 'secret societies' of the non-Christians. In other words, it was made pellucidly clear to the Chinese that social and economic progress was directly linked to cultural assimilation. In addition, it would not have escaped the astute Chinese that if they adopted the religion of the 'master race' it would add to the natural advantage which their light skin colour conferred on them in a society obsessed by 'race' and colour prejudices. Perhaps this is why Look Lai raises the pertinent question whether the Chinese conversions "represented the creation of an active practicing Christian community, and how many were simply symbolic or cosmetic conversions for the purpose of acknowledging the customs of the new society . . ."[86]

The Christian priests, however, entertained no doubt about the sincerity of the Chinese converts. They were considered model believers. None was said to surpass them in their devotion or in their contributions to their several church funds.[87]

> There is something so thorough in their devotion, so single-minded in their charity, and so consistent in their whole walk and conversation, as to be quite refreshing to those who are accustomed only to the conventional Christianity in which we have been brought up . . . They have taken up the new religion—not as a garment that may be laid aside when convenience suit but as an energizing principle that gives the spring of action to a new life.[88]

There was also a noticeable correlation between their conversion and the decline of the nocturnal activities of the Chinese gangs. If this signified a dissolution of the secret societies, then Christianity certainly was a highly successful mechanism of social control among the Chinese.

As in Australia,[89] the Chinese converts were given English (so-called 'Christian') names on baptism and were required to abandon traditional cultural practices which were considered incompatible with Christian morality. Yet their conversion did not seem to entail complete 'de-Sinosization' or an overt acceptance of white superiority. Christian worship was from the outset conducted in the Chinese language (presumably Cantonese) by Chinese catechists;[90] and from the 1870s onwards the Chinese sought to preserve their ethnic identity even while becoming Christians by constructing their own churches in several parts of the colony. The first of these was St. Saviour's in Georgetown on a grant of land from the Anglican body. Opened in 1875, the building cost $3,408 (£710) to construct. It was plain but well proportioned, consisting of a nave fifty by twenty feet, and north-south aisles fifty by eight feet. The site was enclosed and the building painted. The roof was provided with guttering. The original structure did not have a chancel, porch, font or harmonium.[91] The erection of this church is a classic demonstration of the British colonial attitude which favoured the cultural assimilation of the subordinate ethnic populations while maintaining their social distance. Other Chinese churches were erected at Plantation Met-en-Meerzorg, West Coast Demerara, in 1878; at No. 78 Village, Corentyne coast, Berbice and Plantation Enmore, East Coast Demerara, in 1884; at Bagotville, West Coast Demerara, in 1886; and in New Amsterdam (St. Clement's) in 1891.[92]

As further proof that Chinese Christians did not forego the core of their ethnicity, converts (as we shall see below) continued to celebrate the Chinese New Year simply by adding special Christian church services to the traditional practices.[93] Although enjoined by their missionary mentors to desist, they also continued to gamble and smoke opium. This suggests that as in the United States there was a certain amount of syncretism in their religio-cultural beliefs and behaviour. In this regard, the Chinese displayed a high degree of selectivity in accommodating to the elite culture of the host society: for while adopting the dominant religion, they were able to determine the form which their observances would take and to retain a high degree of ethnic exclusivity at the same time. Their adoption of Christianity, therefore (as indeed other aspects of western culture), represented limited cultural assimilation. Look Lai thus asserts that such assimilation never amounted to "a process of *absorption* by the larger culture, but more a subtle process of *hybridization*, a blend of the Old World and the New, the New World here meaning the Euro-African melting-pot tradition that was unique to the Americas".[94]

Western Education

Closely related to the issue of cultural assimilation via Christianity was the influence of western education which for the most part was in the hands of the religious bodies. As Look Lai notes, "The school became the major socializing agency of the larger colonial society, since it was in this environment that the children of immigrants would have the most intimate contact with others from another race".[95] There is very little documentary data, however, on the education of the Chinese immigrants during the nineteenth century. As indentured immigrants, education was not considered useful for the Chinese by the estates' management who, as we saw with respect to the Indians, felt that they stood to lose labour, and furthermore that education made them 'uppity' and unstable. But unlike the Indians, and recognizing that Guyana (or one of the neighbouring colonies) would be

282

*Cultural
Power,
Resistance,
and
Pluralism*

their permanent home, the Chinese opted to avail themselves of whatever limited educational opportunities came their way as a means of social mobility.

The 1870 commission thus observed that they had a strong desire for schooling *both* in English and Chinese.[96] Schools existed at Plantations Skeldon and Eliza & Mary on the Corentyne where there were notable Chinese communities.[97] On other estates, Chinese attended schools where available along with Indian children; and even though, because of their small numbers, they generally formed a minority, they were reputedly the most regular and attentive pupils both during the week and on Sundays, and made great progress in reading (both religious and secular), writing, arithmetic, and English grammar.[98] As they moved off the estates during and after the 1860s they attended schools in the villages and towns where they mingled with children of other ethnic groups. Despite their desire for Chinese language teaching, however, in the schools both on and off the estates the medium of instruction was English, and this contributed to the decline in use of Chinese languages among the *t'usheng*. As was the case with the Portuguese, this trend caused concern among some Chinese in Georgetown who, disliking the growing inability of their children to read and write in Chinese, attempted to resist by petitioning the governor in 1881 for financial assistance to hire a Chinese teacher and rent a school house. Elite opinion, however, was firmly against this and they used their cultural power to refuse the request. Chinese-language education was not expressly prohibited, but it had to be entirely at the expense of the Chinese; and since they could hardly afford it, their languages eventually died.[99]

Leisure

The Chinese immigrants faced the same restrictions relating to leisure as did the Indians. As indentured workers they were required to work long hours each day and on Saturdays as well in order to complete their assigned tasks, or face *criminal* charges; and similarly those who worked in the factory during the grinding season routinely exceeded the statutory ten hours a day and, as we have seen, on occasion could be required to work in excess of twenty continuous hours. For these workers, therefore, leisure was a scarce luxury. Not that the Chinese demanded much by way of leisure time: for they came from a culture which did not have regular holidays; hence festival days were generally the only time employees got a break from work. This habit of working all year round except on festal days was taken by them overseas,[100] and was certainly maintained in Guyana where, before their mass conversion, they tended to work voluntarily on Christian holidays like Easter and Christmas.[101]

Most traditional Chinese festivals are family oriented,[102] but as we have seen, the severe shortage of women rendered it extremely difficult to reconstruct the Chinese family in Guyana. This, however, was not the main reason why many Chinese festivities did not seem to survive the crossing, for all Chinese communities overseas suffered that same disability. Yet it did not prevent several Chinese festivals from being observed in Southeast Asia and North America, for instance. One major reason for this difference was the regular physical contact which those *hua-qiao* were able to maintain with the motherland which was generally lacking in Guyana and the Caribbean. There was far more traffic of persons back and forth between those areas and China. In addition, far more Chinese in those areas engaged in independent self-employment and thus had greater control over their leisure time than their counterparts in Guyana and the Caribbean whose free time was strictly controlled by their employers. The need to conform to the work routine of the plantations meant that the Chinese immigrants could only celebrate traditional cultural events when granted time off by the management. But perhaps the most decisive factor in determining the continuity of Chinese cultural festivals in Guyana was the large-scale conversion of the vast majority of the Chinese there (as in Trinidad) to Christianity within three decades of their first arrival. This meant that they had to give up many of their 'pagan' cultural customs. Those that they retained not only had to conform to the plantation work cycle, but also had to have significance to all the Chinese regardless of origin. That would make it easier to iron out differences in observance and practice, thus making homogenization possible.

According to Ching-Hwang, the observance of Chinese festivals was one of the major functions of the clan in overseas communities. Unlike Euro-Christian festivals which are largely religious, Chinese festivals were connected with tradition or with peasant economic activities influenced by seasonal changes. The major tradition-bound Chinese festivals were the *Qing-ming (Ch'ing-ming)* in early April which involved visiting ancestral graves and offering food to the spirits of the dead; the May festival (also known in the United States as the Dragon Boat festival) in memory of the patriotic poet Ch'u Yuan (343-290 B.C.); the *Chung-yuan* in the seventh moon (feeding the hungry ghosts); and the Moon (Mid-Autumn) festival on the fifteenth day of the eighth lunar month when gifts were offered to the Moon Goddess. Those connected with seasonal peasant economic activities were the spring festival, Winter Solstice Day, and the Chinese lunar New Year on the second new moon after the winter solstice (i.e., either in January or February).[103]

284

*Cultural
Power,
Resistance,
and
Pluralism*

Ching-Hwang further notes that the early Chinese immigrants in Singapore and Malaya tended to observe all these festivals despite changes in environment and climate. This he attributes partly to their unquestioning loyalty to tradition, and partly to the fact that those were the only times that they were accustomed to enjoying leisure.[104] In Guyana, however, several of the Chinese were already Christians on arrival, and with the subsequent mass conversion of the rest, festivals such as the *Qing-ming/Ch'ing-ming* (*Gah San* in Jamaica) which remained very central to the religious and cultural life of the *hua-qiao* in Southeast Asia and North America eventually lost their significance. It is also true that given their small numbers on individual estates, and dispersed as they were all over the coast, not much attention was paid to their cultural activities (except of course the most colourful or public) and undoubtedly many aspects of Chinese culture in the colony simply went unnoticed and unrecorded. So it is very probable that some of the traditional festivals might indeed have been observed quietly by the Chinese without attracting public attention.

As a result, the only Chinese festival which received attention from the colonial elites was the lunar New Year festival largely because it brought together Chinese from different parts of the colony in one very colourful public celebration, and at the same time by its very nature aroused elite concern about public safety. In many respects, the New Year festival stood at the centre of the homogenized *hua-qiao* culture of the Chinese immigrants. The traditional celebration usually lasts about one month with preparations beginning at the start of the twelfth lunar month and reaching a climax in the last ten days.[105] But for a start the demanding work routine on the plantations ruled out any likelihood that Chinese would have sufficient time to make all the preparations required. As a rule the plantations granted only about five days for the celebration of this festival.[106] It is not surprising, therefore, that there is no documentary record of the *sao-chen* (sweeping the dust). This tradition requires that the kitchen god should be sent out of the home before a major house-cleaning exercise is undertaken. Everything in the house is moved out, cleaned, and rearranged, and major domestic repairs done. On the twenty-third day a farewell sacrifice is prepared for the kitchen god, and on the days immediately preceding the New Year, food is prepared in sufficient quantity to last for the fifteen days of the celebration, as well as for ancestor worship and religious ceremonies. Pictures, fireworks, incense sticks, papers, and sweets are bought for decorating the house and for use in the ceremonies.[107] But it seems that this tradition was considerably modified in Guyana and certainly the religious rituals associated with it were eradicated. This was so not only because of the heavy work schedules on the plantations, but also because the traditional Chinese family unit upon which it so heavily depends was not reconstituted in Guyana. Furthermore, since it is also based on traditional Chinese religious beliefs and practices, the rapid conversion of the Chinese immigrants under missionary influence prohibited the preservation of the religious aspects of this tradition.

The grand climax of the New Year festivities was reached on the fifteenth day of the first month with *Cheng Yueh Shih Wu*, the lantern festival. In keeping with their new condition as converted Christians, many of the Chinese started the day by attending special church services.[108] In China, one the main features of this celebration is the consumption of the last of the New Year food,[109] and certainly the immigrants preserved this custom with a lavish display of food, fruit and drink. Their rooms and homes were tastefully decorated, and they all visited one another and ate and drank as they wished. Indeed the quantity consumed was a gauge of the prestige of the host.[110] Fireworks were also exploded to mark the beginning of the new year although this caused considerable annoyance to the colonial elites.[111]

The high point of the day's festivities was the lantern parade. The immigrants evidently spent long hours at night after work on their lamps and lanterns. According to Chinese tradition, "the more ingenious the lantern, the higher the prestige of the family who shows it".[112] The display of lanterns symbolizes the brightness and good luck that the family hopes for, and the chasing out of the darkness and bad luck that they wish to avoid.[113] In Guyana, large Chinese processions paraded through the streets with paper lanterns made with great artistic ingenuity of various sizes, shapes and sparkling colours, depicting immense birds, fishes, etc.[114] "The lanterns themselves are well worth examining, they are no paltry shams, but really deserve the name of works of art, ingenious in design and finished with the most careful neatness."[115] In one procession there was a majestic peacock which strutted along in all the bedizenment of bright pigment and glittering tinsel. Behind it was a gigantic fish with glossy scales and an 'automatic mouth' that kept ceaselessly gasping the breeze; then came temples aglow with painted gauze and blazing lamps, followed by the dumpy sun-fish, round and ruddy, and the quaint Trigger fires.[116] In another, the huge birds and fish were so cleverly made that the wind gave a lifelike motion to the wings and gills respectively.[117] They were usually accompanied by the loud music of bagpipe, gongs, cymbals and 'tom-toms' (drums), and by the display of fireworks and crackers[118] as a manifestation of happiness, and to scare away demons.[119]

As with the Indian *tadja* processions, the Chinese lantern processions posed a direct challenge to the idea of the cultural dominance of the colonial elites and were thus both a symbol of cultural resistance and of Chinese ethnic identity. Moreover, the processions attracted considerable working class Creole participation which threatened to nullify the divide and rule policies of the colonial elites in the racially segmented society. Not surprisingly they attracted some measure of hostility from the elites who used their cultural power to subject them to official harassment. One such incident occurred in 1881. The revellers were in the habit of serenading government officials such as the governor, the immigration agent general, and others of similar standing, during their street parades.[120] On this occasion, however, while the procession was in front of Government House (the governor's residence), a police inspector charged the revellers with his horse causing several with their lanterns to be thrown into the trench. Surprisingly none drowned.[121] That the celebrations survived this kind of elite pressure is indicative of the cultural resistance of the Chinese and the high value which they placed on maintaining a distinct ethnic identity even after the majority had converted to Christianity.

Apart from the New Year festivities, the Chinese immigrants found other ways to amuse themselves. Despite their small numbers and the sparsity of women, the Chinese immigrants practised some of their traditional arts, particularly theatre, which was common to the two major groups. Tsai notes that Chinese opera is a dramatic art form that possesses the elements of action, dialogue, and singing.[122] New arrivals in Guyana celebrated their safe passage to the colony with a series of theatricals in the evening under the portico of the Immigration Office.[123] Similarly some of the very first Chinese immigrants in 1853 at Plantation Blankenburg staged plays on Sundays when they were not working. On one occasion they represented, upon a cleverly ornamented stage, the life and works of a Chinese hero with good action; and at the end of the performance they held a grand feast.[124] Given the shortage of females, it is reasonable to imagine that as in the United States female roles were played by beardless males.[125]

In 1877 a much more sophisticated acrobatic performance was held in the Philharmonic Hall in Georgetown when a group of Chinese dramatists toured the colony. This was patronized by Chinese from all over the country and was described as a fine exhibition. The actors were dressed in rich Chinese costumes, and their faces were masked or painted. "The suspension by the hair of a sturdy young Celestial . . . was . . . performed, as well as many feats of contortioning, rope climbing and tumbling, in which they excelled."[126] Music, both vocal and instrumental, was almost continuous throughout the performance although not to the appreciation of the cultural elites in the audience: "we confess that to us their music hath no charms".[127]

The elites never allowed an opportunity to slip by without deprecating Chinese musical sounds. In fact they considered the word 'music' a misnomer for Chinese sounds. "To ears apt to the linked harmonies of our master tone poets, melody is an essential part of music . . . But so do not the Chinese 'musicianers'. A tom-tom, a gong, and a pair of cymbals are not provocative of 'moonlight tenderness', nor are they capable of selection on the gamut."[128] To them the tones of Chinese music were fixed: "The uncertain bass of the cymbals, the fundamental note and its shrill harmonic from the gong, and the monotonous chattering of the tom-tom, do not afford notes enough for even an incipient melody, such for example as the croonings of a savage".[129] It was rare to find one who was prepared to acknowledge that genius in the Chinese musicians which enabled them to produce the most varied rhythmic changes:

> These the performers execute with the most remarkable exactness. The tom-tom player, though he holds the sticks in a manner that a thoroughbred drummer would go mad over, does some surprising feats on the cow-skin. His rolls are rapid and distinct enough for a guardsman . . . The tom-tom man is evidently the chief of the party, it is he who gives the time, and indicates the endless changes of rhythm which on ears celestial induce the delight which 'Home, sweet home', or some kindred air, produces on our terrestrial drums.[130]

If Chinese music did not win many fans among the cultural elites, the rhythm of the drum and cymbals probably helped to account for the participation of working class Creoles in the New Year processions. But on the other hand, there is no evidence of Chinese adopting creole music and dance forms. This suggests that there may have been very little acculturation at this level.

The cultural elites were revolted by the Chinese habits of opium smoking and gambling. These were considered twin evils and accordingly deplored as inherently bad for the physical and spiritual well-being of the perpetrators. It is also very likely that their link with the organized crime of Chinese 'secret societies' was an added factor in determining elite attitudes to them. Yet that did not impede the Chinese from indulging freely. These were habits which both *Punti* and *Hakka* shared in common, and formed important features of the homogenized *hua-qiao* culture. As was the case in all other areas of the world to which Chinese migrated, after a long day's work several of them----regardless of tribal origin—sought to 'wind down' by smoking or chewing opium (*bhang*).[131] This addiction was acquired in China where British drug traffickers, with the full connivance and support of their government, smuggled the drug and even went to war in 1839 to force it 'down the throats' of the Chinese people. Opium was consumed both by eating and by smoking with deleterious effects. Thus, "It is a disgusting spectacle to go into an opium shop on an estate, and see them in all stages of intoxication".[132]

Opium was abused by some Chinese who became quite emaciated and almost unfit for work as a result of over-consumption.[133] Indeed, several deaths among Chinese immigrants on the estates were attributed to such abuse; and it appears that in many instances this was due to premeditation and design on their part, i.e., suicide, which the planters and the legal authorities covered up by failing to conduct inquests on the bodies.[134] Yet it was feared that to prohibit the use of opium would lead to even more deaths since large numbers of Chinese had become totally addicted to the drug.[135] But it was not only the Chinese who were involved in opium consumption. Their club rooms were visited by one or two Creoles and Indians.[136] It was consequently necessary to introduce legislation to control both the sale and excessive use of opium.

Opium was in fact legally imported into the colony during the nineteenth century and, as in Australia and the United States, sold without restrictions by any general retailer or druggist. Between 1853 and 1858, the average annual importation of opium was 752 pounds; in 1859 it rose to 1,174 pounds, and in 1860 to 3,191 pounds. In the first six months of 1861, some 3,021 pounds were legally imported, in addition to considerable quantities smuggled into the local market. By 1861, therefore, trade in opium had become a regular branch of commerce in the colony, and one Portuguese retailer alone in Georgetown was reported to have in stock opium worth $7,000 (£1,458.33).[137] Legal imports of this drug continued to increase: from 3,991¾ pounds in 1861 to a peak of 28,963½ pounds in 1883.[138] These figures do not include an unknown quantity of illegal imports due to rampant smuggling.[139] In March 1876, for instance, 455 pounds of smuggled opium were seized by the Customs—a drop in the ocean.[140]

The importation of opium into Guyana (and other British colonies) cannot, however, be related exclusively to its use (or abuse) by Chinese immigrants. Virginia Berridge points out that substantial quantities of the drug were imported into metropolitan Britain itself, and until 1868 sold freely by pharmacists, grocers, market vendors and even itinerant hawkers to anyone who wanted to buy it. It was not only used by adults both for medicinal and recreational purposes, but also given to children; and just as in Guyana and elsewhere, deaths by opium poisoning in Britain were sufficiently high to cause concern.[141] So widespread and commonplace was the use of the drug that James Walvin could wittily turn Marx on his head by stating that opium was the religion of the masses in nineteenth century Britain.[142]

What is perhaps surprising is that the Guyanese cultural elites acted before the British authorities to try to bring the sale and use of opium under control. Hence Ordinance No. 22/1861 required retailers to take out special licences, and prohibited druggists from selling the drug over the counter. They were only permitted to sell opium upon prescription of a doctor, or if it was a bona fide medicinal compound. The issue of opium licences was also restricted, and licensed dealers

could only sell limited quantities within prescribed hours.[143] This law
was made more stringent in 1870[144] though without much practical
effect since imports continued to climb as use of the drug spread much
beyond the Chinese immigrants to the Indians and Creoles. This worrying situation spurred the passage of new restrictive laws in 1883 and
1889 with the result that imports declined to 10,674 pounds by 1891
and continued to fall.[145] But as Howard Johnson noted in Trinidad,[146]
the Chinese had already made a significant contribution to the local
cultural matrix which despite its debilitating effects, promoted ethnic
integration.

As with opium, the habit of gambling attracted official concern by
1861 when the idea of suppressing it was openly discussed.[147] Gambling was, of course, antithetical to Victorian middle class Christian
morality, but it was not deemed prudent to invest estate managers
with "those unusual powers of police" to curb it.[148] Consequently it
remained a flourishing pastime among the Chinese beyond the end of
the century despite their conversion to Christianity. As was the case
everywhere in the Chinese diaspora, "Gambling is the chief delight of
John Chinaman, the chances on which he will stake money are as
ingenious as they are endless; the number of pips in an orange, the
weight of a fish, odd or even in a handful of 'cash' (the coin of his
country), are enticements that will induce him to risk his all, even to
the very clothes on his back".[149] Some Chinese were such inveterate
gamblers that it was not unusual for them to squander $50 or $100 in
one night (equivalent to 40-80 weeks' wages at the statutory rate!).[150]
Even more extraordinary was the case of one Chinese gambler who,
according to Kirke, ". . . lost all his money, then his house and furniture, then his wife, and then he staked himself as a slave for six months
and lost that, and strange to say, he faithfully worked out his debt of
honour, toiling for his master without wages for the allotted time, and
then began life afresh, a saddened, and let us hope, a wiser man".[151]

As we have noted before, gambling, linked with secret society activity, was conducted in dens (along with opium smoking) called 'Chinese Hells' which could either be a specially appointed barrack-room
on an estate or the back room of a Chinese shop anywhere in the
country. Night after night the Chinese gathered at their 'club' to
gamble: "quiet orderly people who sit or stand around the table, stolid
and passive in their appearance; as unconcerned when they lose as
when they win, satisfied that the game is being played on the square
and that they are having the full benefit of their luck, good or bad".[152]

Chinese gambling in Guyana was no different from elsewhere in
the diaspora. One form of gambling was the game of *dominoes* in
which the seductive *bitt* (eight cents/four pence) was the highest risk
that appeared on the board. Very noticeable at the table was the ex-

290

Cultural
Power,
Resistance,
and
Pluralism

traordinary rapidity with which the players counted their pieces, evidently knowing the total of every possible combination of figures at a glance.[153]

Mich-han or Michahan (Fan-tan in the United States and Canada) was another very popular game of fortune. This was very simple and appeared to admit no duplicity. There was a board on which was painted the numbers 1, 2, 3, 4. There were also very many little brass circlets with a square cut in the centre of each. A brass dome, much like a cup cover, completed the paraphernalia of the game. Betting was made on the numbers given above and any amount could be placed on any of them according to the bettor's choice. When all bets were made, the banker effortlessly swept an indefinite number of brass circlets under the little brass dome, and from under this he took them or raked them by the end of a little stick, in quantities of four until there were four, three, two or one left. If one counter remained, those who had backed the number 1 on the board were paid in proportion to the sums staked, and likewise for the other three numbers. Winners paid the bank a token sum out of their winnings.[154]

Another game, perhaps a variation of michahan, employed a small square very shallow copper box. Its bottom was painted partly white and partly black or red. Gamblers staked on one of the colours, the banker receiving and paying according as the bettors hit or missed the right colour. As with michahan, this seemed to be wholly a game of chance with no advantage to the banker.[155]

Far less straightforward and above suspicion, however, was the lottery called chefa (whé-whé in Trinidad, peaka peow in Jamaica, policy in Canada, and white dover card sweepstakes in the United States[156]) where the chances were generally 36-1 against the bettor; yet if he won he received an amount equalling just twenty-eight times his stake (plus his stake). On the wall, over against a table presided over by a man who sold the tickets, was a pictorial chart with thirty-six figures or pictures representing animals, birds, fish, shell-woman, fire dragon, etc. Everyday except Sunday (since most Chinese were converted to Christianity by the early 1880s) the game was carried on from 9.30 a.m. to 9.30 p.m.; and at every hour during that period the result of each lottery was declared.[157]

The banker was usually concealed in a small box-like structure attached to the partition of the room. For each lottery, he attached one of the pictorial characters to a canvas which he rolled and placed in a cylindrical tin. Using a pulley, this tin was suspended from the ceiling in full view of gamblers gathered. Thereafter the sale of lottery tickets proceeded, in some cases by 'clerks' who went out into the streets. Each ticket represented one of the characters which the purchaser chose. Suspicious elite observers claimed that the banker kept a note of the amount wagered on the various symbols so that at a glance he could tell upon which most money had been staked. Then when the list was closed, he would disappear across the street and return a few minutes later to announce the winning character.[158] But it is highly unlikely that the gamblers would have permitted him to take down the cylindrical tin and open it in private before disclosing its contents.

At the same time, as is the case with gambling everywhere, all is never above board, and so too among the Chinese. Cheating led to disputes which, because they were prepared to stake so much, occasionally led to murderous assaults and to suicides. Unfair practices were even more dangerous when Chinese gambling houses began to open their doors to the general public. As in both Trinidad and Jamaica, the Chinese lottery became very popular among working class Creoles. But many unlucky people did feel that they had been cheated by unscrupulous Chinese gambling managers. Fortunately this never boiled over into racial violence against the Chinese.[159] Gambling in fact facilitated a measure of cultural integration between the Chinese and members of the host society, not on the basis of Chinese acculturation, but rather the reverse. Even though the opium dens which were previously associated with gambling were actively discouraged by the cultural elites and consequently went into decline along with the use of opium, by opening gambling to the wider community the Chinese were able to retain one of their most cherished cultural activities while adding something new to the culture of the host society which at the same time fostered cultural integration. But their continued attachment to gambling, even after their conversion to Christianity, and in direct contravention not only with Victorian Christian morality, but with all the entreaties by the elites to desist and in the face of legal action to eradicate that 'vice', was a classic example of cultural resistance by a subordinate ethnic group.

While contracted to the estates, the Chinese also participated in the leisure activities organized by the management after the grinding season. As noted before, a holiday was usually set aside to 'fête' and reward the labourers for their hard work which offered the Chinese a chance to mingle informally and 'play' with workers of other ethnic groups. Sporting events were organized, and the best workers were given gifts of sugar, rice, and money bonuses. At one such gala day held at Plantation La Jalousie on new year's day 1883, a greased pole was erected and ham, some bottles of brandy, and other niceties were placed at the top to be taken by the first person to get there. After many attempts by several workers, an enterprising Chinese was successful.[160]

It was on occasions like these (and of course in the 'Negro yard') that the Chinese learned to play cricket; but in keeping with the

292

*Cultural
Power,
Resistance,
and
Pluralism*

separatist tendencies in the society they were forced to form their own ethnic cricket teams.[161] As we have seen before, cricket simultaneously differentiated *and* integrated the cultural segments in the colonial society. Thus while obliged to form their own teams, the Chinese were not too shy to challenge teams composed of players of other ethnic groups including the supra-elite Georgetown Cricket Club—although they were generally no match for their opponents. What is clear, however, is that the value system embodied in the game was not fully inculcated by the Chinese who continued to be very selective in what they incorporated. Kirke noted, for instance, that although given out on two occasions (once leg before wicket, the other caught behind) in a match against the G.C.C. second eleven, the Chinese team captain refused to leave the wicket until he was clean bowled, middle stump, by a yorker! Even then he stalked off to the pavilion muttering "strange Chinese oaths".[162] Such values as playing by the rules ('fair play') and unquestioningly obeying the decisions of the umpire simply did not hold good with the Chinese. This is probably because, like the Indians, cricket was not regarded as a means of achieving social respectability and mobility, even though the Chinese did embrace both Christianity and western education. The role of cricket (and of sport generally) in aiding their assimilation of British socio-cultural values thus seems to have been quite limited during the nineteenth century.

Summary

The Chinese immigrants, like the Indians, went to Guyana with a perception that their sojourn would be temporary, and that they would return to China some day after the expiration of their indenture contracts. But the chances of that ever becoming reality were slim since, unlike the Indians, they were not offered assisted return passages; and the likelihood of their accumulating enough savings to pay the return fare and have some money to take back from their paltry earnings on the plantations was rather remote. The result was that very few were able to afford to go back home, though some did move to other Caribbean territories. For the majority, however, the reality soon dawned that Guyana would be their final resting place, and this tended to make them more amenable and adaptable to local cultural influences.

The cultural adaptation of the Chinese was not easy since it meant reconciling strong ethnic differences between the *Punti* and *Hakka* immigrants. But the need to survive in a hostile social and physical environment forced them to evolve a homogenized culture based on those elements common to both factions, in addition to making accommodations with the host culture. Their cultural adaptation was also considerably influenced by the acute shortage of females among them, and by the small and irregular importations of new immigrants. The shortage of females rendered it virtually impossible for them to recreate the traditional Chinese family in Guyana around which many cultural activities are organized. But then this was not unique to the Chinese in Guyana; and female shortage certainly did not prevent other Chinese overseas from preserving their cultural traditions. In those situations, the clans and secret societies substituted for the family. But small numbers and the scattering of the Chinese must have militated against strong clans and secret societies developing in Guyana. One further consequence of the shortage of females, though, is that in the absence of continuous imports of fresh Chinese immigrants, this posed a fundamental problem of sheer survival as a community, for they could not even sustain their already small numbers further depleted by out-migration.

The smallness of their (dwindling) numbers was thus perhaps most critical in determining their cultural adaptation. They never were afforded the opportunity to create large, self-contained ethnic communities like the Indians on the plantations; instead they were scattered in very small numbers all over the coastal belt. Although they did make a few efforts to set up ethnic agricultural settlements once freed of their contractual obligations, these were not long lasting particularly since many of the Chinese gravitated towards the retail trade which meant setting up shops in scattered locations. Furthermore, the small and infrequent batches of new Chinese immigrant arrivals meant that the vital reinforcing cultural link with the motherland was never secure. For the most part, therefore, they had to sustain themselves culturally by their own inner resources.

These circumstances left the Chinese in a culturally vulnerable position wherefrom it was extremely difficult to ward off the pressures of the cultural elites to assimilate. This was most vividly seen in their dramatic conversion almost *en masse* to Christianity in a relatively short period, made more attractive and acceptable by the fact that the principal missionary working among them for a brief period was himself ethnically Chinese. Yet this did not amount to cultural capitulation, for they practised their new religion within exclusive ethnic boundaries and in a distinctly Chinese manner; and at no time did they give the slightest indication that they regarded Victorian elite culture as superior to theirs. Nor did the tendency to adapt behind ethnic walls signify a disinclination to integrate: for they never prevented Creole participation in their lottery activities and New Year festivities, and they in turn mixed easily and mated with Creole women, 'rubbed shoulders' with other ethnic groups at horse-racing meetings, learnt cricket and other creole pastimes.

294

*Cultural
Power,
Resistance,
and
Pluralism*

The adaptation of the Chinese was characterized by a process of selective accommodation which ensured that they were not culturally integrated by being submerged within the dominant culture of the host society. Instead it enabled them to adopt significant elements of the host culture and adapt them to suit their own tastes, needs and purposes, while preserving important aspects of their own cultural traditions and values. This undoubtedly involved very fundamental cultural changes, but the resulting synthesis was a functionally whole culture which was sufficiently distinctive to provide the Chinese with a clearly defined ethnic identity.

Nevertheless, culture played a patently subordinate role to 'race' in determining the social position and status of the Chinese throughout the nineteenth century. While their wholesale adoption of Christianity, for instance, endeared them to the cultural elites, it did not in any way alter their racially defined social status as they continued to be seen as quaint Oriental strangers, relegated to the lower margins of the host society. Cultural assimilation, therefore, did not promote social equality for the simple reason that 'race' presented a seemingly insurmountable obstacle to that process. Besides, given their small and ever-dwindling numbers, the sense of a distinctive ethnicity which their culture, however radically altered, provided the Chinese was essential to preserving ethnic unity and cohesion in a race conscious society.

The case of the Chinese *hua-qiao* culture, however, does not support the notion of cultural pluralism. As enunciated by M.G. Smith, religion is one of the *basic* or *compulsory* institutions of a cultural group. Hence the large-scale conversion of the Chinese to Christianity meant that no matter how 'ethnic' their form of worship, they shared the same *basic* institution as the cultural elites. This negates the idea of cultural pluralism.[163] But, as we have seen, their adoption of Christianity (or of cricket, for that matter) did not signify an acceptance of the dominant value system which accorded a position of superiority to British culture. Thus the Chinese did not share perhaps the most important socio-cultural value of the host society. Instead they continued to preserve traditional *exclusive* institutions with their associated values. This, therefore, indicates that they cannot be considered as being culturally integrated in accordance with the theory advanced by Braithwaite, R.T. Smith, et al. Thus, not unlike that of the Portuguese, the Chinese culture does not conform to either the integrationist or the pluralist theory. But it would appear there is a greater degree of divergence from the values of the host culture(s) than convergence.

CONCLUSION:
Cultural Power, Resistance
and Pluralism

This book has had three principal concerns. First, it has sought to determine how and with what effects the colonial elites made use of their cultural power in an effort to mould a consensus of values among all sections of the population around the notion of the superiority of Victorian culture. Second, it has dealt with the responses of the subordinate ethnic groups to this attempt at cultural imposition and the extent to which they were successful in resisting the forces and influences of cultural domination. Third, it has analysed the extent of cultural divergence and integration among the several ethnic groups, and their impact on the organization of the colonial society in relation to the competing consensual and pluralist theories.

The cultural power of the colonial elites was derived from their position of social, political and economic dominance. In nineteenth century Guyana this gave them monopoly control over the apparatus of the state (both the legislative and security branches), and over the commanding heights of the economy (the plantation system). Through the former they could, if necessary, make laws and regulations, and employ punitive measures and violence, either to impose their own cultural values and institutions on the subordinate population or to outlaw and suppress those cultural practices of the subject peoples which they considered abhorrent; through the latter, especially by means of the system of indentured labour, they could, by restricting the leisure time and freedom of movement of the dependent labourers, impose severe constraints on their cultural activities. This enormous cultural power was further augmented by elite control of the press (the major newspapers), the educational system (especially the cultural content of the curriculum), and the churches (sermons and missionary proselytization). Through these media they were able to thrust their opinions and cultural propaganda on the powerless in the society who might, after constant (almost daily) badgering, relent.

296

*Cultural
Power,
Resistance,
and
Pluralism*

No less critical to the armoury of elite cultural power were invented imperial traditions, the most important of which was the exaltation of the British monarchy into a symbol of grandeur, majesty and omnipotence. Through the repetition of rituals related to the monarchy (and the accompanying show of armed force associated with military parades), a sense of awe and loyalty was fostered among the subordinate population in support of the broader ideology and system of imperial rule.

Less compelling perhaps, but no less effective, was the influence of sport (particularly cricket) in transmitting British cultural values. This was altogether a voluntary (and insidious) process of cultural transmission largely through example and encouragement, but which at the same time served to reinforce the social distance between elite and mass. Because of the subtlety of inculcation (no enforced laws or loud propaganda), and the pleasure and social respectability derived, it engendered little or no resistance from the subordinate populations and consequently was to some extent effective in promoting value consensus.

No discussion of the cultural power of the elites could be complete without reference to the force of ridicule. This was very effectively used to belittle both those who persisted in preserving 'primitive' and 'barbaric' traditions, as well as those who assimilated ('imitated') elite culture. The reason for the latter was to make it absolutely clear that, unlike the French policy of *Assimilation,* social equality was not on offer by the British with their cultural package.

This broad-based cultural power was skilfully employed by the colonial elites. But it is important to note that only very rarely in the postemancipation period did they resort to draconian measures (i.e., legislation, judicial punishment, and armed force) to **impose** their cultural values on the subordinate ethnic groups, even though those were the primary mechanisms for maintaining law and order, and social stability. Generally such strong-armed measures were only used to **prohibit or control/regulate** subordinate cultural behaviour that was considered inhumane and barbarous (e.g., the Indian *charak puja*), grossly immoral (e.g., Creole dignity balls), an intolerable nuisance (e.g., drumming of all kinds and the use of fireworks), or a threat to their security (e.g., obeah and the Indian *tadja*). Such regulations and prohibitions in effect set the broad parameters within which the cultural self-expression of each ethnic group was allowed to take place.

Unlike the French, at no time did the British colonial state itself get actively involved in the business of promoting cultural assimilation. Yet each time it legislated or enforced a cultural prohibition, it did in fact seek to impose certain elite cultural *values.* No less important was the fact that although the subordinate ethnic groups were allowed the freedom of cultural self-expression within certain legally prescribed limits, the cultural elites made it pellucidly clear that social mobility and respectability were premised on cultural assimilation. Therein lay perhaps their most subtle, yet coercive use of their cultural power.

It was, of course, the white British elites in whom, as the bearers and custodians of imperial culture, were vested the power to transmit it. Yet although they had the greatest stake in the colony, both financially and politically, and as a social group who were long present there, as individuals they harboured an immigrant mentality since they saw their colonial residence as temporary, to be endured only for as long as they could amass enough wealth with which to return home. In addition, being at the apex of the social hierarchy as the primary colonizers, they considered themselves to be the standard bearers of a superior culture with which they had a moral obligation to civilize the ex-slaves and indentured immigrants—'the white man's burden'. There was, therefore, no question of their adapting to the clearly 'inferior' cultures of the natives and immigrants. Consequently, their emphasis lay in preserving their 'superior' Victorian middle class culture as closely to the metropolitan model as was humanly possible on the 'frontiers of civilization' and transmitting it, consciously or unconsciously, to the subordinate masses. In this they experienced varying degrees of success very largely through the efforts of the missionaries.

But ironically, because their pedigree was long present in the colony, they were in reverse unconsciously 'tainted' by the 'inferior' culture of the Afro-Creoles which affected their speech patterns and accent, general demeanour, habits, food, customs and even beliefs to some extent. Thus, although the new planter elite of the postemancipation period was more capitalistic and less paternalistic than the old-style Anglo-Dutch class which they replaced, a Euro-Creole socio-cultural model was already well established to which all newcomers sooner or later acculturated; and, of course, the minority who were born in the colony were raised in that cultural framework. Thus whether they chose to admit it or not, there continued even after emancipation to be a symbiotic relationship between Europe and Africa in the plantation society which formed an integrated creole cultural world. All whites who resided for any significant period in the colony became an integral part of that world.

It is important, however, to note that as travel between colony and metropolis became quicker, cheaper and more frequent as a result of steamships, metropolitan cultural influences became stronger. This was aided after slavery by the weakening of some of the old links between black and white in the society consequent on the large-scale movement of ex-slaves off the plantations. But even though the black or coloured 'concubine', for instance, became less prevalent (especially

298

*Cultural
Power,
Resistance,
and
Pluralism*

in the towns) as more white metropolitan women were brought out as wives, sexual promiscuity between white men and brown-black women persisted especially in the rural areas, thus ensuring that the cultural links between white and black continued to be nurtured. These were further preserved by the presence of an army of service retainers in many elite households which was considered essential as a symbol of their elevated social status. These servants included cooks, maids, butlers, houseboys, nannies, grooms, gardeners, etc., all of whom both culturally influenced, and were influenced by, their elite employers. Elite culture, therefore, was never wholly British, though those influences became much stronger in the later nineteenth century. And although the European cultural bias or orientation was employed to reinforce their sense of racial superiority, elite culture was not coterminous with the racial boundaries of the white section for the simple reason that several educated coloureds and blacks also acquired it after emancipation. In fact the whites themselves considered this to be desirable if a consensus of values were to be created, and thus actively used their cultural power to that end.

White elite opinion was generally critical of the cultures of the subordinate peoples. At best they were regarded as alien (Portuguese), at worst as idolatrous paganism (Indian), or downright barbarism (African and Afro-Creole). But there was a cautious measure of pragmatic tolerance of cultural pluralism in certain quarters. This was related to the fact that the dominant planting interest wanted a contented labour force and recognized that not to interfere in the cultural behaviour of their indentured workers, however much they abhorred it privately, was sound policy. Besides, they harboured a feeling that Christian converts were a destabilizing element in the work force, and consequently were not terribly supportive of missionary efforts. The missionaries, on the other hand, were often overzealous in their efforts to impose their religious culture and values on non-Europeans, and were generally intolerant and arrogant. Their 'best' work was done among the Creoles and the Chinese, most of whom were christianized. But success among the Indians was rare as the missionaries were too few to start with, encountered strong resistance from organized religions, and only lukewarm support from the planters.

Thus, as we have seen, the responses of the subordinate ethnic groups to the elite exercise of their cultural power were quite varied. Of all the ethnic groups in the plantation society, the Creoles were the only group who had a relatively clear perception of Guyana as home. Africa was a distant memory although it may have been revived by the periodic arrivals of African immigrants after emancipation. But even then, there was no realistic hope of ever returning there, and there was nowhere else to go. Neighbouring West Indian islands were hardly beckoning. In fact, the flow was in the other direction as significant numbers of West Indian ex-slaves found their way to Guyana to benefit from higher wages and land. So even though their status was very subordinate (second-class subjects), Guyana was home. This perception had very important consequences for the cultural behaviour and attitudes of the Creoles.

Ideas imposed over generations of slavery to the effect that things white and European were superior, and things black and African were inferior, were reinforced and emphasized after emancipation by the cultural elites who used their enormous power to good effect. So much so that, as we saw, Africans were feared and regarded with suspicion; and even their children did not seek to preserve their languages and carry on their traditions. Thus a long tradition of enforced accommodation to white cultural values, institutions, customs, etc., was continued after emancipation, reinforced by the notion that one important criterion for social advancement was possession of the 'right' cultural attributes. It was their insatiable desire to attain a measure of social respectability within the colonial context which to a very large extent made the Creoles highly receptive to the dominant Anglo-Creole culture. Hence they displayed a general tendency to look down on their own Afro-Creole cultural heritage, even though at the same time their day to day behaviour, nurtured in the yards and streets of the villages and urban ghettos, portrayed very many aspects of that tradition. Not surprisingly, both as individuals and as an ethnic group they were characterized by cultural ambivalence: despising the very things that could unite them and give them a sense of self-esteem, dignity and identity.

This is not to say that all Afro-Creoles were thus confused. There always existed a persistent strain of resistance, both conscious and subconscious, to the imposition of Victorian cultural values and practices. One might find it natural for the small settlements of new African immigrants to retain pride in their cultural traditions. But even among the native Creoles, those persons living in remote rural areas seemed to preserve with a certain amount of pride their African-based cultural roots; and that trend seemed to take on new force between 1848 and 1860 when significant numbers of Creoles in different parts of the country began to turn their backs on the institutions and symbols of white civilization, including Christianity. The key figures of such cultural resistance were the obeah and *cumfo* practitioners who were even prepared to defy the law and elite opinion in order to practise their 'black' arts. This tradition of resistance, as has already been pointed out, was an integral part of the social milieu of the urban and village yard and street which spawned a vibrant counter-culture of values that were wholly antithetical to those being imposed from

300

*Cultural
Power,
Resistance,
and
Pluralism*

above. Even so, for the most part, Creole cultural resistance was not consciously organized, articulated or mounted to effectively counter the strong influences of elite cultural power.

Thus the majority of Creoles, having inculcated the disparaging ideas disseminated by the cultural elites about Afro-Creole folk traditions devalued the culture of their everyday lives, and in an often vain quest of social respectability idealized and imbibed that of a world into which they were for a long time denied access by virtue of their 'race'. Afro-Creole folk culture was thus never wholly African, although the African element was very substantial particularly among persons at the lower end of the social hierarchy. However, as British education and Christian values spread, more and more European elements were incorporated especially among the socially aspiring Creole *évolués*. These formed an important bridge linking the two great cultural traditions of creoledom, Afro-Creole and Victorian, but their conscious bias was clearly towards the latter. Thus like the elite culture, the Afro-Creole folk culture was not coterminous with the racial boundaries of the Creoles. For most of the postemancipation period, the culture overlapped those racial boundaries.

With respect to the subordinate immigrant groups, all felt alien and considered home to be elsewhere. Hence their inclination to assimilate the host cultures was generally weak. All immigrants perceived their sojourn in the colony as temporary, and thus saw no good reason to become acculturated. The focus of their cultural adjustments lay in making their ethnic traditions compatible with their 'temporary' way of life in the colony. This work shows that, with the possible exception of the Chinese, the emphasis was on redefining and restructuring traditional institutions, customs, ideas and beliefs to suit the altered circumstances, rather than adopting local cultural forms. While some ethnic groups were successful in this regard, others had to make significant modifications. But the general objective was the same—to make as little change as was necessary to survive their temporary stay.

Several factors determined the nature of the cultural adaptation of immigrant groups. Firstly, the size and regularity of the immigration process were important. The larger the number of any given category of immigrants and the higher the frequency of their arrivals, the better able they were to resist the cultural power of the elites and to reconstitute and maintain their ethnic traditions in the colony. In other words, a strong cultural link with the motherland could be maintained. In Guyana, the Indians as well as the Portuguese were best favoured in this regard, whilst the Chinese and Africans were the least favoured. Secondly, if they were located in large numbers on plantations, this favoured the reconstitution and preservation processes. Again the Indians and Chinese were at opposite poles where this is concerned.

The size of the female population played an important role since in the traditional cultures imported into Guyana, many of the customs and practices centered around the family, and women played a crucial part in that context. Also women as the principal child rearers were mainly responsible for transmitting cultural traditions and values from one generation to the next. Here the Portuguese were best favoured since their migration was characterized by a relative balance between the sexes. But among the Indians and Chinese there was a gross disproportion of males to females which adversely affected the onward transmission of traditional culture.

The existence of a highly organized religion with its hierarchy of priests also played a vital role in the retention of traditional culture. This was to be found strongest among the Indian immigrants, both Hindus and Muslims, as well as the Portuguese. Indeed when one considers that the Muslims only numbered 16.3 percent of Indian immigrants and yet were able to preserve intact their religious beliefs and practices in the face of hostility not only from the cultural elites, but also from the Creoles and their Hindu counterparts, it demonstrates how important an organized religious system was. So far as the Portuguese were concerned, their whole cultural matrix was centered around the preservation of Roman Catholicism, Madeira-style. What is very striking is that among each of the above religious groupings, priests were instrumental in defending and protecting the religion from external assaults. On the other hand, the Chinese who lacked such a highly organized religious system in the colony actually converted *en masse* to Christianity. Africans likewise were encouraged to do so by the example of the native Creoles.

Of the several subordinate ethnic groups present in the colony, the Indians were perhaps the most successful at resisting elite cultural power and preserving their cultural traditions in the alien environment despite the severe shortage of women. They benefitted from large numbers, large concentrations, regular reinforcements of fresh immigrants from India, and highly organized religions. Moreover, their position of marginality in relation to the host society meant that they never considered themselves bound by the values of that society. There was no strong impulse on their part, therefore, to acquire Anglo-elite culture in order to achieve social respectability in quite the same way as the Creoles. Even when creole Indians adopted cricket, for instance, they did so more for pure entertainment and to demonstrate their prowess than in a quest for social respectability.

The emphasis of the Indian immigrants, therefore, was on preserving their traditional culture and value system. They were thus better able to reconstitute their cultural institutions both on and off the estates. Even so, however, they had to make significant adjustments

302

*Cultural
Power,
Resistance,
and
Pluralism*

necessitated by the great sexual imbalance in their composition and by conditions of life and work under indenture on the estates. Mating relationships and ultimately marriage and the family unit itself underwent considerable change as women became more liberated; residence in estate housing imposed severe restraints on reconstituting the traditional joint family; the conditions of life and work on the plantations made nonsense of the fine distinctions in the caste system which separated persons of different *jatis* and their 'subcastes'; while the rigid work routine on the plantations imposed very real constraints on the preparations for and celebration of the great Hindu and Muslim festivals, thus forcing very significant modifications.

But the Indians were sufficiently large in number (forming over 40 percent of the population by 1900) and self-assured as a community to overcome many of those hurdles. Eventually they were able to redefine and restructure their cultural institutions and practices within a traditional all-India framework which ironed out minor regional or caste differences. This enabled them to reconstruct a homogenized/Brahmanized Bhojpuri-based cultural matrix adapted to their way of life in the plantation environment, but which kept faith with their great Indian tradition. This Bhojpuri culture formed the basis of a positive sense of ethnicity whose function it was to provide the Indians with inner group solidarity and resilience against a hostile society beyond. They were thus able to resist the pressures of the cultural elites to assimilate, particularly emanating from the white missionaries, because they had a viable counter-culture to what was on offer. This homogenized culture, therefore, provided the critical means for sustaining the Indians as a self-contained ethnic community behind the racial boundaries which isolated them from the society at large. Thus while 'race' continued to be the principal determinant of the social position of the Indians, culture played a vitally important role in reinforcing that racial differentiation. The case of the Indians, therefore, is very supportive of the notion of cultural pluralism.

The Portuguese, too, were highly successful in reconstituting and preserving their ethnic (Latin) traditions. Although not nearly as large in number as the Indians and, by nature of their primary economic activity (retail trading) not as concentrated residentially (except in a few places, e.g., in Georgetown, on the west bank of Demerara, and to a lesser extent on the Pomeroon river in Essequibo), they were favoured by a regular traffic between the colony and Madeira (both migration and commerce), a balance of the sexes, and an organized religion. This enabled them to successfully resist pressures to conform to English religio-cultural practices associated with Roman Catholicism; and, with the assistance of Italian Jesuit priests, they were eventually able to establish their own ethnic churches and related cultural institutions thereby ensuring the preservation of Madeiran religious and secular customs, as well as their language and a strong sense of Portuguese nationality. Not least of all, the success of the Portuguese in the retail trade provided them with the economic wealth, social status and ethnic pride with which to promote and exhibit aspects of their Latin culture. Thus, unlike the Creoles who depended on inculcating Anglo-elite culture to achieve social respectability, for the Portuguese such respectability was attained largely through their accumulation of wealth which obviated the need to make cultural compromises.

So, even though they too were forced by circumstances on the ground to make modifications, these were aimed mainly at adjusting to the reality of life in the colony rather than adopting local cultural forms. Besides, the level of racial hostility between the Portuguese and Creoles was a strong disincentive to such acculturation. Thus, great emphasis was understandably placed by the Portuguese on cultural autonomy and ethnic pride. This is why they were so concerned about losing their language late in the century, why they agitated for ethnic Portuguese rather than Italian priests, and why they refused to renounce their Portuguese nationality. So, as with the Indians, the Portuguese Latin culture was vitally important for moulding ethnic solidarity. Nevertheless, they shared certain basic values with the British cultural elites stemming from a common historical antiquity, a shared adherence to Christian civilization and western capitalism, and similar racial attitudes. In addition, by the end of the century there was some evidence of cultural change as the process of creolization slowly influenced the Portuguese, even though their socio-racial boundaries held firm. The case of the Portuguese, therefore, does not support the idea of cultural pluralism, but rather of cultural heterogeneity as defined by M.G. Smith.

The Chinese offered an interesting contrast to the Indians and Portuguese. They were not favoured with the advantage of large numbers, regular reinforcements from China, or large concentrations in any part of the colony. Furthermore, of all the immigrant groups, they suffered from the worst imbalance between the sexes. Finally, they were not able to preserve strong organized religions largely because their numbers were too small to sustain the three great Chinese religions *and* Christianity which was also represented among them. This unique combination of adverse factors meant that the preservation of their traditional culture was always an uphill task, and even the maintenance of their already small numbers was under constant threat. Although they, like all other immigrants, came with a perception that their stay would be temporary, they would probably have been among the first to realize that the prospect of ever returning home was very remote indeed in the absence of any financial assistance from the

304

Cultural
Power,
Resistance,
and
Pluralism

government. They were thus eventually much more reconciled to the fact that Guyana was in reality their new home. Those who did not, migrated to other Caribbean territories, not back (with a few exceptions, of course) to China.

It is not surprising, therefore, that it was the Chinese who made the most significant cultural accommodation to the host society. Certainly more than any other new immigrant group the Chinese acquired the desire to attain social respectability within the existing colonial society which entailed making important cultural compromises. And it was mainly in the very fundamental area of religion that such compromise was most apparent. In the space of just a few years between the mid-sixties and early eighties, virtually all the Chinese were converted to Christianity. Yet that did not represent a cultural capitulation to a 'superior' civilization; for that accommodation was made within the framework of a distinct sense of Chinese ethnicity which enabled them to preserve some of their traditional values. What they did was to incorporate Christian (*not Victorian*) beliefs, principles and practices into their cultural fabric. The result was Christianity Chinese-style, in the same way that the Portuguese practised theirs Madeira-style. The religion might have been alien, but the forms of worship and the language used were distinctly Chinese. They also played cricket, but in accordance with their own notions of 'fair play'.

Thus even in their cultural accommodation the Chinese were selective and were able to preserve a separate and distinct value system and ethnic identity. This view is reinforced by the fact that they did not cease to practise those aspects of traditional secular Chinese culture that could be preserved, albeit in a modified manner, of which the *Cheng Yueh Shih Wu* (the Chinese lunar new year festival) is a classic example. The case of the modified Chinese *hua-qiao* culture, therefore, is neither supportive of cultural pluralism nor of integration, but rather of cultural heterogeneity.

What therefore emanates from this study is that at the end of the nineteenth century no all-inclusive integrated cultural matrix based on a *universally* shared system of values could be said to have emerged in Guyana. But there were certainly signs of an integrative process at work, particularly within the Creole and white sections where the cultural power of the British elites was highly effective in moulding a consensus of values centered on the superiority of Victorian culture. Within the colonial context this emergent integrated Creole cultural matrix provided a framework within which the new immigrant groups could be assimilated. However, except for the Chinese, the cultural power of the elites was not sufficiently potent among the immigrants to produce that desired result; while on the other hand in their determination to resist that power, both the Indians and the

Portuguese fought to hold as fast as they could to modified versions of their traditional cultures and their accompanying value systems. In the process, they displayed an inclination to eschew close cultural links with the Creole population. This was clearly reflected, for instance, in the Portuguese (and Italian priests') discouragement of Creole participation in their church organizations, and the Indian withdrawal from the *tadja* celebration when Creole involvement grew.

The outcome of the counteractive interplay between the cultural power of the elites and the cultural resistance of the immigrants was a tendency towards the preservation of cultural difference rather than integration. The only major attribute shared by all ethnic groups was language since new immigrants found it necessary to acquire *Creolese* in order to function in the plantation society. But even then its use was largely confined to the points of contact, most notably in the work and market places.

The question that arises now addresses the influence of this study on the theoretical debate (alluded to in the introduction) about the issues of cultural integration or cultural pluralism. The empirical evidence examined here would (once again)[1] seem to indicate that neither the theory of cultural integration (and class stratification) around a system of shared values (as advanced by L. Braithwaite, E. Brathwaite, R.T. Smith, Hall, Cross, and others[2]) nor that of cultural pluralism (as advanced by M.G. Smith, Despres, van den Berghe, van Lier, and others[3]) where there is no common value system, is sufficient to explain or analyse the reality of a society like Guyana in the late nineteenth century.

The high degree of cultural integration within the traditional creole white/coloured/black sector of the society around a core of ideas and values which stressed the superiority of Victorian culture is certainly strongly supportive of the integrationist viewpoint. There was also a small measure of interculturation among the newer immigrant groups and the constituents of the creole host society which might seem to reinforce the concept of cultural integration. But the failure of the elites' use of their cultural power to forge a body of common values with which to unite the *whole* society points to the weakness of the integrationist theory as it applies to nineteenth century Guyana; although it might conceivably be argued that the general long-term tendency was towards value consensus.

Contrary to that perception, it is apparent from this study that with the exception of the white/black Creole socio-cultural continuum, Guyanese society even at the *end* of the nineteenth century was comprised of a number of discrete cultural sections which shared very little with one another other than a common commitment to making money in the plantation economy (acquisitive materialism). That ex-

306

*Cultural
Power,
Resistance,
and
Pluralism*

ception, however, is in itself sufficient to demonstrate the limitations of the theory of cultural pluralism in analysing a society in the process of change. This weakness is further demonstrated when one takes into account the Portuguese and the Chinese immigrants, both of whom ended up sharing some of the same *basic* institutions as members of the host society by the end of the century, while espousing different value systems.

Yet, since generally speaking it is true that each immigrant group tried to preserve its own *exclusive* institutions and values based on its traditional cultural model, both as an essential mechanism for resisting the cultural power of the elites and for moulding ethnic group consciousness and solidarity, the theory of pluralism would seem to be more relevant to Guyanese society at this stage of its development than its integrationist rival. Even though the physical and social environment wrought some change to the immigrant cultures, for the most part this led to consolidation *within* existing ethnic boundaries rather than cultural integration *across* those boundaries. The amalgam made for a rich diversity of culture, but there was no rapid momentum towards the evolution of a truly *national* Guyanese culture or value system integrating *all* ethnic groups. Thus the small indications of cultural integration which became more perceptible as time went on did not go far enough by the end of the century to fundamentally alter the overall picture of cultural pluralism.

This is why the colonial authorities of Guyana did not in the final analysis embrace consensus creation mechanisms, as the exercise of the cultural power at their disposal, heavy-handed though it was, was slow in realizing the desired results and consequently very unreliable for maintaining social stability. Not a great deal of resources, either human or financial, were employed in pursuit of this objective (especially relative to what were outlaid on the police, the military, the judiciary, jails and asylums), and the results were commensurate. The one area which seemed to offer the prospect of creating a consensual society was sport, particularly cricket. All ethnic groups, even the ultra-resistant Indian immigrants, inculcated an enduring love for the game. But the cricket culture was designed to preserve social divisions based on 'race' and class differences. Moreover, unlike the Creoles who saw cricket (like western education and Christianity) as a means of achieving social respectability and mobility, the Indians in particular resisted inculcating the social values with which it was packaged because these were fundamentally at variance with their reconstructed *Bhojpuri* value system. In short, intent on preserving their cultural autonomy, the Indian immigrants were not playing the *social* game. Cricket's potential as an integrative force, both socially and culturally, was thus severely hampered. Its socio-cultural impact in Guyana, therefore, was not nearly as powerful before the end of the nineteenth century as Stoddart found in Barbados where, he suggests, it superseded coercion as a mechanism of social order and stability.[4]

As pointed out elsewhere[5] the racially divided society of Guyana thus remained continuously unstable for the duration of the postemancipation nineteenth century. In contrast to Barbados, great reliance was placed on the threat and use of force to ensure social stability, although it was not employed to stamp British culture on the subordinate populations. For most of the period under review, therefore, cultural assimilation played second fiddle to coercion as a mechanism of social control in the ethnically compartmentalized society of nineteenth century Guyana. It was only when the society itself underwent change as the Creole *évolués* gradually broke through the racial barriers and eventually forced their way into government during the 1890s that coercion began to give way to cultural assimilation and value consensus as the main instrument of social control.

APPENDIX

TABLE 1   *Population Statistics, 1841-1911*

Category	1841	1851	1861	1871	1881	1891	1911
Whites	2,776	3,630	2,881	2,903	3,225	4,558	3,937
Blacks & Mixed	91,074	108,438	110,216	122,862	143,319	144,619	145,737
Indians	343	7,682	22,081	48,363	79,929	105,463	126,517
Portuguese	2,619	7,928	9,859	12,029	11,926	12,164	10,084
Chinese	-	-	2,629	6,880	5,234	3,714	2,622
*Amerindians and others	1,321	8,316	8,241	454	9,485	7,810	7,144
Total	98,133	135,994	155,907	193,491	253,118	278,328	296,041

* The census statistics for the Amerindian population were crude estimates since they were generally out of reach of the census takers. In any event the Amerindians do not form a part of this study.

Sources: Decennial censuses, 1841-1911. There was no census in 1901.

TABLE 2   *Residential Distribution*

Category	Location	1851	1861	1871	1881	1891
Whites	Rural	1,539	1,199	1,309	1,194	1,701
	Urban	2,091	1,682	1,594	2,031	2,857
Blacks & Mixed	Rural	81,380	82,265	89,948	107,709	109,305
	Urban	25,055	27,951	32,914	35,610	35,314
Indians	Rural	6,658	21,499	46,781	77,341	100,225
	Urban	1,024	582	1,582	2,588	5,238
Portuguese	Rural	5,966	6,567	6,611	5,378	6,105
	Urban	1,962	3,292	5,416	6,548	6,059
Chinese	Rural	-	2,441	6,562	4,439	2,761
	Urban	-	188	318	795	953

The figures for 1881 and 1891 are estimates.
Sources: Decennial censuses, 1851-1891.

TABLE 3   Gender Statistics

Year	Whites		Black & Mixed		Indians		Portuguese		Chinese	
	M	F	M	F	M	F	M	F	M	F
1851	2,369	1,261	54,118	54,320	6,038	1,644	4,726	3,202	-*	-*
1891	2,728	1,830	71,625	72,992	64,703	40,760	6,042	6,124	2,583	1,131

* Chinese migration to Guyana began in 1853, hence no figures.
Sources: Decennial censuses, 1851 and 1891.

TABLE 4   Narcotics Imports

OPIUM/BHANG		GANJA/MARIJUANA	
Period	Average Annual Amount (pounds)	Period	Average Annual Amount (pounds)
1850-1853	Not available	1850-1856	Not available
1854-1861	1,557.2	1857-1862	6,915.6
1862-1871	8,690.3	1863-1873	Not available
1872-1881	19,490.7	1874-1881	7,054.1
1882-1891	13,564.6	1882-1891	12,745.5

Sources: C.O. 116—Blue Books of Statistics, 1850-1891

NOTES

Abbreviations

1. Journals and Documents

AA	American Anthropologist
AJS	American Journal of Sociology
AQ	Anthropological Quarterly
BELC	Boletín de Estudios Latinoamericanos y del Caribe
BG	Berbice Gazette
BJS	British Journal of Sociology
CI	Caribbean Issues
CO	Colonial Office papers. Great Britain
CQ	Caribbean Quarterly
CS	Caribbean Studies
CSSH	Comparative Studies in Society and History
(D)DC	(Demerara) Daily Chronicle
DT	Demerara Times
EA	Eastern Anthropologist
EPW	Economic and Political Weekly
ERS	Ethnic and Racial Studies
GT	Guiana Times
IJCS	International Journal of Comparative Sociology
IJHS	International Journal of the History of Sport
IM	Immigrants and Minorities
JBS	Journal of British Studies
JCH	Journal of Caribbean History
JCS	Journal of Caribbean Studies
JFI	Journal of the Folklore Institute
JHR	Jamaica Historical Review
JICH	Journal of Imperial and Commonwealth History
JSAH	Journal of Southeast Asian History
JSAS	Journal of Southeast Asian Studies
JSH	Journal of Social History
LMS	London Missionary Society papers
MMS	(Wesleyan) Methodist Missionary Society papers
PP	(British) Parliamentary Papers
PS	Population Studies
RG	Royal Gazette
RI	Revista Interamericana
SES	Social and Economic Studies
SH	Social History
SJ/BG	Society of Jesus papers on British Guiana
SPG	(United) Society for the Propagation of the Gospel in Foreign Parts (papers)
VS	Victorian Studies
WIQ	West India Quarterly
WP	Weekly Penny

2. Miscellaneous

Bce.	Berbice
Dem.	Demerara
Encl.	Enclosure (in a document)

Chapter One

1. See the essays by John Breuilly, Keith Hopkins and David Cannadine in Juliet Gardiner, *What is History Today...?* (London, 1988), 48-57. Each writer, however, treats cultural history as a branch of social history.

2. The most notable of these are: Edward Brathwaite, *The Development of Creole Society in Jamaica 1770-1820* (Oxford, 1971), Bridget Brereton, *Race Relations in Colonial Trinidad 1870-1900* (Cambridge, 1979), and Patrick Bryan, *The Jamaican People 1880-1902* (London, 1991).

3. It is important to stress that the focus of this work is **the plantation society of Guyana** as opposed to the entire country. In strict geographical terms, this confines it to the coastal plains and extending inland for just a few miles along the banks of the main rivers, viz., the Essequibo, Demerara, Berbice and Corentyne. This means that the indigenous peoples, the Amerindians, who lived in the hinterland behind the plantations (and their culture), do not form part of this study. In one or two instances, however, Amerindian cultural influences did become part of the culture of the plantation society. These influences predate the ending of slavery when there was greater contact between Amerindians and the plantation sector, largely through their roles either in capturing and returning runaway slaves or assisting them to form maroon settlements in the bush. One Amerindian influence in particular, a dish called *pepperpot* (see chapter 5), was adopted by practically all of the newer immigrant groups to become the national dish of Guyana.

4. Brian L. Moore, *Race, Power and Social Segmentation in Colonial Society: Guyana after Slavery,* *1838-1891* (New York, 1987), 191-211.

5. Brian Stoddart, "Sport, cultural imperialism, and colonial response in the British empire", *CSSH* 30 (1988): 650-52.

6. Throughout this study, the term "ethnic group" is used in accordance with Schermerhorn's definition as a "collectivity within a larger society having real or putative common ancestry, memories of a shared historical past, and a cultural focus on one or more symbolic elements defined as the epitome of their peoplehood . . . A necessary accompaniment is some consciousness of kind among members of the group". See R.A. Schermerhorn, *Comparative Ethnic Relations: A Framework for Theory and Research* (New York, 1970), 12.

7. M.G. Smith, *The Plural Society in the British West Indies* (Berkley, 1965); *idem, Culture, Race and Class in the Commonwealth Caribbean* (Kingston, 1984); Leo A. Despres, *Cultural Pluralism and Nationalist Politics in British Guiana,* (Chicago, 1967); Pierre van den Berghe, *Race and Racism* (New York, 1967); R.A.J. van Lier, *The Development and Nature of Society in the West Indies* (Amsterdam, 1950).

8. Ibid. Smith listed kinship, education, religion, property and economy, recreation, "and certain soldalities" as the basic institutions. Despres makes a similar differentiation between cultural and heterogeneity and pluralism, but based on the functions of the institutions.

9. See L. Braithwaite, "Social stratification and cultural pluralism", in *Social and Cultural Pluralism in the Caribbean,* edited by V. Rubin. Annals New York Academy of Sciences, vol. 83, art. 5, 1960: 819-22; R.T. Smith, *British Guiana* (London, 1962). Numerous other scholars have contributed to this point of view.

10. Moore, 213-23.

Chapter Two

1. The data for this chapter are taken from a previous book by the author entitled *Race, Power and Social Segmentation in Colonial Society: Guyana after Slavery, 1838-1891* (New York: Gordon and Breach Science Publishers, 1987).
2. A total of 41,027 West Indians (1834-90) and 14,060 Africans (1834-67) went to Guyana. See G.W. Roberts and M.A. Johnson, "Factors involved in immigration and movements in the working force of British Guiana in the nineteenth century", *SES* 23, no. 1 (1974). While the West Indians, mainly Barbadians, settled among the local black population, many of the Africans tried to recreate tribal units either in villages of their own or in sections of Creole villages. For instance, a substantial African community, mainly Kongo, Yoruba and Kru, was formed at Canal No.1, West Bank Demerara, after their indentures expired. Plantation Guineve was bought by the Kongo and became known as "Kongo Heart Burn". Most of the Africans in this area were, however, Yoruba (Aku). They were located mainly at Plantations L'Oratoire (also called "Oku tedu/Oku town"), L'Heureuse ("Sabakay"), Beau Voisin ("Cornet"), and Vauxhall. Several migrated there from other parts of the colony, attracted by relatively cheap land prices. (See J.G. Cruickshank, "Among the 'Aku' (Yoruba) in Canal No. 1, West Bank, Demerara River", *Timehri* IV (3rd. ser.), 1917).
3. Brackette F. Williams, *Stains on My Name, War in My Veins: Guyana and the Politics of Cultural Struggle* (Durham, 1991), 127-74.

Chapter Three

1. See decennial censuses, 1851-1891. In 1840 there were only 71 Dutch residents still remaining in the colony (Light to Russell, No. 160, 24 December 1840, C.O.111/173; see also Brian L. Moore, *Race, Power and Social Segmentation in Colonial Society* (New York, 1987), 51-53.
2. Letter by 'Creole of Demerara' in *RG*, 14 June 1879. According to this source, in 1879 coloureds numbered 19 (16.8%) of the 113 estate managers in Guyana.
3. Moore, 131-32.
4. J.R. Moore, *A Handbook of the the causes of non-success and degradation of the Negro race in British Guiana* (Demerara, 1874).
5. B. Brereton, *Race Relations in Colonial Trinidad, 1870-1900* (Cambridge, 1979), 94.
6. P. Bryan, *The Jamaican People, 1880-1902* (London, 1991), 80.
7. E. Jenkins, *The Coolie: His Rights and Wrongs* (London, 1871), 45.
8. B. Premium, *Eight Years in British Guiana* (London, 1850), 12-13.
9. L. Crookall, *British Guiana* (London, 1898), 87-88; see also J.W. Boddam-Whetham, *Roraima and British Guiana* (London, 1879), 125-26.
10. Crookall, 85-95.
11. "A Demerara planter's hospitality", *RG*, 4 October 1888; R. Schomburgk, *Travels in British Guiana, 1840-44*, vol. 1 (Georgetown, 1922), 41; Crookall, 66-70; encl. in Scott to Boyce, No. 481, 1 May 1875, MMS/W.v/2. See also the advertisements in the local press. The Berbice or planter's chair was an elongated reclining chair with a sloping back and long flat arms which extended beyond the normal length of the chair to enable the user to stretch out his legs on the arm itself. Given the style of dress used by women in the 19th century, it was clearly a man's chair. Why it was linked specifically with Ber-

bice is not clear, because it appears to have originally been imported from India where it was commonplace among planters.

12. Schomburgk, loc. cit.
13. See note 11.
14. Ibid.
15. Boddam-Whetham, 126-27.
16. Ibid. 121-22; see also *RG*, 15 March 1877—letter by "Clarinda".
17. D. Wood, *Trinidad in Transition* (London, 1968), 82-84; Bryan,– 75-76.
18. *RG*, 10 June 1879–"A glimpse of overseeing in Demerara"; and *RG*, 21 June 1879–"Overseeing in Demerara".
19. W. Arthur Sawtell,"First impressions of the colony", *Echo*, 4 September 1897 (extracted from his paper published in the June 1897 issue of *Timehri*).
20. J.A. Heatley, *A Visit to the West Indies* (Alnwick, 1891), 54.
21. Ibid.
22. *RG*, 29 January 1881, letter by a visitor.
23. *RG*, 17 February and 10 March 1877, letters by "A lady correspondent".
24. See Jihang Park, "Sport, dress reform and the emancipation of women in Victorian England: a reappraisal", *IJHS* 6, no. 1 (1989): 10-30.
25. Edna Bradlow, "The culture of a colonial elite: the Cape of Good Hope in the 1850s", *VS 29*, no. 3 (1986): 391.
26. Heatley, 44-45.
27. Jenkins, 33.
28. Bradlow notes that imperialism and its corollary, loyalty to the royal family, were widespread among British settlers in the Cape Colony (Bradlow, 391-92).
29. Cannadine states that royal ceremony was not for the delight of the masses, but a group rite for the elite sections of society—the royal family, the aristocracy, and the church. The monarchy was thus not a symbol of national unity, but the head of the elite corporate groups. In fact celebrations focusing on national heroes such as Nelson and Wellington were far more popular than even coronations. The growth of the monarchy as a symbol of national and imperial unity was aided by Victoria's longevity, the growth of a new empire, of a national press which made use of new photographic techniques, and of new modes of transportation (bicycles, tramcars, railways, buses and cars). See David Cannadine, "The context, performance and meaning of ritual: the British monarchy and the 'Invention of Tradition', c. 1820-1977", in *The Invention of Tradition*, edited by E. Hobsbawn and T. Ranger (Cambridge, 1983), 101-64.
30. The term "invented tradition" is used here in Hobsbawm's sense, "a set of practices, normally governed by overtly or tacitly accepted rules and of a ritual or symbolic nature, which seek to inculcate certain values and norms of behaviour by repetition, which automatically implies continuity with the past" (see Eric Hobsbawm, "Introduction: inventing traditions", in Hobsbawm & Ranger (eds.), 1.
31. See for instance *RG*, 25 May 1844; 28 May 1859; *Creole*, 25 May 1861; *Colonist*, 15 June 1865; *Argosy*, 31 May 1890; *BG*, 11 May 1892.
32. *RG*, 26 August 1854.
33. *Colonist*, 11 March 1863; *Creole*, 13 March 1863.
34. *Colonist*, 10 February 1864.
35. *Colonist*, 11 March 1864.
36. *Echo*, 18 June 1887. The Barbadians had a reputation for being fiercely loyal to the imperial monarch. According to the *Argosy*, they had "unbounded loyalty to... the Queen", called their country 'little England', and boasted that they would always defend the Crown against all comers: "As long as Her Majesty has Barbados and the Barbadians on her side no harm can come to Her" (*Argosy*, 29 March 1884).

37. *RG*, 19 June 1887; 20 & 21 September 1887; *Echo*, 24 September 1887; Irving to Holland, No. 146, 14 April 1887, C.O.111/438; Bruce to Holland, No. 370, 1 October 1887, C.O.111/440; *DC*, 20 & 22 June 1897, 28 October 1898.

38. *Creole*, 6, 16, 23 & 27 February 1861.

39. *Echo*, 24 October 1896; *DC*, 15 & 22 October 1898.

40. *DDC*, 1 December 1881 and 1 December 1883; *BG*, 2 December 1891.

41. *RG*, 5 December 1888. In Jamaica there were two similar organizations, the Jamaica Scottish Society and the Jamaica Caledonian Society (Bryan, 73-74).

42. Father Woollett's "Notes", S.J/B.G/9.

43. Bradlow, 391.

44. *RG*, 14 September 1878.

45. *RG*, 3 July 1880–"Local Sketches".

46. Ibid.

47. Ibid.

48. *RG*, 23 October 1880–"Local Sketches".

49. *RG*, 7 August 1880–"Local Sketches".

50. *RG*, 9 January 1875, letter by "Paterfamilias".

51. *RG*, 26 January 1875, letter to the editor.

52. Ibid.

53. "Paterfamilias", loc. cit.

54. Ibid.

55. *RG*, 7 August 1880–"Local Sketches".

56. *RG*, 23 October 1880–"Local Sketches".

57. *Colonist*, 27 October 1874.

58. *RG*, 23 October 1880–"Local Sketches"; see also *RG*, 28 May 1859; *Creole*, 25 May 1861; *Argosy*, 31 May 1890.

59. Bradlow, 390.

60. Brereton, 61-62.

61. *RG*, 22 & 26 February 1876. Andrews notes that a duel was a formal and well-mannered event. Although the cause might vary from case to case, the general reason was "that the man of honour must above all 'suffer no affront, which is a term of Art for every

Action designedly done to undervalue him' ". She notes that the most serious affront was "giving the lie" or publicly impugning the veracity, honesty or courage of another gentleman. See Donna T. Andrews, "The code of honour and its critics: the opposition to duelling in England, 1700-1850", *SH* 5, no. 3 (1980): 409-34.

62. *RG*, 21 February 1885.

63. *RG*, 16 October 1880–"Local Sketches".

64. Comment of A. Macrae, encl'd in Light to Stanley, No. 83, 18 April 1845, C.O.111/227.

65. H. Bronkhurst, *Among the Hindus and Creoles of British Guiana* (London, 1888), 51-52.

66. Decennial censuses, 1851-91.

67. H. Kirke, *Twenty-Five Years in British Guiana* (London, 1898), 99.

68. Jenkins, 31; Schomburgk, 40; *RG*, 18 March 1875–"Sketches by Nemo".

69. Boddam-Whetham, 124-25.

70. "Nemo", loc. cit.

71. Ibid.

72. Schomburgk, loc. cit.

73. Cannadine, 112.

74. *RG*, 14 April 1877–"Mr. Pepps' Diary in Georgetown".

75. Comment of M. Macpherson, encl'd. in Light, No. 83, loc. cit.

76. Kirke, 34; Schomburgk, 46.

77. Moore, 61-74 and 130-33.

78. Letter by "A Country Curate", *Colonist*, 30 May 1866; Schomburgk, 46; Bronkhurst, 200.

79. Bryan notes that in Jamaica bookkeepers (and overseers) were not encouraged to marry since the estate had a vested interest in collecting a portion of their salary for room and board. That portion of salary would be lost if they married. Thus to satisfy their sexual desires, they resorted to women on the estates over whom they had power (see Bryan, 76). In Indonesia, estates refused to hire married applicants and did not allow them to marry while in service because marriages took up too much of the employee's time and salary.

As in the Caribbean during slavery, concubinage was actively encouraged. This marriage restriction lasted until this century in Sumatra. See Ann Laura Stoler, "Rethinking colonial categories: European communities and the boundaries of rule", *CSSH* 31 (1989): 143.

80. *Colonist*, 30 May 1866, letter by "A Country Curate"; Wood, 83; see also Brereton, 60.

81. Greathead to Boyce, No. 891, 7 September 1871, and Silcox to Boyce, no. 962, 21 September 1871, MMS/W.v/2. Three Wesleyan Methodist missionaries were accused to having affairs with unmarried women, viz., Irvine, Dickson, and Bronkhurst. It is not clear if they were married, although reference to the fashion of having two wives would suggest so.

82. Comments of F. Fothergill and R. Hancock, encl'd in Light, No. 83, loc. cit.

83. Kirke, 34-35.

84. Stoler, 146-49.

85. Ibid., 144.

86. *RG*, 4 October 1888, "A Demerara planter's hospitality".

87. Heatley, 42.

88. Light to Stanley, 23 November 1843, C.O.111/203; see also comments of Messrs J. Edgehill and R. Hancock in Light to Stanley, No. 83, loc. cit.

89. *RG*, 11 January 1881.

90. Ronald Hyam, "Empire and sexual opportunity", *JICH* 14, no. 2 (1986): 41- 42.

91. *RG*, 22 February 1877–letter by "Clarinda"; *RG*, 17 March 1877, letter by "Jessie".

92. R. Hancock's comment in Light, No. 83, loc. cit.

93. *RG*, 11 January 1881.

94. Kirke, 58.

95. *RG*, 25 May 1878, "Argus" column.

96. *RG*, 11 January 1881.

97. Hyam, 54-63.

98. *RG*, 30 October 1880, "Local Sketches".

99. "Clarinda", loc. cit.

100. *RG*, 1 February 1876, letter by "Censor".

101. *RG*, 15 March 1877–second letter by "Clarinda".

102. Ibid.

103. "Jessie", loc. cit.

104. *RG*, 13 April 1878, "Argus" column.

105. Schomburgk, 43.

106. Brereton notes that in addition to doing no housework, upper class women in Trinidad never marketed and rarely cooked, though they did direct their private armies of domestics (Brereton, 59-60).

107. See decennial censuses, 1851-1891.

108. *RG*, 8 May 1866.

109. *RG*, 5 August 1873.

110. See the Henry Bullock family papers 1861-1915, Essex Record Office, D/DVv 74.

111. *DC*, 5 October 1887–H.V.P.Bronkhurst's serialized "The religion and religious system of our East Indian population".

112. *DC*, 1 February 1889.

113. *Argosy*, 2 February 1889.

114. Ibid.

115. *DC*, 1 February 1889. For descriptions of some other upper class weddings see *BG*, 26 January 1889; *Argosy*, 26 April 1890; *DC*, 22 November 1898.

116. Bryan, 95.

117. Kirke, 19; R. Hancock's comment in Light, no. 83, loc. cit.

118. Ibid.

119. *Colonist*, 23 October 1874.

120. The Henry Bullock family papers, Essex Record Office, D/DVv 74.

121. Bronkhurst, *Among the Hindus and Creoles*, 159-61.

Chapter four

1. J.W. Boddam-Whetham, *Roraima and British Guiana* (London, 1878), 128-29; Richard Schomburgk, *Travels in British Guiana, 1840-44*, vol. 1 (Georgetown, 1922), 41-42; L. Crookall, *British Guiana* (London, 1898), 72-76.

2. Crookall, loc. cit.

3. Schomburgk, 43.

4. Boddam-Whetham, loc. cit.; J.A. Heatley, *A Visit to the West Indies* (Alnwick, 1891), 54.
5. Crookall, loc. cit.
6. Ibid.
7. Boddam-Whetham, loc. cit.
8. Heatley, 54.
9. B. Brereton, *Race Relations in Colonial Trinidad, 1870-1900* (Cambridge, 1979), 61.
10. Tricia Foley, *The Romance of Colonial Style* (London, 1993), 114-47. See also Brereton, 57, and P. Bryan, *The Jamaican People, 1880-1902* (London, 1991), 73-74.
11. H. Kirke, *Twenty-five Years in British Guiana* (London, 1898), 24-25; *RG*, 18 March 1875.
12. *RG*, 12 January 1878— "Argus" column.
13. *Colonist*, 11 March 1871.
14. J. Amphlett, *Under a Tropical Sky* (London, 1873), 75.
15. *RG*, 18 March 1875.
16. *RG*, 13 March 1875.
17. *DC*, 24 March 1885.
18. *RG*, 14 December 1880. This club was actually originated by a Portuguese, Mr. Menzies.
19. *RG*, 18 December 1880—"Notes by a Rambler".
20. *DC*, 26 August 1885.
21. Bryan, 72.
22. Kirke, 24-25.
23. *RG*, 18 March 1875.
24. Kirke, loc. cit.; Amphlett, loc. cit.
25. Brereton, 59.
26. Ibid.
27. Boddam-Whetham, 128-29.
28. *RG*, 20 and 30 March 1875– letters to the editor.
29. *RG*, 25 March 1875–letter to the editor.
30. Ibid.
31. *RG*, 27 March 1875–letter to the editor.
32. *Colonist*, 1 February 1889.
33. Answers to the Anti-Slavery Society's Queries encl'd in Light to Stanley, No. 255, 12 December 1844, C.O.111/215.
34. E. Bradlow, "The culture of a colonial elite: The Cape of Good Hope in the 1850s", *VS* 29 (1986): 393-97. Brereton, however, seems to portray a somewhat different picture for Trini-

dad claiming that "literary activity was often an integral part of the social round, and the whites were unquestionably the leaders of society" (Brereton, 58).
35. Bradlow, 396.
36. Reports of Stipendiary Magistrates Fothergill and Macpherson, encl'd in Light to Stanley, 18 April 1845, No. 83, C.O.111/227.
37. Ibid. Bradlow notes that in the Cape Colony "by contrast with Victorian England, the habit of reading, in the sense of a private activity associated with solitary enjoyment or acquisition of knowledge, was rare" (Bradlow, 393).
38. The Queen's College was located during the nineteenth century at the corner of Main and Murray streets. See Norman E. Cameron, *A History of the Queen's College of British Guiana* (Georgetown, 1951), 1-57.
39. Kirke, 8-9.
40. Light to Stanley, No. 96, 3 May 1844, C.O.111/210; No. 166, 31 July 1844, C.O.111/212; also No. 264, 29 December 1844, C.O.111/215. In September 1844, the Secretary of State informed the governor of the queen's accession to patronage of the society (Stanley to Light, No.451, 27 September 1844, C.O.111/212).
41. *RG*, 15 June 1844.
42. Ordinance No. 19 of 1866, C.O.113/5.
43. *RG*, 4 April 1866; *Colonist*, 6 March 1868.
44. Blue Books of Statistics for 1869-1891. (C.O.116).
45. *Colonist*, 13 February 1868; *RG*, 5 August 1869.
46. Barkly to Pakington, No.159, 9 October 1852, C.O.111/291; Blue Books of Statistics for 1869-1900.
47. *RG*, 16 October 1875.
48. *BG*, 20 February 1889.
49. Blue Books of Statistics, 1869-1891.
50. *BG*, 22 June 1889; 4 December 1889; 20 & 24 June 1891; 4 July 1891; 6 January 1892; and 12 October 1892.

51. *RG*, 4 October 1851.
52. *RG*, 4 March 1854; 18 August 1859; 24 November 1866; *Colonist*, 5 December 1866.
53. Blue Books of Statistics, 1869-1891.
54. *Colonist*, 20 January 1866; *RG*, 18 & 27 January 1866.
55. See, for instance, *BG*, 19 August 1882; 2 & 16 October, 1889; 3 May and 2 August 1890; *DC*, 1, 13, 14, 23 September 1898; 26 October 1898.
56. *Colonist*, 10 February 1864; 4 November 1865; 15 December 1866.
57. *RG*, 8 May 1873; *Colonist*, 20 March 1875.
58. *Colonist*, 18 September 1869.
59. *RG*, 11 April 1874.
60. *RG*, 12 April 1883; 13 November 1883; *DDC*, 14 November 1883; *Argosy*, 3 May 1890; 15 November 1890; *DC*, 27 January 1885.
61. *DC*, 8 April 1885; 31 August 1885; 15 June 1886.
62. *RG*, 6 December 1860.
63. *RG*, 17, 24 & 28 December 1844.
64. *RG*, 16 January 1851.
65. *Creole*, 31 May 1862.
66. *BG*, 28 March 1891.
67. *RG*, 11 January 1849.
68. *RG*, 12 July 1849.
69. Anonymous letter to the editor, *RG*, 19 May 1859.
70. *BG*, 18 February 1865; *Creole*, 20 December 1866; 15 March 1867; *Colonist*, 12 January & 16 April 1867.
71. See *BG*, 2 October 1889; *DC*, 4 & 7 September 1898; 4 & 5 October 1898; and 2 November 1898.
72. *RG*, 25 October & 18 December 1849; *Creole*, 12 April 1862; 18 February 1863; *BG*, 23 & 27 June 1888; 31 October 1888.
73. See, for instance, *RG*, 1 August 1844; 26 January 1878; 5 March 1878; 22 May 1883.
74. *Echo*, 2 & 30 September 1893.
75. Heatley, 45.
76. Ibid., 45-46.
77. *RG*, 19 January 1858; see also Ordinance No. 7 of 1858 and Walker to Labouchere, No. 21, 21 March 1858, C.O.111/319.
78. *RG*, 18 March 1875–"Sketches of Demerara by 'Nemo' ".

79. *RG*, 13 February 1858.
80. See for instance *RG*, 22 June 1844, 15 February 1849, 18 December 1849, 11 April 1863, 2 May 1863, 16 October 1875; *Colonist*, 14 September 1865, 19 May 1866, 30 January 1867, 2 January 1872; *DC*, 11 October 1885; *BG*, 18 August 1888, 1 May 1889; Schomburgk, 43.
81. *RG*, 20 December 1851.
82. *RG*, 29 December 1860.
83. *RG*, 7 January 1875; *Colonist*, 7 January 1875.
84. *RG*, 9 January 1875–letter by "Paterfamilias".
85. See footnotes 81-83.
86. *RG*, 16 February 1875.
87. Ibid. Other fancy dress balls were held both in Georgetown and in New Amsterdam. See for instance, *RG*, 5 January 1878 and *BG*, 9 January 1892.
88. *BG*, 5 October 1864.
89. *Colonist*, 15 April 1871.
90. Ibid.
91. *RG*, 1 December 1874 –letter by "Paterfamilias".
92. *RG*, 14 April 1877–'Mr. Pepps' Diary in Georgetown".
93. *RG*, 1 December 1874–letter by "Paterfamilias"; see also *RG*, 29 January 1881–letter by a visitor; and Kirke, 11.
94. "Paterfamilias", loc. cit.
95. Kirke, 11.
96. Querriman is a local scale fish.
97. *RG*, 2 September 1886.
98. *RG*, 29 January 1881–letter by a visitor.
99. Father Woollett's "Notes", 1858-1860, S.J/B.G/9.
100. Peter Bailey, *Leisure and Class in Victorian England* (London, 1987), 69-153; Keith A.P. Sandiford, "The Victorians at play: problems in historiographical methodology", *JSH* 15, no. 2 (1981): 271-78; Timothy J.L. Chandler, "Games at Oxbridge and the public schools, 1830-80: the diffusion of an innovation", *IJHS* 8, no. 2 (1991): 171-201. There is a fast growing body of literature on sports in Victorian Britain and the empire. See, for instance, Richard Holt, *Sport and*

the British: A Modern History
(London, 1989); J.A. Mangan,
The Games Ethic and Imperialism
(London, 1986), and his *Pleasure,
Profit and Proselytism: British Cul-
ture and Sport at Home and
Abroad, 1700-1914* (London,
1988), and Brian Stoddart,
"Sport, cultural imperialism, and
colonial response in the British
empire", *CSSH* 30, 1988.

101. Sandiford, loc. cit.; also his
"Cricket and the Victorian soci-
ety', *JSH* 17, no. 2 (1983): 305;
Stoddart, 653.

102. Benny Green, *A History of
Cricket* (London, 1988), 192.

103. Holt, 207-08.

104. Bailey, loc. cit.; Sandiford,
"The Victorians", 279-80.

105. Holt, 221.

106. Stoddart, 650-56; Holt, 212-23.

107. Kathleen E. McCrone, "Play up!
play up! and play the game! sport
at the late Victorian Girls' Public
School", *JBS* 23, no. 2 (1984): 107-
08. See also, Sandiford, "The Victorians", 281-82; and J.A. Mangan, "The social construction of
Victorian femininity: emancipation, education and exercise",
IJHS 1-4.

108. McCrone, 108-34; Mangan, "The
social construction", 4-7.

109. Jihang Park, "Sport, dress reform
and the emancipation of women
in Victorian England: a reappraisal", *IJHS* 6, no. 1 (1989): 11.

110. Bailey, 98.

111. Holt, 208.

112. Kirke, 19.

113. Ibid., 97-98.

114. Barton Premium, *Eight Years in
British Guiana, 1840-48* (London,
1850), 118-120.

115. Kirke, 62-64.

116. Ibid.

117. Ibid.

118. *Colonist*, 21 March 1875; 13 June
1876; *RG*, 9 October 1880–"Local Sketches".

119. *BG*, 27 August 1864, 11 February
1865, 6 August 1884, 25 August
1888, 18 September 1889, 22 February 1893; *Colonist*, 3 & 25 June
1867; Hincks to Buckingham &

Chandos, No. 52, 18 April 1868,
C.O.111/367; *RG*, 27 July 1869,
18 September 1880–"Local
Sketches"; *DC*, 24 March 1885,
6 March 1891, 7 September 1898.

120. *BG*, 19 July 1865.

121. *BG*, 27 September 1893.

122. Brereton, 6; Bryan, 194-95.

123. Stoddart, 656-57.

124. *RG*, 9 February 1878.

125. Kirke, 61-63.

126. For a complete history of the Demerara Turf Club, see the serialized column "Records of the Demerara Turf Club", *RG*, 8, 11, &
29 September; 2, 6, 9, 13, 16 & 23
October; 27 November; 4, 8, 11,
18 December 1886.

127. Kirke, loc. cit.

128. *Argosy*, 14 June and 5 July 1890.

129. See *RG*, 13 August 1878, 3 January 1880; *BG*, 28 December 1864.

130. Kirke, 63; also, Schomburgk, 50;
RG, 13 August 1878, 3 January
1880.

131. Kirke, 61-63.

132. *RG*, 20 April 1876.

133. Kirke, 63. Interestingly, although
obeahmen were reputedly in
great demand on race days, the
white elites were prepared to defend horse-racing against the
charge that it encouraged obeah
practices. The promoters disclaimed any responsibility for
obeah at the races, and argued
that the two grand race meetings
each year were a source of great
entertainment to all echelons of
society. In other words, if obeah
was indeed practised, that should
not be allowed to detract from
the benefits offered by horse-racing (letter by "One of the Promoters", 10 May 1878 in *RG*, 11
May 1878).

134. *Creole*, 7 April 1858. Another fra-
cas occurred at the Race Course
in October 1869 in which there
were a few casualties including
the secretary, Mr. Boelin, who
sustained a dislocated shoulder after being thrown (*Creole*, 31 October 1869 and *WP*, 1 November
1869).

135. *Colonist*, 2 February 1878.

136. Kirke, loc. cit. see also Park, 17.

137. Heatley, 54 & 56; Cameron, 46.

138. *RG*, 12 March 1884; *BG*, 23 June, 4 July, 15 August 1888, 30 January, 8 May, and 22 June 1889; *DC*, 29 March 1891.

139. Park, 17; Stoddart, 657-58; *BG*, 23 June 1888, 30 January 1889, and 22 June 1889; *DC*, 29 March 1891.

140. Sandiford, "Cricket and the Victorian society", 307-11.

141. Stoddart, 658.

142. *RG*, 23 October 1858.

143. *Colonist*, 22 January 1872.

144. *Colonist*, 12 September 1865.

145. *RG*, 31 December 1863, 6 January and 26 February 1864; *Colonist*, 4 January and 26 February 1864.

146. Cameron, 32-62; *RG*, 29 January 1884; Jimmy Richards & Mervyn Wong, *Statistics of West Indies Cricket 1865-1989* (Kingston, 1990), 5.

147. *RG*, 17 March 1859.

148. *Colonist*, 23 February 1865, 12 September 1865.

149. *RG*, 28 January 1869.

150. Kirke, 63-64.

151. Richards & Wong, 4 & 9. Up to 1900, the Guyana winning record was 4-7 against Barbados, 5-2 against Trinidad, and 2-0 against Jamaica. Edward Fortescue Wright was the best of the elite cricketers to play for Guyana in the 19th century. He was a fine all-round cricketer who was well known in that capacity in his native Gloucester before he went to the colony to take up a post as Inspector of Police (Kirke, 49).

152. *RG*, 26 August 1869. Hawke's team played two games against supposedly representative Guyanese teams, but which were composed entirely of members of the GCC (see *Echo*, 27 February, 3, 10 and 24 April 1897).

153. Hilary McD. Beckles, "The making of the first 'West Indian' teams, 1886-1906", unpublished paper (Barbados, 1993), 7.

154. *RG*, 19 January and 18 June 1884, 30 November and 28 December 1885.

155. Heatley, 54.

156. *BG*, 19 August 1865.

157. *BG*, 6 March 1889 and 9 September 1891.

158. *RG*, 14 December 1880.

159. *Argosy*, 2 October 1880; *DC*, 18 and 22 January, 22 February 1885, 20 February, 8 and 10 March 1891.

160. See, for instance, *DC*, 18 & 21 January 1885, 20 February 1885, 20 February 1891, 8 & 10 March 1891.

161. Cameron, loc. cit.

162. Chandler, loc. cit.

163. *RG*, 29 May & 25 August 1849; *BG*, 2 January 1864.

164. *BG*, 2 January, 5 October and 28 December 1864.

165. *DC*, 8 February 1885, 13 September and 14 October 1898.

166. *Colonist*, 26 January 1878; *RG*, 2 February 1882. The Berbice Cycling Club was opened in 1893 with a ride from New Amsterdam to Plantation Everton (see *BG*, 11 March 1893). Bryan has observed similar developments in Jamaica with the formation of the Jamaica Bicycle Club in 1886 with the same membership fee as in Guyana (Bryan, 200-01).

167. David Rubenstein, "Cycling in the 1890s", *VS 21*, no. 1 (1977): 47-72; Park, 18-20; Bryan, loc. cit.

168. *DDC*, 15 August 1882. While formed largely for track and field purposes, this club served more as a general sports club and played cricket as well. See the report on the GCC, [*RG*, 29 January 1884].

169. *RG*, 21 April and 17 May 1884.

170. *DC*, 25 October 1898; Cameron, loc. cit.

171. Sandiford, "The Victorians at play", 281.

172. Holt, 210.

173. *Colonist*, 11 March 1871; *DC*, 17 September 1898; Kirke, 23-25.

174. *RG*, 17 November 1866; *Colonist*, 8 April 1867.

175. *DT*, 9 August 1875; *RG*, 8 July 1876. The DCA endured to the end of the century (see for instance *Echo*, 7 November 1896).

176. *BG*, 29 June 1889; *Argosy*, 15 March 1890.

177. *RG*, 30 August 1877. Bryan has observed similar Scottish associations in late 19th century Jamaica (Bryan, 73-74).

178. *RG*, 12 November 1878.

179. *Colonist*, 19 January 1878. For a description of British middle class attitudes towards gambling, see Bailey, 142-43.

180. *RG*, 26 January 1878.

181. Brian L. Moore, *Race, Power and Social Segmentation in Colonial Society* (New York, 1987), 191-212.

Chapter Five

1. For full details on the establishment of free villages in Guyana after emancipation, see Brian L. Moore, *Race, Power and Social Segmentation in Colonial Society* (New York, 1987), 34-37.

2. W. Rodney, *A History of the Guyanese Working People* (Kingston 1981), 61.

3. A. Adamson, *Sugar without Slaves* (New Haven, 1972), 58.

4. Letter by "A Country Curate", in *Colonist*, 30 May 1866.

5. John Candler, Extract from Diary (edited by Prof. Boromé), *CS* 4 (1964): 56.

6. Adamson, 58-60.

7. A. Trollope, *The West Indies* (London, 1860), 183-84.

8. E. Jenkins, *The Coolie: His Rights and Wrongs* (London, 1871), 44.

9. J. Brumell a.k.a. "A Landowner", *Demerara After Fifteen Years of Freedom* (London, 1853), 51.

10. I. Scoles, *Sketches of African and Indian Life in British Guiana* (Demerara, 1885), 5.

11. Ibid.

12. H. Dalton, *The History of British Guiana*, vol. 2 (London, 1855), 5.

13. Scoles, 15-19.

14. Dalton, loc. cit. The "palm-loaf" is the spine of the branch of the coconut or palm tree.

15. H.V.P. Bronkhurst, *The Colony of British Guiana* (London, 1883), 254; Report of Stipendiary Magistrate [hereafter SM] Ware encl'd

in Walker to Grey, No. 20, 13 June 1848, *P.P.*1847-48. XLVI.

16. *RG*, 15 September 1888.

17. Ibid.

18. B. Premium, *Eight Years in British Guiana 1840-1848* (London, 1850), 73-74.

19. Dalton, 10. Scoles too observed the penchant of Creole women for verbal abuse. "True the poor African [woman] has only *broken* English at her command, but certain it is she makes the most of the *broken pieces* flinging them at you right and left in a most offensive or hurtful form when her monkey is fairly up; or when her ire or indignation has been fairly roused, then her language becomes every bit as saucy and quite as savage as that of any of the wicked wily and unwashed ones in the nooks and miserable corners of our model *European* cities. But . . . an African indignation and hot anger soon cools down without as a rule leaving behind it the ordinary residue of vindictive feeling or the wicked desire of seeking revenge." See I. Scoles, "Sketches of African life in British Guiana", *DC*, 15 March 1885.

20. "H.R.", 'Local Sketches', *RG*, 28 August 1880.

21. D. V. Trotman, *Crime in Trinidad* (Knoxville, 1986), 257.

22. Orlando Patterson, "The ritual of cricket", *Jamaica Journal* 3 (1969): 22-25. Patterson developed this idea in relation to cricket as a symbol of English culture in the Caribbean.

23. Bronkhurst, *The Colony*, 221.

24. Ibid.; Light to Grey, No. 18, 3 May 1848, *P.P.*1847-48. XLVI.

25. John R. Rickford, *Dimensions of a Creole Continuum* (Stanford, 1987), 59.

26. Bronkhurst, *The Colony*, 220-21.

27. J.G. Pearson, "Guiana's alien peasantry", *Argosy*, 16 January 1886.

28. Rickford, 71-72.

29. Richard Schomburgk, *Travels in British Guiana, 1840-44*, vol. 1 (Georgetown, 1922), 44.

30. Rickford, 57-58.
31. J. van Sertima, *The Creole Tongue* (Demerara, 1905), 4-5.
32. J.G. Cruickshank, *Black Talk* (Demerara, 1916), 6-12.
33. Scoles, 52.
34. Bronkhurst, *The Colony*, 222.
35. A. Hardy, *Life and Adventure in British Guiana* (London, 1913), 67.
36. Ibid., 70.
37. Trotman, 256.
38. L. Crookall, *British Guiana* (London, 1898), 130.
39. J.G. Cruickshank, "Among the 'Aku' (Yoruba) in Canal No. 1, West Bank Demerara River", *Timehri* 7, 3rd. ser. (1917): 77.
40. Cruickshank, loc. cit. The meanings of these names were supplied by Dr. Waibinte Wariboko of Nigeria.
41. H.V.P. Bronkhurst, *Among the Hindus and Creoles of British Guiana* (London, 1888), 152-53.
42. This information has been supplied by Dr. W. Wariboko of Nigeria.
43. Ibid.
44. H. Kirke, *Twenty-five Years in British Guiana* (London, 1898), 197.
45. Ibid.
46. Pearson, loc. cit.
47. Kirke, loc. cit.
48. Ibid.; Pearson, loc. cit.
49. Dalton, 5.
50. Bronkhurst, *Among the Hindus and Creoles,* 208.
51. Bronkhurst, *The Colony*, 209.
52. J. Gerard, "Inter Guianese" (ms. A–Society of Jesus, 1899-1901).
53. Premium, 25-26.
54. Dalton, loc. cit.; Jenkins, 34; Bronkhurst, *The Colony*, 209; encl. 4 in Light to Stanley, No. 255, 12 December 1844, C.O.111/227.
55. W. Arthur Sawtell, "First Impressions of the Colony", *Echo*, 4 September 1897.
56. Dalton, 5; Jenkins, 34; Bronkhurst, *The Colony*, 209; Crookall, 119.
57. Premium, loc. cit.
58. Bronkhurst, *The Colony*, 209.
59. Schomburgk, 48-49.
60. "A Landowner", 14-15; Dalton, loc. cit.
61. Premium, loc. cit.
62. Crookall, 119.
63. Barkly to Grey, No. 102, 26 June 1850, *P.P.*1851. XXXIX.
64. Ibid.
65. Scoles, 20; Bronkhurst, *The Colony*, 255.
66. Ibid.; Anon., "The overseer's manual", *Argosy*, 22 March 1884.
67. Cruickshank, *Black Talk*, 6-7.
68. Anon., loc. cit.
69. Ibid.
70. Cruickshank, *Black Talk*, 8. The Jamaican equivalent is called *Dukunoo*.
71. Scoles, loc. cit.
72. Hardy, 75-76.
73. Anon., loc. cit. Bronkhurst, *The Colony*, loc. cit.
74. Scoles, loc. cit.
75. R. Bastide, *African Civilizations in the New World* (New York, 1972), 100.
76. C. Dance, *Chapters from a Guianese Log-Book* (Demerara, 1881), 84.
77. R.T. Smith, "The family in the Caribbean", in *Caribbean Studies: A Symposium*, edited by V. Rubin (Seattle, 1960), 67.
78. N. Solien, "Household and family in the Caribbean: some definitions and concepts", *SES* 9, no. 1 (1960): 104-06. See also S. Greenfield, "Households, families and kinship systems in the West Indies," *AQ* 35 (1962): 130.
79. R.T. Smith, *The Negro Family in British Guiana* (London, 1956), 51.
80. Veness to Sect., 31 March 1871, SPG/E.26.
81. Limmex to Gen. Sect., 12 August 1851, MMS/W.iv/5.
82. Reports of [SM] J.D. Fraser for June 1851, C.O.116/168.
83. Report of [SM] W H. Ware, C.O.116/168.
84. Candler, 59.
85. Bronkhurst, *Among the Hindus*, 200; see also a letter from "A Country Curate" to the editor of the *Colonist*, 30 May 1866, in which he states that if things were vastly improved at that time, he wonders "what a sink of iniquity the colony must have been" before.

86. M.J. Herskovits, *The Myth of the Negro Past* (Boston, 1941), 171.

87. Walker to Newcastle, No. 102, 20 October 1853, C.O.111/297; Stipendiary Magistrates' reports, 1848-54, C.O.116. In this period, legal marriages fluctuated between a low of 504 and a high of 554.

88. Report of [SM] W.H. Ware, 30 June 1853, C.O.116/169. Ware claimed that parents considered a period of living together essential before they gave their formal consent to legal marriage. This assumes of course that such consent was necessary (see Report of [SM] W.H. Ware, 30 June 1850, C.O.116/168).

89. Dalton, 11; Report of Ware (1853), loc. cit.

90. J. Pearson, loc. cit.

91. Dalton, loc. cit.

92. R. T. Smith, "The family in the Caribbean", 68.

93. R. Duff, *British Guiana* (Glasglow, 1866).

94. Dalton, loc. cit.

95. Callier to Perks, No.409, 22 April 1870, MMS/W.v/2.

96. Duff, loc. cit.

97. Report of Ware (1853), C.O.116/169; report of [SM] Carbery, 31 December 1850, C.O.116/168.

98. Report of Ware, 30 June 1854, C.O.116/169; Barkly to Grey, No. 102, 20 June 1850, *P.P.*1851.XXXIX. The structural features of common-law unions have persisted into the later twentieth century, and modern sociological research has demonstrated that once the new household is established the relationship becomes more stable whether or not sanctioned by legal marriage, and that the majority of unions endure at least until the woman finishes her period of child-bearing (see R.T. Smith, "The family", loc. cit.).

99. Report of Ware (1850), loc. cit.

100. Limmex to Gen. Sect., 12 August 1851, MMS/W.iv/5; Iitchin to Sect., September 1866, SPG/E.19. The problem of infidelity, especially on the part of males, is supported by modern sociological findings; but Smith notes that females tend to be quite faithful especially during the child-bearing period (see R.T. Smith, *The Negro Family*, 114). Freilich has argued that there is a basic contradiction in the black male's attitude to sexual life. While he claims monopolistic sexual rights over his wife, he considers all other women (including other men's wives) sexually accessible to him. And since the black community lionizes the man who has had many sexual affairs, there is a strong incentive to "lay" as many women as possible. But it is important to note that sexual promiscuity does not necessarily entail dissolution of the "marriage" and abandonment of the family (see M. Freilich, "Serial polygyny, negro peasants and model analysis", *AA* 63, no. 5 (1961): 961 & 965.

101. Report of [SM] Carbery, 31 December 1853, C.O.116/169.

102. Limmex, loc. cit.; Candler, 57.

103. Premium, 138-39.

104. Kortright to Kimberley, No. 224, 18 October 1880, C.O. 111/417.

105. Ibid.

106. Comment by Marshall, encl. in Light to Stanley, No. 897, 18 April 1845, C.O.111/227.

107. Candler, 57.

108. Premium, loc. cit.; Limmex, loc. cit. *RG*, 29 April 1875.

109. Barrett to Tidman, 12 August 1847, LMS 7/2 (Dem.).

110. Bronkhurst, *The Colony*, 350.

111. Ibid., 348.

112. Trotman, 176-77.

113. "H.R.", 'Local Sketches: Etiquette', *RG*, 16 October 1880.

114. Premium, 137-38. Modern sociological research by Freilich shows that in Trinidad no third party is brought into such a "divorce" whether or not the marriage is religiously sanctioned. The wife usually leaves the house with her children and moves to her mother's home or to a new household. Because of this, how-

ever, Freilich regards black marriage as a temporary phenomenon, not designed to be permanent, but only for as long as the couple can "cooperate". He thus claims that blacks conceive of marriage as a "now-for-now" affair (see Freilich, 960-61). This conclusion appears rather superficial, and is certainly contradicted by other researchers. Bell notes that between the ages of 14 and 45, black women spend 38 percent of that time or 11.8 years in legal marriage. When added to the time spent in common-law unions, the overall average is 19.3 years or 59 percent of the child-bearing span (see R. Bell, "Marriage and family differences among lower class Negro and East Indian women in Trinidad," *Race*, 1970, 64-65). This seems to endorse Smith's point that women remain faithful during the child-bearing period, and points to a high degree of stability in the union during those years, regardless of male promiscuity (see Smith, *The Negro Family*, 114-15).

115. Bronkhurst, *The Colony*, 350.
116. Kirke, 36.
117. Bronkhurst, *The Colony*, loc. cit.
118. Bronkhurst, *Among the Hindus*, 208.
119. Pearson, loc. cit.; comments of Messrs. Fothergill, Pearson, Matheson and Cruickshank encl'd in Light, No. 83, loc. cit.
120. Ordinance No. 12 of 1854. See Wodehouse to George Grey, No. 40, 21 July 1854, C.O.111/301; *Creole*, 23 December 1857—letter d/d 21 December; *Creole*, 9 October 1858; *RG*, 9 January 1869.
121. Comments of Messrs. Macpherson, Hancock, Crichton, Watt, Merry, Verbeke, & Croal encl'd in Light, No. 83, loc. cit. This is supported by sociological research in Trinidad by Green who has demonstrated that black parents do pay great attention to child-rearing. Green asserts that in this sphere, mothers are dominant: they are the task leaders,

value leaders and expressive leaders in the family, and are also responsible for the training and disciplining of the children. Fathers assist, but the role of the mother is emphasized where the father is weak or absent. He further notes that black women also often share one another's child care in a way which leaves much unsupervised activity to the child. "This early independence training leads to much independent behaviour as well as flexibility and achievement in later years." The result is that the children's social range is unrestricted and they are free to move about the community and to have social activities of their own choice (see H. Green, "Socialization values in the Negro and East Indian subcultures of Trinidad", Ph.D. diss., University of Connectict, 1964, 30-33).

122. Callier to Gen. Sect., No. 74, 23 December 1869, MMS/W.v/2.
123. Comments of M.J. Retemeyer encl'd in Light, No. 83, loc. cit.
124. Callier, No. 74, loc. cit.
125. M.J. Retemeyer, loc. cit.
126. Kirke, 35.
127. *Colonist*, 14 March 1864 & 11 April 1874; *DDC*, 6 September 1883; *RG*, 20 January 1887.
128. *DDC*, 16 August 1884; *RG*, 6 May 1876.
129. *Colonist*, 17 September 1868.
130. Schomburgk, 51.
131. Trotman, 174.
132. R.T. Smith, *The Negro Family*, 70 & 143; *idem*, "The family in the Caribbean", 70.
133. Kirke, 36.
134. Pearson, loc. cit.
135. M.J. Field, *Religion and Medicine of the Ga People* (London, 1961), 171-73; S.F. Nadel, *Nupe Religion* (London, 1954), 23.
136. Hincks to Newcastle, No. 183, 16 November 1863, C.O.111/342.
137. Bronkhurst, *The Colony*, 342-43.
138. Bronkhurst, *Among the Hindus*, 149; Kirke, 195; *Echo*, 17 January 1891.
139. Veness to Sect., 31 March 1871, SPG/E.26.

140. Bronkhurst, *The Colony*, loc. cit.
141. *BG*, 22 May & 2 June 1889.
142. Veness, loc. cit.
143. Ibid.
144. Encl. in Light, No. 83, loc. cit.; Premium, 137.
145. Crookall, 130.
146. R.T. Smith, "Culture and social structure in the Caribbean: some recent work on family and kinship studies", *CSSH* 6, no. 1 (1963): 35-36; idem, *The Negro Family*, 149 & 233.
147. M. Alleyne, *Roots of Jamaican Culture* (London, 1988), 78.
148. Dance, 85.
149. Bronkhurst, *Among the Hindus*, 160-61.
150. W.L.B. [excerpt from the *Wesleyan Greeting*] in *DC*, 20 November 1898.
151. J.S. Wallbridge, "Fifty years recollection of British Guiana", *Timehri* I, 3rd. ser. (1911): 266.
152. W.L.B., loc. cit. In an article quoted by the *Echo*, Gilbert Ward writing in the English paper *Church Gazette* noted that the English rural folk drowned their bereavement in considerable consumption of alcoholic beverages; there were "hours of continuous, but resigned soaking". These 'wakes' were by no means the quiet, solemn affairs that the white colonial elites tried to convey (see *Echo*, 26 November 1898).
153. B. Brereton, *Race Relations in Colonial Trinidad, 1870-1900* (Cambridge, 1979), 156-57.
154. Field, 199; also M.J. Herskovits, *Trinidad Village* (New York, 1947), 137.
155. Pearson, loc. cit.
156. Herskovits, *Trinidad Village*, 138.
157. Field, 200.
158. Wallbridge, loc. cit.
159. Pearson, loc. cit.
160. Stipendiary Magistrates' reports for the half year ending 31 December 1851, C.O.116/168.
161. Dance, 90-91.
162. Pearson, loc. cit.
163. Field, 202; Nadel, 128.
164. Trotman, 259.
165. Herskovits, *Myth*, 161.
166. Brian L. Moore, *Race, Power and Social Segmentation in Colonial Society* (New York, 1987), 35-38.
167. Cruickshank, "Among the 'Aku' ", 75.
168. M. Herskovits, *Life in a Haitian Valley* (1937), 70-75; Bastide, 28-29.
169. See R.T. Smith, "Ethnic difference and peasant economy in British Guiana", in *Capital, Saving and Credit in Peasant Societies*, edited by R. Firth and B. Yamey (London, 1964), 316.
170. P. Bryan, *The Jamaican People, 1880-1902* (London, 1991), 203-4.
171. Wallbridge, 266.
172. Stipendiary Magistrates' reports of W.H. Ware, 30 June 1848, C.O.116/167; and of Fraser, 30 June 1851, C.O.116/168.
173. Herskovits, *Myth*, 161-62.
174. Stipendiary Magistrates' reports, 1848-54, C.O.116.
175. *RG*, 5 January 1878.
176. Blue Books of Statistics, 1851-91, C.O.116.
177. Foreman to Mullens, 18 February 1875, LMS 10/1 (Dem.).
178. Encl. 2 in Irving to Derby, No. 295, 25 October 1883, C.O.111/429; *Argosy*, 1 February 1883.
179. *(D)DC*, 20 January 1884, 3 January 1886 & 18 February 1887.
180. Attorney-General's report, 24 October, encl'd in Irving to Derby, No. 295, 25 October 1883, and Ludlow to Wingfield, Misc., 29 November 1883, C.O.111/429.
181. Encl. in Bruce to Holland, No. 19, 16 January 1888, C.O.111/444; encl. in Irving to Holland, No. 156, 15 April 1887, C.O.111/438. The 1880s witnessed an upsurge in political activity in Guyana among the Creole middle classes which ultimately led to constitutional change in 1891 that gave non-whites representation in the colonial legislature for the first time (see Moore, 68-76).
182. Blue Books of Statistics, 1887-1890, C.O.116.
183. Attorney-General's report, 7 March, in Gormanston to Ri-

pon, No. 43, 6 March 1893, C.O.111/467.

184. *RG*, 7 March 1854 & 5 January 1878; *Argosy*, 8 September 1883; *DDC*, 18 November 1881, 6 July 1883, 19 June & 7 August 1884. See also Bryan, 204.

185. *RG*, 29 November 1883; *Colonist*, 7 November 1883.

186. *DDC*, 28 September 1882; *Colonist*, 7 November 1882.

187. *DDC*, 11 November 1882; *Colonist*, 25 July 1882.

188. *RG*, 5 November 1878; *Argosy*, 5 March 1881 & 12 July 1884; *DDC*, 13 July 1884.

189. *RG*, 17 June 1879; *DC*, 28 February 1885.

190. *RG*, 6 June 1883; *Echo*, 16 April 1887; *Colonist*, 2 January 1883 & 19 May 1883; *DDC*, 26 August 1883.

191. *RG*, 17 January 1885. On the occasion of the 50th anniversary of the final emancipation in 1888, the following friendly societies and lodges, comprising about 1400 participants, took part in a grand parade in Georgetown: the Grand United Order of Odd fellows, the British Order of Ancient Free Gardeners, the Loyal Order of Shepherds, the Hand of Justice Lodge, the Union Friendly Society, Smith's Church Sunday School Band of Hope, St. George's Burial Society, the British Guyana Reform Tobits Society, St. Barnabas' Benevolent Society, the Independent Order of Oddfellows (London Unity), Myrtle Female Lodge, the Grand Triumphal Car, the Foundry Band, the Georgetown Lily Lodge, and the Ancient Order of Foresters (Georgetown Diamond Lodge). Many of these societies included women. See Bronkhurst, *Among the Hindus and Creoles*, 303.

192. *DC*, 3 January 1885.

193. Bronkhurst, *The Colony*, 386-87.

194. Everard Im Thurn, "Occasional Notes", *Timehri* I, 1911.

195. Anon, loc. cit.

196. Premium, 13-14.

197. Anon, loc. cit.

198. Cruickshank, "Among the 'Aku' ", 78.

199. Ibid., 77-78; Schomburgk, 47. See also Alleyne, 109-112.

200. Cruickshank, loc. cit.

201. Ibid. See also Alleyne, 110.

202. Schomburgk, loc. cit.

203. *RG*, 6 January 1859.

204. *Creole*, 15 September 1858.

205. "H.R.", 'Local Sketches: Dancing Parties', *RG*, 25 September 1880.

206. Kirke, 49-50.

207. Schomburgk, 48.

208. Bronkhurst, *The Colony*, 387.

209. "H.R.", 'Local Sketches: Dancing Parties', loc. cit.

210. *RG*, 27 June & 10 July 1866.

211. Ibid.; *Colonist*, 1 June 1877.

212. Ibid.

213. Ibid.

214. "H.R.", 'Local Sketches: Dancing Parties', loc. cit.

215. *Creole*, 15 September 1858 & 24 August 1864; *Colonist*, 10 July 1866, 1 June & 3 October 1877.

216. Hardy, 76.

217. Harris to Sect., 31 December 1866, SPG/E.22.

218. J. van Sertima, *Scenes and Sketches of Demerara Life* (Georgetown, 1899), 99-102. Although carnival was the main Creole festival in Trinidad, Brereton notes that the urban poor black nevertheless celebrated Christmas in similar vein to their Guyanese counterparts—by parading on the streets, with drumming and dancing, some masked in the 'nègre-jardin' costume (Brereton, 157).

219. Van Sertima, loc. cit.

220. Ibid.

221. *Echo*, 30 December 1893.

222. Ibid.

223. *RG*, 4 January 1881. Brereton notes similar attitudes of disgust towards the Christmas street parades and carnival celebrations in Trinidad (Brereton, 157, 171-73).

224. Bryan, 207.

225. Kirke, 42-44.

226. Ibid. In one rally held at Zoar Congregational Chapel in August 1899, $369 were raised (see *Echo*, 9 August 1899).

227. C.D. Dance, "Chapters from a Guianese Log-Book", *RG*, 19 October 1878.

228. Bryan, 207-08.

229. Duerwaarder to Gen. Sect., No. 111, 22 January 1864, MMS/W.v/5.

230. Bronkhurst, *The Colony*, 387-88.

231. Ibid.; see also Bryan, 208.

232. Letter by "A Villager" (23 May), *Argosy*, 27 May 1882; Bronkhurst, *The Colony*, 260.

233. Light to Stanley, No. 143, 2 July 1845, C.O.111/224; encl. in Light to Grey, No. 176, 2 September 1846, *P.P.*1847.(in 325) XXXIX; Barrett to Tidman, 12 August 1847, LMS.7/2 (Dem.); encl. in Light to Grey, No. 49, 18 March 1848, *P.P.*1847-48 (in 399) XLV; encl. in Barkly to Grey, No. 159, 31 October 1849, *P.P.*1850.(21) XXXIX; encls. 1 & 2 in Barkly to Grey, No. 60, 17 April and encl. 2 in No. 136, 24 September 1850, *P.P.*1851 (624) XXXIX; *Creole*, 28 March 1860; *BG*, 22 July 1882. For the situation in Trinidad, see Trotman,161-163.

234. *Argosy*, 11 April 1885; *RG*, 15 May 1883; *DC*, 8 April 1885 & 4 April 1888.

235. *RG*, 8 May 1866.

236. Ibid.; *RG*, 14 May 1866.

237. Ibid.

238. *Colonist*, 29 March 1869.

239. *RG*, 1 May 1869.

240. *Creole*, 27 July 1863; *RG*, 27 November 1855; letter to the editor (13 August), *DDC*, 14 August 1884. Schomburgk, 49-50. For the suppression of cockfighting in Trinidad, see Trotman, 261.

241. Kirke, 63; Bryan, 194-95; Trotman, loc. cit.

242. *RG*, 30 March 1875 & 14 December 1876.

243. Schomburgk, 50.

244. Letter by "Nemo" (8 May 1878), *RG*, 8 May 1878.

245. Letter by "One of the Promoters" (10 May 1878), *RG*, 11 May 1878.

246. Schomburgk, 50.

247. B. Stoddart, "Sport, cultural imperialism, and colonial response in the British empire", *CSSH* 30 (1988): 649-73.

248. B. Stoddart, "Cricket, social formation and cultural continuity in barbados: a preliminary ethnohistory", *JSH* 14, no. 3 (1987).

249. B. Stoddart, "Sport", 649-73.

250. *Colonist*, 14 October 1864.

251. *Colonist*, 21 February 1883; *RG*, 1 January 1878 & 29 July 1884; *DC*, 4 & 29 September, 25 October 1898. Some of these clubs were the "Royal Bedford" of Victoria, the "Royal Rainbow" of Ann's Grove, the "Invincible Fundanius" of Belfield, the "Wondrous C.C." of Buxton, the "Planatics" of Golden Grove. Very interestingly all of these were located on the east coast of Demerara. The cricket team of the "Crescent Club" of Belfield (1884) included four schoolmasters and a Portuguese shopkeeper which suggests middle class membership. Whether this was the case of the other Creole country clubs is unknown. Certainly, however, the two main Creole clubs in Georgetown, the "Demerara C.C." and the "B.G. Churchmen's Union C.C." were solidly middle class in membership. The latter also demonstrates the spread of "muscular Christianity" to the colony.

252. *Liberator*, 31 March 1869.

253. Kirke, 49

254. Heatley, 54.

255. The newspapers of the 1890s generally reported on cricket matches and the scores made. See also Kirke, 49.

256. *RG*, 1 January 1878.

257. Kirke, 49.

258. In July 1881 a cricket match was organized at Victoria between two female teams composed of members of the "Velveteen Club".

259. I. Scoles, *Sketches of African and Indian Life* (Demerara, 1885).

260. "Argus" column, *RG*, 2 February 1878.

Chapter Six

1. Brian L. Moore, *Race, Power and Social Segmentation in Colonial Society* (New York, 1987), 197-98.

2. See Henderson to Tidman, 18 April 1849, LMS.7/4 (Dem.); and McKenzie to Sect., 3 January 1856, SPG/E.Pre E. Jamaica experienced a similar upsurge in Afro-Creole religion, in particular *Myalism*, while ex-slave attendance at churches and chapels declined during the 1850s. This was followed (as was the case in Guyana) by a great revival in 1860. (See R.J. Stewart, *Religion and Society in Post-Emancipation Jamaica* (Knoxville, 1992), and P.D. Curtin, *Two Jamaicas* (New York, 1955).

3. This strike to resist the forced reduction of wages by the planters was bitter and lasted for three months at the beginning of 1848. Hitherto the missionaries had posed as the friends and advisors of the ex-slaves, and indeed in a previous strike in 1842 had supported their right to strike for better wages and working conditions. But during the severe economic recession of the late 1840s in the wake of the Sugar Duties Act, the white colonists as a body–including the colonial officials, merchants, and the missionaries–almost unanimously agreed that the planters simply could not afford to pay the high wages demanded by the ex-slaves, and that if the latter were successful the plantation sector would literally go out of existence and with it "civilization". The ex-slaves were thus isolated in this bitter, and indeed violent, struggle; and in the process became quite disillusioned with the institutions and values of white civilization, not least of all the church (see B. L. Moore, 41).

4. L. Crookall, *British Guiana* (London, 1898), 132; Woollett's Notes, 1858-60, SJ/*BG*/9; R. Bastide, *African Civilizations in the New World* (New York, 1972), 108. Both Schuler and Alleyne note that in St. Thomas, Jamaica, where significant numbers of Bantu people from the Congo region were located, *Kumina* became the dominant Afro-Creole religious form (see M. Schuler, *"Alas, Alas, Kongo": A Social History of Indentured African Immigration into Jamaica* and M. Alleyne, *Roots of Jamaican Culture* (London, 1988), 92-93). In Guyana, whatever religion was practised by the Congolese probably went into decline by the end of the century by which time even the use of the names of the gods became corrupted. Crookall (loc. cit.) for instance, noted that the name *Gorgonzambe* was actually applied to him as priest by an old African: "you am de doctah for a' we soul; and de African name for de minister am Gorgonzambe, which mean God-doctor".

5. Ibid., 100. The word *Komfo* is found also among the Asante whose priests are called *Obi O Komfo* (ibid., 103).

6. G. Parrinder, *West African Religion* (London, 1949), 54-55; J. Lucas, *The Religion of the Yorubas* (Lagos, 1948), 162; S.F. Nadel, *Nupe Religion* (London, 1954), 90-91; M. J. Field, *Religion and Medicine of the Ga People* (London, 1961), 10-91; J. Mbiti, *African Religions and Philosophy* (London, 1969), 54-55.

7. C.D. Dance, *Chapters from a Guianese Log-Book* (Dem., 1881), 78; *RG*, 6 & 8 March 1877. At Mara, Berbice, in 1876 *Cumfo* ceremonies were organized by a *Cumfo*-man named Brocker Quio and a woman named Betty Ann Moore. Quio was reported to have rejected Christianity. When a Christian priest remonstrated against the *Cumfo* proceedings, Quio and Moore not only threatened to beat him or anyone else who interfered, but held their ceremony simultaneously with the Sunday evening church service which was seri-

ously disturbed by the open air drumming and singing (*Colonist*, 15 January 1876).

8. Levi to Tidman, 12 January 1866, LMS.9/3 (Bce); Rattray to Tidman, 4 March 1850, LMS.7/5 (Dem.).

9. Dance, 78-79.

10. R. Duff, *British Guiana* (Glasgow, 1866), 134-40.

11. *DC*, 18 November 1885.

12. B.W. Higman, "Terms of kin in the British West Indian slave community: differing perceptions of masters and slaves", in *Kinship Ideology and Practice in Latin America*, edited by R.T. Smith (Chapel Hill, 1984), 66-70.

13. *DC*, 18 November 1885. In a more recent description of *Cumfo*, Ovid Abrams (1970) writes that before the dance begins "there is a grand preparation of various dishes, cakes, white rum, wine and sometimes whisky. There must also be blood sacrifice of a white fowl, a lamb or goat, the blood of which is thrown around the yard. The yard is also adulterated with broken eggs, white rum and appropriate drugs. When the drums begin beating all those persons who are possessed with spirits which enjoy that type of music, begin to dance and enjoy themselves: in some cases they dance for hours and never stop until the spirits are satisfied. In Cumfa, the person no longer has control over his body, the spirits take over. It is not until the drum stops beating and the spirit is satisfied that it has enjoyed itself that it leaves the medium and he regains consciousness. Cumfa dance is a very skilful and marvelous dance to look at. Sometimes the dancers lie flat on the ground and perform very acrobatic feats when they catch the cumfa. After long hours of dancing the feasting begins and everyone present is expected to participate". See O. Abrams, *Guyana Metagee* (Dem., 1970), 114.

14. I. Scoles, *Sketches of African and Indian Life in British Guiana* (Demerara, 1885), 59-61; Jansen to Tidman, 6 February 1862, LMS.9/1 (Dem.).

15. *Colonist*, 15 January 1876.

16. Duff, loc. cit.

17. R. Schomburgk, *Travels in British Guiana, 1840-44*, vol. 1 (Georgetown, 1922), 48.

18. *Colonist*, 15 January 1876.

19. Duff, loc. cit.

20. J. Beattie and J. Middleton, "Introduction" in their *Spirit Mediumship and Society in Africa* (London, 1969), xviii.

21. R. Firth, "Foreword", in *Spirit Mediumship*, edited by Beattie and Middleton, x-xi.

22. W & F. Mischel, "Psychological aspects of spirit possession", *AA* 60 (1958): 254-57; and the following papers in *Spirit Mediumship*: edited by Beattie and Middleton: R. Firth, "Foreword", xi-xiv; M.J. Field, "Spirit possession in Ghana", 11-13; R. Horton, "Types of spirit possession in Kalabari religion", 22, 24, 28, 45-46; P. Verger, "Trance and convention in Nago-Yoruba spirit mediumship", 52, 65; and G. Parrinder, "Witchcraft", 138.

23. The word "witch" is not being used here in a gender-specific manner, but includes both males and females.

24. Field, 137. "A *won* . . . is 'anything that can work but not be seen' and includes the smaller beings of specialized and limited activity associated with medicines and magic . . ." (ibid., 4). "A *won*–which usually has no name–will act for any one, provided that the person has observed the proper ceremonies in becoming owner of the medicine, and provided that he is careful about any taboos attached to its use. There is an automatic quality about a *won*–press the right button and the machine works for you whoever you are" (ibid., 111).

25. G. Parrinder, *Withcraft: European and African* (London, 1963), 135; Bastide, 103.

26. Alleyne, 59.

27. P. Curtin, *Two Jamaicas* (New York, 1970), 39.

28. O. Patterson, *The Sociology of Slavery* (London, 1967), 188.

29. X, "Stray notes on obeah", *Timehri* VI, 3rd. ser. (1919): 128-30.

30. Ibid. Two descriptions should suffice to indicate how the obeahmen worked. In 1860 a boy, James Forester, became ill while at work for Sandy Cuffy. He complained of feeling something in his skin. With the boy's mother's consent Cuffy sent for old Cupido, an obeahman, who arrived with a basket with his implements and cures. On entering the room where young James was lying, Cupido asked for a glass of water into which he put a "horse-eye" berry and drank it. Then placing an egg in the palm of his hand, he began to sing an African song. He then made an incision on the boy's temple with a razor. After "sterilizing" his razor by wiping off the blood with a Guinea pepper, he applied a cow's horn to the incision and sucked through it. On withdrawing it, he produced a piece of glass which was supposed to have been taken from the incision. This procedure was repeated on the other temple, the back, and both legs. From each leg a piece of flint and a dead person's tooth respectively were removed instead of glass. On completing his operation, he packed up, asked for a glass of rum and was paid. Cupido was subsequently arrested and jailed (see *Colonist*, 21 November 1866). The second instance occurred in 1870 when another "doctor" was taken before the court for "malpractice". A man named Allan took his wife to the "doctor" to cure an internal pain. The latter at first gave her a decoction of herbs, and when that did not work, decided to "operate" on her in the presence of a midwife. He made an incision in her side, "and then commenced certain very curious operations which resulted . . . in the supposed delivery of an enormous living crapaud [frog]. . ." (see *RG*, 11 January 1870).

31. Light to Russell, separate, 21 December 1840, C.O.111/173.

32. Ibid.

33. Alfred Hardy, *Life and Adventure in British Guiana* (London, 1913), 100.

34. Duff, 140-51.

35. In one incident at Victoria village in 1876, an African who was allowed to rest in the house of a "good Samaritan" responded by throwing something in the face of his host's daughter which caused her to faint. When ordered out of the house, he threw a small parcel of dried blood, hair and other matter into the hedge. Apparently this was what he had used to harm the child (*RG*, 10 June 1876).

36. Ibid., 99-100; *Colonist*, 21 November 1860; *RG*, 11 January 1870; *Creole*, 21 March 1864; *Echo*, 21 September 1889.

37. H.V.P. Bronkhurst, *The Colony of British Guiana and its Labouring Inhabitants* (London, 1883), 382; Rattray to Tidman, 21 March 1849, LMS.7/4 (Dem.); Walker to Newcastle, No. 102, 20 October 1853, C.O.111/297; Duff, loc. cit. Jansen to Tidman, 6 February 1862, LMS.9/1 (Bce); Deurwaarder to Gen. Sect., No. 111, 22 January 1864, MMS/W.v/5.

38. Rattray to Tidman, 4 March 1850, LMS.7/5 (Dem.), and 27 March 1851, LMS.7/6 (Dem.). Rattray claimed that the "Kroomen" in the Canal No. 1 area on the Demerara river were corrupting the Creoles by practising as doctors, wizards and obeahmen.

39. Barton Premium, *Eight Years in British Guiana, 1840-48* (London, 1850), 94-95. The missionaries were overtly hostile to obeah and its practitioners ever since they began working among the slaves early in the century, and it was they who for the most part sus-

pected Africans as the main perpetrators and encouraged hostility towards them as such. It seems to have been the only way they could explain the resurgence of obeah after emancipation after they thought that they had succeeded in almost eradicating it in the last years of slavery (see in particular Rattray's letters of 21 March 1849, 4 March 1850, and 27 March 1851 [cited before]).

40. Ibid. Missionaries felt that some people were afraid to talk out against obeahmen lest they be victimized. "Thus between mystery and terror, they [obeahmen] hold almost supreme sway in certain circles; and become objects of fear, if not also of a certain degree of veneration; that shields them from exposure and punishment". *WP*, 5 February 1870.

41. *Colonist*, 21 November 1866; *RG*, 19 June 1873.

42. Letter by "Sympathetic" (5 September), *RG*, 9 September 1873.

43. Light to Russell, Separate, 21 December 1840, C.O.111/173; and *DC, 16 March 1889*.

44. Duff, 141-42. Kirke cited the case of a jealous mulatto woman, "concubine" of her white master, who reputedly obtained a love philtre from an obeahman to retain her master's affection. The man, however, gradually wasted away after being given the potion in his coffee daily. H. Kirke, *Twenty-five Years in British Guiana* (London, 1898), 208.

45. Ordinance No. 1 of 1855, C.O.113/3; Wodehouse to Grey, No. 15, 24 January 1855; Grey to Wodehouse, No. 1, 2 March 1855; Wodehouse to Russell, No. 51, 21 March 1855; and Russell to Wodehouse, No. 25, 26 June 1855, C.O.111/304.

46. *RG*, 27 August 1859, 11 August 1860; *Colonist*, 6 October 1866, 4 February 1870.

47. *Creole*, 3 May 1872.

48. *DC*, 26 November 1885.

49. *Creole*, 3 May 1872; *Colonist,* 21 November 1866; *RG*, 11 August 1860.

50. E.A. Weinstein, *Cultural Aspects of Delusion* (New York, 1962), 148-53.

51. Scoles, 59.

52. Bastide, 110; Alleyne, 92.

53. Scoles, loc. cit.; Nadel, 26-27.

54. Hardy, 96-97. Alleyne notes that among the Bantu of Congo, spirits of the departed are called *bamvumbi* or *banzambi* who "constantly intervene in the world of the living. They come back to frighten the living and are endowed with unusual powers" (Alleyne, 57).

55. Field, 196-97.

56. Scoles, 61. Among the Ga, food when given to dead spirits is sprinkled above the ground for the ghost to come and eat. No food made especially for the dead ever contains salt or pepper (Field, 200).

57. Dance, 78-80.

58. Ibid., 81-83.

59. Ibid., 79.

60. Ibid., 61-62.

61. Ibid., 63-64.

62. Ibid.

63. Ibid., 58-59.

64. Scoles, 59-61.

65. Ibid.

66. Parrinder, *Witchcraft*, 138.

67. Dance, 81. The "halo" is probably an indication of syncretism with European witchcraft superstitions (see Parrinder, *Witchcraft*, loc. cit.).

68. Field, 133-37.

69. *Colonist*, 20 June 1877.

70. Nadel, 168.

71. Dance, loc. cit.

72. Ibid.; *RG*, 5 April & 8 May 1877.

Chapter Seven

1. Brian L. Moore, *Race, Power and Social Segmentation in Colonial Society* (New York, 1987), 162.

2. R.T. Smith, "Some social characteristics of Indian immigrants to British Guiana", *PS* 13, no. 1 (1959): 39; Basdeo Mangru, "Disparity in Bengal and Madras emigration to British Guiana in the

nineteenth century", *RI* 13 (1983): 99-107.

3. Steven Vertovec, *Hindu Trinidad: Religion, Ethnicity and Socio-Economic Change* (London, 1992), 11-13.

4. Report of Dr. Shier (supplement), 23 May 1865, in *Colonist*, 1 June 1865.

5. *Report of the* [1870] *Commissioners Appointed to Inquire into the Treatment of Immigrants in British Guiana* (Dem., 1871), 129-31.

6. Ibid.

7. Report of the Medical Officer of the Immigration Dept., 30 April 1877, *Administrative Reports*, 1876; Report of the Immigration Agent General [hereafter I.A.G.] (ag.), 4 August 1882, *Administrative Reports*, 1881.

8. *Report of the* [1870] *Commissioners*, loc. cit.

9. Report of Dr. Shier, loc. cit.

10. *Report of the* [1870] *Commissioners*, 132; J. Candler, "Diary", *CS* 4, no. 2 (1964).

11. Report of Dr. Shier, loc. cit.

12. Ibid.

13. G. DesVoeux, *Experiences of a Demerara Magistrate* (Georgetown, 1948), 132.

14. *Report of the* [1870] *Commissioners*, 130-31.

15. H.V.P. Bronkhurst, *The Colony of British Guiana* (London, 1883), 255; idem, *The Origin of the Guyanian Indians* (Dem., 1881), 21; L. Crookall, *British Guiana* (London, 1898), 114-15.

16. Crookall, loc. cit.

17. Dale A. Bisnauth, "The East Indian immigrant society in British Guiana 1891-1930", unpublished Ph.D. thesis (U.W.I., 1977), 184.

18. Report of Dr. Shier, loc. cit.

19. Ibid.

20. Bisnauth, 185.

21. Bronkhurst, *The Colony*, 253-54.

22. Ibid.

23. Ibid.

24. Bronkhurst, *The Origin*, 21; Crookall, 113-14.

25. Vertovec, 93; F. Josa, "The languages of India", *Timehri* III, no. 2 (1915): 267-68.

26. For a detailed analysis of the development and decline of Guyanese Bhojpuri, see Surendra K. Gambhir, "The East Indian speech community in Guyana: a sociolinguistic study with special reference to Koine formation", Ph.D. diss., University of Pennsylvania, 1981.

27. Ibid; see also R.C. Chaudhury, *Bihar District Gazetteers: Shahabad* (Patna, 1966) 122-26; M.A. Durbin, "Formal changes in Trinidad Hindi as a result of language adaptation", *AA* 75 (1973): 1290-304. According to Devonish, Bhojpuri has a vocabulary which is quite similar to that of standard Hindi/Urdu, but has quite a different grammatical system (H. Devonish, "Nature of African-East Indian contact in 19th century Guyana: the linguistic evidence", Seminar Paper, UWI, Mona, June 1991, 6).

28. Lutchmee Parsad Ramyead, "Indian languages in Mauritius: a perspective", in *Indians Overseas: The Mauritian Experience*, edited by U. Bissoondoyal (Mauritius, 1984), 142.

29. Report of the [1870] Commissioners (ms.), sec.25, C.O.111/380.

30. See John R. Rickford, *Dimensions of a Creole Continuum* (Stanford, 1987), 65.

31. Devonish, 6-14.

32. Ramyead, 145.

33. For a fuller discussion of the education of the Indians, see chapter 8.

34. Bronkhurst, *The Colony*, 210; J. Amphlett, *Under a Tropical Sky* (London, 1873), 68-69; E. Jenkins, *The Coolie: His Rights and Wrongs* (London, 1871), 36-37.

35. Bronkhurst, *The Colony*, 210-11.

36. Ibid.; idem, *Among the Hindus and Creoles of British Guiana* (London, 1888), 50; R. Duff, British Guiana (Glasgow, 1866), 234; Amphlett, loc. cit.

37. Bronkhurst, *The Colony*, loc. cit. Duff, loc. cit.

38. Ibid.

39. D.W.D. Comins, *Notes on Emigration from India to British*

Guiana (Calcutta, 1893), loc. cit.; 10.

40. Bronkhurst, *The Colony, idem, Among the Hindus*, 17 & 50; Duff, loc. cit.; J.E. Hewick, "Our people", *Timehri* I, no. 1 (1911): 234-35.

41. This is true wherever in the diaspora Indians migrated in relatively substantial numbers, e.g., Trinidad, Surinam, Mauritius, Fiji. But where, as in Jamaica, they were small in number and scattered, traditional forms of dress disappeared in favour of the western styles of the host society. See Verene Shepherd, *Transients to Settlers: The Experience of Indians in Jamaica 1845-1950* (Leeds, 1994), 206.

42. See Edward Brathwaite, *Contradictory Omens: Cultural Diversity and Integration in the Caribbean* (Kingston, 1974).

43. Encl. in Walker to Labouchere, No. 24, 5 October 1857, *P.P.*1859.XX.

44. Bronkhurst, *The Colony*, 256; *idem, The Origin* 19.

45. Ibid.

46. Bronkhurst, *The Colony*, 252-53.

47. Ibid., 257; *idem, The Origin*, loc. cit.

48. Even in Jamaica where Indians were/are a scattered minority who consequently lost many aspects of their traditional culture, their cuisine still remains distinctly Indian in provenance, although they have incorporated some Creole food (Shepherd, 206).

49. See H. Tinker, *A New System of Slavery: The Export of Indian Labour Overseas 1830-1920* (Oxford, 1974); Moore, *Race, Power and Social Segmentation* (New York, 1987); Mangru, *Benevolent Neutrality* (London, 1987); B. Brereton, *Race Relations in Colonial Trinidad* (Cambridge, 1979); D. Wood, *Trinidad in Transition* (Oxford, 1968); Pieter Emmer, "The great escape: the migration of female indentured servants from British India to Suriname", *Abolition and its Aftermath: The*

Historical Context 1790-1916, edited by David Richardson (London, 1985), 245-66; Rosemarijn Hoefte, "Female indentured labor in Surinam: for better or for worse?", *BELC* 42 (1987): 55-70; Rhoda Reddock, "Freedom denied: Indian women and indentureship in Trinidad and Tobago 1845-1917", *EPW* 20 (1985): 79-87.

50. Hincks to Buckingham & Chandos, No.178, 22 December 1868, sub-enclosure in enclosure 1, C.O.111/369.

51. Barkly to Pakington, No.86, 21 April 1852, encl., *P.P.* 1852. XXXI; Scott to Kimberley, No.65, 2 May 1871, C.O.111/385; Report of the IAG for 1891, C.O.114/53. See also Basdeo Mangru, "The sex-ratio disparity and its consequences under the indenture in British Guiana", in *India in the Caribbean* edited by D. Dabydeen and B. Samaroo (London, 1987), 223.

52. Scott to Kimberley, No.119, 20 October 1870, C.O.111/377; Mangru, "Sex-ratio", loc. cit.

53. Report of the IAG for 1882, C.O.114/34.

54. Labouchere to Wodehouse, No.94, 30 June 1856, C.O.112/33; Hincks to Buckingham & Chandos, No. 178, 22 December 1868, encl. C.O.111/369.

55. Report of the IAG, 29 October 1877, in *Administration Reports* for 1876.

56. Duff, 320; *RG*, 1 January 1861.

57. Mangru, "Sex-ratio", 217.

58. See footnote 56. The general rarity of sexual relations between Indians and Creoles in both Trinidad and Guyana is noted by Wood, Brereton and Mangru as well. See D. Wood, 138; Brereton, 183; Mangru, "Sex-ratio", 216.

59. Scott to Kimberley, No.100, 15 August 1870, C.O.111/376; Johnson to Hawkins, 15 September 1856, SPG/E.1.

60. *DC*, 25 August 1887.

61. *DC*, 28 June 1888, and *BG*, 30 June 1888.

62. Ibid.

63. Ibid.

64. Barkly to Grey, No.60 17 April
1850, encl.2, *P.P.* 1851. XXXIX;
Irving to Stanley, 16 October
1885, No. 295, encl.,
C.O.384/155; H. Kirke, *Twenty-
Five Years in British Guiana* (London, 1898), 101. See also Mangru,
"Sex-ratio", 227; K.L. Gillion,
Fiji's Indian Migrants (Melbourne, 1962), 125; and Shepherd, 209.

65. *Colonist*, 14 October 1869.

66. Mangru, "Sex-ratio", 225. This is
a very contentious point with
which I would take issue. The
giving of a dowry before marriage is an old Hindu custom. As
I shall show later, in Guyana and
other plantation colonies where
women were in high demand,
the upper caste practice of the
bride's parents providing the
dowry to those of the bridegroom appeared to have been reversed. This may imply an intrusion of market forces of demand
and supply, and could lend credibility to contemporary European
misinterpretations that in fact
brides were actually being *sold* to
the highest bidder. But as Hoefte
points out what appears to be an
aberration in the plantation colonies was in fact fairly common
practice among the lower castes
and untouchables in northern India (Hoefte, 65).

67. Gillion, 144.

68. Brereton, 182-83; David Dodd,
"The well-springs of violence:
some historical notes on East Indian criminality in Guyana", *CI*
2 (1976): 3-16.

69. In March 1870, an Indian man
mutilated the body of his wife,
cutting off both arms, her
breasts, and slashing her cheeks
and body. Most wife murders
were similarly gruesome. See
WP, 19 March and 16 April
1870; also Duff, loc. cit.; Hincks
to Newcastle, No.21, 3 March
1862 & No. 74, 19 May 1862,
C.O.111/334; Hincks to Buckingham & Chandos, No.164, 5 De-

cember 1867, C.O.111/364; *Colonist*, 18 & 20 April 1864, 27 September 1864, 20 July 1865, 22
June 1866, & 13 February 1869;
Watson to General Secretary,
No.442, n.d., MMS/W.v/5. The
point about men resorting to
physical violence in an attempt
to cow women to remain with
them has been forcefully made
by Reddock, 79-87.

70. Hincks to Newcastle, No. 89,
4 May 1869, encl., C.O.111/345;
Scott to Kimberley, No.100,
supra cit.; Report of the IAG,
4 August 1882, in *Administration
Reports* for 1881; also see the governors' despatches for 1882-1890
in C.O.384.

71. The statistics for Trinidad are
strikingly similar to those for
Guyana. Wood notes that between 1859 and 1863, there were
27 murders of Indian women
(wives or mistresses of the murderer) (Wood, 154); and Brereton
further points to another 87 murders of Indian women between
1872 and 1900, of which 65 were
wife-murders (Brereton, 182);
also Reddock, loc. cit; and
Hoefte, loc. cit; David V. Trotman, *Crime in Trinidad*
(Knoxville, 1986), 170-74.

72. Irving to Derby, No. 339, 5 December 1883, C.O. 384/144; see
also Scott to Kimberley, No.106,
18 July 1871, C.O.111/386.

73. Ordinance No.10 of 1860, sec.11,
C.O.113/3; Irving to Stanley,
No. 257, 18 September 1885,
encl., IAG to Government Secretary, 23 February 1885,
C.O.384/155.

74. Ordinance No.2 of 1887,
C.O.113/7; Report of the IAG
for 1888, C.O. 114/44.

75. Irving to Derby, No.339, 5 December 1883, C.O.384/144. According to Mangru, wife murders
in British India between 1866-70
was .0007% of the total population, whereas in Guyana it was
.71% (1859-64) and .209% (1865-70) among the Indian population. However, he cautions
against such raw comparisons

since the two populations were significantly different in composition (Mangru, "Sex-ratio", 218).

76. Hincks to Newcastle, No.89, 4 May 1864, C.O.111/345; Scott to Kimberley, No.106, 18 July 1871, C.O.111/386; Bronkhurst, *The Colony*, 351; *RG*, 30 July 1878, letter to the Editor.

77. Scott to Granville, No.43, 1 March 1869, C.O.111/371.

78. *Colonist*, 14 October 1869.

79. IAG to Government Secretary, 23 February 1885, encl. in Irving to Stanley, No.257, 18 September 1885, C.O.384/155.

80. Comins, 31-33; Report of the [1870] Commissioners (ms.), sec. 25, C.O.111/380.

81. Ordinance No.25 of 1891, secs. 151-152, C.O.113/8. Although the elective section of the Court of Policy [the British Guiana legislature] unanimously agreed in January 1889 that it was desirable to give validity to marriages of Indians celebrated according to their own religion and personal law (see Bruce to Knutsford, No.48, 39 January 1889, C.O.384/173), and this was duly legislated in the 1891 ordinance, that law was suspended for three years until other issues relating to the indenture system were settled. See also Mangru, "Sex-ratio", 213-14.

82. Encl. in Irving to Stanley, No. 257.

83. Hoefte, 65; Brereton, 182.

84. Ibid.; Report of the [1870] Commissioners (m.s), sec.25, loc. cit.; Comins, 31; Reports of the IAG for 1884, C.O.114/38, for 1892-93, C.O.114/57, and for 1893-94, C.O.114/61.

85. Ibid.

86. Report of the [1870] Commissioners (m.s), sec. 25, Irving to Derby, No. 339, loc. cit..

87. Ordinance No.2 of 1887; Report of the IAG for 1887, C.O.114/43.

88. Encl. in Irving to Stanley, No. 257. loc. cit.

89. Bronkhurst to Boyce, No.716, 24 August 1872, MMS/W.v/2.

90. Ordinance No.25 of 1891, C.O.113/8.

91. These figures exclude those for the year 1898-1899.

92. See Reports of the IAG for 1894-95, 1895-96, 1896-97, 1897-98, 1899-1900 in C.O.114/64, 114/68, 114/74, 114/78, and 114/87.

93. Mangru, "Sex-ratio", 213-14.

94. Bisnauth, 201-15.

95. Ibid., 227.

96. Ordinance No.10 of 1860, C.O.113/3; Wodehouse to Newcastle, No.45, 22 March 1860, C.O.111/326; Ordinance No.25 of 1891, sec.146, C.O. 113/8.

97. Irving to Holland, No.55, 5 February 1887, encl., minute of Haynes Smith, C.O.384/165.

98. M.N. Srinivas, *Religion and Society among the Coorgs of South India* (London, 1952), 156-57; S.C. Dube, *Indian Village* (London, 1955), 141-42; Bronkhurst, *The Origin*, 23.

99. Dube, loc. cit.

100. *BG*, 29 March 1865.

101. F. Josa, "The Hindus in the West Indies", *Timehri* III (1), 1913, 26.

102. Bronkhurst, *Origin*, 22

103. Kirke, 173.

104. J.G. Pearson (ed.), *New Overseer's Manual* (Georgetown, 1890), 54

105. J.D.Speckmann, *Marriage and Kinship among the Indians in Surinam* (Assen, 1965), 186.

106. This view is endorsed by more recent sociological research on Guyana by C. Jayawardena and R.T. Smith, "Marriage and family amongst East Indians in British Guiana", *SES* 13, no. 3 (1964): 346.

107. J.D. Pearson, "The life history of an East Indian", *Timehri* 10, (1897): 143.

108. Kirke, 173.

109. Brereton, 183.

110. Vertovec, 105-06; see also J.S. & L.D. MacDonald, "Transformation of African and India family traditions in the Southern Caribbean", *CSSH* 15, (1973): 171-98; and Joseph Nevadomsky, "Social change and the East Indian in rural Trinidad: a critique of methodologies", *SES* 31 (1982): 90-126.

111. Gerad Tikasingh, "Social change in the emerging East Indian community in the late 19th century", *JCS* 1(1980): 129.

112. Bronkhurst, *Among the Hindus*, 143.

113. Bronkhurst, *Origin*, 24.

114. V.P. Vatuk, 'Craving for a child in the folksongs of East Indians in British Guiana', *JFI* 2, no. 1 (1965): 60.

115. Bronkhurst, *Among the Hindus*, 143-44.

116. Vatuk, loc. cit.

117. F. Josa, "The Hindus in the West Indies", *Timehri* III, no. 1 (1913): 26.

118. Bronkhurst, *The Colony*, 370; *idem, Among the Hindus*, 152. See also Dube, 118.

119. Bronkhurst, *The Colony*, 373; Dube, 117; O. Lewis, *Village Life in Northern India* (Illinois, 1958), 48; B.Benedict, *Indians in a Plural Society* (London, 1961), 111; M. Freilich, "Cultural diversity among Trinidadian peasants", Ph.D. diss., Columbia Univ., 1960, 106; M. Klass, *East Indians in Trinidad* (New York, 1961), 118-19. In Trinidad, this ceremony is held either on the sixth day (the *catthi/catee*) at which the mother and baby are bathed and purified, or on the twelfth day (*barahi*).

120. Benedict, 113.

121. Bronkhurst, *The Colony*, 370-71; *idem, The Origins*, 24.

122. Bronkhurst, "The religion and religious system of our East Indian population", loc. cit.; *DC*, 5 October 1887.

123. Klass, loc. cit.; Freilich, Benedict, 111.

124. Bronkhurst, *Origin*, 24-25; *idem, The Ancestry or Origin of our East India Immigrants* (Demerara., 1886), 58-60.

125. Lewis, 49; Dube, 117.

126. Bronkhurst, *Among the Hindus*, 153; *idem, Origin*, 24-25; *idem, Ancestry*, loc. cit.

127. Bronkhurst, *Among the Hindus*, 153. Muslims in India hold the *chhatti* ceremony on the sixth day. On the seventh day the child is shaved and named. Both days are marked by feasts as well as the fortieth when the mother is again bathed (Dube, 118). In Trinidad the child is shaved at the same ceremony since the presence of hair at birth is considered unclean. (R.J. Smith, "Muslim East Indians in Trinidad", Ph.D.diss., Univ. of Penn., 1964, 83-84).

128. Bronkhurst, *The Colony*, 373.

129. Robert Smith, 84.

130. Bronkhurst, *The Colony*, loc. cit.; *idem, Among the Hindus*, 152.

131. Bronkhurst, *Among the Hindus*, 148.

132. Vatuk, 57-58.

133. Bronkhurst, *The Colony*, 352.

134. Speckmann, *Marriage and Kinship*, 153.

135. Bronkhurst, *The Colony*, 334 & 336

136. Brereton, 183.

137. Josa (1913), 29.

138. Bronkhurst, *The Colony*, 340; This ceremony is called the *lagan* (Speckmann, 137; Lewis, 170-71).

139. Speckmann, *Marriage and Kinship*, 138-39; Jayawardena and Smith, "Hindu marriage customs in British Guiana," *SES* , no. 2 (1958): 179-80; Benedict, 95-96; Klass, 123.

140. Speckmann, *Marriage*, 147-48; Dube, 122; Hoefte, 65.

141. Josa (1913), 30; Shepherd, 210.

142. Bronkhurst, *Among the Hindus*, 146.

143. *DC*, 1 July 1888.

144. *RG*, 17 May 1881.

145. Speckmann, *Marriage*, 139. Jayawardena and Smith, "Hindu marriage", 183; Lewis, 179.

146. Bronkhurst, *The Colony*, 340; Anon., *A Missionary Present about the Children in British Guiana* (London, n.d.), 23. The nuptial shed is built by a *nao* or *nau* (technically a barber, though the title is given to an assistant in ritual preparations). See Speckmann, *Marriage*, 139; Jayawardena & Smith, "Hindu marriage customs", 183.

147. Anon., 23-27; Bronkhurst, *The Colony*, 340-41.

148. See Jayawardena & Smith, "Hindu marriage customs", 178-94; Speckmann, *Marriage*, 135-57; Benedict, cha VIII; Klass, 121-27.

149. Bronkhurst, *The Colony*, 339.

150. Josa (1913), 29; Jayawardena & Smith, "Hindu marriage customs", 186-88; Speckmann, *Marriage*, 144; Benedict, 98.

151. Ibid.

152. Bronkhurst, *The Colony*, 339-40.

153. Ibid., 338

154. Bronkhurst, *Among the Hindus*, 148.

155. Josa (1913), 29.

156. First petition of East Indians, 27 August, encl'd in Hemming to Chamberlain, No.285, 14 September 1896, C.O.111/487.

157. Josa, loc. cit.

158. *Colonist*, 14 April 1871.

159. Josa (1913), loc. cit.

160. Smith & Jayawardena, "Marriage and family", 356 & 364.

161. See encls. in Hemming to Chamberlain, No.285, C.O.111/487. Brereton notes that in Trinidad a "Music Bill" was drafted in 1883 in direct response to drum-beating by Indians which annoyed the officers at St. James Barracks. But it was so clearly aimed at just one section of the population, that there was a great outcry in the press and it was withdrawn (Brereton, 161).

162. Bronkhurst, *Among the Hindus*, 125-26.

163. Klass, 129.

164. Bronkhurst, *Among the Hindus*, 158-162.

165. George E. Ross, "A Seunarain funeral", *The Presbyterian Witness*, January 1901, quoted in Bisnauth, 249.

166. Ibid., 154; *idem, The Colony*, 367-68. This is very similar to the funerary customs in India (Dube, 125).

167. *RG*, 18 April 1863.

168. P. Ruhoman, *Centenary History of the East Indians in British Guiana* (Georgetown, 1947), 116; Klass, 130.

169. Bisnauth, 245-46.

170. Gillion, 124; and Shepherd, 221-223.

171. J.A. Dubois, *Description of the character, manners and customs if the people of India; and of their institutions, religious and civil* (London, 1817), 362-64. Bisnauth claims that the Hindu funerary practices were essentially those of the Sieunaraini movement which was by far the most popular religious expression of Hinduism among the Indian immigrants. He thus argues that perhaps since there was no tradition of cremation in the host society, and no encouragement of it among the immigrants, the Hindus drew on burial rites already practised by them, i.e., those of the Sieunaraini; and once started they proved self-perpetuating (Bisnauth, 246).

172. See P. van der Veer & S. Vertovec, "Brahmanism abroad: on Caribbean Hinduism as an ethnic religion", *Ethnology* XXX, no. 2 (1991): 158-59. Rodney suggested that the Indians were directly influenced by Creole African funerary customs (creolization). See W. Rodney, *A History of the Guyanese Working People, 1881-1905* (Kingston, 1981), 179. No hard evidence has been found for the 19th century to indicate that cremation was either banned by law or by estate management although it seems reasonable to assume that it was discouraged.

173. Ross, loc. cit.

174. Bronkhurst, *The Colony*, 368; *Among the Hindus*, 154; Ruhoman, 116; Dube, 125; Klass, 130; Benedict, 119.

175. Dubois, 364.

176. *DC*, 9 October 1888.

177. Bronkhurst, *The Colony*, 367.

178. I. Scoles, *Sketches of African and Indian Life in British Guiana* (Georgetown, 1885), 61.

179. Dube, 125.

180. Smith, These figures are generally in line with those for all Indian emigrants leaving the port of Calcutta extracted from the Annual Reports of the Calcutta

Protector of Emigrants between 1874 and 1917. According to those data, the emigrants comprised 12.03% Brahmins and other high castes, 36.82% agricultural castes, 6.39% artisan castes, 33.16% low castes, 11.56% Muslims, and 0.04% Christians (Vertovec, 33). The figures for Indians migrating to Trinidad between 1876 and 1917 are strikingly close to those for Guyana (Vertovec, 96).

181. Report of the IAG for 1881, 4 August 1882, *Administration Reports*, 1881.

182. E.A.V. Abraham, "The East Indian coolie in British Guiana," *WIQ*, (1886): 400.

183. J.H. Hutton, *Caste in India: Its Nature, Structure and Origin* (London, 1961), 88.

184. Capt. and Mrs. Swinton, *Journal of a Voyage with Coolie Emigrants from Calcutta to Trinidad* (London, 1859).

185. Bronkhurst, *Among the Hindus*, 18.

186. B. Schwartz, "Ritual aspects of caste in Trinidad", *AQ* 37 (1964): 1.

187. Dube, 36-39.

188. Bronkhurst, *The Colony*, 281-87.

189. H.V.P. Bronkhurst, "The religion and religious system of our East Indian population," *DC* 21 July 1887.

190. Abraham, 400.

191. Comins, 79.

192. *Colonist*, 27 & 29 March 1875.

193. G. DesVoeux, *Experiences of a Demerara Magistrate, 1863-1869* (Georgetown, 1948), 131; Comins, 79.

194. Scott to Kimberley, No.100, 15 August 1870, C.O.111/376; Kirke, 101.

195. Bronkhurst, *The Colony*, 287.

196. Abraham, loc. cit.

197. *RG*, 25 March 1876.

198. Bronkhurst, *The Colony*, 287.

199. Vertovec, 99. Vertovec quotes Comins who seemed to suggest that hypogamy was mainly a male phenomenon: "Members of the Chattri, Rajput and Thakur class frequently get married to or

form connections with women of a lower class" (D. Comins, *Notes on Emigration from India to Trinidad*, Calcutta, 1893, 79).

200. R.T. Smith and C. Jayawardena, "Caste and social status among the Indians of Guyana", in *Caste in Overseas Indian Communities*, edited by B. Schwartz (California, 1967), 53.

201. Klass, 58.

202. Comins, 38.

203. Bronkhurst, *The Colony*, 285.

204. F.L.P. Josa, "The Hindus in the West Indies," *Timehri* II, no. 2 (1912): 308.

205. Dube, 36.

206. A. Niehoff, "The survival of Hindu institutions in an alien environment," *EA*, 12 (1958): 174. According to him, the ranking system in Trinidad is as follows: high castes—Brahmin, Gosain, Chattri; middle castes—Kurmi, Ahir, Koiri, Lohar, Barria, Kayasth; low castes—Chamar, Dom, Dhobie.

207. Klass, 153.

208. Ibid.

209. Speckmann, *Marriage and Kinship*, 32-33.

210. Srinivas, 24-25

211. R. Fox, "Varna Schemes and ideological integration in Indian society", *CSSH* 11, 1 (1969): 29 & 43.

212. J.D. Speckmann, "The caste system and the Hindustani group in Surinam", in *Caste...Overseas*, 208.

213. Speckmann, *Marriage and Kinship*, 32; see also the quotation associated with footnote .

214. G.D. Berreman, "Caste in India and the United States", *AJS* 66 (1960): 120-21.

215. G.S. Ghurye, *Caste and Race in India* (London, 1932), 104-11.

216. A. Béteille, *Caste, Class and Power* (Berkeley, 1969), 48.

217. I am indebted to Bridget Brereton for this observation.

218. Bronkhurst, *The Colony*, 286 & 294.

219. Report of the [1870] Commissioners (ms.), Appendix C—III, C.O.111/382.

220. Report of the [1870] Commissioners (ms.), sec.3, C.O.111/379.

221. Report of the [1870] Commissioners (ms.), sec. 14, C.O.111/379.
222. Comins, 80. According to Vertovec, these Vaishnavite *bhakti* practices included small gatherings for singing *bhajans*, reciting the *Ramayana*, and for listening to sermons on the *Bhagavata Purana* (Vertovec, 56).
223. Comins, loc. cit.
224. Bronkhurst, *Among the Hindus*, 142.
225. Comins, 82; Gillion, 147. According to Gillion, *Ramlila* was staged in Fiji after about 1902. In both Trinidad (comment by Brereton) and Guyana, such performances were regularly held from the 1870s.
226. Bronkhurst, *The Colony*, 389.
227. Comins, 80.
228. *DC*, 18 October 1898.
229. Bronkhurst, *The Colony*, 252.
230. Comins, 80, 82; Pearson, "The life history of an East Indian", 138.
231. Comins, "Diary", 31 (in Appendix of *Notes on Emigration From Calcutta to British Guiana*). It is interesting to note that Pln. Port Mourant was the source of the first Guyanese Indians to play for the West Indies cricket team from the 1950s onwards, viz., Rohan Kanhai, Joe Solomon, Ivan Madray, and Alvin Kalicharran. Two Creole cricketers from Port Mourant also represented the West Indies–John Trim and Basil Butcher.
232. *Colonist*, 18 & 25 January 1882, 2 January 1883; *DC*, 26 February 1886. In 1886 the planters and their staffs of Plantations Anna Regina, La Belle Alliance, Richmond, Henrietta and Bush Lot in Essequibo organized a cricket match between the all white Essequibo Cricket Club and its sister Georgetown Cricket Club while the workers (Indian, Chinese and Creole) had fun doing other things or as spectators.
233. Walker to Newcastle, No.102, 20 October 1853, C.O.111/297; Ferrier to Tidman, 14 March 1855, LMS.8a/1 (Dem.); Bronkhurst to Gen. Sect., No.583, 6 September 1861, MMS/W.v/5; *DC*, 11 May 1888.
234. *Creole*, 29 December 1858—letter to the editor; *RG*, 1 January 1880.
235. Bronkhurst, *The Colony*, 242.
236. Bronkhurst, *The Origins*, 20.
237. Ibid.
238. Encl. in Hincks to Buckingham & Chandos, No. 148, 30 October 1867, C.O.111/364; Attorney-General's report, 5 August, encl'd in Rushworth to Kimberley, No.126, 7 August 1873, C.O.111/398; see Ordinances No.6 of 1867 and No.29 of 1869, C.O.113/5.
239. Report of the [1870] Commissioners (ms.), sec.13, C.O.111/379; *(D)DC*, 13 July & 16 October 1884, 18 and 20 October 1888.
240. Report of the IAG for 1882, C.O.114/34; *DDC*, 12 & 26 January, and (letter to the editor) 12 June 1884.
241. See the Blue Books of Statistics, 1860-1883, C.O.116.
242. Irving to Kimberley, No.121, 4 May 1883, C.O.384/144.
243. Ordinance No.22 of 1860, C.O.113/4; Ordinance No.26 of 1880, C.O.113/6; Ordinance No.4 of 1889, C.O.113/8; Report of the IAG for 1882, C.O.114/34.
244. Blue Books of Statistics, C.O.116; Report on the Customs Dept. for 1889, C.O.114/47.
245. Ibid.; *DDC*, 12 June 1884.
246. Report of the IAG for 1882, C.O.114/34; Irving, No. 121, loc. cit.
247. *DC*, 3, 6 & 7 November 1898.

Chapter Eight

1. H.V.P. Bronkhurst, *Among the Hindus and Creoles of British Guiana* (London, 1888), 16-17, & 72; *Colonist*, 22 May 1883—letter by Bronkhurst; C. Jayawardena, "Religious belief and social change: aspects of the develop-

ment of Hinduism in British Guiana", *CSSH* 8, no. 2 (1966): 216.

2. S. Vertovec, *Hindu Trinidad* (London, 1992), 106.
3. Dale A. Bisnauth, "The East Indian immigrant society in British Guiana 1891-1930", Ph.D. thesis, U.W.I., 1977, 253-58.
4. Ibid., 54-55.
5. Jayawardena, loc. cit.
6. *RG*, 26 February 1880.
7. Bronkhurst, *Among the Hindus*, 86.
8. Jayawardena, loc. cit.
9. Bronkhurst, *Among the Hindus*, 16.
10. Jayawardena, loc. cit.
11. F.P.L. Josa, "The Hindus in the West Indies", *Timehri* II (1912): 305.
12. Suchita Ramdin, "Folk religion of the Hindu immigrant: a case study". In *Indians Overseas: The Mauritian Experience*, edited by U. Bissoondoyal (Mauritius, 1984), 109-37.
13. Report of the [1870] Commissioners Appointed to Inquire into the Treatment of Immigrants in British Guiana (ms.), sec.25, C.O.111/380.
14. Vertovec, 110.
15. *Colonist*, 14 April 1883—letter by Bronkhurst.
16. Ibid.
17. *DC*, 25 July 1886; *BG*, 12 February 1890.
18. D.W.D. Comins, *Notes on Emigration from India to British Guiana* (Calcutta, 1893), 99.
19. Josa, 306; see also Ramdin, footnote 4, 137.
20. Vertovec, 107; and Josa, *Timehri* II (1912): 305.
21. *Colonist*, 2 February 1883 (Bronkhurst).
22. A. Hardy, *Life and Adventure in British Guiana* (London, 1913), 82-83.
23. Bronkhurst, *Among the Hindus and Creoles*, 17.
24. K.L. Gillion, *Fiji's Indian Migrants: A History to the end of Indenture in 1920* (Melbourne: OUP, 1962), 149.
25. *Colonist*, 28 April 1883 (Bronkhurst).
26. *Colonist*, 14 May 1883 (Bronkhurst).
27. Josa (1912): 306.
28. J. Candler, "Extract from Diary" (edited by Prof. Boromé), *Caribbean Studies* 4 (1964): 55.
29. *Colonist*, 14 May 1883 (Bronkhurst).
30. *Colonist*, 5 June 1883 (Bronkhurst).
31. D. Wood, *Trinidad in Transition* (Oxford, 1968), 150. While the *charakh puja* was not present in Trinidad, there is no evidence that the South Indian fire-walking ceremony taken there was practised in Guyana.
32. *RG*, 1 February 1866; H.V.P. Bronkhurst, *The Colony of British Guiana* (London, 1883), 356.
33. Ibid.
34. Encl. in Barkly to Newcastle, No. 60, 14 April 1852, C.O.111/294.
35. Ibid.
36. Ingram to Tidman, 23 February 1856, LMS.7/4 (Bce); H.V.P. Bronkhurst, *The Origin of the Guyanian Indians* (Demerara, 1881), 43.
37. Bronkhurst to Gen. Sect., No. 349, 6 June 1861, MMS/W.v/5.
38. Bronkhurst, *Among the Hindus*, 92.
39. Ibid., 86.
40. J.G. Pearson (ed.), *New Overseer's Manual* (Georgetown, 1890), 49-50.
41. Bronkhurst, *Among the Hindus*, 17, 83-86.
42. J.D. Speckmann, *Marriage and Kinship among the Indians of Surinam* (Assen, 1965), 33; C. Jayawardena, "The disintegration of caste in Fiji Indian rural society", in *Anthropology in Oceania*, edited by L.R. Hiatt & C. Jayawardena (Sydney, 1971), 94; *idem*, "Religious belief and social change", 227-29.
43. R.J. Moore, "East Indians and Negroes in British Guiana, 1838-1880", D.Phil. thesis (Univ. of Sussex, 1970), 355-56.
44. P. van der Veer & S. Vertovec, "Brahmanism abroad: on Caribbean Hinduism as an ethnic religion", *Ethnology* XXX, no. 2 (1991): 158.

45. Bronkhurst, *Among the Hindus*, 83-86; *idem, The Colony*, 291-92; *Colonist*, 19 March 1883–letter by Bronkhurst.

46. Veer & Vertovec, loc. cit., 157.

47. See notes 42, 43. Gillion notes the same activities performed by *sadhus* in Fiji (Gillion, 147). Vertovec claims that in Trinidad a single Brahmin served as *purohit* for all families, as well as "god-father" (*guru*) to virtually all individuals, especially males. See Vertovec, 114.

48. Pearson, *Manual*, 49-51.

49. Ibid.

50. Bronkhurst, *The Colony*, 279.

51. R.J. Moore, 356.

52. Bronkhurst, *Among the Hindus*, 72 & 90.

53. Report of the [1870] Commissioners (ms.), Appendix C—III, C.O.111/382. There was no standard number of holidays adhered to by the plantations. Each plantation acted individually. For instance, whereas La Hague claimed that it granted the Indians a week for *tadja*, Ruimveldt, Better Hope and Vryheid's Lust granted just three days, while Enmore left it optional with the immigrants whether to work or not.

54. *Creole*, 5 May 1882.

55. See S.C. Dube, *Indian Village* (London, 1955), 99; and M. Klass, *East Indians in Trinidad* (New York, 1961), 171-72.

56. Bronkhurst, *Among the Hindus*, 122-23; O. Lewis, *Village Life in Northern India* (Illinois, 1958), 221; Klass, 160-61; Dube, 104-05.

57. *RG*, 1 February 1866; Bronkhurst to General Sect., No.389, 2 April 1864, MMS/W.v/5; and his *The Colony*, 357. See also Dube, 103-04.

58. Dube, loc. cit.

59. Klass, 108; Lewis, 229; Dube, 107.

60. Report of the [1870] Commissioners, sec.25, C.O.111/380. Gillion notes that both *Mohurrum* and *Holi* were celebrated in Fiji (Gillion, 124). Bisnauth notes that *Holi* was celebrated every year, but all of his evidence pertains to the 20th century and is mostly from oral sources. According to these, on the night of the full moon of *Phagun*, a bonfire was set alight generally on the outskirts of the estate. Around this the people walked or ran shouting "*Holi, Holi*". When the flames died down, water was poured over the embers and the people streaked their foreheads with ashes for good luck. Early the next morning, the *Holi Kelna* or *Holi* "play" began with men and women dunking each other in nearby trenches or squirting or pouring muddy water on passersby. *Abir* was also used. On *Phagwah* day visits were paid to friends and relatives (Bisnauth, 269-71).

61. Ibid.; Bronkhurst to Gen.Sect., No. 389, loc. cit.; Edun notes that the Mauritian term *Yamseh* is unknown in India. It is a local corruption of the cries of "Ya Hossein! O Hossein!" used in the Mohurrum procession (see Enayet Hossen Edun, "Tajjia (Tazzia)", in U. Bissoondoyal, 28.

62. *Colonist*, 29 January 1877.

63. Kelvin Singh, *Bloodstained Tombs: The Muharram Massacre 1884* (London, 1988), 6; Wood, 151.

64. Singh, loc. cit.

65. *Colonist*, 15 February 1878.

66. *Colonist*, 16 February 1876.

67. P. Ruhoman, *Centenary History of the East Indians in British Guiana, 1838-1938* (Georgetown, 1947), 110; Klass, 165-68; Dube, 97 & 108; Lewis, 231.

68. Bronkhurst, *The Colony*, 357; Bisnauth, 272-76; see also his *History of Religions in the Caribbean* (Kingston, 1989), 159.

69. *Creole*, 12 May 1865 & 19 April 1867; *RG*, 28 February & 3 March 1874; Bronkhurst, *The Colony*, 358-59. Bisnauth also considers the clashes to be essentially between Hindus and Muslims (Bisnauth, *History*, loc. cit.). In India during the nineteenth century (and even today), clashes between rival *Mohurrum* bands

were reported. These were/are mainly conflicts between *Sunni* and *Shiite* processions. In Guyana, however, it appears that since the Muslims as a whole were so small in number, such differences were minimized in favour of Islamic solidarity and did not, it seems, play any role in the violence between rival *tadja* processions.

70. *Creole*, 19 April 1867; *RG*, 4 March 1874.

71. Report of the [1870] Commissioners (ms.), appendix C, C.O.111/382.

72. *RG*, 1 February 1866; Bronkhurst, *The Colony*, 357.

73. Johnson to Hawkins, 15 September 1865, SPG/E.1.; Hardy, 81-82. It is not surprising that contemporary white commentators should have failed to distinguish between Muslim and Hindu processions. The Hindu *tadja* differed only slightly in appearance. Indeed the only major differentiating feature seems to be the contents of the structure. Muslims had coffins, Hindus had images of the goddess *Durga*. For a description of the *tazzia* in Mauritius, see Edun, 30.

74. *RG*, 1 February 1866; Bronkhurst, *The Colony*, 358-59.

75. Edun, 31. He states that in Mauritius mock combats with sticks were fought during the procession and "prisoners" taken. On their way the processionists shouted "Ya Ali; Ya Hussein" in chorus. Very interestingly he observes that the processions died out, but cites no reason. It is very probable that as in Guyana it may have been due to official restrictions.

76. Ibid.; Edun notes that *gatka* and *ratiffe* were special features of the *Mohurrum* celebrations in Mauritius (Edun, 31-32).

77. Edun, 31-32. He also notes that *kushti* (wrestling) was done at night at a special place called *Akhaara*.

78. *RG*, 27 January 1877.

79. *RG*, 1 February 1866; also "The Tazzia Festival in India", *RG*, 4 March 1884.

80. *RG*, 2 January 1879—letter to the editor.

81. *RG*, 9 January 1879—letter to the editor.

82. *RG*, 2 January 1879—letter.

83. *DDC*, 28 November 1882.

84. *RG*, 11 December 1883.

85. *DC*, 18 November 1885.

86. *DC*, 21 October 1885.

87. *DC*, 25 October 1885.

88. *RG*, 11 August 1860. Wood and Singh note Creole participation in the festival in Trinidad from the 1850s (Wood, 152-53; Singh, 7). See also Patrick Beaton, *Creoles and Coolies or Five Years in Mauritius* (London, 1859), 182, where a similar phenomenon was observed in Mauritius.

89. Watson to Gen. Sect., No. 442, n.d. [1862], MMS/W.v/5.

90. *Creole*, 3 May 1872.

91. *Argosy*, 11 December 1880.

92. Wodehouse to Newcastle, No. 31, 25 February 1860, C.O.111/326.

93. Bronkhurst, *The Colony*, 362.

94. *RG*, 24 January 1878.

95. *DC*, 25 October 1885.

96. R.J. Moore, 373-75.

97. Letter to the editor, *Argosy*, 2 April 1904.

98. *Colonist*, 18 April 1873.

99. *RG*, 11 December 1883; Bronkhurst, *Among the Hindus*, 63.

100. *RG*, 10 May 1873.

101. *DC*, 18 November 1885; *Creole*, 19 April 1867 & 6 September 1869; *Colonist*, 8 April 1868.

102. *Creole*, 19 April 1867.

103. *Colonist*, 14 & 15 March 1870; *RG*, 20 August 1853 and 10 January 1880; *Creole*, 19 April 1867.

104. Bronkhurst to Gen. Sect., No. 432, 23 June 1866, MMS/W.v/5; idem, *The Colony*, 362-63; *RG*, 11 August 1860.

105. Singh, 8.

106. *RG*, 11 August 1860.

107. Singh, 15.

108. Scott to Granville, No. 144, 8 November 1869, C.O.111/373; Ordinance No. 16 of 1869, C.O.113/5; *RG*, 10 May 1873.

The power to define routes for the processions was used in 1875 by Governor Longden when stipendiary magistrates on the west coast of Demerara and the Essequibo islands anticipated serious disturbances among the celebrants on a few estates who were banding to attack others, and had even enlisted Chinese immigrants, reputedly the best and strongest fighters, on their side. Specific routes were therefore arranged to prevent different processions from clashing, and large bodies of armed police were also deployed to maintain order (Longden to Carnarvon, No. 38, 20 February 1875, C.O.384/106).

109. *RG*, 10 May 1873; *Colonist*, 14 January 1878; *DDC*, 18 & 30 November 1883.
110. Comins, 81.
111. *DC*, 22 & 29 October 1885.
112. *DC*, 19 March 1885; *RG*, 3 July 1897; *Argosy*, 26 March and 13 April 1904. See also Bisnauth, "The East Indian immigrant society", 272-77.
113. See Singh, 17-26.
114. *RG*, 12 November 1884.
115. I. Marrat, *In the Tropics* (London, 1881), 129-31.
116. J. Jones, "Mission of British Guiana", *Letters and Notices*, vol. 1, 1862-63, footnote, 152; Gillion, 151-52.
117. *RG*, 7 March 1872.
118. Williams to Gen. Sect., 27 March 1852, MMS/W.iv/5.
119. Shrewsbury to Gen. Sect., 21 December 1858, MMS/W.v/5.
120. Bronkhurst to Hoole, No. 74, 27 December 1860, MMS/W.v/5.
121. *Report of the Guiana Diocesan Church Society for 1860* (Demerara, 1861), 15; *Report of the* [1870] *Commissioners* (Georgetown, 1871), 193.
122. Bhose's report quoted in the *Report of the* [1870] *Commissioners*, 193.
123. Hore to Sect., n.d., SPG/D.44.
124. Ruhoman, 214-20.
125. Hardy, 68.
126. Bhose to the bishop, 23 January 1863 in *Report of the Guiana Diocesan Church Society* (Demerara, 1864), 24;
127. Williams to Gen. Sect., 27 April 1852, MMS/W.iv/5.
128. Bronkhurst to Gen. Sect., No. 400, 6 May 1862, MMS/W.v/5.
129. Bhose to the bishop, loc. cit.
130. Williams, 27 April 1852, loc. cit.
131. Bronkhurst to Gen. Sect., No. 322, 22 April 1863, MMS/W.v/5.
132. Bronkhurst to Boyce, No. 527, 24 May 1869, MMS/W.v/2.
133. Bhose's report for 1869 quoted in the *Report of the* [1870] *Commissioners*, 193.
134. Bronkhurst to Osborn, 17 March 1881, MMS/W.v/2.
135. Bronkhurst to Gen. Sect., No. 389, 2 April 1864, MMS/W.v/5; Gillion, 151.
136. Bronkhurst to Gen. Sect., No. 680, 22 August 1862, MMS/W.v/5.
137. Williams to Gen. Sect., 25 June 1852, MMS/W.iv/5.
138. Bronkhurst to Gen. Sect., No. 1057, 30 November 1877, MMS/W.v/2.
139. Bronkhurst to Hoole, No. 117, 28 February 1861, MMS/W.v/5.
140. Bronkhurst to Hoole, No. 311, 26 March 1872, MMS/W.v/2.
141. Bronkhurst to Gen. Sect., No. 349, 6 June 1861, MMS/W.v/5.
142. Bronkhurst to Gen. Sect., No. 262, 23 April 1867, MMS/W.v/5.
143. Brett to Austin, 18 July 1852, SPG/D.16.
144. H. Bronkhurst, "The religion and religious system of our East Indian population", *DC*, 28 July 1887.
145. Ibid.; Comins, 61; Bhose, loc. cit.; Brett, loc. cit.
146. Bhose to Jones, 26 January 1865, in *Report of the GDCS for 1864*, 31; Bronkhurst to Boyce, No. 527, 24 May 1869, MMS/W.v/2; Bronkhurst to Gen. Sect., No. 245, 8 April 1867, MMS/W.v/5.
147. Bhose to Jones, 26 January 1865, loc. cit.
148. Bronkhurst to Boyce, 7 November 1872, MMS/W.v/2; Bhose to the bishop, 23 January 1863, in *Report of the GDCS for 1862*.

149. Bronkhurst, *The Colony*, 286.
150. *Report of the* [1870] *Commissioners*, 193.
151. Bronkhurst to Gen. Sect., 22 November 1866, MMS/W.v/5.
152. Bronkhurst, *The Colony*, 286.
153. Bronkhurst to Hoole, No. 475, 19 July 1861, MMS/W.v/5.
154. Pearson to Bullock, 30 September 1878, SPG/E.33.
155. E. Sloman, "Coolie missions in British Guiana", *WIQ* 3 (1887): 236; Brett to Austin, 18 July 1852, SPG/D.16; Shrewsbury to Sects., 5 July 1860, MMS/W.v/5; *Report of the GDCS for 1858* (Demerara, 1859).
156. Bronkhurst to Boyce, 6 January 1869, MMS/W.v/2.
157. Bronkhurst, *Among the Hindus*, 52-53; Sloman, loc. cit.
158. Bronkhurst to Gen. Sect., No. 718, 24 July 1875, MMS/W.v/2; and No. 680, 22 August 1862, MMS/W.v/5; extract from *The Villager, DDC*, 9 January 1883.
159. R.J. Moore, 360.
160. Bronkhurst to Gen. Sect., 22 January 1867, MMS/W.v/5; *idem*, No. 196, 22 February 1868, MMS/W.v/2; Brett to Bullock, 31 December 1867, SPG/E.33; *RG*, 12 September 1878 & 22 February 1879.
161. *Colonist*, 28 February 1876; *RG, 2 January 1879.*
162. Johnson to Hawkins, 15 September 1856, SPG/E.1; *RG*, 13 March 1877.
163. Bronkhurst to Gen. Sect., 27 January 1868, MMS/W.v/2; extract from the *Guiana Diocesan Church Society Magazine*, 1 August 1881, SPG/E.36.
164. Josa to Sect., 31 December 1883, SPG/E.38.
165. Bronkhurst to Gen. Sects., No. 1057, 30 November 1877, MMS/W.v/2.
166. Josa, loc. cit.
167. E.A.V. Abrahams, "The East Indian Coolie in British Guiana", *WIQ* 2 (1886): 404; Bronkhurst, *The Origin*, 44.
168. Letter by Bronkhurst in *DC*, 2 September 1885; *idem*, *The Origin*, 44.

169. Bronkhurst to Gen. Sects., No. 907, 5 November 1864, MMS/W.v/5; letter by Bronkhurst in *DC*, 2 September 1885. See chapter 9 for an account of the authentic Portuguese custom.
170. Bronkhurst, No. 907, *idem*, No. 711, 7 September 1865, MMS/W.v/5.
171. *Colonist*, 10 May 1876.
172. *RG*, 6 February 1877.
173. Grey to Light, No. 35, 24 September 1846, *P.P.* 1847.XXXIX. 115.
174. Lugar to Hawkins, 18 February 1850. SPG/D.16.
175. *Report of the GDCS for 1860*, 13.
176. *Colonist*, 18 May 1860.
177. Report of the [1870] Commissioners (ms.), sec. 25, C.O. 111/380; see also sec. 3, C.O. 111/379.
178. Comins, 60.
179. Report of the [1870] Commissioners (ms.), sec. 3, C.O. 111/379.
180. *RG*, 8 February 1879; *Colonist*, 16 September 1881.
181. Letter to the editor, *Colonist*, 24 June 1866.
182. Harris to Secretary, 31 December 1866, SPG/E.22.
183. Bhose to Jones, 26 January 1865, in *Report of the GDCS* for 1864 (Demerara, 1865).
184. Christian to Committee, 4 January 1865, SPG/E.16.
185. Comins, 56; Wodehouse to Newcastle, No. 31, 25 February 1860, C.O.111 326; Veness to Bullock, 2 July 1861, SPG/E.8; Bronkhurst to General Secretaries, No. 400, 6 May 1862, MMS/W.v/5.
186. Report of the [1870] Commissioners (ms.), sec. 25, C.O. 111/380; Christian to Committee, loc. cit.
187. Encl. in Walker to Grey, No. 137, 4 November 1848, C.O. 111/259.
188. Bronkhurst to Boyce, No. 716, 24 August 1872, MMS/W.v/2.
189. Report of the IAG, 25 October 1881, in *Administration Reports* for 1880.
190. Report of the IAG (ag.), 4 August 1882, in *Administration Reports* for 1881.
191. Abraham, loc. cit., 405; Comins, 61.

192. Comins, 56-57.
193. Bronkhurst to General Secretaries, No. 400, 6 May 1862, MMS/W.v/5.
194. Comins, 53 and 60; *Colonist*, 18 May 1860.
195. Bronkhurst, *The Origin*, 33.
196. Bronkhurst, *Among the Hindus*, 17.
197. Comins, 8.
198. W. Look Lai, *Indentured Labor, Caribbean Sugar* (Baltimore, 1993), 257.
199. Bronkhurst, *Among the Hindus*, 50.
200. Dube, 93.
201. Bronkhurst, *Among the Hindus*, 127.
202. Klass, 181-82.
203. Bronkhurst, *The Colony*, 379.
204. Bronkhurst, *Among the Hindus*, 122.
205. *Creole*, 3 May 1872.
206. J.A. Dubois, *Hindu Manners, Customs and Ceremonies* (Oxford, 1906), 341-49.
207. *Creole*, 22 September 1858.
208. *Colonist*, 10 September 1877. In 1889 when a large snake was found on Plantation Vryheid's Lust, it was presumed to have belonged to an Indian man who was believed to be an obeahman. He had erected a long pole on which he used to place a red light at night. It was feared that he had had some "devilish dealings" with the snake which he left to wander about the estate after moving to another location (see *Echo*, 29 June 1889).

Chapter Nine

1. M. Menezes, *Scenes from the History of the Portuguese in Guyana* (London, 1986), 8.
2. Brian L. Moore, "The social impact of Portuguese immigration into British Guiana after emancipation", *BELC*, no. 19 (1975): 5-6.
3. K.O. Laurence, "The establishment of the Portuguese community in British Guiana", *JHR* 5, no. 2 (1965): 72-73.
4. Brian L. Moore, *Race, Power and Social Segmentation in Colonial Society* (New York, 1987), 157.
5. W. Rodney, *A History of the Guyanese Working People, 1881-1905* (Kingston, 1981), 178.
6. H.V.P. Bronkhurst, *The Colony of British Guiana and its Labouring Inhabitants* (London, 1883), 254.
7. Rattray to Tidman, 25 February 1856, LMS (Dem.) 8a/2.
8. Light to Stanley, No. 17, 21 January 1842, C.O.111/196.
9. Light to Grey, No. 150, 16 July 1847, *PP* 1847-48. XXIII. Pt.I.
10. Bronkhurst, 255.
11. Menezes, 31 & 158.
12. For a good account of the relationship between the Portuguese immigrants and the Catholic church, see M.N. Menezes, "The Madeiran Portuguese and the establishment of the Catholic church in British Guiana, 1835-1898", in *After the Crossing: Immigrants and Minorities in Caribbean Creole Society*, edited by Howard Johnson (London, 1988), 57-78.
13. Stanley to Light, No. 47, 27 December 1841, C.O.111/183; Light to Stanley, No. 73, 24 January 1842, GNA.
14. Petition from "Members of the Catholic Committee", 17 March 1845, GNA.
15. Light to Gladstone, No. 112, 12 June 1846, C.O.111/233; and No. 140, 14 July 1846, C.O.111/234.
16. Encl. in Barkly to Grey, No. 166, 17 November 1849, C.O.111/270; No. 170, 23 November 1849; and No. 16, 10 January 1850, C.O.111/272.
17. Blue Book of Statistics for 1851, C.O.116/220.
18. Menezes, "The Maderian Portuguese", 60.
19. Sherlock to Barrow, 25 May 1858, SJ/*BG*/12.
20. Johnson to Hawkins, 13 August & 24 December 1855, and Conyers to Hawkins, 14 January 1856, SPG/E.Pre E; also Shrewsbury to Hoole, 21 December

1858 and Spratt to General Secretary, 23 December 1858, MMS/W.v/5.

21. J. Jones, "Mission in British Guiana," *Letters and Notices* [SJ] 1 (1862-63): 163.

22. Walker to Fr. Provincial, 7 October 1862, SJ/*BG*/16.

23. Etheridge to Johnson, 10 July 1857, SJ/*BG*/11.

24. *Colonist*, 7 March 1877—letter to the editor.

25. Fr. Woollett's "Notes", SJ/*BG*/9.

26. Walker to Fr. Provincial, loc. cit.

27. "Obituary" [of Schembri], 1898, *Letters & Notices* 24 (1897-98).

28. Etheridge to Fr. Provincial, 9 April 1858, SJ/*BG*/12; *DDC*, 10 December 1882.

29. Etheridge to Fr. Provincial, 9 April 1858, SJ/*BG*/12.

30. "Obituary" [Schembri], loc. cit.

31. Jones, 163-64.

32. "Obituary" [Schembri], loc. cit.

33. Woollett's "Notes", loc. cit.

34. Woollett to Fr. Provincial, 7 February 1859, SJ/*BG*/13.

35. Ibid.

36. Walker to Fr. Provincial, private, 6 November 1861, SJ/*BG*/15.

37. Woollett's "Notes", loc. cit.

38. Walker to Fr. Provincial, 22 November 1861, SJ/*BG*/15.

39. Walker to Fr. Provincial, 6 November 186, loc. cit.

40. Ibid.

41. Woollett's "Notes", loc. cit. Walker to Fr. Provincial, 6 November 1861, Etheridge to Fr. Provincial, n.d., SJ/*BG*/19.

42. Etheridge to Fr. Provincial, 9 March 1863, SJ/*BG*/17.

43. Bishop Etheridge's Diary, 1858-1877, SJ/*BG*/8.

44. "Obituary" [Schembri], loc. cit. According to Roman Catholic religious legend, the Sacred Heart of Jesus burning with love for mankind was revealed in an apparition to St Margaret Alacoque in France in the 17th century. She was a French Visitandine nun. She initiated the feast of the Sacred Heart on the Friday after the octave of Corpus Christi.

45. J. Gerard, "Inter-Guianese" (ms.A, Society of Jesus, 1900).

46. Etheridge to Fr. Provincial, loc. cit.

47. "Obituary" [Schembri], loc. cit. Etheridge to Fr. Provincial,

48. *DDC*, 25 November and 10 December 1882.

49. *DDC*, 27 June 1883.

50. Walker to Fr. Provincial, 7 October 1862, SJ/*BG*/16.

51. Galton to Knight, 11 November 1897, SJ/*BG*/20.

52. H. Bronkhurst, *The Colony of British Guiana and its Labouring Inhabitants* (London, 1883), 220. In 1897, Bishop Galton noted that "the rising generation and the majority of the younger Portuguese had lost the Portuguese language" (Galton to Knight, 11 November 1897, SJ/*BG*/20).

53. *Echo*, 25 July 1896.

54. W. DesVoeux, *Experiences of a Demerara Magistrate* (Georgetown, 1948), 147.

55. Walker to Fr. Provincial, 7 October 1862, loc. cit.

56. Ordinance No.14 of 1876, C.O.113/6.

57. Galton to Knight, loc. cit.

58. *RG*, 21 December 1872.

59. Anonymous letter about the Church of the Ascension, New Amsterdam, in *Letters and Notices* 13 (1880): 301.

60. Barker, 24 February 1891, *Letters and Notices* 21 (1891-92).

61. Walker to Fr. Prov., 23 December 1862, S.J/B.G./16.

62. Fr. Woollett's "Notes", 1858-1860, SJ/*BG*/9.

63. Barker, loc. cit.

64. Woollett's, loc. cit.; "Notes", *RG*, 8 January 1866 and 4 January 1877; *Colonist*, 2 January 1883. At the best of times, the use of fireworks in a country composed almost wholly of wooden buildings was dangerous. But this was even more so when fireworks were homemade by the Portuguese. In one instance the fireworks accidentally exploded while being made, not only burning the building but also seriously injuring the two persons making them. See *WP*, 20 November 1869.

65. Woollett's "Notes", loc. cit.

66. Ibid.
67. *BG*, 24 August 1892.
68. Anonymous letter, loc. cit.; *RG*, 18 August 1877.
69. Scoles, 8 October 1869, in *Letters and Notices*, 7, 1871.
70. *RG*, 18 August 1877
71. Anonymous letter, loc. cit.; *RG*, 16 August 1864.
72. *RG*, 18 August 1877.
73. Anonymous letter, loc. cit.; *BG*, 19 August 1882.
74. *DDC*, 29 August 1882; *Colonist*, 17 August 1883.
75. Woollett's "Notes", loc. cit.
76. Anonymous letter, loc. cit.
77. Menezes, "The Maderian Portuguese", 66.
78. Ibid.; *Colonist*, 6 June 1876, 19 May 1877.
79. *RG*, 26 May 1875.
80. *RG*, 18 May 1875, 22 May 1877.
81. *DDC*, 29 May 1883.
82. *Argosy*, 22 March 1884; *DC*, 28 April 1885, 6 & 13 May 1885, 17 September 1886, 13 September 1898. The Society of St Joseph was formed in 1884 by one of the Italian priests, Fr De Moura in collaboration with Messrs A. Gonsalves, Jr., Mr de Souza, and J.J. Fernandes (see *DDC*, 26 June 1884).
83. *RG*, 14 August 1883.
84. Menezes, "The Madeiran Portuguese", 67.
85. Woollett's "Notes", loc. cit.
86. M.N. Menezes, *Scenes*, 156.
87. *DDC*, 26 June 1888; *Reflector*, 25 June 1892
88. Menezes, "The Madeiran Portuguese", 67.
89. Woollett's "Notes", loc. cit.; *Colonist*, 2 June 1883; *DDC*, 5 June 1883.
90. *DDC*, 24 May 1883.
91. *DC*, 8 October 1898.
92. *DDC*, 25 July 1883, 13 November 1883.
93. *Colonist*, 31 July 1871; *DC*, 4 January 1888.
94. *DC*, 25 July 1893
95. Anonymous letter, loc. cit.
96. Encl. in Irving to Stanhope, No. 290, 27 October 1886, C.O.111/436.
97. Encl. in Bruce to Knutsford, No. 392, 6 December 1888, C.O.111/448.
98. *Colonist*, 15 & 17 February 1875; *RG*, 26 February 1878.
99. *Colonist*, 31 October 1879.
100. Bronkhurst, *The Colony*, 344.
101. *Colonist*, 12 April 1883.
102. *BG*, 19 August 1893.
103. Scoles, 8 October 1869, in *Letters and Notices* [SJ] 7 (1871).
104. Ibid.
105. Ibid.
106. Laws, September 1872, in *Letters and Notices* 8 (1872).
107. Ibid.
108. J. Cutileiro, *A Portuguese Rural Society* (London, 1971), 271-272.
109. Minutes of the Court of Policy, December quarter 1872, C.O.114/26; Bruce to Knutsford [& encl.], No. 392, 6 December 1888, C.O.111/448.
110. *Creole*, 10 September 1866; *Colonist*, 3 December 1870; *DDC*, 26 June 1884; *DC*, 17 February 1885; *RG*, 10 July 1886; *Argosy*, 28 June 1890.
111. *Creole*, 21 January 1863; *Colonist*, 1 November 1871; 21, August 1872; 30 August 1872; 13 August 1874; 11 April 1878; 25 January 1883; *Watchman*, 26 November 1876; *DC*, 19 March 1885; 4 May 1894; 7 June 1894; *RG*, 26 July 1883; 25 August 1888; *BG*, 29 August 1888.
112. Barrett to Tidman, 12 August 1847, LMS.7/2 (Dem.).
113. *RG*, 15 February 1849.
114. *Watchman*, 8 December 1876; *Colonist*, 5 April 1877; 2 May 1879; *Argosy*, 28 October 1882; *RG*, 25 September 1888; *BG*, 26 May 1886; *DC*, 25 January 1893; 2 December 1898.
115. *Watchman*, 21 September 1877; *BG*, 8 May 1889.
116. *BG*, 15 June 1892.
117. *DC*, 9 October 1898.
118. See, for instance, *RG.*, 29 July 1884.
119. The first all-Portuguese cricket club was formed in Georgetown in 1878 (*Colonist*, 28 December 1878). Another one was the North Cummingsburg C.C. (*DC*, 11 July 1897).

120. *Colonist*, 6 October 1866; 'X', "Stray notes on obeah", *Timehri* VI, 3rd. ser. (1919): 129.

121. According to Smith, cultural heterogeneity occurs when the members of different ethnic groups share the same basic or compulsory institutions but practise different alternative and/or exclusive institutions. Cultural pluralism occurs when there is an absence of shared basic institutions. See M.G. Smith, *The Plural Society in the British West Indies* (Berkeley, 1965), 79-82.

Chapter Ten

1. *Hua-qiao/hua-ch'iao* means "a Chinese person or a Chinese community residing abroad". For a discussion on the evolution of use of this term in Chinese history writing, see Wang Gungwu, "Southeast Asian *Hua-Ch'iao* in Chinese history-writing", *JSAS* XII, no. 1 (1981): 1-14.

2. Encl. 4 in Walker to Newcastle, 19 November 1861, No. 83, C.O.111/332; Mundy to Carnarvon, 4 April 1866, No. 37, C.O.111/362. According to Fried, the difference between these two groups is essentially linguistic. *Punti* is spoken by the Cantonese who "are descended from the more or less indigenous peoples of Yueh, the pre-Han country that extended over much of modern Kwangtung, adjacent provinces, and into modern Indo-China". The *Hakka*, "the guest people", originated in northern China but migrated over a long period of time to Fukien and Kwangtung "where they live side by side with Cantonese without fusion". See M.H. Fried, "Some observations on the Chinese in British Guiana", *SES* 5 (1956): 61-62.

3. Walton Look Lai, *Indentured Labor, Caribbean Sugar: Chinese and Indian Migrants to the British West Indies, 1838-1918* (Baltimore, 1993), 40; C.C. Clementi, *The Chinese in British Guiana* (Georgetown, 1915), 333-49; H. Ly-Tio-Fane Pineo, *Chinese Diaspora in Western Indian Ocean* (Mauritius, 1984), 35-37.

4. J. Levy, "The economic role of the Chinese in Jamaica: the grocery retail trade", *JHR* 15 (1986): 32-33; Look Lai, 97.

5. At Victoria, British Columbia, the principal port of entry for Chinese immigrants into Canada there were less than 100 women and well over 3,000 men as late 1902. In the United States the number of men per 100 women in 1900 was 1,887. A similar pattern emerged in Australia and New Zealand. In Victoria, Australia, there were just three women to 25,421 men in 1857; by 1901 although the ratio had increased there still only 609 women to 6,740 men. In New Zealand there were in 1906 just 55 Chinese women to over 2,500 men. In Mauritius there were 3,457 males to 58 women in 1901, while in Singapore only 20 percent of the Chinese population was female in 1900. In Manila the ratio was 6:1 until the 1940s. See Anthony B. Chan, "Chinese bachelor workers in nineteenth-century Canada", *ERS* 5, no. 4 (1982): 515-16; Shih-Shan Tsai, *The Chinese Experience in America* (Bloomington, 1986), 40; Kathryn Cronin, *Colonial Casualties: Chinese in Early Victoria* (Melbourne, 1982), 19 and 136; Kwen Fee Lian, "The sociopolitical process of identity formation in an ethnic community: the Chinese in New Zealand", *ERS* 11, no. 4 (1988): 514-17; Chinben See, "Chinese Clanship in the Philippine Setting", *JSAS* XII, no. 1 (1981): 230; L.W. Crissman, "The segmentary structure of urban overseas Chinese communities", *Man* 2, no. 2 (1967): 186-87; Ly-Tio-Fane Pineo, 267-80.

6. Look Lai, 45-46, 74 and 94.

7. Report of the IAG, 15 October 1881, in *Administration Reports*, 1880.
8. Decennial census for 1891.
9. Cronin, 19.
10. Barkly to Grey, 31 October 1851, No. 152, *PP* 1852-53.LXVIII.
11. Ly-Tio-Fane Pineo, 264.
12. Chan, loc. cit.; Lian, loc. cit.; Wealthy Chinese felt that their wives were too delicate to face the rigours of colonial life (see Cronin, 19).
13. Ching-Hwang, "Early Chinese clan organizations in Singapore and Malaya, 1819-1911", *JSAS* XII (1981): 84; Ronald Hyam, "Empire and sexual opportunity", *JICH* 14, no. 2 (1986): 68; Tsai, 40; Anthony B. Chan, *Gold Mountain: The Chinese in the New World* (Vancouver, 1983), 80-83.
14. E. Jenkins, *The Coolie: His Rights and Wrongs* (London, 1871), 63.
15. *Report of the* [1870] *Commissioners*, 129, 131. The barrack type accommodation of the Guyanese plantations was similar to that which the Chinese indentured workers were offered in Hawaii (see Tsai, 29). Chan notes that largely to cut their living expenses the Chinese bachelor immigrants in Canada lived in crowded boarding houses which in some ways resembled barracks (see A.B. Chan, "Chinese bachelor workers in nineteenth-century Canada", *ERS* 5, no. 4 (1982): 527). A similar picture is painted by Chinben See for the Philippines. See his "Chinese clanship in the Philippine setting", *JSAS* XII, no. 1 (1981): 226. Since the Chinese who went to Australia were essentially voluntary gold prospectors, accommodation was manifestly different and took the form of sprawling tent villages. Even so, however, their tents were noticeably clean and neat with furniture, books and musical instruments (Cronin, 23).
16. Ibid.

17. Report of the [1870] Commissioners (ms.), sec.24, C.O.111/380.
18. H. Bronkhurst, *The Colony of British Guiana* (London, 1883), 211-12; L. Crookall, *British Guiana* (London, 1898), 119.
19. Bronkhurst, *The Colony*, 253.
20. *BG*, 17 June 1865.
21. H. Kirke, *Twenty-five Years in British Guiana* (London, 1898), 158.
22. *BG*, 17 June 1865.
23. Kirke, 158-60.
24. *RG*, 23 & 31 May 1866.
25. *BG*, 17 June 1865.
26. M. Freedman, "Chinese kinship and marriage in Singapore", *JSAH* 3 (1962): 70.
27. Chinben See, 230.
28. *Report of the* [1870] *Commissioners*, 137. In 1871 children under 15 years amounted to only 9.2 percent of the Chinese population. But as Chinese immigration declined, the number of children born to Chinese parents increased significantly, even though their total numbers continued to fall. In 1881 out of 5,234 Chinese, 841 (16.1%) were local born; and by 1891, out of 3,714, some 1,239 (33.4%) were locals (see Look Lai, Appendix 1, 302).
29. According to Clementi, 2,141 Chinese left the colony between 1881 and 1902 (Clementi, 332). Look Lai thinks that this out-migration began from the 1870s (Look Lai, 201).
30. Barkly to Newcastle, No. 9, 26 February 1853, *P.P.* 1852-53.LXVIII.
31. *Colonist*, 25 August 1864. In one such incident the woman was actually killed by her husband Yip-Yow. He was condemned to death, but subsequently reprieved on grounds of insanity (see *Echo*, 28 October and 4 November 1893).
32. J. Amphlett, *Under a Tropical Sky* (London, 1873).
33. *RG*, 27 July 1876.
34. Decennial census for 1891.
35. Fried, 58-59.

36. Encls. 3 & 4 in Walker to New-castle, No. 83, 9 November 1861, C.O. 111/332.

37. Report of the [1870] Commis-sioners (ms.), sec. 13, C.O. 111/379.

38. Hincks to Buckingham & Chan-dos, No. 177, 18 December 1868, C.O. 111/369; also Scott to Kim-berley, No. 106, 18 July 1871, C.O. 111/386.

39. Report of the [1870] Commis-sioners (ms.), sec. 25, C.O. 111/380; Spooner to Hawkins, 19 January 1857, SPG/E.1.

40. Ly-Tio-Fane Pineo, 282; Brian L. Moore, *Race, Power and Social Segmentation in Colonial Society* (New York, 1987), 181-82. Mat-ing between Chinese men and Creole women in the later nine-teenth century seems to have been more widespread than I indi-cated in that book.

41. Kirke, 160.

42. Fried, 58-59.

43. *RG.*, 25 July 1876; Comins, 95. In 1892 the Immigration Agent General reported six marriages between Chinese men and Indian women (Look Lai, 210).

44. Ly-Tio-Fane Pineo, 283-84; Freed-man, 70-71.

45. Look Lai, 207.

46. Moore, 181-82.

47. R. Hyam, "Empire and sexual op-portunity", *JICH* 14 (1986): 58-59 and 68.

48. Cronin, 122.

49. Look Lai, 208; Hyam, loc. cit.

50. Tsai, 46.

51. Freedman, 72; Yen Ching-Hwang, "Early Chinese clan or-ganizations in Singapore and Ma-laya, 1819-1911", *JSAS* XII, no. 1 (1981): 62-63; see also Chinben See, 225-30.

52. Look Lai, 211.

53. Freedman, loc. cit.; Crissman, 190-91.

54. Tsai, 46-47.

55. Ching-Hwang, loc. cit.; Chinben See, loc. cit.

56. Look Lai points out that these districts can be classified as fol-lows: (i) the Sze Yup (Four Dis-tricts) area west of Macao, com-posed of Toishan (Hsinning be-fore 1914), Hsinhui (Sun Wui), Kai Ping, and Enping; (ii) the Sam Yup (Three Districts) area to the north of Canton, compris-ing Nanhai (Nam Hoy), Pan Yu, and Hsun-tak (Shunde); and (iii) other districts scattered around the Cantonese Pearl river delta, but dominated by Chungshan to the north of Macao (Look Lai, 42).

57. Crissman, 197-99; M. Topley, "The emergence and social func-tion of Chinese religious societies in Singapore", in *Immigrants and Associations*, edited by L.A. Fal-lers (The Hague, 1967), 62-63. Tsai states that "the Triad soci-ety was originally a quasi-relig-ious fraternity established in the 17th century by a sect of militant Buddhist monks of the Shaolin Monastery in the Fuzhou area. The name Triad, or Three United Society, is apparently de-rived from the trinity of Heaven, Earth and Man; hence it was also known as the Society of the Three Dots and as the Heaven and Earth Society. Because of its connection with the Ming Dy-nasty (1368-1644) founded by the Emperor Hongwu, it also re-ceived the names of Sect of Hong, Family of Hong, and Red League" (Tsai, 51).

58. Tsai, loc. cit.

59. Marlene Kwok Crawford, *Scenes from the History of the Chinese in Guyana* (Georgetown, 1989), 67-69; Cronin, 33.

60. Cronin, 18 & 32.

61. Cronin, 31-40; Tsai, 51-54; Freed-man, 73; *idem*, "Immigrants and associations: Chinese in nine-teenth century Singapore", *CSSH* 3, no. 1 (1960): 30-35; Topley, loc. cit.; Crissman, loc. cit.

62. B.L. Moore, "The settlement of Chinese in Guyana in the nine-teenth century", *IM* 7 (1988): 44.

63. Freedman, "Immigrants and asso-ciations", 37.

64. *RG*, 4 July 1863; Report of the [1870] Commissioners (ms.), sec.13, loc. cit.

65. *Argosy*, 4 November 1882; *DC*, 11 & 30 May 1888; J.A. Heatley, *A Visit to the West Indies* (Alnwick, 1891), 41.
66. *RG*, 4 July 1863.
67. L.W. Crissman, loc. cit.; Under this system, the Dutch appointed a *kapitan* from among the Chinese who was responsible for administering the community and maintaining law and order. It was a form of indirect rule, with the *kapitans* serving as brokers between the Chinese and the colonial authorities.
68. Moore, "The settlement of Chinese", 44.
69. Walker to Newcastle, No. 83 and encl. 4, loc. cit.
70. Tsai, 42.
71. Lobscheid to the Bishop, 20 December 1859, SPG/E.6; Report of the [1870] Commissioners (ms.), sec.25, loc. cit. *DC*, 2 March 1889.
72. Look Lai, 74-75.
73. Rattray to Tidman, 25 January 1853, LMS 7/8 (Dem.).
74. Barkly to Newcastle, No. 32, 20 February 1853, *P.P.* 852-53.LXVIII; Shrewsbury to Gen. Sect., No. 260, 2 April 1860, MMS/W.v/5.
75. Walker to Newcastle, No. 83, loc. cit.
76. *Report of the Guiana Diocesan Church Society for 1861* (Demerara, 1862), 15; extract from *The Guiana Magazine*, SPG/E.14; Shrewsbury to Gen. Sect., 2 April 1860, MMS/W.v/5.
77. Encl. in Murdoch to Rogers, No.3340, 10 April 1865, C.O.318/245; Austin to Bulloch, 20 August 1866, SPG/D.28.
78. Hincks to Cardwell, No. 27, 21 February 1865, C.O.111/350; Mundy to Cardwell, No. 30, 3 August 1866, C.O.111/360.
79. Hincks to Cardwell, No. 27, loc. cit.; Report of the [1870] Commissioners (ms.), sec.24, loc. cit.
80. *Colonist*, 19 November 1869; Bridger to Sect., 30 December 1873, SPG/E.28; *RG*, 6 May 1879; F. Josa, *Tale of A Roaming Catholic* (London, 1920).
81. Josa to Sect., 31 December 1887, SPG/E.42.
82. I am indebted to Bridget Brereton for this observation.
83. Cronin, 104-118.
84. Tsai, 42-45.
85. Look Lai, 258.
86. Ibid., 212.
87. F. Josa, *Tale*, loc. cit.
88. *Colonist*, 25 April 1876; Josa, *Tale*, loc. cit.
89. Cronin notes that their old amusements were forbidden, and the hours formerly spent gambling or in idle club-house chatter were now devoted to evangelizing (Cronin, 118-19).
90. Extract from *The Guiana Magazine* (1862) in SPG/E.14.
91. *Colonist*, 28 January, 8 August 1874; Longden to Carnarvon, No. 153, 15 August 1874, C.O.111/402; No. 249, 4 December 1875, C.O.111/406; *RG*, 4 December 1875; *DT*, 26 November 1875. The cornerstone was laid by Governor Longden in August 1874. Of the $3,408 to build the church, $1,349 were raised by the Chinese themselves, and the rest by voluntary subscriptions. The church was built on the site of the old St. Philip's church at the corner of Broad and Saffon streets.
92. *Colonist*, 10 February 1876; *RG*, 9 February 1878; *(D)DC*, 13 June 1884, 16 November 1886; *Argosy*, 5 July 1884; *BG*, 11 February 1891. St. Clement's in New Amsterdam was 55 by 22 feet in size, and stood on brick pillars four feet high. It had a height of 18 feet from pillar to plate, and could accommodate 200 persons. At the eastern end of the steep zinc-covered roof was an ornamented cross carved by a Chinese cabinetmaker, Edward Yee Foo. On the western end was the belfry, and a porch which was the entrance. The furniture, made of polished crabwood and mahogany, included the altar, reredos, and special chairs for the bishop, rector, visiting clergy and catechist, reading desk, choir

stalls, harmonium, and a number of pretty and powerful lamps.

93. *DDC*, 10 February 1883; *Argosy*, 6 February 1886.

94. Look Lai, 211.

95. Ibid., 214.

96. Report of the [1870] Commissioners (ms.), sec. 25, C.O. 111/380.

97. Veness to Hawkins, 13 January 1862, SPG/E.14.

98. May to Secretary, 22 January 1862, SPG/E.10, and 15 February 1864, SPG/E.14.

99. Petition (translation) by Chinese (Peter, James and Thomas) 16 September 1881, and office minute, in Government Secretary's Office document No. 4650/81, 22 April 1882, GNA.

100. Ching-Hwang, 79-80. These festivals were also celebrated in the United States and Australia. See Tsai, 36, and Cronin, 26.

101. Report of the [1870] Commissioners (ms.), Appendix C, C.O. 111/382.

102. W. Eberhard, *Chinese Festivals* (New York, 1952), 4.

103. Ching-Hwang, 79-80.

104. Ibid.

105. M.C. Yang, *A Chinese Village* (London, 1948), 90.

106. Report of the [1870] Commissioners (ms.), Appendix C—III, C.O.111/382.

107. Yang, 90-92.

108. *DDC*, 10 February 1883; *Argosy*, 6 February 1886; *BG*, 22 January 1890 and 3 February 1892.

109. Yang, 95.

110. Pearson, *The Overseer's Manual*, loc. cit.

111. *BG*, 18 February 1893. A New Amsterdam resident, John King, complained that every year the Chinese prevented other persons from sleeping by exploding their fireworks all night.

112. Eberhard, 62-63.

113. Yang, loc. cit.

114. *RG*, 24 February 1880; *Argosy*, 2 February 1884; Bronkhurst, 365.

115. *Colonist*, 11 February 1880.

116. Ibid.

117. *Argosy*, 2 February 1884.

118. Heatley, 41; *RG*, 24 February 1880; *Colonist*, 23 January 1879; *Argosy*, 14 February 1885.

119. Yang, 94.

120. *Colonist*, 1 February 1881; *Argosy*, 21 February 1885; *DC*, 17 February 1885.

121. *Colonist*, 2 February 1881.

122. Tsai, 36-37.

123. *RG*, 10 March 1874; Kirke, 160.

124. *RG*, 14 February 1854.

125. Tsai, loc. cit.

126. *Colonist*, 1 November 1877.

127. Ibid.

128. *Colonist*, 11 February 1880.

129. Ibid.

130. Ibid.

131. Howard Johnson, "The Chinese in Trinidad in the late nineteenth century", *ERS* 10, no. 1 (1987): 92-93; Anthony B. Chan, "Chinese bachelor workers", 527-29; Crissman, 185-204; Freedman, "Immigrants and associations", 25-48; Tsai, 39-40; Cronin, 26.

132. *Argosy*, 5 April 1884. Chan notes that "opium addicts in Canada needed a pipe about the length and thickness of a common flute. The tip of the pipe taken into the mouth was flattened to accommodate the person's lips. On the other end was a bowl of terracotta about the size of a demitasse that was connected to the stem. The opium smoked ... was a dark gummy paste made by roasting a pea-sized amount of opium. Placed in the hole of the bowl, the drug was then ready for consumption. The average addict took about twelve pipes in one sitting for a total ascent to the edge of reality". See Chan, loc. cit.

133. Report of the [1870] Commissioners (ms.), sec.13, C.O.111/379.

134. *Creole*, 18 July 1860.

135. Report of the [1879] Commissioners (ms.), sec.13, loc. cit

136. *Report of the* [1870] *Commissioners*, 131; *Creole*, 6 September 1869.

137. Attorney-General's Report, 7 November 1861, in Walker to Newcastle, No. 82, s.d., C.O.111/332. In the United States, there were

no specific laws against the sale or use of opium; hence it was openly sold in the streets (Tsai, 39). In Australia, opium dormitories were always open (Cronin, 26).

138. Blue Books of Statistics, 1861-1883, C.O.116.

139. *Colonist*, 26 August 1874, 28 September 1875.

140. *Colonist*, 9 March 1876.

141. V. Berridge, "Victorian opium eating: responses to opiate use in nineteenth-century England", *VS* 21, no. 4 (1978): 437-62.

142. Remark by James Walvin at the twenty-fifth conference of the Association of Caribbean Historians, Kingston, Jamaica, March 1993.

143. Encl. 1 in Walker to Newcastle, No.83, 19 November 1861, C.O.111/332; Berridge, loc. cit

144. *Creole*, 6 September 1869; Minutes of the Court of Policy, C.O.114/25.

145. Irving to Kimberley, No. 121, 4 May 1883, C.O.384/144; report of the Attorney-General, encl'd in Gormanston to Knutsford, No. 96, 25 March 1889, C.O.111/451; Blue Book of Statistics, 1891.

146. Johnson, loc. cit.

147. Encl. 4 in Walker, No.83, loc. cit.

148. Encl. 3 in Walker, No.83, loc. cit.

149. *Colonist*, 11 February 1880.

150. *Argosy*, 4 November 1882.

151. Kirke, 158.

152. *Argosy*, 4 November 1882.

153. *Colonist*, 11 February 1880.

154. *DC*, 30 May 1888; *Argosy*, 4 November 1882. See also Chan, 530, and Tsai, 38.

155. *RG*, 4 July 1863.

156. See Wood, 163; Johnson, 91-92; A.W. Lind, "Adjustment patterns among the Jamaican Chinese", *SES* 7, no. 2 (1958) 163; Chan, 530; Tsai, 38-39.

157. J. van Sertima, *Scenes and Sketches of Demerara Life* (Georgetown, 1899), 87-91; *DC*, 11 May 1888; *Argosy*, 4 November 1882.

158. See note 19.

159. Ibid.; *Argosy*, 4 November 1882; *DC*, 30 May 1888. See also P. Bryan, *The Jamaican People, 1880-*

1902 (London, 1991), 194, for a brief description of the lottery in Jamaica; and Johnson, loc. cit., on *whé-whé* in Trinidad.

160. *Colonist*, 2 January 1883. See also *Colonist*, 18 & 25 January 1882 and *DC*, 26 February 1886.

161. In February 1885 it was reported that a cricket match was played between a Chinese team and an East Coast XI. The Chinese lost (*DC*, 19 February 1885).

162. See *DC*, 19 February 1885, and Kirke, 49.

163. M.G. Smith, *The Plural Society in the British West Indies* (Berkeley, 1965), 79-82.

Chapter Eleven

1. For a full discussion of rival theories as they can be applied to Guyanese society towards the end of the nineteenth century, see the author's *Race, Power and Social Segmentation in Colonial Society* (New York, 1987), 220-23.

2. See, for instance, Lloyd Braithwaite, "Social stratification in Trinidad", *SES* 2 (1953); E.K. Brathwaite, *Contradictory Omens: Cultural Diversity and Integration in the Caribbean* (Mona, 1974); M. Cross, "Cultural pluralism and sociological theory: a critique and reevaluation", *SES* 17 (1968); Stuart Hall, " Pluralism, race and class in Caribbean society", in UNESCO, *Race and Class in Post-Colonial Society* (Paris, 1977); and R.T. Smith, "Social stratification, cultural pluralism, and integration in West Indian societies", in *Caribbean Integration*, edited by S. Lewis & T.G. Mathews (Puerto Rico, 1967).

3. See, for instance, M.G. Smith, *Culture, Race and Class in the Commonwealth Caribbean* (Kingston, 1984); Leo Despres, *Cultural Pluralism and Nationalist Politics in British Guiana* (Chicago, 1967); Pierre van den Berghe, "Pluralism and the polity: a theoretical exploration", in *Plu-*

ralism in Africa, edited by L. Kuper & M.G. Smith (Berkeley, 1971); and, R.A.J. van Lier, *The Development and Nature of Society in the West Indies* (Amsterdam, 1950).

4. Brian Stoddart, "Cricket, social formation and cultural continuity in Barbados", *JSH* 14, no. 3 (1987).

5. Moore, *Race, Power and Social Segmentation*, 191-211.

BIBLIOGRAPHY

PRIMARY SOURCES

British Colonial Office Records (Public Record Office)

C.O.111	British Guiana: original correspondence.
C.O.112	British Guiana: letters from the Secretary of State.
C.O.113	British Guiana: acts/ordinances.
C.O.114	British Guiana: sessional papers and administration reports.
C.O.116	British Guiana: stipendiary magistrates' reports and blue books of statistics.
C.O.318	West Indies: original correspondence.
C.O.384	Emigration: original correspondence.
C.O.537	Colonies (General), Supplementary: original correspondence.

Great Britain—Parliamentary Papers

Miscellaneous documents were used covering the period 1840-1872.

Essex Record Office, Chelmsford

D/DVv 74   Correspondence and photographs, Henry Bullock 1861-1915.

Guyana National Archives Records

Governors' Despatches to the Secretary of State (incomplete).
British Guiana: Despatches from the Secretary of State for the Colonies (incomplete).
Government Secretary's Office Letter Books.
Laws of British Guiana, 1838-1900.
Proclamations, 1859-1900.
Administration Reports.
Minutes of the Court of Policy, 1838-1900.
Minutes of the Combined Court, 1838-1900.
Immigration Certificates.
Official Gazette, 1845-1900.
British Guiana Blue Books, 1844-1900 (incomplete).

Wesleyan Methodist Missionary Society

Stack W.iv/5   West Indies: correspondence, 1848-1857.
Stack W.v/2   British Guiana and Leewards, 1868-1891.
Stack W.v/5   St. Vincent and Demerara, 1858-1890.

London Missionary Society

Boxes 7-11   Demerara: original correspondence, 1846-1894.
Boxes 7-11   Berbice: original correspondence, 1850-1899.

Society of Jesus, English Province

BG/8-20   British Guiana: correspondence, 1857-1902.
Letters and Notices, vols. 1-25, 1862-1900.

United Society for the Propagation of the Gospel

Class D   Letters received, vols. 16-99, 1850-1891.
Class E   Missionary reports, vols. 1- 45, 1856-1890.

Newspapers (Guyana National Archives & British Library Newspaper Library)

Argosy, 1881-1900
Berbice Gazette, 1838-1900
Colonist, 1848-1884
Creole, 1856-1882
Daily Chronicle, 1885-1900
Demerara Daily Chronicle, 1881-1884
Demerara Times, 1875-1876
Echo, 1887-1899
Guiana Herald, 1843, 1885
Guiana Times, 1840-1848, 1866
Liberator, 1868-1869
Royal Gazette, 1838-1889
Reflector, 1889-1892.
Watchman, 1871-1879
Weekly Penny, 1869-1870.

SECONDARY SOURCES

Contemporary

Abraham, E.A.V. 1886. "The East Indian Coolie in British Guiana". *West Indian Quarterly* 2.

Amphlett, John. 1873. *Under a Tropical Sky: A Journal of First Impressions of the West Indies*. London: Sampson Low, Marton, Low & Searle.

Beaton, Patrick. 1859. *Creoles and Coolies or Five Years in Mauritius*. London: J. Nisbet & Co.

Bennett, George W. 1875. *An Illustrated History of British Guiana*. Georgetown: L. McDermott.

Boddam-Whetham, J.W. 1879. *Roraima and British Guiana*. London: Hurst & Blackett.

Bronkhurst, H.V.P. 1881. *The Origin of the Guyanian Indians*. Demerara: Colonist.

_____. 1886. *The Ancestry or Origin of Our East Indian Immigrants, being an Ethnological and Philological Paper*. Georgetown: Argosy.

_____. 1887 "The religion and religious system of our East Indian population". *Daily Chronicle* (5 October).

_____. 1888. *Among the Hindus and Creoles of British Guiana*. London: T. Woolmer.

_____. 1888. *The Colony of British Guiana and Its Labouring Inhabitants*. London: T. Woolmer.

Brumell, J. [A Landowner]. 1853. *Demerara After Fifteen Years of Freedom*. London: T. Bosworth.

Candler, John. 1964. "Extract from Diary". Edited by Prof. Boromé. *Caribbean Studies* 4.

Clementi, C.C. 1915. *The Chinese in British Guiana*. Georgetown: Argosy.

Comins, D.W.D. 1893. *Notes on Emigration from India to British Guiana*. Calcutta: Bengal Secretariat Press.

Crookall, Lawrence. 1898. *British Guiana: or Work and Wanderings among the Creoles and Coolies, the Africans and Indians of the Wild Country*. London: T. Fisher Unwin.

Crooke, W. 1896. *The Popular Religion and Folk-lore of Northern India*. London: Archibald Constable & Co.

_____. 1896. *The Tribes and Castes of the North-Western Provinces and Oudh*. Calcutta: Central Printing Office.

Cruickshank, J.G. 1916. *Black Talk*. Demerara.

_____. 1917. "Among the 'Aku' (Yoruba) in Canal No.1, West Bank, Demerara River". *Timehri* IV, 3rd ser.

Dalton, Henry. 1855. *The History of British Guiana*. 2 vols. London: Longman, Brown, Green, & Longmans.

Dance, C.D. 1881. *Chapters from a Guianese Log-Book*. Demerara: Royal Gazette.

DesVoeux, George W. 1903. *My Colonial Service in British Guiana*. London: Murray.

_____. 1948. *Experiences of a Demerara Magistrate, 1863-1869*. Edited by V. Roth. Georgetown: Daily Chronicle.

Dubois, Jean Antoine. 1817. *Descriptions of the character, manners and customs of the people of India; and of their institutions, religious and civil*. London.

_____. 1906. *Hindu Manners, Customs and Ceremonies*. Oxford: Clarendon Press.

Duff, R. 1866. *British Guiana: Being Notes on a Few of the Natural Productions, Industrial Occupations and Social Institutions*. Glasgow: Thomas Murray & Sons.

Eves, Charles W. 1889. *The West Indies*. London: Sampson Low, Marston, Searle, & Rivington.

Farrar, Thomas. 1892. *Notes of the History of the Church in Guiana*. New Amsterdam: W. MacDonald.

Gerard, John. 1899-1900. "Inter-Guianese" (ms.). Society of Jesus, London.

Grierson, George A. 1883. *Report on Colonial Emigration from the Bengal Residency*. Calcutta (official publication).

Hardy, Alfred. 1913. *Life and Adventure in British Guiana*. London: Epworth Press.

Heatley, J.A. 1891. *A Visit to the West Indies*. Alnwick, Northumberland: H.H. Blair.

Hewick, J.E. 1911. "Our people". *Timehri* I.

Im Thurn, Everard. 1882. "Occasional notes". *Timehri* I.

Jenkins, Edward. 1871. *The Coolie: His Rights and Wrongs*. London: Strahan & Co.

Josa, F.P. Luigi. 1912 and 1913. "The Hindus in the West Indies". *Timehri* II; III, no. 1.

_____. 1915. "The languages of India". *Timehri* III, no. 2.

Kirke, Henry. 1898. *Twenty-five Years in British Guiana*. London: Sampson Low & Co.

Luckhoo, E.A. 1912. "East Indians in British Guiana". *Timehri* II.

MacArthur, J. Sidney. 1912. "Our people". *Timehri*, II.

Marrat, Jabez. 1881. *In the Tropics*. London: Wesleyan Conference Office.

Moore, J.R. 1874. *A Handbook of the Causes of Non-Success and Degradation of the Negro Race in British Guiana*. Demerara: A.C. Taylor.

Pearson, J.G. 1886. "Guiana's alien peasantry". *Argosy* (16 January).

_____, ed. 1890. *New Overseer's Manual: or the Reason Why of Julius Jugler*. Georgetown: Argosy.

_____. 1897. "The life history of an East Indian". *Timehri* 10.

Premium, Barton. 1850. *Eight Years in British Guiana, 1840-48*. London: Longman, Brown, Green & Longmans.

Rodway, James. 1885. "On some of the domestic medicines used in Guiana". *Timehri* 4.

_____. 1893. "Occasional notes: negro folklore". *Timehri* 7.

_____. 1918. "Occasional notes: Surinam folk tales". *Timehri* V.

Sawtell, W. Arthur. 1897. "First impressions of the colony". *Echo*.

Schomburgk, Richard. 1922. *Travels in British Guiana, 1840-1844*. 2 vols. Translated by W.E. Roth. Georgetown: Daily Chronicle.

Scoles, Ignatius. 1885. *Sketches of African and Indian Life in British Guiana*. Demerara: Argosy.

Sloman, E. 1887. "Coolie missions in British Guiana". *West India Quarterly* 3.

Speirs, James. 1902. *The Proverbs of British Guiana*. Demerara: Argosy.

Swinton, Capt., and Mrs., 1859. *Journal of a Voyage with Coolie Emigrants from Calcutta to Trinidad*. Edited by J. Carlisle. London: Alfred W. Bennett.

Thorne, J.T. 1899. *Some Haphazard Notes of a Forty-Two Years' Residence in British Guiana*. Demerara: Argosy.

Trollope, Anthony. [1860] 1968. *The West Indies and the Spanish Main*. Reprint, London: Dawsons.

Van Sertima, J. 1897. *Among the Common People of British Guiana*. Georgetown: C.K. Jardine.

_____. 1899. *Scenes and Sketches of Demerara Life*. Georgetown: C.K. Jardine.

_____. 1905. *The Creole Tongue of British Guiana*. New Amsterdam: Berbice Gazette.

Wallbridge, J.S. 1911. "Fifty years recollections of British Guiana". *Timehri* I.

"X". 1919. "Stray notes on obeah". *Timehri* VI.

Modern

Abrams, O. 1970. *Guyana Metagee*. Demerara.

Adamson, Alan H. 1972. *Sugar Without Slaves: The Political Economy of British Guiana, 1838-1904*. New Haven: Yale University Press.

Alleyne, Mervyn. 1988. *Roots of Jamaican Culture*. London: Pluto Press.

Andrews, Donna T. 1980. "The code of honour and its critics: the opposition to duelling in England, 1700-1850". *Social History* 5.

Angrosino, M.V. 1976. "Sexual politics in the East Indian family in Trinidad. *Caribbean Studies* 16.

Anon. 1987. "Chinese new year galas". *Beijing Review* 30.

Appiah, Anthony. 1992. *In my Father's House: Africa in the Philosophy of Culture.* N.Y.: O.U.P.

Bailey, Peter. 1977. "A mingled mass of perfectly legitimate pleasures: the Victorian middle class and the problem of leisure". *Victorian Studies* 21.

_____. 1987. *Leisure and Class in Victorian England: Rational Recreation and the Contest for Control, 1830-1885.* London: Methuen.

Baksh, Ishmael. 1979. "Stereotypes of Negroes and East Indians in Trinidad: a re-examination". *Caribbean Studies* 25.

Barber, Karin. 1987. "Popular arts in Africa". *African Studies Review* 30.

Bastide, Roger. 1972. *African Civilizations in the New World.* N.Y.: Harper and Row.

Beattie, John, & John Middleton, eds. 1969. *Spirit Mediumship and Society in Africa.* London: Routledge and Kegan Paul.

Beckles, Hilary McD. 1993. "The making of the first 'West Indian' teams, 1886-1906" (unpublished paper). Barbados.

Bell, R. 1970. "Marriage and family differences among lower class Negro and East Indian women in Trinidad". *Race* 12, no. 1.

Benedict, Burton. 1961. *Indians in a Plural Society.* London: H.M.S.O.

Bently, Gerald. 1967. *Some Preliminary Observations on the Chinese in Trinidad.* Montreal: McGill.

Berger, Mark T. 1988. "Imperialism and sexual exploitation: a response to Ronald Hyam's 'Empire and sexual opportunity'". *Journal of Imperial and Commonwealth History* 17.

Berreman, G.D. 1960. "Caste in India and the United States". *American Journal of Sociology* 66.

Berridge, Virginia. 1978. "Victorian opium eating: responses to opiate use in nineteenth-century England". *Victorian Studies* 21, no. 4.

Béteille, André. 1969. *Caste, Class and Power.* Berkeley: University of California Press.

Bhattacharyya, Narendra Nath. 1975. *Ancient Indian Rituals and their Social Contents.* London: Curzon Press.

Bisnauth, Dale. 1989. *History of Religions in the Caribbean.* Kingston: Kingston Publishers.

_____. 1977. "The East Indian immigrant society in British Guiana, 1891-1930". Ph.D. thesis, University of the West Indies.

Bissoondoyal, U. 1984. *Indians Overseas: The Mauritian Experience.* Moka, Mauritius: Mahatma Gandhi Institute.

Bodde, Derk. 1957. *China's Cultural Tradition, What and Whither?* N. Y: Rinehart.

Boodhoo, Ken. 1981. "East Indian labourers". In *Readings in Caribbean History and Economics,* edited by Roberta M. Delson. New York: Gordon & Breach.

Bose, Hirmal E. 1967. *Culture and Society in India.* Bombay: Asia Pub. Ho.

Bradlow, Edna. 1986. "The culture of a colonial elite: the Cape of Good Hope in the 1850s". *Victorian Studies* 29.

Brathwaite, Edward. 1970. *Folk Culture of the Slaves in Jamaica.* London: New Beacon Books.

_____. 1971. *The Development of Creole Society in Jamaica 1770-1820.* Oxford: Clarendon Press.

_____. 1974. *Contradictory Omens: Cultural Diversity and Integration in the Caribbean*. Kingston: Savacou.

Braithwaite, L. 1953. "Social stratification in Trinidad". *Social & Economic Studies* 2.

_____. 1960. "Social stratification and cultural pluralism". In *Social and Cultural Pluralism in the Caribbean*, edited by V. Rubin. Annals of the New York Academy of Sciences. Vol. 83. Art 5.

Brereton, Bridget. 1979. *Race Relations in Colonial Trinidad, 1870-1900*. Cambridge: C.U.P.

Brenneis, Donald. 1987. "Talk and transformation". *Man* 22.

Bryan, Patrick. 1991. *The Jamaican People 1880-1902*. London: Macmillan.

Bushaway, Bob. 1982. *By Rite; Custom, Ceremony and Community in England 1700-1880*. London: Junction Books.

Cameron, Norman E. 1951. *A History of the Queen's College of British Guiana*. Georgetown: F.H. Persick.

Cannadine, David. 1983. "The context, performance and meaning of ritual: the British monarchy and the 'invention of tradition', c. 1820-1977". In *The Invention of Tradition*, edited by E. Hobsbawm and T. Ranger. Cambridge: CUP.

Chan, Anthony B. 1982. "Chinese bachelor workers in nineteenth-century Canada". *Ethnic and Racial Studies* 5.

_____. 1983. *Gold Mountain: The Chinese in the New World*. Vancouver: New Star Books.

Chandler, Timothy J.L. 1991. "Games at Oxbridge and the public schools, 1830-80: the diffusion of an innovation". *International Journal of the History of Sport* 8.

Chaudhury, R.C. Roy. 1966. *Bihar District Gazetteers: Shahabad*. Patna: Govt. of Bihar.

Chevannes, Barry. 1988. "Race and culture in Jamaica". *World Marxist Review* 31.

Ching, Annette M.T. 1985. "Ethnicity reconsidered with reference to sugar and society in Trinidad". D.Phil. thesis, University of Sussex.

Ching-Hwang, Yen. 1981. "Early Chinese clan organizations in Singapore and Malaya, 1819-1911". *Journal of Southeast Asian Studies* XII.

Clarke, Colin, Ceri Peach, & Steven Vertovec, eds. 1990. *South Asians Overseas*. Cambridge, C.U.P.

Cohn, Bernard S. 1983. "Representing authority in Victorian India" In *The Invention of Tradition*, edited by E. Hobsbawm and T. Ranger. Cambridge: CUP.

Coughlin, R.J. 1955. "The Chinese in Bangkok". *American Sociological Review* 20.

Cronin, Kathryn. 1982. *Colonial Casualties: Chinese in Early Victoria*. Melbourne: MUP.

Cross, M. 1968. "Cultural pluralism and sociological theory: a critique and reevaluation". *Social & Economic Studies* 17.

_____.1978. "Colonialism and ethnicity". *Ethnic and Racial Studies* 1.

Crissman, L.W. 1967. "The segmentary structure of urban overseas Chinese communities". *Man* 2.

Curtin, P.D. 1970. *Two Jamaicas: The Role of Ideas in a Tropical Colony, 1830-1865*. N.Y.: Harvard University Press.

Cutileiro, Jose. 1971. *A Portuguese Rural Society*. Oxford: Clarendon Press.

Dabydeen, D., and B. Samaroo, eds. 1987. *India in the Caribbean*. London: Hansib.

Davids, Leo. 1964. "The East Indian family overseas", *Social and Economic Studies* 13.

Despres, Leo, A. 1967. *Cultural Pluralism and Nationalist Politics in British Guiana*. Chicago: Rand McNally.

Devonish, Hubert. 1991. "Nature of African-East Indian contact in 19th century Guyana: the linguistic evidence". Seminar paper, Department of History, UWI, Mona.

Dodd, David J. 1976. "The well-springs of violence: some historical notes on East Indian criminality in Guyana". *Caribbean Issues* 2, no. 3.

Dube, S.C. 1955. *Indian Village*. London. Routledge & Kegan Paul.

Durbin, Mridula Adenwala. 1973. "Formal changes in Trinidad Hindi as a result of language adaptation". *American Anthropologist* 75.

Eberhard, Wolfram. 1952. *Chinese Festivals*. N.Y.: H. Schuman.

Edun, E. Hossen. 1984. "Tajjia (Tazzia)". In *Indians Overseas: The MauritianExperience*, edited by U. Bissoondoyal. Moka, Mauritius: Mahatma Gandhi Institute.

Ehrlich, Allen S. 1971. "History, ecology and demography in the British Caribbean: an analysis of East Indian ethnicity". *South Western Journal of Anthropology* 27.

Emmer, Pieter. 1986. "The great escape: the migration of female indentured servants from British India to Surinam, 1873-1916". In *Abolition and Its Aftermath*, edited by P.D. Richardson. London: Frank Cass.

_____. 1987. "The position of Indian women in Surinam". *Boletín de Estudios Latinoamericanos y del Caribe* 43 (Dec).

Fallers, L.A., ed. 1967. *Immigrants and Associations*. The Hague: Mouton.

Field, Margaret J. 1961. *Religion and Medicine of the Ga People*. Accra: Presbyterian Book Depot.

Firth, R., and B. Yamey, eds. 1964. *Capital Saving and Credit in Peasant Societies*. Chicago: Aldine Pub. Co.

Foley, Tricia. 1993. *The Romance of Colonial Style*. London: Thames & Hudson.

Fox, Richard. 1969. "Varna schemes and ideological integration in Indian society". *Comparative Studies in Society and History* 11.

Freedman, M. 1960. "Immigrants and associations: Chinese in 19th century Singapore". *Comparative Studies in Society and History* 3.

_____. 1961. "Overseas Chinese associations: a comment". *Comparative Studies in Society and History* 3.

_____. 1962. "Chinese kinship and marriage in Singapore". *Journal of Southeast Asian History* 3.

Freilich, M. 1960. "Cultural diversity among Trinidian peasants". Ph.D. diss., Colombia Univ.

_____. 1961. "Serial polygyny, negro peasants, and model analysis". *American Anthropologist* 63.

Fried, Morton H. 1956. "Some observations on the Chinese in British Guiana". *Social and Economic Studies* 5.

Frucht, Richard, ed. 1971. *Black Society in the New World*. N.Y.: Random House.

Gallop, Rodney. 1961. *Portugal: A Book of Folkways*. Cambridge: The University Press.

Gambhir, Surendra K. 1981. "The East Indian speech community in Guyana: a sociolinguistic study with special reference to Koine formation". Ph.D. diss., University of Pennsylvania.

Gardiner, Juliet. 1988. *What is History Today . . . ?* New Jersey: Humanities Pr. International.

Ghurye, G.S. 1932. *Caste and Race in India*. London: K. Paul, Trench, Trubner & Co.

Gillion, K.L. 1962. *Fiji's Indian Migrants: A History to the End of Indenture in 1920*. Melbourne: OUP.

Goldstein, Rhoda, ed. 1971. *Black Life and Culture in the United States*. N.Y.: Crowell.

Gosling, P.L.A., & L.Y.C. Lim, eds. 1983. *The Chinese in Southeast Asia*. 2 vols. Singapore: Maruzen Asia.

Gould, Harold A. 1987. *The Hindu Caste System: The Sacralization of a Social Order*. Delhi: Chanakya Pubs.

Green, Benny. 1988. *A History of Cricket*. London: Barrie & Jenkins.

Green, H. 1964. "Socialization values in the Negro and East Indian sub-cultures of Trinidad". Ph.D. diss., University of Connecticut.

Greenfield, Sidney. 1962. "Households, families, and kinships systems in the West Indies". *Anthropological Quarterly* 35.

Gungwu, Wang. 1981. "Southeast Asian *Hua-ch'iao* in Chinese history-writing". *Journal of Southeast Asian Studies* XII.

Gunputh, Veena Devi. 1984. "Sex disproportion among Indian immigrants". In *Indians Overseas: The Mauritian Experience*, edited by U. Bissoondoyal. Moka, Mauritius: Mahatma Gandhi Institute.

Hadfield, John. 1987. *Victorian Delights: Reflections of Taste in the Nineteenth Century*. N.Y.: Meredith Press.

Hall, Stuart. 1977. "Pluralism, race and class in Caribbean society". In *Race and Class in Post-colonial Society*, edited by UNESCO. Paris: UNESCO.

Haraksingh, Kusha R. 1988. "Structure, process and Indian culture in Trinidad". *Immigrants and Minorities* 7.

Herskovits, Melville J. 1937. *Life in a Haitian Valley*. N.Y.: A. Knopf.

———. 1941. *The Myth of the Negro Past*. N.Y.: Harper & bros.

———. 1947. *Trinidad Village*. N.Y.: A. Knopf.

Hiatt, L.R., and C. Jayawardena. 1971. *Anthropology in Oceania*. Sydney: Augus and Robertson.

Higman, B.W. 1984. "Terms of kin in the British West Indian slave community: differing perceptions of masters and slaves". In *Kinship Ideology and Practice in Latin America*, edited by Raymond T. Smith. Chapel Hill: Univ. of North Carolina Press.

Hobsbawm, Eric. 1983. "Introduction: inventing traditions". In *The Invention of Tradition*, edited by E. Hobsbawm and T. Ranger. Cambridge: CUP.

Hobsbawm, Eric, & Terence Ranger, eds. 1983. *The Invention of Tradition*. Cambridge: CUP.

Hoefte, Rosemarijn. 1987. "Female indentured labor in Suriname: for better of for worse?". *Boletín de Estudios Latinoamericanos y del Caribe* 42.

———. 1987. "The position of female British Indian and Javanese contract laborers in Suriname: a last word". *Boletín de Estudios Lationamericanos y del Caribe* 43 (Dec).

Holt, Richard. 1989. *Sport and the British: A Modern History*. Oxford: OUP.

Hutton, J.H. 1961. *Caste in India: Its Nature, Function, and Origin*. London: O.U.P.

Hyam, Ronald. 1986. "Empire and sexual opportunity". *Journal of Imperial and Commonwealth History* 14.

———. 1988. " 'Imperialism and sexual exploitation': a reply". *Journal of Imperial and Commonwealth History* 17.

———. 1990. *Empire and Sexuality: The British Experience*. Manchester: MUP.

Jain, Ravindra K. 1986. "Freedom denied? Indian women and indenturship". *Economic and Political Weekly* 21.

———. 1988. "Overseas Indians in Malaysia and the Caribbean: comparative notes". *Immigrants and Minorities* 7.

Jayawardena, C. 1960. "Marital stability in two Guianese sugar estates". *Social and Economic Studies* 9.

_____. 1966. "Religious belief and social change: aspects of development of Hinduism in British Guiana". *Comparative Studies in Society and History* 8.

_____. 1971. "The disintegration of caste in Fiji Indian rural society". In *Anthropology in Oceania*, edited by L. R. Hiatt and C. Jayawardena, Sydney: Angus and Robertson.

_____. 1980. "Culture and ethnicity in Guyana and Fiji". *Man* (ns) 15.

Jayawardena, C., & R. T. Smith. 1958. "Hindu marriage customs in British Guiana". *Social and Economic Studies* 7.

_____. 1964. "Marriage and the family amongst East Indians in British Guiana". *Social and Economic Studies* 13, no. 3.

Jha, J.C. 1974. "Indian heritage in Trinidad (West Indies)". *Eastern Anthropologist* 27.

_____. 1982. "The background of the legislation of non-Christian marriages in Trinidad and Tobago". In *East Indians in the Caribbean*, edited by B. Brereton and W. Dookeran. New York: Kraus.

Johnson, Howard. 1987. "The Chinese in Trinidad in the late nineteenth century". *Ethnic and Racial Studies* 10.

_____, ed. 1988. *After the Crossing: Immigrants and Minorities in Caribbean Creole Society*. London: Frank Cass.

Kayongo-Male, Diane. 1984. *The Sociology of the African Family*. London: Longman.

Kelly, John D. 1988. "From Holi to Diwali in Fiji: an essay on ritual and history". *Man*. (ns) 23.

Klass, Morton. 1961. *East Indians in Trinidad*. N.Y.: Columbia University Press.

Kuper, L., and M.G. Smith. 1969. *Pluralism in Africa*. Berkeley: Univ. of Calif. Press.

Kwok Crawford, Marlene. 1989. *Scenes from the Histroy of the Chinese in Guyana*. Georgetown: the author.

Laurence, K.O. 1965. "The establishment of the Portugese community in British Guiana". *Jamaica Historical Review* 5, no. 2.

Lasdun, Susan. 1981. *Victorians at Home*. London: Weidenfeld & Nicolson.

Leach, E.R., ed. 1960. *Aspects of Caste in South India, Ceylon and North-West Pakistan*. Cambridge: C.U.P.

Lemon, Anthony. 1980. "The Indian communities of East Africa and the Caribbean". In *Studies in Overseas Settlement and Population*, edited by A. Lemon and N. Pollock. London: Longman.

Lewis, Oscar. 1958. *Village Life in Northern India*. Illinois: University of Illinois Press.

Lewis, S., and T.G. Mathews. 1967. *Caribbean Integration*. Univ. of Puerto Rico: Institute of Caribbean Studies.

Levy, J. 1986. "The economic role of the Chinese in Jamaica: the grocery retail trade". *Jamaica Historical Review* 15.

Lian, Kwen Fee. 1988. "The sociopolitical process of identity formation in an ethnic community: the Chinese in New Zealand". *Ethnic and Racial Studies* 11.

Lind, Andrew W. 1958. "Adjustment patterns among the Jamaican Chinese". *Social and Economic Studies* 7, no. 2.

Look Lai, Walton. 1993. *Indentured Labor, Caribbean Sugar: Chinese and Indian Migrants to the British West Indies, 1838-1918*. Baltimore: Johns Hopkins U.P.

Lowerson, John & John Myerscough. 1977. *Time to Spare in Victorian England*. Hassocks. Harvester Press.

Lucas, J. 1948. *The Religion of the Yorubas*. Lagos: C.M.S. Bookshop.

Lyman, S.M. 1974. *Chinese Americans.* N.Y.: Random House.

Ly-Tio-Fane Pineo, Huguette. 1985. *Chinese Diaspora in Western Indian Ocean.* Mauritius: Chinese Catholic Mission.

MacDonald, J.S., & L.D. MacDonald. 1973. "Transformation of African and Indian family traditions in the southern Caribbean". *Comparative Studies in Society and History* 15.

MacKenzie, J.M. 1986. *Imperialism and Popular Culture.* Manchester: M.U.P.

McCrone, Kathleen E. 1984. "Play up! play up! and play the game! Sport at the late Victorian Girls' Public School". *Journal of British Studies* 23.

Mangan, J.A. 1986. *The Games Ethic and Imperialism.* London: Viking.

_____. 1987. *Pleasure, Profit and Proselytism: British Culture and Sport at Home and Abroad, 1700-1914.* London: Frank Cass.

_____. 1989. "The social construction of Victorian femininity: emancipation, education and exercise". *International Journal of the History of Sport* 6.

Mangru, Basdeo. 1983. "Disparity in Bengal and Madras emigration to British Guiana in the nineteenth century". *Revista Interamericana* 13.

_____. 1987 (a). *Benevolent Neutrality.* London: Hansib.

_____. 1987 (b). "The sex-ratio disparity and its consequences under the indenture in British Guiana". In *India in the Caribbean*, edited by D. Dabydeen and B. Samaroo. London: Hansib.

_____. 1993. *Indenture and Abolition: Sacrifice and Survival on the Guyanese Sugar Plantations.* Toronto: Tsar Publns.

Mayer, Adrian. 1960. *Caste and Kinship in Central India.* Berkeley: Univ. of California Press.

Mbiti, John. 1971. *African Religions and Philosophy.* London: Heinemann.

McClendon, W.H. 1983. "The foundations of Black culture". *The Black Scholar* 14.

McClenon, James. 1990. "Chinese and American anomalous experiences: the role of religiosity". *Sociological Analysis* 51.

Menezes, M.N. 1986. *Scenes from the History of the Portuguese in Guyana.* London:. Sr M.N. Menezes, R.S.M.

_____. 1988. "The Madeiran Portuguese and the establishment of the Catholic church in British Guiana, 1835-98". *Immigrants and Minorities* 7.

Mischel, W., & F. Mischel. 1958. "Psychological aspects of spirit possession". *American Anthropologist* 60.

Moore, Brian L. 1975. "The social impact of Portuguese immigration into British Guiana after emancipation". *Boletín de Estudios Latinoamericianos y del Caribe*, no. 19: 5-6

_____. 1977. "The retention of caste notions mong the Indian immigrants in British Guiana during the nineteenth century". *Comparative Studies in Society and History* 19.

_____. 1984. "Sex and marriage among Indian immigrants in British Guiana during the nineteenth century". Presented at the Third Conference of East Indians in the Caribbean, UWI, St. Augustine, Trinidad.

_____. 1987. *Race, Power and Social Segmentation in Colonial Society: Guyana after Slavery 1839-1891.* N.Y.: Gordon and Breach.

_____. 1988. "The settlement of Chinese in Guyana in the nineteenth century". *Immigrants and Minorities* 7.

_____. 1991. "Mating and gender relations among Indians in nineteenth century Guyana". *Guyana Historical Journal* 3.

Moore, Robert J. 1970. "East Indians and Negroes in British Guiana, 1838-1880". D. Phil. thesis, Sussex Univ.

Morris, H.S. 1957. "Communal rivalry among Indians in Uganda". *British Journal of Sociology* 8.

_____. 1956. "Indians in East Africa: a study in a plural society". *British Journal of Sociology* 7.

Mosher, Steven W. 1983. *Broken Earth: the Rural Chinese*. N.Y.: Free Press.

Nadel, S.F. 1954. *Nupe Religion*. London: Routledge & Kegan Paul.

Nath, Dwarka. 1950. *A History of the Indians in British Guiana*. London: Nelson.

Nelson, Donna. 1973. "Caste hierarchy and competition in an overseas Indian community". *Contributions to Indian Sociology* (n.s.) 7.

Nevadomsky, Joseph. 1980. "Changes in Hindu institutions in an alien environment". *Eastern Anthropologist* 33.

_____. 1982. "Social change and the East Indian in rural Trinidad: a critique of methodologies". *Social and Economic Studies* 31.

_____. 1983. "Changes over time and space in the East Indian family in Trinidad". In *Overseas Indians*, edited by George Kurian and Ram P. Srivastava. New Delhi: Vikas.

Niehoff, Arthur. 1959. "The survival of Hindu institutions in an alien environment". *Eastern Anthropologist* 12.

_____. 1960. *East Indians in the West Indies*. Milwaukee: Milwaukee Public Museum.

_____. 1967. "The function of caste among Indians of the Oropuche Lagoon". In *Caste in Overseas Indian Communities*, edited by Barton M. Schwartz. San Francisco: Chandler.

Park, Jihang. 1989. "Sport, dress reform and the emancipation of women in Victorian England: a reappraisal". *International Journal of the History of Sport* 6.

Parrinder, G. 1949. *West African Religion*. London: Epworth Press.

_____. 1951. *West African Psychology*. London: Lutterworth Press.

_____. 1963. *Witchcraft: European and African*. N.Y.: Barnes & Noble.

_____. 1969. *Religion in Africa*. London: Penguin.

Patterson, Orlando. 1967. *The Sociology of Slavery*. London: MacGibbon and Kee.

_____. 1969. "The ritual of cricket". *Jamaica Journal* 3.

Ramdin, Suchita. 1984. "Folk religion of the Hindu immigrants—a case study". In *Indians Overseas: The Mauritian Experience*, edited by U. Bissoondoyal. Moka, Mauritius: Mahatma Gandhi Institute.

Ramyead, Lutchmee P. 1984. "Indian languages in Mauritius: a perspective". In *Indians Overseas: The Mauritian Experience*, ediited by U. Bissoondoyal. Mauritius: Mahatma Ghandi Institute.

Ranger, Terrence. 1983. "The invention of tradition in colonial Africa". In *The Invention of Tradition*, edited by E. Hobsbawm and T. Ranger. Cambridge: CUP.

Reddock, Rhoda. 1985. "Freedom denied: Indian women and indentureship in Trinidad and Tobago, 1845-1917". *Economic and Political Weekly* 20.

Richards, J., & M. Wong. 1990. *Statistics of West Indies Cricket 1865-1989*. Kingston: Heinemann.

Richardson, David P., ed. 1985. *Abolition and its Aftermath: The Historical Context 1790-1916*. London: Frank Cass.

Rickford, John. 1987. *Dimensions of a Creole Continuum: History, Texts and Linguistic Analysis of Guyanese Creole*. Stanford: S.U.P.

Rodney, Walter. 1981. *A History of the Guyanese Working People, 1881-1905*. Baltimore: Johns Hopkins U.P.

Roberts G.W., and M.A. Johnson. 1974. "Factors involved in immigration and movements in the working force of British Guiana in the nineteenth century". *Social & Economic Studies* 23, no. 1.

Rogers, Charles. 1971. *Social Life in Scotland, from Early to Recent Times*. Port Washington, N.Y.: Kennikat Press.

Rubenstein, David. 1977. "Cycling in the 1890s". *Victorian Studies* 21.

Rubin, V., ed. 1960. *Social and Cultural Pluralism in the Caribbean*. Annals of the New York Academy of Sciences. Vol. 83, art.5.

Ruhoman, Peter. 1947. *Centenary History of the East Indians in British Guiana, 1838-1938*. Georgetown: Daily Chronicle.

Sakai, Tadao. 1981. "Some aspects of Chinese religious practices and customs in Malaysia and Singapore". *Journal of Southeast Asian Studies* XII.

Sandiford, Keith A.P. 1981. "The Victorians at play: problems in historiographical methodology". *Journal of Social History* 15.

_____. 1983. "Cricket and the Victorian society". *Journal of Social History* 17.

Sargent, Carolyn Fishel. 1988. "Born to die: witchcraft and infanticide in Bariba culture". *Ethnology* 27.

Schermerhorn, R.A. 1970. *Comparative Ethnic Relations: A Framework for Theory and Research*. N.Y.: Random House.

Schuler, M. 1980. *"Alas, Alas, Kongo": A Social History of Indentured African Immigration into Jamaica*. Baltimore: Johns Hopkins Univ. Press.

Schwartz, Barton M. 1963. "The dissolution of caste in Trinidad". Ph.D. diss., U.C.L.A.

_____. 1964 (a). "Caste and endogamy in Trinidad". *South Western Journal of Anthropology* 20.

_____.1964 (b). "Ritual aspects of caste in Trinidad". *Anthropological Quarterly* 37, no. 1.

_____. 1965. "Patterns of East Indian family organization in Trinidad". *Caribbean Studies* 5.

_____. 1967 (a). "Differential socio-religious adaptation". *Social and Economic Studies* 16.

_____. ed. 1967 (b). *Caste in Overseas Indian Communities*. San Francisco: Chandler. See, Chinben. 1981. "Chinese clanship in the Philippine setting". *Journal of Southeast Asian Studies* XII.

Shaw, Thomas A. 1985. "To be or not to be Chinese: differential expressions of Chinese culture and solidarity in the British West Indies". *Ethnic Groups* 6.

Shepherd, Verene A. 1994. *Transients to Settlers: The Experience of Indians in Jamaica 1845-1950*. Leeds: Peepal Tree Press.

Simpson, G. E. 1955. "Political cultism in West Kingston, Jamaica". *Social and Economic Studies* 4.

_____. 1956. "Jamaican revival cults". *Social and Economic Studies* 5.

_____. 1962 (a). "Folk medicine in Trinidad". *Journal of American Folklore* 75.

_____. 1962 (b). "The Shango cult in Nigeria and Trinidad". *American Anthropologist* 64.

_____. 1964. "The acculturative process in Trinidadian Shango". *Anthropological Quarterly* 37.

Singer, P., & E. Araneta. 1967. "Hinduism and creolization in Guyana: the plural society and basic personality". *Social and Economic Studies* 16.

Singh, Kelvin. 1988. *Bloodstained Tombs: the Muharram Massacre 1884*. London: Macmillan.

Sinha, Raghuvir. 1977. *Religion and Culture of North-eastern India*. New Delhi: Abhinov Pubs.

Smith, M.G. 1965. *The Plural Society in the British West Indies*. Berkeley: Univ. of Calif. Press.

_____. 1984. *Culture, Race and Class in the Commonwealth Caribbean.* Kingston: Univ. of the West Indies.

Smith, R.T. 1956. *The Negro Family in British Guiana.* London: Rontledge and Kegan Paul.

_____. 1959 (a). "Family structure and plantation systems of the New World". In *Plantation Systems of the New World*, edited by S.W. Mintz. Social Science Monographs VII. Washington: Pan American Union.

_____. 1959 (b). "Some social characteristics of Indian immigrants to British Guiana". *Population Studies* 13.

_____. 1960. "The family in the Caribbean". *Caribbean Studies: A Symposium*, edited by V. Rubin. Seattle: Univ. of Washington.

_____. 1963. "Culture and social structure in the Caribbean: some recent work on family and kinship studies". *Comparative Studies in Society and History* 6.

_____. 1964. "Ethnic difference and peasant economy in British Guiana". In *Capital, Saving and Credit in Peasant Societies*, edited by R. Firth and B. Yamey. Chicago: Aldine Pub. Co.

_____. 1967. "Social stratification, cultural pluralism and integration in West Indian societies". In *Caribbean Integration*, edited by S. Lewis and T.G. Mathews. Univ. of Puerto Rico: Institute of Caribbean Studies.

_____. 1978. "The family and the modern world system: some observations from the Caribbean". *Journal of Family History* 3.

_____. 1982. "Family, social change, and social policy in the West Indies". *Nieuwe West-Indische Gids* 56.

_____. 1984. *Kinship, Ideology and Practice in Latin America.* Chapel Hill: University of Carolina Press.

_____. 1988. *Kinship and Class in the West Indies: A Genealogical Study of Jamaica and Guyana.* Cambridge: C.U.P.

Smith, R.T., and Chandra Jayawardena. 1967. "Caste and social status among the Indians of Guyana". In *Caste in Overseas Indian Communities*, edited by Barton M. Schwartz. San Francisco: Chandler.

Smith, Robert Jack. 1964. "Muslim East Indians in Trinidad: retention of ethnic identity under acculturative conditions". Ph.D. diss., U. of Penn.

Solien, Nancie. 1960. "Household and family in the Caribbean". *Social and Economic Studies* 9.

Sow, Alpha I., et al. 1979. *Introduction to African Culture: General Aspects.* Paris: UNESCO.

Speckmann, Johan D. 1965. *Marriage and Kinship among the Indians in Surinam.* Assen: van Gorcum & Co.

_____. 1967. "The caste system and the Hindustani group in Surinam". In *Caste in Overseas Indian Communities*, edited by Barton M. Schwartz. San Francisco: Chandler.

Srinivas, M.N. 1952. *Religion and Society among the Coorgs of South India.* Oxford: Clarendon Press.

Stephens, Thomas M. 1987. "The language of ethnicity and self-identity in American Spanish and Brazilian Portuguese". *Ethnic and Racial Studies* 12.

Stewart, R.J. 1992. *Religion and Society in Post-emancipation Jamaica.* Knoxville: Univ. of Tenn. Press.

Stoddart, Brian. 1987. "Cricket, social formation and cultural continuity in Barbados: a preliminary ethnohistory". *Journal of Sport History* 14, no. 1.

_____. 1988. "Sport, cultural imperialism, and colonial response in the British empire". *Comparative Studies in Society and History* 30.

Stoler, Ann Laura. 1989. "Rethinking colonial categories: European communities and the boundaries of rule". *Comparative Studies in Society and History* 31.

Storch, Robert D. 1982. *Popular Culture and Custom in Nineteenth Century England*. London: Croom Helm.

Stover, Leon E. 1976. *China: An Anthropological Perspective*. Pacific Palisades, Calif.: Goodyear Pub. Co.

Survadinata, Leo. 1987. "Ethnic Chinese in Southeast Asia: problems and prospects". *Journal of International Affairs* 41.

Thapar, Romesh. 1977. *Tribe, Caste and Religion in India*. Columbus, Mo.: Sth Asia Bks.

Tikasingh, Gerad. 1980. "Social change in the emerging East Indian community in the late 19th century". *Journal of Caribbean Studies* 1.

Tinker, H. 1974. *A New System of Slavery: The Export of Indian Labour Overseas 1830-1920*. Oxford: O.U.P.

Topley, M. 1967. "The emergence and social function of Chinese religious associations in Singapore". *Comparative Studies in Society and History* 3. (Published 1967. In *Immigrants and Associations*, edited by L.A. Fallers. The Hague: Mouton.)

Trotman, David Vincent. 1986. *Crime in Trinidad: Conflict and Control in a Plantation Society, 1838-1900*. Knoxville: U.T.P.

Trouillot, Michel-Rolph. 1987. "The lost continent of the Americas: recent works on Afro-America and the Caribbean". (Review article) *Latin American Research Review* 24.

Tsai, Shih-Shan Henry. 1986. *The Chinese Experience in America*. Bloomington/Indianapolis: Indiana U.P.

van den Berghe, Pierre. 1967. *Race and Racism*. New York: Wiley.

van den Berghe, Pierre. 1969. "Pluralism and the polity: a theoretical exploration". In *Pluralism in Africa*, edited by L. Kuper and M.G. Smith. Berkeley: Univ. of Calif. Press.

van Lier, R.A.J. 1950. *The Development and Nature of Society in the West Indies*. Amsterdam: Koninklijk Instit. voor de Tropen.

Vatuk, Ved P. 1965. "Craving for a child in the folksongs of East Indians in British Guiana". *Journal of the Folklore Institute* 2.

Veer, Peter van der, & Steven Vertovec. 1991. "Brahamanism abroad: on Caribbean Hinduism as an ethnic religion". *Ethnology* xxx, no.2.

Vertovec, Steven. 1992. *Hindu Trinidad: Religion, Ethnicity and Socio-economic Change*. London: Macmillan Caribbean.

Weightman, George. 1954. "Community organization of Chinese living in Manila". *Philippine Social Sciences and Humanities Review* 29.

Weinstein, E.A. 1962. *Cultural Aspects of Delusion: A Psychiatric Study of the Virgin Islands*. N.Y.: Free Press of Glencoe.

White, Naomi Rosh. 1978. "Ethnicity, culture and cultural pluralism". *Ethnic and Racial Studies* 1.

Williams, Brackette F. 1991. *Stains On my Name, War in my Veins: Guyana and the Politics of Cultural Struggle*. Durham: Duke Univ. Press.

Wood, Donald. 1968. *Trinidad in Transition: The Years after Slavery*. London: O.U.P.

Yang, M.C. 1948. *A Chinese Village*. London: Kegan Paul, Trench, Trubner.

INDEX

Abortions: and obeahmen, 143
Accommodation: Chinese, 266-267; Creoles, 86-89; elites, 19-24; Indians, 156-160; Portuguese, 242-243
Acculturation: 153, 190, 287, 291; reverse, 53, 101
Adelphi Theatre, 62
Adopi, 148
Africa, West: 95, 112, 150
Africans: 298, 300; cooperative activity, 114; dress, 95, 98; languages, 91-92; names, 94; religion, 138; tribes, 93-94
Akan: 93, 143; names, 94
Amerindians: 7, 100, 101, 118, 153, 247
Anansi: 125-126
Archery: 72
Architecture: Creole, 86-89; elite, 19-24; Indian, 232
Assembly Rooms: 29, 54, 59, 61, 62, 63, 65, 120
Athenaeum Society: 59, 60
Athletics: 80-81
Austin, Bishop William Piercy: 58
Australia: British settlers in, 26,82; Chinese in, 265, 273, 275, 276, 279, 280, 288

Balls: elite, 32, 44, 64-66; Creole, 117, 120-121, 296; fancy dress, 32, 33, 65, 120-121; queen's birthday, 27, 33, 63
Bands: Georgetown Militia, 66, 121, 261; Portuguese, 254, 255, 258, 261; *Primeiro de Dezembro*, 256, 261
Barbadians: 11, 101, 130
Barbados: 29, 31, 74, 76, 78, 130, 170, 307
Bazaars: 62
Belfield: 74, 131
Berbice: 11, 17, 39, 59, 60, 72, 74, 80, 86, 92, 102, 110, 117, 139, 160, 169, 193, 209, 228, 230, 232, 233, 234, 254, 278, 280
Berbice Cricket Club, 79
Berbice (Amateur) Dramatic and Musical Club, 62
Berbice Lawn Tennis Club, 75
Berbice Public Library: 60

Berbice Reading Society: 59-60
Bhaktism: appeal of, in Guyana, 208
Bhojpuri-based culture: emergence of, 205; role of, 240
Bhojpuri language: as form of cultural resistance, 163; as lingua franca of Indian immigrants, 162
Bhose, Rev. E.B.: 227, 228, 232, 234
Bicycle club: formation of, 80
Birth customs: among Creoles, 108-109; among elites, 44-45; among Hindus, 180-181; of Indians, as form of cultural resistance, 182; among Muslims, 181-182
Blacks and coloreds. *See* Creoles
Boat-racing (rowing): 80
Bourda: new elite cricket ground, 79, 80
Brahminization process: in the Caribbean, 214
Braithwaite, Lloyd: 5, 154, 294, 305
Brathwaite, E.K.: 167, 305
Brazil: 138, 147
Britain (British Isles): 17, 22, 26, 27, 29, 31, 33, 34, 40, 47, 54, 59, 68, 70, 73, 75, 80, 81, 82, 96, 115, 127, 132, 204, 288
British. *See* Whites (British)
British Guiana Club, 54
British Guiana Museum Company, 59
British Guiana Mechanics Society, 117
British Isles. *See* Britain
British Medical Association: Guyana branch of, 67
Bronkhurst, H.V.P.: 91, 93, 106, 118, 161, 170, 179, 180, 181, 182, 183, 188, 195, 207, 208, 211, 212, 214, 217, 220, 227, 228, 229, 230, 231, 232, 236
Bunsee, Richard: 170-171

Camoenie Creek: Chinese settlement at, 279
Canada: British settlers, 26, 82; Chinese, 290; cricket, 79
Canadian Presbyterians: 228, 231, 240
Cape Colony (see also South Africa): 26, 30, 57, 58
Caste: 160, 161, 184, 191-199, 203, 272, 302; breakdown in system of, 184, 192,

193; and cultural resistance, 199; features of, in Guyanese society, 197-198; as frame of reference for Indian immigrants, 196-197, 199; passing, 194-195; retention of idea of, by Indians, 191, 195, 198

Charak puja: banning of, 213

Chefa: among Chinese, 290-291

Chess, 81; club in Berbice, 81

Children: abuse of, among Creoles, 107-108; adoption of, among Creoles, 108; Chinese, 271; Creole, 106-109; elites, 44-45; importance of male, to Indians, 179; Indian attitude to female, 180; law regarding maintenance of, 105; Portuguese, 248-249, 251, 252

China: 267, 270, 271, 304; immigrants from, 2, 8, 265, 274; religions, 277-278; drugs, 287

Chinese: 65, 101, 123, 128, 151, 153, 298, 300, 301, 303-304, 306; accommodation of, 266-267; children, 271; accommodation to elite culture, 281; conversion to Christianity, 268, 271, 277, 278-281, 283, 293, 303, 304; construction of churches, 280-281; clans, 273-274, 293; creation of homogenized culture among, 268; cultural adaptation of, 292-293, 304; and cultural integration theory, 294; and desire for language teaching, 282; double family, 273; dress, 268; drinking, 73; education, 281-282; family, 267, 270, 271, 285, 293; female shortage, 8, 265-266, 267, 270-271, 293; festivals, 283-286; food, 268-270, 285; furniture, 271; gambling among, 73, 267, 281, 287, 289-291; gangs, 275-277, 280; *Hakka*, 265, 266, 268, 287, 292; historical data on, 6; homosexuality, 273; horse-racing, 73; language, 278, 280, 282; laws to curb criminal gangs among, 277; lodge, 275; male dominance among, 271; mating with Indian women, 272, 273; mating with Creole women, 271, 272; music, 286-287; names, 280; new year celebration, 281, 284-286, (Creole participation in), 286, 293, 304; and preservation of ethnic identity, 280; occupations, 12, 14; opium, 204, 265, 267, 281, 287-289; *Punti* (Cantonese), 265, 268, 292; retail trade, 293; secret societies, 273, 275-277, 280, 287, 293; stereotypes, 13; theatre, 286

Chinese hell: 276, 289

Christianity: conversion of Chinese, 271, 277-281; conversion of Indians, 226-233; Creoles, 137, 138, 139, 142, 306; and education, 233; reasons for success of, among Chinese, 279-280

Christmas: Chinese, 282; Creole festivities, 122-124; elite fancy dress balls, 65; elite sports, 75; Indians, 199; Portuguese, 253-254

Church: as medium of Euro-Christian values, 125

Church of England: 39, 227

Church of the Sacred Heart: establishment of, 250

Church of Scotland: 39, 227

Churches: construction of by Chinese, 280-281

Circus: 62

Clan organizations: of Chinese, 273-274; and festival celebrations, 283; function of, 274

Clarinda: views of, on marriage, 41-42

Clubs: elite, 32, 51, 54-57; Portuguese, 261

Coalpot: 23; use by Creoles, 99

Cockfighting: Creoles, 128-129; elites, 72; Indians, 203

Coconut toddy: manufacture and sale of, by Indians, 203-204

Colonial Office: 116, 168-169

Colonial state: control of, 295; and social unity, 13

Combined Court: 73, 244

Concerts: 61

Concubinage: among Creoles, 102-104; among elites, 36-38; among Indians, 173; among Portuguese, 245, 255

Consensus: cultural, 2, 83; social, 27, 48, 83; of values, 14, 205, 295, 296, 304, 307

Cooking facilities: for Indians on estates, 161

Correa de Natividade, Joaquim A.: 244

Court of Crown Cases Reserved: 146

Court of Policy: 28, 29, 146, 211

Cremation: among Indians, 189

Creole newspaper: elitist attitude of, 18

Creoles: 243, 249, 298-300, 306; accommodation, 86-89; Amerindian influence on culture of, 153; anti-Portuguese riots, 11; attitude to immigrants, 11; birth customs, 108-109; breaking down political barriers, 84; Christianity and church-going, 124, 299; Christmas celebrations, 122-124; and contemporary observers, 6; cooperative activity, 114-117; cricket, 129-133; cultural impact on whites, 83; death customs, 112-114; dignity balls, 121-122, 296; dinners, 117; domestic servants, 67; drama, 118-119; dress, 95-98; drinking, 73, 112, 127; and elite culture, 17-19, 23, 85; family, 101-108; food, 99-101; Friendly and Burial societies, 114-117, 152; gambling, 73, 128-129, (in Chinese lottery) 291; horse-racing, 73, 129; influence of missionaries on, 152; kite flying, 127-128; language, 91-93; lodges, 115-117; loyalty to British monarchy, 18, 28; male infidelity, 104; marriage, 102-104, 109, 111; marriage customs, 109-111; music and dance, 110, 117-124, 126, 137, 140, 152; names, 94-95; obeah belief and practice, 129, 139, 142-147, 152, 296, 299; occupations, 12, 14; pastimes, 124-129; peasant villages, 9; perception of Guyana, 151-152; population, 7-8; quest for social respectability, 91, 93, 94, 95, 99, 103, 111, 124, 130, 132, 133, 134, 142, 147, 151, 152; religion, 117,

137-142, 152, 299; sexual promiscuity, 104; small farming, 9; spirit possession, 127, 140-142; spirit belief, 147-149, 152; stereotypes, 13; superstitions, 149, 151, 152; taxation for immigration, 155; use of opium, 289; wakes, 47, 112-113, 152; witchcraft, 142, 150-151, 152; women, 36, 95, 96, 102-106, 125, 127, 132, 145

Creolization: 132, 145; of Creoles, 109, 115, 121; of Indians, 167, 168, 189, 203, 219; of Portuguese, 252-253; 263; of whites (British), 30, 51, 83

Cricket: 28, 32, 51, 75, 76-79, 81, 296; and character training, 76-78; among Chinese, 291-292, 304; among creole Indians, 202; among Creoles, 129-133; playing of, by Creole women, 132; and the military, 76-78; and moulding social values, 76; among Portuguese, 261-262; and social control, 130; and social respectability, 132; and socio-cultural integration, 12, 202, 306, 307

Cricket clubs, 55; in villages, 131

Criminal gangs: among Chinese, 275-276; as symbols of Chinese resistance, 276

Cross, Malcolm: 5, 305

Cuba: 2

Cultural alienation: of Indian children, 236

Cultural ambivalence: of Creoles, 91, 142, 147, 153, 299

Cultural assimilation: 15, 133, 134, 153, 154, 205, 224, 233, 236, 249, 280, 281, 294, 296, 297, 307; Portuguese and, 261; promotion of, through sport, 129; and social mobility, 83

Cultural borrowing: by Creoles, 101, 224; by Indians, 187, 188, 189, 190, 216, 232

Cultural compartmentalization: 4

Cultural divergence: 5, 295

Cultural history: 1, 238

Cultural heterogeneity: 264, 303

Cultural integration: 4, 5, 154, 202, 205, 224, 239, 240, 252, 262, 263, 264, 295, 305, 306; promotion of, by colonial elite, 15

Cultural pluralism: 154, 240, 264, 294, 298, 302, 303, 305; indicators of, 15; limitations of theory of, 306; theory of, 4-5; tolerance of, by elites, 298

Cultural power: 29, 48, 83, 93, 94, 116, 122, 128, 129, 142, 145, 149, 151, 179, 187, 199, 200, 205, 211, 213, 216, 226, 233, 239, 245, 247, 249, 250, 252, 255, 259, 260, 262, 276, 277, 278, 280, 282, 286, 295, 296, 297, 298, 300, 304, 305, 306; concept and definition of, 3, 5, 15; and elite dress code, 26; and horse riding, 75; and sport, 70, 71, 72, 76, 78

Cultural resistance: 4, 5, 83, 295, 305; by Chinese, 268, 270, 273, 276, 285, 286; by Creoles, 67, 89, 91, 93, 115, 117, 118, 122, 132, 133, 134, 138, 142, 149, 152, 154, 299, 300; by Indians, 164, 166, 167, 179, 190, 199, 205, 211, 214,

216, 226, 228, 229, 231, 233, 234, 236, 238, 301-302, 306; by Portuguese, 246, 249, 250, 252, 260, 262

Culture: factors determining immigrants' adaptation of, 300-301; preservation of, among Indian immigrants, 238; role of, in nineteenth century Guyana, 84; and social identification, 12-13, 15, 154; strengthening of metropolitan influences on, 297

Cumfo (*Watermamma*): 118, 138-142, 152, 153, 299; and link with obeah, 139; purpose of, 142; as symbol of Afro-Creole cultural resistance, 142, 299

Cycling: among elites, 80

Dahomey: 114

Dances: Creoles, 117-124, 152; creolization of European, 121; elites, 53, 64-65; Indians, 201

Dasserah, 217-218

Death customs: of Creoles, 112-114; of elites, 46-47; of Indians, 188-190

Demerara: 11, 28, 35, 39, 62, 72, 74, 78, 80, 86, 106, 114, 139, 150, 170, 188, 190, 211, 220, 222, 225, 234, 237, 245, 247, 267, 278, 279, 280, 302

Demerara Chess Association, 81

Demerara Club, 55

Demerara Dramatic Club, 62

Demerara Musical Institute, 61

Demerara Musical Society, 61

Demerara Rowing Club, 80

Demerara United Amusement Club: and elite entertainment, 65

Denmark, Princess of: 28

Despres, Leo: 4, 240, 305

Dholuk: restrictions on use of, 187

Dinners: among Creoles, 117; among elites, 32, 53, 66-68; among Indians, 201

Diwali celebrations, 217

Dog racing: 128-129

Dominoes: playing of, among Chinese, 289-290

Dowry: presentation of, among Indians, 183-184, 187

Drainage: along Demerara coast, 86

Drama: among Chinese, 286; among Creoles, 118-119; among elites, 61, 62; among Indians, 201. *See also* Theatre

Dramatic clubs: formation of, 62

Dress: of Africans, 98; of Chinese, 268; of Creoles, 95-99; and cultural power, 26; of elites, 24-26, 31, 45, 64, 65, 66; of Indians, 164-167; of Portuguese immigrants, 243; role of, in process of Chinese cultural homogenization, 268; as symbol of Chinese cultural resistance, 268; as symbol of Indian cultural resistance, 166-167

Drinking: and horse-racing, 73, 74; among Chinese, 73; among Creoles, 73, 112, 127; among elites, 31, 34, 44, 47, 55, 62, 68, 72, 82; among Indians, 73, 202, 203; among Portuguese, 73, 74

D'Urban Course: races at, 73-74

Duelling, 34

Dutch. *See* whites (Dutch)
Dutch East Indies: 36, 38
Dutch Reformed Church: 39
Dutch West Indies: 2

Easter: 255, 256, 282, 199
Eating habits: of Chinese, 268; of Indians, 167-168
Echo newspaper: elitist attitude of, 18
Education: 295, 306; attitude of estate managers to, 235; Chinese, 281-282; compulsory education law (1876), 163, 234, 235; and cultural alienation of children, 236; Indians, 163, 233-236; and link to Christianity, 233; Portuguese, 248-249, 252
Edward VII: 27
Elite Victorian culture: and social mobility, 17-19
Elites: and creation of value consensus 83; creolizing influences on, 83; and criticism of subordinate cultures, 298; mentality of, 82; and undermining of African influence on Creoles, 152
England. *See* Britain
English (people). *See* Whites (British)
English (language). *See* Language
Essequibo: 11, 72, 74, 92, 209, 223, 234, 247, 302
Estates: 86, 155, 161, 178, 192, 199, 213, 220, 225, 228, 234, 242, 243, 266, 267, 291
Etheridge, Bishop James: 246, 250
Ethnic conflict: 11-12
Eversham Mutual Aid Society: 117
Evolués: 17-19, 47, 82, 84, 300, 307
Exhibitions: of produce, 62
Ex-slaves: 99, 152, 242, 297, 299; cooperative activity, 114; and missionaries, 137; move off plantations, 86, 297

Family: Chinese, 267, 270, 273; Creoles, 101-108, 152; definition, 102; Indians, 178-179, 180, 302; Portuguese, 241; whites (British), 83
Fasting: among Hindus, 212
Females. *See* Women
Fêtes: organization of, 62
Fiji: 171, 189, 212, 214, 215, 217, 219, 226, 229
Food: of Barbadian Creoles, 101; of Chinese, 268-270; of Creoles, 99-101; Creole influence on, 53; of elites, 51, 53, 66-68; European style, 66-67; as example of reverse acculturation, 101; of Portuguese, 243-244, 255; taboos concerning, among Creoles, 101
Football: among elites, 79-80
Fortune-telling: among Indians, 201
French West Indies: 2
Friendly and Burial Societies: 152; as example of creolization process, 115; as form of cultural resistance, 115, 117; legislation regulating, 116; role of, 116-117

Funerals: among Creoles, 113; among elites, 46-47; among Indians, 189-190
Furniture: of Chinese, 271; of Creoles, 88; of elites, 19-23; of Indians, 160, 161

Ga: 142
Gambling: among Chinese, 73, 287; and Chinese cultural resistance, 291; among Creoles, 73, 128-129; among elites, 34, 81-82; and facilitation of Chinese cultural integration, 291; and horse-racing, 73, 74; among Indians, 73, 202, 203; among Portuguese, 73
Ganja: use of by Indians, 204
Gender relations: among Indians, 171
Georgetown: 11, 17, 23, 29, 39, 40, 45, 51, 58, 60, 61, 62, 72, 73, 74, 75, 81, 88, 106, 115, 117, 120, 121, 123, 127, 128, 129, 131, 146, 174, 201, 230, 234; residential areas of nineteenth century, 19
Georgetown Chess Club: 81
Georgetown Club: 54
Georgetown Cricket Club: 76, 78, 79, 80, 292
Georgetown Football Club: 79
Georgetown Gymnastic Club: membership of, 81
Georgetown Histrionic Club: 62
Georgetown Militia Band: 66
Georgetown Philharmonic Club: 61
Gibson, Rev. John: 227
Gilbert, J.T.: 60
Golf: among the elite, 75
Goverment House: 28, 29, 33, 63, 82
Governors: and entertainment, 63
Grenada: 170
Guiana Diocesan Church Society: 233, 234

Haiti: 114, 147
Hakka: differences between *Punti* and, 268
Hawke, Lord: 79
Haynes, Richard: 60
Hinduism: 216, 217, 233; *bhakti*, 200; consolidation of, 209; divorce, 173; eating proscriptions, 167; fasting, 212; female subordination, 176; *Krya Sutra*, 213; prohibition of alcohol, 203
Hindus: 207, 301; priests, 214-216; reaction to missionaries, 228ff; worship, 211-212
Hindu temples: in nineteenth century Guyana, 209, 211
Hogg, Quintin, 227
Holi: celebration of, 218, 220
Homosexuality: among Chinese, 273; among elites, 40
Horse-racing: 73-74; and Chinese, 73, 293; and Creoles, 73, 129; among elites, 72, 73-74; and Indians, 73, 202; and integration, 12; and Portuguese, 73
Horse-riding: among elite, 51, 53, 74-75
Horseshoes: superstitions regarding, 149
Household, concept of: 101-102

Hunting: among elite, 70-71
Illandun, Mary: 169-171
Immigrants: 2, 7-8, 155, 300; objective of enrichment, 11
Immigration: 2; of Chinese, 271; and population increase, 7-8; of Portuguese, 241
Immigration Ordinance: civil marriages under, 174
Indentureship: 9
India: 162, 163, 165, 168, 171, 172, 176, 181, 182, 189, 190, 191, 192, 194, 196, 197, 203, 204, 207, 211, 214, 217, 219, 228, 229; British settlers in, 26; immigrants from, 2, 8, 155; empress of, 27
Indians: 101, 123, 151, 153, 298, 300, 301-302; arrival of, in Guyana, 155-156; ancestor veneration, 190; assimilation of elite culture by creole, 236; *Bhojpuri*, 162, 233; birth customs, 179-182; caste, 160, 161, 184, 191-199, 207, 230, 239, 272, 302; caste passing, 194-195; child marriage, 176; Christianity, 202, 226-233; cock-fighting, 203; concubinage, 173; cremation and burial, 189; *Creolese*, 163, 164, 216; cricket, 202; dance, 201; *Dasserah*, 217ff; *dholuk*, 187; death customs, 188-190; dinners, 201; *Diwali*, 217; dowry, 183-184, 187; dress, 164-167; drinking, 73, 188, 202, 203; education, 163, 202, 233-236; English language, 163, 164, 214; estate housing, 156-160; family, 172, 178-179, 180, 205, 302; female shortage, 8, 265, 168-169; female subordination, 175-178; food, 161, 167-168, 201; fortune-telling, 201; furniture, 160, 161; gambling, 73, 188, 202, 203; Hindu temples, 209, 211; historical data on, 6; *Holi*, 217, 220, 226; horse-racing, 73; interracial marriage, 192; language, 162-164, 205, 214, 230; legal marriage, 173-175; magic, 237; marriage customs, 182-187; marriage laws, 172, 173, 174; *Mohurrum*, 217ff; music, 184, 187, 201; Muslim mosques, 209, 212; names, 181, (christian) 231; naming ceremonies, 180-181; occupations, 12, 14; polyandry, 171, 193; *Rama Navami*, 217; religious festivals, 216-226; sex and marriage, 169-179; social respectability, 202, 203; social mobility, 202; stereotypes, 13; superstition, 237; superstitions, 181; tadja, 218ff; theatre, 201; transformation in religious culture of, 219; use of *ganja*, 204; use of opium, 204, 289; value of boys, 179-180; wakes, 188, 190; wife murder, 172-173, 176, 177, 271; witchcraft, 237; women (dress), 164-165; women (interracial mating), 36; women (cooking and eating), 167-168; women as helpmates in Guyana, 177
Indonesia: 275, 277
Indoor games: Chinese, 267, 289-291; elites, 53, 55, 60, 81
Intellectual activities: 57-60

Irish: 17; wakes, 112
Islam: among Africans and Creoles, 138; among Indians, 138, 203, 212, 216, 233
Italy: 246
Ithaca: village of, 86

Jamaica: 17, 23, 29, 36, 46, 73, 80, 81, 114, 115, 116, 119, 122, 123, 125, 126, 129, 137, 138, 143, 147, 150, 171, 184, 189, 204, 218, 284, 290, 291
Jesuits: 246ff
Jewellery: wearing of, by Indians, 164-165
Jews: 39
Joint family structure: of Indians, 178
Jubilees: papal, 257; Queen Victoria, 27, 28
Jumbi: 147, 149

Kenna, 101
Khan, Ghoolmahumad: 201
King, C.H.: 79
Kite flying: among Creoles, 127-128
Konki, 100

Labour: importation of, in Guyana, 8
Ladies. *See* Women
Language: 251; of Africans, 91-92; of Chinese, 278, 280, 282; *Creolese* 91-92, 163, 164, 239, 241, 251, 252, 305; Dutch-Creole, 92; English, 163, 164, 236, 246; of Indians, 162-164, 230, 233; of Creoles, 91-93; of Portuguese, 245, 246, 249, 251, 252, 262
Lantern parade: as symbol of Chinese cultural resistance, 285-286
La Penitence Lawn Tennis Club: 75
Lawn tennis: 53, 75
Laws of *Manu*: on adultery, 173
Levees: governors', 63
Liche-wake: among elites, 47
Lifestyle: of colonial elites, 30
Literary and Debating Club: 60
Lloyd, Clive: 133
Lobscheid, Rev. William: 278
Lodges: of Chinese, 275; of Creoles, 114-117; of elites, 65-66
Logies: as estate dwellings, 158
London Missionary Society: and hostility to Indian immigration, 227
Long Bubbies, 148
Luckhoo, Edward Alfred, 240; Joseph Alexander, 240

Madeira: 2, 241, 243, 253, 254, 256, 258, 262
Malaya: 275, 284
Manila (Philippines): 270
Mansions: architectural style of, 21-23; furnishings of, 21-22; as symbol of planter dominance, 19; as symbol of power and status, 24
Marooning party: among elites, 71
Marriage: as business venture among Indians, 172; civil, under Immigration Ordinance, 174; among Creoles,

102-104, 109, 111; among elites, 36-38; 39; among Indians, 172-178; among Muslims, 186; negotiations for, among Indians, 183; preservation of Indian customs relating to, 176; recognition of Indian, 173; retention of customs by Indians, 187; views of Clarinda on, 41-42

Marriage customs: Creoles, 109-111; elites, 45-46; Indians, 182-187; Portuguese, 258

Masih Das, Benjamin, 240

Masquerade bands: Creoles, 123-124; Portuguese, 253

Mauritius: 162, 163, 180, 209, 211, 219, 221, 222, 223, 272

Medical facilities: lack of, in rural areas, 106

Michahan: playing of, by Chinese, 290

Missionaries: 152, 209, 214, 298; and attack on Indian culture, 213-214, 226-233; and attempts to convert Portuguese immigrants, 245; attitudes to black family, 102, 103; Bel Air Coolie Mission, 227; Canadian Presbyterian Missionary Society, 228, 231, 240; Church of England (Anglican), 227; Creole preachers, 228; influence on Creoles, 124, 127, 137, 151; London Missionary Society, 227; Methodist Missionary Society, 227; Presbyterian Missionary Society, 227; and reinforcement of white values, 13; support for planters, 138

Mohurrum, 218; celebration of, 220-222

Monarchy, British: 296; and Creoles, 18; symbolism of, in colonies, 27-29; traditions associated with, 27-29; and white elites, 27

Moore, Rev. J.R.: 18

Music: of Chinese, 286-287; of Creoles, 117-124, 126, 152; of elites, 53, 61, 66; of Indians, 184, 187, 201; of Portuguese, 253, 254, 255, 261

Muslims: Africans, 223; distrust of (Indian) priests, by cultural elites, 215-216; dress of, 164; Indians, 207, 209, 211, 212, 214, 301; reaction to Christian missionaries, 228ff; sects of, 207; worship of, 212

Names: Africans, 93-94; Chinese, 280; Creoles, 94-95; Indians, 181, 182, 231

Naming ceremonies: of Creoles, 109; of elites, 44; of Indians, 180-181, 182

New Amsterdam: 17, 39, 53, 60, 61, 72, 75, 79, 184, 186, 232, 245, 254, 255, 261

New Year: Chinese lunar new year, 123, 281, 304; Creole festivities, 124 ; and elite fancy dress balls, 65; and elite sports, 75; and Indian immigrants, 199

New Zealand: British settlers, 26; Chinese immigrants, 265

Obeah: 142-147, 152, 153, 296; fear of, by cultural elites, 143; legislation against, 145-146; link with *Cumfo*, 139; Portuguese, 263; practice of, among Afro-Creoles, 142-147; punishment for

practising, 145; similarity to Indian sorcery, 237, 238; and sport, 129; as symbol of cultural resistance, 299

Obeahmen: and abortions, 143; influence of, 129; as symbol of cultural resistance, 145; and use of poisons, 143-144

Occupational specialization: 12, 14, 197

Ole haig, 150

Opium: 265, 287-289; legislation to control, 288-289; use of, by Chinese, 287-289; use of, by Indians, 204

Overcrowding: among Indians on estates, 158; in urban working class areas, 88-89

Overseers: accommodation, 23; sexual behaviour, 40

Pacific islands: 38

Pandit: function of, 215

Papal jubilees: celebration of, by Portuguese, 257

Parade Ground: 28, 76, 78, 79, 80, 130, 133

Pastimes: Creoles, 124-129; Portuguese, 260-262

Peasant villages: establishment of, by ex-slaves, 9, 86

Pentecost, feast of: celebration by Portuguese, 123, 255

Pepperpot, 100

Percival, Exley: 78

Performing arts: among the elites, 61-62

Performing artistes: visiting, 61

Philharmonic Hall: 61, 62, 286

Picnicking: among elites, 71, 72

Plantations: 180, 191,213, 234, 297; and Chinese, 265, 276, 283, 284; ex-slaves' dependence on, 9; and Indians, 231. *See also* Estates

Pilgrimages: by Indians, 190

Plantation Better Hope: Presbyterian mission at, 227-228

Plantation Diamond: and new type of estate dwelling, 158

Plantation society: 1, 95

Plantation system: 108, 115, 295; in the Caribbean, 2; and Guyanese economy, 13; and immigration, 8; and social unity, 13; vulnerability of, 9

Planters: 9, 155, 160, 163, 191, 200; attitude to Christian missionaries, 230, 231; attitude to immigrants' education, 233, 234, 235, 236, 239; behaviour, 34, 35; hospitality, 35; gambling, 81

Plural society: theories of, 13-14; change in, 84

Population: 7-8; Amerindian, 7; black and coloured, 7-8; British, 7-8; Chinese, 8; Indian, 8; Portuguese, 7-8

Portugal: 244, 246, 257

Portuguese: 97, 101, 108, 117, 121, 123, 127, 232, 298, 300, 301, 302-303, 305, 306; accommodation, 242-243; and adherence to traditions, 258-259, 302; and elite clubs, 54-55; anti-Portuguese riots, 11, 249; brass bands, 254, 258, 261, (*Primeiro de Dezembro* band) 256,

261; clubs and societies, 261; concubinage, 245, 255; cricket, 261-262; and dissatisfaction with English-led church, 246; dress, 243, 258; drinking, 73, 254; education, 248-249, 252; family, 241; festivities, 253-259; food, 243-244, 255; furniture, 243; gambling, 73; historical data on, 6; horse-racing, 73; immigrants, 7-8; language, 241, 245, 246, 249, 251, 252, 253, 262; marriage, 258; masquerade bands, 253; music, 253, 254, 255, 261; obeah, 263; occupations, 12, 14; pastimes, 260-262; religion, 244-257; retail trade, 9, 12, 203, 204, 241; and retention of Madeiran religious culture, 252; and retention of nationality, 262; Roman Catholic church, 39, 243ff; Sacred Heart church, 250, 256; sale of opium, 288; stereotypes, 13; as strike breakers, 242; as sugar workers, 242; women, 241, 243, 253, 256
Portuguese Benevolent Society: 258, 260
Potbury, J.A.: 78
Press (newspapers): 18, 24, 27, 44, 83, 85, 295; *Argosy*, 223; *Berbice Gazette*, 81; *Colonist*, 81, 130, 238; *Creole*, 18, 29; *Daily Chronicle*, 139; *Echo*, 18, 28; role of colonial, 27; *Royal Gazette*, 40, 81, 127, 232
Prince Albert: 28
Prince Alfred: 29
Printers' Benevolent Association, 117
Punti: differences between *Hakka* and, 268

Quayle, George: 60
Queen's College: 58, 75, 78, 80

Racial boundaries: and culture, 83, 263, 300
Racial stereotypes: 12-13
Racoon dance: of Afro-Creoles, 118
Rally of Tribes, 125
Rama Navami: Hindu festival of, 217
Ramlila, 201
Religion: centrality of, to Indian culture, 207; among elite, 38-39; and Indian cultural resistance, 216; practices of Hindus, 212-213; role of, in retention of traditional culture, 301; transformation in culture of, among Indians, 219
Religious customs: of Portuguese, 259-260
Religious education: of Portuguese immigrants, 244
Religious festivals: celebration of, by Portuguese, 253-257; merger of Hindu and Muslim, 218; as symbols of Indian cultural resistance, 226
Religious rituals, West African: retention of, 137, 138
Retail trade: Portuguese dominance of, 9
Reverse acculturation: Afro-Creole food as example of, 53, 101
Ridicule: as tool of elites, 134, 296
Rifle-shooting: 72

Roman Catholic Church: 39; attraction to Indians, 232; and Portuguese, 241, 244ff, 262; Sacred Heart church, 250, 256; threatened schism, 248, 249, 262
Royal Agricultural and Commercial Society: 58, 59
Rugby: 79-80
Ruhoman, Joseph: 240

Schembri, Fr. Benedict: 247, 248ff; disagreement between English Catholics and, 248-251; and promotion of Portuguese ethnic identity, 249; and retention of Madeiran religious customs, 247, 248
Scots: 17, 29, 81. *See also* Whites (British))
Scottish National Association, 29
Sea-wall: elite promenade, 28, 31, 51, 61, 123, 127
Secret societies: of Chinese, 275; efforts to suppress, through Christianity, 277; evolution of, into benevolent societies, 275; and operation of gambling and opium dens, 276
Segmented society: 12, 13
Sexual promiscuity: Creoles, 104; elites, 34, 39-41, 47, 62, 82
Shak-shak, 119
S'iku dances: among Afro-Creoles, 118
Silent Temple Lodge: formation of, by Chinese, 275
Silk-cotton tree: supernatural powers of, 148-149
Singapore: 273, 275, 279, 284
Siva Narayani (Sieunaraini) sect, 208
Slater, Rev. James, 227
Sling-shot: 128
Small farming: 9
Smith, M.G.: plural society theorist, 4, 84, 154, 240, 251, 264, 294, 303, 305
Smith, Raymond T.: 5, 101, 102, 103, 107, 111, 154, 187, 191, 194, 294, 305
Smoking concerts, 61
Snobbery: among elites, 34
Social behaviour: of elite, 31-34
Social clubs: of elite men, 54-57; function of, 55-57
Social distance: 134, 296
Social mobility: 91, 93, 133, 202, 297, 306
Social respectability: 91, 93, 94, 95, 99, 103, 111, 116, 124, 130, 132, 133, 142, 147, 151, 202, 239, 296, 297, 300, 306
Social stability: maintenance of, 2, 83, 306, 307
Social status: of Creoles, 84, 154; quest by elites, 31-47, 48, 57, 82
Social visiting: among elites: 53
Society for Natural History and Geology, 58
South Africa: 82, 273. *See also* Cape Colony
Spirit belief: 147-149, 152
Sports: 68-91; and assimilation, 69-70; 129; and class bias, 69; and gender bias, 70; and racial segregation, 69; value consensus, 70-71, 83, 296
St. Anthony, feast of: 257

St. George's Cathedral: 29
St. Joseph: feast of, 256; Society of, 256
St. Peter, feast of: 256
St. Thomas, Virgin Islands: 40, 170
Stoddart, Brian: concept of cultural power, 3; on cricket, 70, 76, 130, 307
Storytelling: among Afro-Creoles,125-126
Strike: of 1848, 138
Suddie: racecourse at, 74
Sugar exports: 9
Surinam: 2, 138, 172, 173, 178, 184, 196, 204, 214
Swimming: 72
Swizzles: 31, 55, 56, 68

Tadja: 123, 285, 218ff, 296, 305; building and cost of, 222; Creole participation in, 138, 220, 223-224, 225; decline of, 223-224; hostility of elites to, 224-226; Indian hostility to Creole, 224; legislation to curb, 225; Portuguese involvement, 224
Tamils: 165, 183, 188, 190
Tea meetings: Creoles, 126; elites, 62
Temperance societies: 127
Theatre. *See* Drama
Timehri: 59
Tobago: 114
Traditions, invention of by elites: 27, 83, 296
Trafalgar day: 29
Trees: supernatural powers of, 148-149
Trinidad: 2, 9, 18, 23, 34, 36, 54, 73, 74, 78, 89, 108, 112, 114, 123, 124, 127, 128, 129, 147, 150, 164, 169, 170, 171, 172, 173, 178, 179, 180, 181, 182, 188, 193, 194, 196, 204, 209, 213, 215, 217, 218, 219, 220, 223, 225, 226, 228, 231, 237,273, 278, 279, 283, 289, 290, 291

United States of America: 22, 79, 204, 274, 275, 279, 286, 288, 290

Vaishnavism: among Indians in modern Guyana, 208
Vaishnavite *bhakti*, 200
Values: of colonial elites, 47
van den Berghe, Pierre: plural society theorist, 4, 240, 305
van Lier, R.A.J.: plural society theorist, 4, 240, 305
Varna system: as basis for status differentiation among Indians, 197
Victoria, Queen: birthday clebrations of, 27, 33; empress of India, 27; jubilee celebrations of, 27, 28
Village dispensaries: establishment of, 106
Villages: Creole, 9, 86, 114; Indian, 178; raids by Chinese, 276; and revival of Indian traditions, 238-239

Wakes: among Creoles, 47, 112-113, 152; among elites, 47; among Indians, 188, 190
Warning Spirits of Dead Relatives, 148
Watermamma, 118, 138, 139

Wattle and daub cottages: in Berbice, 160-161
Weddings: of Bhojpuri immigrants, 185-186; of Creoles, 109-111; of elites, 45-46; of Portuguese, 258; of Tamils, 185
Wesleyan Methodists: and attempts to minister to Indians, 227
Whites (British): balls, 32, 33, 64-66; birth customs, 44-45; composition, 17, 81; concubinage, 36-38; creolization of, 30, 51, 83; dinners, 32, 35, 66-68; dress, 24-26, 31, 45, 64, 65, 66; drinking, 31, 34, 44, 47, 55, 62, 68, 72, 82; duelling, 34; economic dominance, 12; etiquette, 34; exclusive social circles, 31-33; extravagance, 35-36, 48, 82; family, 83; food, 51, 53, 66-68, 100; funerals, 46-47; gambling, 34, 81-82; homosexuality, 40; hospitality, 35, 55; interracial sex, 36-38; lifestyles, 30-47; marriage, 36-38, 39; occupations, 12, 17; population, 7; quest for high social status, 31-47, 48, 57, 82; racial stereotypes, 12-13; religion, 38-39; snobbery, 31-33; social clubs, 54-57; wakes, 47; weddings, 45-46; womanizing (sexual promiscuity), 34, 36-38, 40-41, 62; women, 17, 24-26, 30, 34, 36-39, 83
Whites (Dutch): 17, 39
Whites (local-born): 17, 30, 44, (women) 30
Wife beating: among Afro-Creole men, 105-106
Wife murder: among Indians, 172-173, 176, 177
Witchcraft: among Creoles, 142, 150, 152; among Indians, 237; as symbol of Indian cultural resistance, 238
Wives: hiring out of, by Indian men, 171
Workman's Helping Hand Society, 117
Women: 301; Chinese, shortage of, 8, 265-266, 267, 270-271; Clarinda, 41-42; Creole, 36, 95, 96, 102-106, 125, 127; Creole, and obeah, 145; Creole, and sports, 132; and elite clubs, 54, 56-57; elite dress, 24-26; elite, and sports, 70, 71, 72, 75, 76; elite, and domestic chores, 42; Illandun, Mary, 169-171; Indian, 184, 188, 228; Indian, cooking and eating, 167-168; Indian, dress of, 164-165; Indian, sexual activity, 36, 169ff; Indian, shortage of, 8, 168-169; influence among elites, 34; Jessie, 42; portrayal of black, by elites, 104-105; Portuguese, 241, 243, 253, 256; role of, in Afro-Creole household, 106; white, 17, 30, 32, 36, 56-57, 60, 83; white, and morality, 38-39; young elite, and marriage, 41-42
Wright, E. F.: 79
Wu Tai Kam: 273, 279
Wyatt, George: 79

Yards (Creole): as sources of Afro-Creole folk culture, 89, 152; values emanating from, 89-91, 134, 299